GLOBAL HISTORY OF PHILOSOPHY

Global History of Philosophy

JOHN C. PLOTT
with
JAMES MICHAEL DOLIN
WALLACE GRAY

Volume V
(Part Two)
The Period of Scholasticism

MOTILAL BANARSIDASS PUBLISHERS
PRIVATE LIMITED • DELHI

First Edition: Delhi, 1989
Reprint: Delhi, 2000

ISBN: 81-208-0552-6 (Vol. V)
ISBN: 81-208-0549-6 (Set)

Also available at:

MOTILAL BANARSIDASS

236, 9th Main III Block, Jayanagar, Bangalore 560 011
41 U.A. Bungalow Road, Jawahar Nagar, Delhi 110 007
8 Mahalaxmi Chamber, Warden Road, Mumbai 400 026
120 Royapettah High Road, Mylapore, Chennai 600 004
Sanas Plaza, 1302 Baji Rao Road, Pune 411 002
8 Camac Street, Calcutta 700 017
Ashok Rajpath, Patna 800 004
Chowk, Varanasi 221 001

Printed in India

BY JAINENDRA PRAKASH JAIN AT SHRI JAINENDRA PRESS,
A-45 NARAINA, PHASE-I, NEW DELHI 110 028
AND PUBLISHED BY NARENDRA PRAKASH JAIN FOR
MOTILAL BANARSIDASS PUBLISHERS PRIVATE LIMITED,
BUNGALOW ROAD, DELHI 110 007

FOREWORD

It is always interesting to find out who one's neighbors are, especially in a place of old-time residents. Those who have visited or lived in the areas of philosophy and religion have usually been to a few homes besides their own, but have seldom tried to get to know the entire neighborhood. Often it is ignorance of our neighbors that keeps us from meeting each other, and it is not until someone does us the favor of introductions that the barriers come down.

John Plott's ambitious *Global History* is an excellent introduction to our neighbors. Actually it is more accurate to say that he creates a neighborhood by bringing together in a single text the major figures of the Western and Asian traditions. This volume covers the 200 years from 1150 to 1350, and, in assigning places according to age, it presents us with the likes of Peter Lombard next to Hemacandra, Chu Hsi next to Maimonides, Madhva next to Nichiren, and on and on from one juxtaposition to another. With Plott and his assistants as our guides, we go from house to remarkable house, and marvel at the existence of such a neighborhood.

The excitement of meeting so many great thinkers in such a small space, however, is tempered by the fact that each visit must necessarily be short. In some cases we leave only with impressions and generalizations, but these introductions are best understood as invitations to further inquiry. For many of us, specialists and beginners alike, a visit to Plott's gathering of thinkers will provoke an interest in studying at homes we would otherwise not visit.

George J. Tanabe, Jr.
University of Hawaii

ACKNOWLEDGMENTS

First acknowledgment must go to Marshall University, Huntington, West Virginia, USA, where I received many considerations. Especially remarkable in an extraordinary way was the patient and good-spirited helpfulness of the library staff. I also express especial appreciation to the librarians at the University of Hawaii and the University of Michigan, as well as the religion, sociology, history and philosophy departments at the University of Hawaii. Special mention should also be given to Madhev Deshpande of the University of Michigan and Len Evan Goodman of the University of Hawaii.

For their assistance with this volume thanks go to Kenneth Huff for his work on the Glossary and to Becky Fife (both of Southwestern College, Kansas) as well as to Margaret O'Neill and Hideo Murakami. And once again we very much appreciate the assistance of Connie Hager, with Sharon Luman, this time for the Index.

For personal assistance in time of great need, thanks go to Harold Carswell, and to the Friends/Quakers of Ann Arbor and Honolulu.

There is no way for me to adequately acknowledge the contribution of Paul D. Mays to this and every other volume of this work, and the same is true in a different way for Russell H. Hatton. Certainly they will understand what I mean.

Unfading gratitude must go to the many students and faculties from many countries on many continents, including fellow members of World Campus Afloat, who have stimulated and challenged me in formal and informal sessions. Finally, the wit and wisdom of Wing-tsit Chan remains indelibly never to be forgotten.

CONTENTS

INTRODUCTION

It was initially hoped that the Period of Scholasticism (800-1350) could have been treated in one volume as the other periods have been. That being not possible due to length and circumstances, the period has been presented in two volumes. Admittedly we have not been able to find subdivisions for this period which are to our satisfaction. Therefore we have used those subdivisions which seem to fit the history of philosophy, although by no means do we propose that periodizing only according to philosophical developments is desirable. Thus, for the Period of Scholasticism (800-1350) we suggest the following divisions: the Earlier Period of Scholasticism or "Monism in Many Moods" (800-900); the Middle Period of Scholasticism or "Exfoliation and Elaboration" (900-1150); and the Later Period of Scholasticism or the "Great Summas" (1150-1350). What we intend by "Monism in Many Moods" and "Exfoliation and Elaboration" should not necessarily be taken in any strict technical sense, but rather as indicating the dominating *trend* in contrast with the architectonic structuring of the "Great Summas" of the Later Scholastic Period. The reader is referred to Volume II of this study for an overview of our periodization scheme, "The Problem of Periodization."

The basic problem for the ninth century is that implicitly set by St. John of Damascus, namely the Formlessness or Indescribability of God and His relation with nature and man. In Erigena, this relation is basically contingent on God's drawing all things back to Himself; in Saadia, it rests primarily on the Semitic doctrine of God's transcendent position as Creator; in al-Ash'arī, primarily on the Unicity of the Godhead; in Śaṅkara, on the unavoidable inference that since everything experienceable must be within *māyā*, there must be That upon which all rests as *adhyāsa*, superimposition; in Kūkai, on the experience of mystical enlightenment or that level of consciousness wherein all things and all possible ideas are seen as fragmentations of a single Continuum of ever-changing Process. A completely synoptic view of these together is our end.

The temper of the ninth century throughout Eurasia was basically monistic. There may have been variations on the same theme, but there was the will to see all things from a God-like perspective, to see all things as not separated from God. Our thesis is that the rallying point for the ninth century throughout the world was that of the absolute Unity of God and the non-departure from that Unity of all things natural and human. Scotus Erigena manifests this through the theology of theophany; Saadia does it through the moral sphere, emphasizing the moral injunctions given to man in prophetic revelation; Śaṅkara does it through his strict ontology of nondivision, even the nondifference of being and becoming; and al-Ash'arī through his emphasis on Predestination. The monistic tendency and its counter-balances are always in a delicate position. Complete equilibrium would mean *pralaya*, dissolution of the whole of the cosmological panoply, and that we do not yet see—history still moves on.

Al-Ash'arī's reaction against "rationalism" may be best taken as a neo-orthodox re-establishment of the absolute dependence of man on the Will of God, insofar as He can be said to "have" a "will" without compromising his non-anthropomorphic transcendence. This neo-orthodox tendency is manifest also in Śaṅkara, to whom the Buddhists are the 'heretics', and in Saadia against the overmuch Hellenizing tendency of those who were following Philo's precedent, and in Scotus Erigena in his assistance to Charlesmagne in establishing the Holy Roman Empire. This same tendency towards neo-orthodoxy is found in China in the beginnings of Neo-Confucianism in the persons of Han Yü and Li Ao. This does not mean, however, that innovations ceased; neo-orthodoxies also have a way of getting broken open and having rivals.

By the close of the ninth century we have at best qualified monisms and often openly dualist and pluralist trends. Out of the unification of Islam in the external world emerged a new metaphysics of unity which was almost monolithic; but as the political and theological unity of Islam became fragmented, so the monist trend was soon lost in proliferation of distinctions and subtleties of scholastic argumentation until we reach the "Great Summas" (1150-1350). This trend from monistic simplicity through elaboration to excessive complexity and ornamentation is remarkably paralleled in architecture in the transition from Romanesque to elaborate Gothic in Europe and in Dravidian India from the solidity of Tanjore to the filigreed fragrance-in-stone of Belur and Halebīd. In Islam likewise we see essentially the same transition from the early puritanical unadorned mosques to the elaborate and even gaudily ornate mosques of the later centuries. In the Buddhist world the halo begins with the pure simplicity of the early Gupta style, but eventually in China, Japan and India it encompasses the entire universe. Similar developments of the halo motif also transpire in Byzantium and even in Gothic Europe. During the Later Period of Scholasticism the greatest works of Bonaventure and Aquinas, al-Ghazālī and Ibn Rushd, Rāmānuja and Madhva, Lu Hsiang-shan and Chu Hsi, Dōgen and Nichiren, emerge systematically out of previous seminal insights and formulations such as the *Sentences* of Peter Lombard, the *Brahma Sūtras*, and the speculations about the Great Ultimate. They mark without doubt the culmination of the cycle of systematization in a way that has seldom been achieved.

Complexity of argumentation soon becomes the chief characteristic of the whole Scholastic Period equally in the Islamic, Christian, Indian and Chinese fields. One needs much patience indeed, although he who acquires this virtue will be plenteously rewarded. Not until Ockham and his contemporaries is there a trimming down of the multiplication of arguments. Logic as well as faith leads to extremes; but it is just this that the best were trying to avoid. The Middle Way must be inclusive, whether it easily does so or not, or else it must resort to a "somehow" or an "as if" or a multiplication of "neverthelesses" in order to avoid disjoining man and nature and God. One is again and again tempted to return to the Zen Buddhists or the Taoists and abandon logic altogether: but this dichotomizing will never do. The One is always in need, so to speak, of logical as well as trans-logical presentation.

The scholastic philosophers ideologically as well as geographically were very much involved in multi-dimensional encounters between civilizations, which is reflected in the supposed conflict between reason and revelation and the efforts at rendering the scriptures consistent in the way that systematic philosophy and theology demand. This basic problem in the traditions entailed the exploration of the limits of reason as well as the full employment of the rational faculty in defending a supra-rational foundation and/or orientation for philosophizing. This age-old controversy was certainly not peculiar to any particular century. But it is difficult to understand any philosophy in any culture during the Scholastic Period without some appreciation of this problem, which again perplexes many minds, especially among Existentialists and those who are fascinated with Zen.

There is always the temptation of "reading history backwards". One may not rightly judge Aristotle a dolt because he did not invent the microscope, or condemn Śaṅkara for not including a treatise on advanced mathematics, nor condemn any of the Byzantine or Islamic scholastics for not inventing symbolic logic. Likewise, one may not historically condemn any of the scholastic philosophers for not questioning the authority of their canon of scriptures. There are always things which human beings take for granted. One may rather marvel that the critical spirit did get as far advanced as it did (indeed, one sometimes wishes that modern philosophers could show the same keenness of dialectical skill that these thinkers did).

The most important point historically to understand is that from the ninth century tradition becomes so firmly established and the problems so set and the possible solutions so exhaustively explored that only commentaries follow and not original discoveries. Not the *individual* but the *tradition* itself becomes the important thing. This cannot be overstressed.

Through the history of philosophy and religion one must be cautious in either affirming or refuting the positions of those who gained the epithet "heretic". Often it is only historical accident or the struggle for political or military power which determines heresy and orthodoxy, whether in Hinduism, Buddhism, or Christianity. The important thing for any of us concerned with the history of ideas, and especially the global history of ideas, is the recognition of what was considered important enough to become controversial.

Although one may not yet point to many great advances in the empirical sciences, the time of ' retreat" which may be noted in Gregory the Great, for example, is at an end. Still, the chief difference between this and the post-Humean world-view is that here nature is a field of reflection of the Glory of God, a matter of contemplation more than an area for investigation. For most scholastic philosophers the whole of human existence is pointed toward transcendence; this world is the *preparation* for the world to come. Some think the ideal did not quite succeed. But that is not the important thing, for "success" is not the criterion of judgment until the advent of American Pragmatism. The establishment of the God-given goal—everything depends on that, and on that alone. If the goal has not yet been attained, it remains to the credit of the scholastic philosophers that they helped to set it clearly.

That *yin/yang* polarizations should occur historically in the drama of development should not be surprising to those familiar with our previous volumes. Philosophies just do not appear in isolation from each other. Normally they develop in contexts of historical controversies—controversies which more often than not continue through many centuries and even down to the present time. That realization involves us in the more general problem of typology of philosophies and the sociology of knowledge question as to whether or to what extent certain types of philosophies occur in particular types of circumstances. For example, do materialisms come from proletarian movements or rebellions? Are all mysticisms "escape mechanisms" or "opiates" as the orthodox Marxists say; and do they prevail in "Times of Troubles" (to invoke Toynbee)? Under what conditions do fanaticisms become historically effective even though open-minded humanisms seem to be more desperately needed? Do we yet have something to learn from the distinction made by Ibn Sīnā and others between prophetic types of philosophies and 'merely' rational metaphysical systems? Should one make still further distinctions between philosophic mysticism and esoterics; and what of the history of philosophies that claim to be trans-historical?

But these are only a few *questiones disputandae* which arise, and often as not remain unanswered in our *explorations*—for that is all that they can thus far claim to be, and no more. No doubt many specialists will complain that our estimation from their particular point of view is out of focus. To them we appeal for corrections, for we hope to present challenges to others to put it all together as it actually transpired in history.

THE GREAT SUMMAS
(1150—1350)

1. Śrīkaṇṭha

In the Southern Śaiva philosopher Śrīkaṇṭha (c. 1150, although it is difficult to separate him from his really greater commentator Appaya Dīkṣita, c. 1550) we have one of the most ardent attempts which India ever produced at merging piety and intelligence without compromising either. The result may or may not be satisfactory, for it entails a certain degree of compromise in systematic ordering of principles; but it is certainly safe to say that it is more than a mere apology that is offered.

It is often argued that the henotheism involved in Śrīkaṇṭha's devotion to Śiva, analogous to that of Rāmānuja and Madhva and others in their devotion to Viṣṇu, is not to be noticed very much since the structure as far as the Upaniṣadic sources are concerned is quite the same. This is basically true, and it is significantly true that there is much more accord on the whole between Śaivas and Vaiṣṇavas than there is between Shī'as and Sunnis or Protestants and Catholics, for in most temple compounds if the chief temple is dedicated to Viṣṇu there will be a temple to Śiva also, and vice versa.

However, the fact that Śiva is primarily a God of Destruction whereas Viṣṇu is the God of Preservation does give a slightly different coloring to the whole system as well as to the cult. But it must not be misunderstood what is meant by 'destruction'. It is *involution* primarily, rather than violent catastrophic upheaval or imposition of calamity. As all reality (including even His own Existence) has emanated from the Undifferentiated 'formless' Form of Śiva, so He and He alone has the power to draw it all back into Himself. That is what destruction is, not the vague amorphous 'absorption' into some still more amorphous Absolute. If God has the power to evolve all reality out of His own Being, to allow or cause some difference or quasi-difference to come into the picture, then He certainly has the comparable power to remove this differentiation and bring all that has gone out from Him back into Himself.

Such a reuniting would constitute a very beatific state indeed. The imaginary picture is very stimulating, and there is nothing as yet in scientific discovery to countervene it. The whole phantasmagoria of all the spiral nebulae and all the invisible and inaudible forces and laws that govern nature's operation, the whole "dance of matter", is Śakti's sport before the invisible formless Śiva, which He could stop in any timeless time and withdraw into formlessness and non-being—or so it appears from our point of view; but from the point of view of the purely spiritual realms it is a withdrawal into the purity of Eternal Being without the imprisonment of form and motion. Of course in the actual iconography the Dance is really that of Śiva himself, but this is after Śiva and Śakti have been merged into the ultimate and erogenous figure in which *yin* and *yang* are no longer in separation.

The Śaiva tendency in regard to ego is also different from what is found in the Vaiṣṇavas, where humility is admittedly cultivated more commonly. The typical Śaiva is more likely to seek to merge his individual ego into the Cosmic Ego of Śiva than to submerge his ego in humble service to Viṣṇu who in his Great Compassion is himself selfless. "Śrīkaṇṭha describes Śiva on the one hand as being the category of *aham* or egohood which forms the individual personality, and at the same time regards it as being of the nature of 'pure being', 'pure consciousness', and 'pure bliss'."[1] The Śaiva mantra *Śivo'ham* (I am Śiva) would seem blasphemous to many a careless Christian critic; but not much more is really meant than St. Paul's "now no longer I but Christ", except for the nuance that instead of elimination of ego altogether quite the opposite is expected, that in absolute universalization of ego an identification with all will be the result.

Perhaps the most difficult thing systematically for Śrīkaṇṭha is the relation between what is called *Sadā* Śiva and Śiva in his state of self-manifestation: the *nirguṇa-saguṇa* problem all over again, the problem of Eckhardt, and to a great extent of Duns Scotus and Lu Hsiang-shan, except here taken into a thoroughgoing uncompromising *theism*. In the strict Advaitic Vedānta of Śaṅkara the theistic level is relegated to the *saguṇa*-Brahman, and that largely for the sake of perpetuation of popular cults for those who are not capable or eligible for the Advaitic *sādhana*, while the *nirguṇa* is, as above relatedness, of such an undifferentiated nature that it would be difficult to say whether it be 'God' or not, being as Nameless as the strictest Jewish conception of *Jahwe*. But with Śrīkaṇṭha and his following this is not so. The *nirguṇa* is not denied or qualified as it is in Rāmānuja, Madhva, Nimbārka and others but is claimed also to be there as the supreme and supremely Personal Deity, giving form to His own Being and to all forms proceeding out of this, although they are subject to "recall without previous notice", so to speak. In short, it is not easy for the Śaiva *siddhāntin* to defend himself from the charge of unsystematic syncretism, trying to satisfy all views without regard to consistency. When so accused, however, he usually resorts to some form of *bhakti* in which it is hoped that the difficulties, or *supposed* difficulties, will disappear in the ardency of devotion to the God "who knows no second" and who eventually will remove all distinctions and thereby abolish all difference in His own primordial unity.

The Śaiva really stresses practice more than theory. Nevertheless a minimum of theory is necessary as a guide to practice, which always means such disciplines as will lead to *mokṣa*. Dasgupta has summarized this minimum:

> Lord Śiva is supposed to be the cause of the creation of the world, its maintenance, and its ultimate dissolution, and the liberation of souls through the cessation of bondage. All these qualities of the production of the world, its maintenance, etc., belong to the phenomenal world of appearance, and cannot therefore be attributed to the Lord Śiva as constituting His essential definition....
>
> Again, the dissolution of the world of appearance is not a magical disappearance, but rather the return of the grosser nature of the *prakṛti* or primal matter into its subtle nature of the same *prakṛti*. The world as a whole is not illusion, but it had at one time manifested itself in a grosser form of apparent reality, and in the end it will again return into the subtle nature of the cosmic matter or *prakṛti*. This return into the nature of the subtle *prakṛti* is due to the conjoint actions of all animate beings as favoured by the grace of God.[2]

It may readily be seen how Śrīkaṇṭha's views on *māyā* will differ from those of the other commentators. For *māyā* to him is not super-imposition, mistake, ignorance, or any of the usual ways of explaining the ambivalence of manifestation and non-manifestation. It is rather the realm of *śakti* (power) primarily, although the concept is much more rich than that, carrying as it does the connotation of "that which brings forth". Pārvatī in the iconography with her varying forms as Kālī, Durgā, Umā, et al, is thus almost always represented as having a two-fold aspect, terrifying and benevolent, which only reflects the systematic primordiality of God-in-Himself and God-in-self-manifestation as Creator, Preserver and Destroyer of the universe. Dasgupta writes:

> So as Brahman cannot remain without His *śakti* or energy, He can be regarded as the material cause of the world, though He in Himself remains transcendent, and it is only His *māyā* that works as an immanent cause of the production of the world. He (Śrīkaṇṭha) thus says that there is a difference between the individual souls and the Brahman, and there is a difference between the *prakṛti* and the Brahman. He would not admit that the world of appearance is entirely different from Brahman; neither would he admit that they are entirely identical....Brahman exists in quite a transcendent manner, apart from the individual souls and the inanimate world. But yet, since the individual souls and the material universe are emanations from His energy, the world of souls and matter may be regarded as parts of Him, though they are completely transcended by Himself.[3]

The same sort of ambiguity is left in regard to the doctrine of matter in this system. On the one hand there is the extreme doctrine of emanation and involution, but on the other hand it is definitely asserted that the cosmos that is projected out of and withdrawn into the Godhead is completely real and not illusory in the sense that Advaita teaches.

Another ambiguity, whether more or less deliberate or not, lies in the field of the relation of individual souls to God. This tradition perhaps faces more directly the problem of the eternity of souls, even though in some sense individuated, created, and subject in all respects to the divine will. From Dasgupta:

> It cannot be argued that before the creation there were no souls, for we know from the Upaniṣadic texts that the souls and God both exist eternally. As the souls have no beginning in time, so their deeds also are beginningless. This may lead to an infinite regress, but this infinite regress is not vicious. The series of births and deaths in the world in different bodies is within the stream of beginningless *karma*. Since God in His omniscience directly knows by intuition the various kinds of deeds that the individual would perform, He arranges suitable bodies and circumstances for the enjoyment or suffering of such deeds already anticipated by Him. So the difference in creation is due to the diversity of one's deeds. The time of destruction comes when the souls become tired and fatigued by the process of birth and death, and require some rest in dreamless sleep.[4]

This may seem relatively naive philosophically, and perhaps it is; but what is attempted is to blend the popular cult and simple faith with the classical tradition without compromising either, and this in any tradition is never easy to do. In all of this the resort to a theology of grace is pivotal. For although in a sense everything is determined by the beginningless law of karma, it is by the grace of Lord Śiva that the devotee is rescued from this inexorable endless chain. Nevertheless this still leaves something to be desired in clarification of the problem of free will since although grace does not operate according to merit only still the injunctions performed to the prescribed rituals cannot easily be put aside. But again, this tradition does not try so hard for a "foolish consistency" but leaves such matters loosely defined and puts the emphasis on *practice* as we have already noted.

The moral fervor in this tradition is quite high, and the spirit of renunciation remains the ideal even among those who are dutifully engaged in worldly pursuits. This does not entail a gross neglect of worldly things in a world-negating perspective but rather a handling of all affairs with a high sense of duty. This is *my* karma, this is *my* way of serving God—such is the attitude that pervades almost all levels of society. The other-worldly perspective is there, but one must not neglect his karma. The *Gītā* enjoins *sva-dharma* very emphatically: better to pursue one's own duties, whether it be sweeping the streets or managing a bank, than the duties of another howsoever well one *might* do that. The other-worldly perspective simply gives detachment; but there is no escape from this world into any other until one's course is completed and one's job is done is this life, and maybe many others yet to come. Blessed is the man who even gains the privilege of planning his next life before leaving this one much less the prospect of 'no return' in final emancipation: such is the attitude.

Although it seems to be more nearly another *bhedābhedavāda*, the system of Śrīkaṇṭha, somewhat like that of Duns Scotus, really does not fall strictly into any systematic characterization, but for the opposite reason. Scotus tries by subtlety of logic to smooth over differences whereas Śrīkaṇṭha tends to let the basic truths stand without undue effort to systematize them or to iron out inconsistencies. Different points of view, different perspectives, are *somehow* put together as they are in actual life, and it is difficult to expect a merely human intellect to force them into any single mould. Or perhaps Śrīkaṇṭha is really somehow trying to deal *from beyond* the realm of definables and prefers to leave the Primordial in its own form. His heart lies in the Tamil *Āgamas*, in which logic and mythology and cultic practice and hagiology are intertwined rather inextricably. But then Śrīkaṇṭha seems quite content not to become involved in any complicated dialectics.

2. Bernard of Clairvaux

St. Bernard of Clairvaux (1091-1153) really deserves as much consideration as Abelard, even though for the most part he is considered to be a mystic of the not-so-philosophical type. St. Bernard is more comparable to his Japanese contemporaries with their poetic bent, or to the Sūfīs or the by now well developed school of *bhakti* of South India, than he is to Abelard his fellow Christian. Bernard is not less paradoxical than Abelard. For in spite of his great works on contemplation he was a very busy man indeed, and his sometimes almost intolerant zeal for orthodoxy is not easy to put together with his ecstatic discourses on the Love of God. Called by the Pope into a post of counsel, he became one of the most politically influential figures of the time. Studied in humility and self-disciplined, one would expect his contemplations to lift him to a place above controversy. But his quarrel with Abelard and success in getting him condemned, stand, in the eyes of many, as a major mark against him. He is nevertheless one of the great saints of all time, as may be attested by the fact that the monastic reform he instituted still survives. For it is one thing to be a philosopher in the academic sense and another thing to embody a philosophy or way of life in an institution that survives the fluctuations of time. In this respect he is ranked with Rāmānuja.

In his major work *De Consideratione* Bernard considers in an artful way the longitude, the latitude, the profundity and the sublimity of God, in a way that includes the impossibility of limiting human discourse to literal meanings when we are dealing with divine things, wherein, in short, the transparency of all things shines with a light that is not of themselves. But this is not a mysticism of a sort that had no societal ramifications. The multidimensionality ramifies through the papacy and other channels into the whole of the medieval mind and society. There is an expression of the ideal that, through the pope, the Church, in spite of her deficiencies, should purify the whole of human society.

Bernard fits into the general characteristics of the eleventh and early twelfth centuries, namely, that the monistic tendency of ninth and tenth centuries begins to exfoliate, and, instead of single univocally affirmed unity, the problem of the relation of the One and the Many comes again into sharper focus, the relation between God and man is more sharply qualified, and, as with Abelard, the univocal, equivocal, diversivocal and multivocal are equally affirmed in any and every proposition concerning universal and particular. So with St. Bernard, God is not only the summit of the mystical ascent, the apex of the pyramid of hierarchies, but also the 'length', 'breadth', 'height' and 'depth' as well. And St. Bernard was quite aware that he was using metalanguage; in fact, he did so explicitly. Multidimensionality, in other words begins to take on a new significance, although it is still within the comprehensive embrace of the One. This, perhaps, is really what is behind the rising importance of the nominalist-realist controversy in Europe, which parallels the Mu'tazilite-Ash'arite controversy in Islam and the Advaita-Bhedābhedavāda-Viśiṣṭādvaita axis in India.

Bernard was born of a noble Burgundian family in France. At the age of twenty-three he entered the monastery of the reformed Benedictines at Citeaux, persuading thirty other nobles and four brothers to enter with him. In only three years he was sent to establish a new monastery at Clairvaux of which he became the first abbot. The fame of his holiness and the miracles told of him and of his power as a preacher soon made his monastery a rival of Cluny in prestige. He helped establish the Knights Templar at the Council of Troyes in 1128, upheld orthodoxy in other councils, successfully advanced the papal claims of Innocent II against the rival pope Anacletus, and preached the Second Crusade so eloquently that its failure fell on him as a judgment of God. Bernard showed himself fully capable of rebuking popes or secular leaders for deviation from the will of God as he perceived it. For a period of thirty years he averaged making two new foundations of monasteries for his order per year. He thus fathered seventy communities directly, and he affiliated others with his spiritual movement, bringing the total to 164 or half the monasteries in the order of Citeaux (also referred to as the Cistercians and later known as Trappists). He was proclaimed a saint in 1173 by Pope Alexander III.

Leclercq says of Bernard that he remains a mystery and his prestige appears ambiguous. He continues to irritate theologians. "In him everything was exceptional, even the human."[1] Leclercq perhaps gives us the most comprehensive and well-documented list of Bernard's characteristics: efficient, shy, dynamic, magnetic, an arouser of passions, mysterious, violent and gentle, quick in intelligence, and, because of illness, often weary and hard to put up with, a man with a pale countenance and flushed cheeks who could be a burden both to others and himself. Leclercq underscores the fact that Bernard was an artist, in words, architecture, calligraphy and probably also in music. If style reflects the man, Bernard's styles reveal several men. As Gilson says: "Bernard found ways to remain a man of letters and to become a saint into the bargain."[2] In his famous sermons on the Canticle (Song of

Songs), he becomes as lyrical as St. Francis. But Thomas Merton correctly adds: "In his letters he is too busy upbraiding the bishops to have time for a sermon to the birds."[3]

One writer said of Bernard, "What power on earth could frighten him?" Indeed, when we see him facing down popes and tyrants, heretics and infidels, we find an intrepid fighter. Whether his causes or methods were always wise and just is another matter. Leclercq says that in politics he acted on faith and on information he did not always check, "and since he was Bernard, he prevailed."[4] Bernard shared some of the prejudices of his age, and of ours. The Abbot of Cluny wanted to help achieve a better understanding of Islam by sponsoring a translation of the Qur'ān. He asked for Bernard's cooperation, but Bernard did not respond. Christendom, he believed, must fight infidels, not as a method of conversion, but to prevent their jeopardizing Christians. Although Bernard shared some of the antisemitic biases of his contemporaries, he nevertheless stepped to the defense of Jews threatened by the Second Crusade.

Bernard, the last of the Church Fathers, marks the end of the patristic period and, by his very resistance, the beginning of the scholastic period. On the question of whether Bernard was a philosopher, Leclercq answers: "He observed and reflected....He had personal opinions on the subject of man, on the union in man of reason and mortal flesh, on the function of the soul (animation, sensitivity, understanding), on its 'parts' (memory, reason and will)....His particular synthesis of these ideas is not elsewhere found."[5] Bernard assimilated Socratic elements (know thyself) and "he knew how to call on reason in his teachings"; but he was not a metaphysician nor a dialectician, and his rhetoric sometimes obscured his logic or interfered with his clarity.

Bernard's purpose was "to arouse desire for an indescribable experience."[6] Most theologians might be content to believe in order to understand (*credo ut intelligam*) but Cistercian theologians, including Bernard as the foremost example, felt led to believe in order to experience (*credo ut experiar*). Bernard, then, was not concerned with technical philosophy but with "celestial philosophy". For him true philosophy means a "practical discernment of the value of things and of the vanity of the world"; not a theory, but "lived wisdom".[7] This spiritual wisdom Bernard tends to set over against the worldly wisdom of the pagan philosophers or of the scholastics such as Abelard who admired them. We might paraphrase the Latin, *Neque enim res quæ in se ipsa non arserit aliud accendit* to read: "If you are not on fire yourself, you cannot ignite anything else," or more literally, "Nothing which does not burn itself can kindle flame in anything else." To enkindle the love of God was the central purpose of Bernard's writing and teaching. While agreeing that St. Bernard was not a metaphysician, Gilson nevertheless says that "he must remain in our eyes a theologian whose speculative vigour and power of synthesis puts him among the greatest."[8] While Bernard's thinking is not lacking in theory, the theory exists not for its own sake as in some metaphysical speculations but for the ordering and inspiring of the spiritual life. In a comment on a passage in the Song of Songs, Bernard wrote: "There are many whom a wise philosophy teaches as to what may be done, while it does not set them in a glow to do it."[9]

In the midst of modernity one hesitates to open the theme of the love of God, for one is sure to be misunderstood. In St. Augustine, for example, there is admittedly, as St. Augustine would be the first to acknowledge quite openly, much that might be misconstrued by a Freudian. Yet one may still insist that the field of mystical theology is much more precise and far-reaching than any modern secular psychoanalysis, which usually wants to push the Godward soul back into the world. But in St. Bernard one seems to find something more undiluted and more nearly without any possible duplicity. The key to this purity lies in the purgation of all selfishness out of the love of God. The knowledge of God is taken for granted; one proceeds from there to eliminate anything whatsoever that is foreign to this one end of selflessly serving the One, Who even more than to the most ardent and pious Ash'arite is the sole initiator of all grace, not to say the Creator of all things. It is really thus in the will that the final union is given, though complete and final union is scarcely possible while the encumbrances of flesh and bones still remain, quite as much as with most of his Buddhist and Hindu contemporaries.

In the following, Bernard, who was known as Doctor Mellifluous, speaks on his favorite subject:

> I have read that God is love, not that he is honor or dignity. ...Honor and glory indeed are due to God and to him alone, but he will accept neither of them if they be not preserved in the honey of love. Love is sufficient of itself; it pleases by itself and on its own account. It is itself merit and is its own reward. Love seeks no cause beyond itself and no fruit. It is its own fruit, its own enjoyment. I love because I love; I love that I may love. Love is a great thing provided it recurs to its beginning, returns to its origin, and draws always from that fountain which is perpetually in flood. Of all the feelings and affections of the soul love is the only one by which the creature, though not on equal terms, is able to respond to the creator and to repay what it has received from him....For when God loves us he desires nothing but to be loved. He loves for no other reason, indeed, than that he may be loved, knowing that by their love itself those who love him are blessed.[10]

A key passage using light, wine and water as metaphors for spiritual transformation reads as follows: "As a tiny drop of water falling in a quantity of wine seems to disappear and take on the taste and color of wine...as air inundated by sunlight seems to become transformed into light itself—so that it is no longer illuminated but is itself a source of illumination, so the saints lose their human passions and are wholly absorbed in God."[11] In only one passage does Bernard speak of the love of God as deifying the soul. The words precede the above quote: "To be thus affected is to be deified (*sic affici, deificari est*)."[12]

Bernard generally does not approach pantheistic monism so closely, but in speaking of the fourth degree of love in which the soul may "love not even himself except for the love of God" he says that the soul "may utterly pass over into God, and, adhering to God, become one spirit with Him." Bernard teaches that in rare and brief moments of this life one might in a certain manner lose oneself, "as though thou wert not." One would then be utterly unconscious of oneself, be emptied of oneself, "and, as it were, brought to nothing."[13] Gilson cautions us to realize that man, when beatified, is *all but* annihilated; however, the dissimilitude of man from God and from himself *is* annihilated. "In short the soul's substance is indestructible; to be annihilated in God is to surrender its own will, that is the separative will that made the man at once different from God and from himself."[14] And Bernard writes: "Man and God, because they are not of one substance or nature, cannot be called 'one thing' ('*unum*', like Father and Son); but they are with strict truth called 'one spirit', if they adhere to one another by the glue of love. But this unity is effected not by coherence of essences, but by concurrence of wills."[15]

Even as Bernard refuses the metaphysician's temptation to let the One swallow up the identity of the individual, so as a teacher of both divine love and human freedom, he likewise refuses the temptation of Augustinian theologians to let God's grace replace the individual's free will. For Bernard, the higher the intensity and quality of the love, the freer is the person. Perhaps no thinker in history has linked love and freedom any more closely than does Bernard. Remembering that "grace" is the theologian's word for effective divine love, Bernard's *Treatise Concerning Grace and Free Will* becomes a kind of magna carta for love and freedom together without any kind of opposition. Indeed, he sees grace and free will working together, at the same time, not by turns: "It is not that grace doeth part and free choice doeth part; but each doeth the entire work by its individual energy. Free choice, in truth, doeth the entire work, and so also doth grace, but, even as the whole is done in the former (by co-operation), so is the whole done in the latter (by origination)."[16]

Bernard distinguishes four modes of freedom: freedom from sin, freedom from misery, freedom from necessity, and freedom from the State if it commands evil. The first two freedoms cannot be complete here but must await restoration and perfection in heaven. But every human being should be free from fate or necessity here and now. What Bernard wrote concerning secular rulers he also acted upon relative to ecclesiastical authorities when he found them in the wrong. When a monk obeyed an unworthy superior too slavishly, Bernard told him he ought to have discussed his scruple with his superior and not simply obeyed blindly or endured patiently like an ox. "I cannot, I confess, help being angry with this most questionable patience. You saw that he was scattered, yet you followed him, you heard him directing what was scandalous, yet you obeyed him."[17]

The chief fruit of nearness to God is love. Bernard believes love "overcomes and transforms all other feelings." He himself does not claim any vision like that of St. Paul, but he does emphasize joy and other spiritual states in a highly personal way. In a famous passage he writes that God entered his soul in such a way that he felt His presence but never felt His coming or departure. God does not come by eye, ear or nose; neither by mouth nor touch. God blends Himself with the mind. Though Leclercq makes much of the close similarity between Bernard's famous description of his spiritual experiences and Origen's, we might rather stress the highly traditional character of all his utterances, as well as note that this particular one echoes St. Paul and Augustine as well as Origen. Moreover, many have been able to express spiritual reality in the same terms as a well-loved author because they have made his language their own. At any rate, whatever its intrinsic merit or metaphysical validity, Bernard's is truly a practical mysticism which produced great devotional hymns and helped rescue from "high Christologies" the human Jesus, whom Bernard doubtless also helped sentimentalize.

Bernard was the last of the Church Fathers while Abelard (with Anselm) can perhaps be counted as the first of the scholastics. The intellectual and spiritual issues which divided them can be located in three main categories: the definition of love, the role of faith and reason, and the status of universals. Abelard, inspired by Cicero and Héloise, saw God's love to be entirely disinterested love. We, imitating God, ought to love Him for Himself and not for any reward of attainment, not even beatitude. The mystic Bernard, on the other hand, instead of defining love for God in dialectical seclusion from beatitude, rather asserts that such love *is* beatitude.

Before Abelard, theology was viewed as praise of God. The new tradition which Abelard was joining and helping shape, if not create, was quite willing to subject St. Paul's epistles to an objective, impersonal method, the same kind of scrutiny applied to other literature. This approach was abhorrent to Bernard and to twelfth-century monastics generally. The theology of Abelard look its departure from doubt and could never wholly deny its origin. This perspective "would clash with Bernard's conception of faith, as a grace divinely infused, spiritual in nature, decisive in affirmation, and sovereign in regency over thought as over life."[18]

The third major clash between the two men was over universals. Briefly it can be illustrated by Bernard's contention that virtue is a reality, not a name, as he perceived that Abelard was saying. In a sentence: "Justice, veracity, benevolence, are not collective terms to describe certain qualities, but vital essences, eternal as God."[19] In addition there were important contrasts of thinking on the Trinity and other doctrinal matters, not to mention the broader contrast of sharply different styles of life and thought. For example, it is clear how Bernard would react to this position of Abelard: "No matter what Augustine says, we affirm that as the Lord assumed a true human nature he took with it all the real defects of human infirmity."[20] An historical irony in this is that Bernard did more to rescue the humanity of Jesus for Christian devotion and imitation than did Abelard.

If there is a bottom line to the fundamental divergencies of viewpoint between Abelard and Bernard it is clarity vs. mystery. "It seemed as if the Church till that time had been stammering, while Abelard spoke out. All became smooth and easy; he treated religion politely, he handled her gently, but she melted away under his hands."[21] If that overstates the case against Abelard, as Bernard tended to do, Michelet doubtless records the truth which agitated Bernard: "The bold (Abelard) simplified, explained, humanized everything."[22] In Abelard's hands nothing hidden or divine was left in the mysteries as far as Bernard was concerned.

Although Bernard's intellectual heirs were not as numerous as his spiritual heirs, among the former we can mention not only Pascal but also Hugo of St. Victor, who was indebted to both sides of the Bernard-Abelard controversy. Also, Bonaventura is explicitly dependent on Bernard for his own position on free will. One warning issued by Bernard seems apropos to all subsequent thinkers: "What is the effect of learning without love? Pride, What is the effect of love without learning? Error."[23] Thomas Merton has written: "Perhaps our own century needs nothing so much as the combined anger and gentleness of another Bernard."[24]

3. Peter Lombard

The fame of Peter Lombard (c. 1095-1160) rests forever on the *Book of Sentences*, his unique formulation which became the backbone of Latin scholasticism from the time he brought it together. The scholastic method as so well exemplified in Peter Lombard had been the practice in India since at least the Han-Hellenistic-Bactrian period if not much earlier, and the same was essentially true in China. Islam was a relatively late-comer into this scholastic method, although it was adopted in essence by al-Kindī if not the Mu'tazilites before him. Many if not most of the Latin scholastics after Lombard accepted the *Sentences* outright as the basis for commentaries, as with Bonaventure, or, as with Aquinas, accepted them indirectly and followed virtually the same outline. Peter Lombard has been called the true founder of Latin scholastic theology, preluding the great works which the union of faith and reason was to bring forth in the thirteenth century. Nevertheless he is too often not given the importance that he deserves historically for the simple reason that his *Sentences* as such are eclipsed almost entirely by the commentaries on them.

Peter Lombard came from the region of Navarre in northern Italy; but we have very little specific information about his family or his origin, except that he probably came from a relatively humble family. His career was rather unexciting and followed the usual pattern. He was educated in Paris schools mostly and gradually passed through the usual stages of the Church hierarchical order until he became Bishop of Paris, which put him in a position of administrative responsibility. As Bishop of Paris he had to be a peace-maker, a reconciler, not only among the philosophers themselves but also between the philosophers and the theologians—no easy task in any age. Like so many all across Eurasia and not merely in Latin Europe, he wrote most of his work for the sake of his students; hence it was done for almost purely pedagogical purposes. It was at the request of his students that he finally finalized the format for the *Sentences* which really had been his lecture notes. Nevertheless, through that form of instruction his genuine spirit of contemplation and prayer shines through and reveals a theology which is "less speculative than affective, less argumentative than religious".

Rather than presenting a fresh revelation *ex nihilo*, as it were, what Peter Lombard did was *formalize* what the current trends already were manifesting. And established custom demanded clarity of presentation in a systematically structured way that admittedly allowed only a minimal margin for individualistic creative freedom, but nevertheless eased comprehension by virtue of clarity of theme and proper structuring of details and illustrations within that framework, which, like the medieval cathedrals (and for that matter also the Dravidian temples of the same period), seldom left any unembellished spaces. Thus the work is really nothing radically new but simply an effective compilation, expertly done, of what had become standard in the universities—no doubt leaving the extremists at both ends, e.g., the 'fundamentalists' who would do away with all the Hellenic heritage and go literally straight back to the sacred text, and those who were already anticipating the expertise in logic and linguistic analysis in the "Positivists of Paris". Félix Protois describes the work as follows: "The immense vogue which the *Book of Sentences* set in motion is sufficient exemplification of its intrinsic qualities: 1) the clear and methodical classification of all the doctrinal questions, 2) the neatness of the exposition, 3) the justness of the solutions, 4) the force and the richness of the testimonies, 5) the concision of the text, 6) the sobriety of the philosophical developments which leave to commentators a very free reign in dealing with the contributions." Of course this description would likewise fit the *Brahma Sūtras* very well.

Indeed, we should make a parallel arrangement of the *Sentences* of Peter Lombard alongside the *Brahma Sūtras* of Bādarāyaṇa to dramatize their remarkable similarity—so remarkable indeed that one is tempted to believe that somewhere in obscurity there must have been some influence howsoever indirect. One may of course simply surmise that such is the function of the human mind that sooner or later it comes out with essentially the same universal problems treated in a more or less universal way. Meanwhile we do not intend to exaggerate the similarities over against the differences, since in detail indeed there are variations, just as there is such a vastly differing variety of commentaries on both sets of *Sūtras/Sentences*, ranging from esoteric monism to outright realism in both cases.

Again, the most elementary basics of both the *Sentences* and the *Brahma Sūtras* are remarkably similar, and the topical outlines are almost identical. To quickly survey a very rich complexity remarkably well controlled, they proceed from the pivotal importance of the Inquiry into the Nature of the Ultimate (Brahman or God), including the problem of the One-and-the-many as applied to rational theology; then, down the hierarchical order through the angels (or plurality of deities) to the nature of God's operation in the created world; in due course the focus changes to the nature of man in relation to the rest of nature, to fellow human beings, and to the rest of creation, culminating in the consideration of the forms of immortality. Thus the typical anthropocentric universe emerges. After this the ethical considerations come into play as related to the question of who is worthy of salvation, *Brahma-vidyā* or heaven, *nirvāṇa*. Then there is generally a shift to the necessity of some social organ to propagate the *Dharma*. Thus the nature of the *saṅgha* follows after the exposition of the *Dharma* and the place of saints, avatars, incarnation(s) and prophets—in short, the Church as the normal channel of God's operating in this world. Man being partly of nature and partly of the 'other' world, there are rites, ceremonies and rituals, the cycle of feasts and fasts harmonious with nature, to give us the greatest freedom from nature possible according to season and within reason.

Of course it is not possible to point to exact parallels in all details, such as the discrepancy in the theories of immortality and future lives (even though Origen had believed in metempsychosis whereas evidently Peter Lombard did not). The Christian sacramental system of course is not exactly but only proximately parallel with the Hindu system. The Christian Trinity, nevertheless, is paralleled in the Vaiṣṇava commentaries by the Avatārs, Jesus himself having long since, along with the Buddha, been accepted as such; and the Holy Spirit with the *Antaryāmī* or even the *Sākṣī* furnishes a remarkable close parallel. The problem of the attributes of God is also closely parallel and the treatment in the commentaries on both sides runs through an equal range of positions, as is likewise the case with free will, determination and grace. But the most notable thing over all is the basic outline, starting with the nature of Brahman/God, then consideration of the creation of the world, proceeding on to the nature of man and the ethical predicament of man between physical necessities and spiritual aspirations, and of course *mokṣa* and salvation naturally occupy highest priority in the end.

We marvel that more has not been written demonstrating this remarkable basic parallel, and again the question of possible influence imposes itself to explain the similarities, which are so basic, the differences turning up in many details but without blotting or blurring the original pattern. Certainly Bādarāyaṇa chronologically came first whatever may have been his direct and indirect sources; hence the notion that there might have been influence from the Latin world to India is ruled out. Of course we may look back to our previous discussions of the possible influences of Neo-Platonism on both worlds, the Buddhists being the in-between transmitters, but beyond those basics we cannot go with any ease at all. The other hypothesis is simpler but perhaps even more difficult to prove, namely the inherent nature of man and our place in the natural and trans-natural such as all mythologies point towards. These considerations are inherently universal, for as Kant said so firmly and clearly later on, we are indeed citizens of two worlds (whether we like it or not). Of course some gnostics and others asserted the notion of many and not just two worlds, but that is not so critically important. In spite of occasional assertions of atheism in world history at large, there is that inalienable 'Something' that leaves human beings dissatisfied in the end with merely material comforts and pleasures, including even the capacity to build philosophical systems and keep them alive as traditions for many centuries.

By 1179 the third Lateran Council was already accepting the *Sentences* as authoritative, and in that document we find repeatedly the expression. We believe with Peter Lombard.... Even so, it was typical of him not to assert too much, leaving matters often open for further discussion. He was, as we might say, more socratic than dogmatic. His method is a happy mixture of the spirit of an investigator such as was Abelard and the conservative spirit of such as St. Bernard of Clairvaux. Between the virtual literalism of Peter Damian and the near 'Advaitic' ontological mysticism of the Carthusians, the Lombard seems to have found a fairly safe middle-ground.

It was Abelard's famous *Sic et Non* that really had set the pace for Peter Lombard's work. Of course it was not only Abelard who influenced the Lombard but virtually every Latin philosopher and/or theologian up to his own time. But more important is the long and very impressive list of those who were influenced by the *Sentences*. However, this does not mean that there was no opposition to this manner of philosophizing, from Robert of Merlun and Maurice de Sully for example. But he was able to vindicate his work as really not radical but simply basic. Indeed he preferred peace and reconciliation rather than encounter. And the famous Joachim of Fiori, who was in full sympathy with the so-called 'Spiritual' Franciscans who chose not to compromise the Holy Vow of Poverty (as he thought even Bonaventure and others were doing), probably did not like these systematizings—almost mechanizing, so to speak, the living vital organic spirituality of their conception of the mission and teaching of Jesus. Even so, this work, whose author is so little acknowledged compared to such as Thomas Aquinas, Ockham and others, was still being cultivated even as late as the seventeenth century.

Peter Lombard can easily be ranked with the rather substantial list of writers who became famous for only one great work, but in the Lombard's case a work of such historical importance that the person has often been forgotten even though the work itself became a basic textbook for all. Thus we leave him with a deep sense of dissatisfaction, since as a sort of man-behind-the-scenes in the formulation and characterization of the Latin Summas that were to follow, his influence is so much far greater than his reputation that he certainly deserves more attention For form being a dogmatist, Peter Lombard, whether by inspiration or by just plain hard thinking, does formulate a heritage with great simplicity and clarity that still persists as a very workable framework for a complete philosophical system. The genius of his compilations is in his selfless and detached manner of dealing with very controversial issues. That Peter Lombard was a compiler rather than an originator cannot be denied; but that his compilations took root and produced such fruit through the centuries is the better index of his genius and even a good measure of his seldom acknowledged charisma.

4. Hemacandra

The Jaina scholar Hemacandra (1088-1172) has been referred to by his contemporaries and later admirers as the greatest encyclopaedic mind in medieval India, the greatest doctor of Jainism, maker of an epoch, polymath of the modern world, the creator of Gujarati consciousness, the omniscient one of the Kali age. It seems that those who are familiar with Hemacandra are almost unanimous in their praise of this scholar, his works and his effectiveness in causing historical change. Some, no doubt, are overly enthusiastic about his standing among the greatest minds in the world history of philosophy when he is compared to such as Patañjali, Śaṅkara, Plato, Aristotle, and such moderns as Tilak, Tagore, and Gandhi. Hemacandra is not popularly known today among Jainas themselves, nor could he be said to be very well known among scholars outside of India.

Hemacandra was born in Gujarat. His name means "golden moon", which name he was given supposedly because he had the lustre of gold (*hema*) and was attractive as a moon (*candra*). Though his father was a Śaiva Hindu, his mother, a pious Jaina, put Hemacandra at the age of nine under the guidance of the famous Jaina teacher Devacandra. Hemacandra quickly gained a reputation for his erudition and sincerity, and eventually acquired the patronage of the powerful Hindu ruler Jayasiṁha. After the death of Jayasiṁha, Hemacandra not only received patronage from the successor, Kumārapāla, but converted him to Jainism and became his personal counsellor and teacher. It is thus through Kumārapāla that Hemacandra was able to establish the foundations of a Jaina state in Gujarat. Kumārapāla was evidently very sincere in his conversion to Jainism and, at least according to legend, "enforced *ahiṃsā* so rigorously that two merchants were mulcted of all their wealth for the crime of killing fleas."[1] In accordance with the highest Jaina discipline, both Hemacandra and his pupil Kumārapāla departed this realm by fasting to death. Even today Jainism is strongest in Gujarat, in no small part because of Hemacandra and his royal patron. According to Sharma, Hemacandra "became one of the three noblest personalities associated with that region. He stands beside the earlier Krisna and later political figure, Gandhi."[2]

Hemacandra was a real polymath who produced not only philosophical treatises but works on grammar, poetics, politics, history, mythology, and other topics. He wrote on Sanskrit, Prakrit, and Apabhramśa, and is recognized as the one who gave complete legitimacy to Apabhraṁśa language and literature, which before him had been considered unfit for religious and philosophical expression. Hemacandra was also an exceptional poet and indeed is perhaps best known for his epic work *The Lives of the Sixty-three Illustrious Persons* (*Triṣaṣṭiśalākāpuruṣa*) which relates the myths and legends of the traditional heroes of Jainism. According to Sharma, "the main purpose of the work is instruction and edification, for the author himself says: 'To sing in praise of the pious, lends to liberation.' "[3]

While the work on *Illustrious Persons* was written at the request of Kumārapāla, Hemacandra's *Yogaśāstra* was written for Kumārapāla and is credited with being the cause of his conversion to Jainism. The *Yogaśāstra* is basically an ethical work, encyclopedic in scope, detailing the duties of laymen and monks. In Hindu ethics such as in the *Gītā* violence was allowed under control and detachment. Jaina ethics was then and still is the strictest general code that remains a major challenge to all other systems. The general opinion is that it is unduly strict. Nevertheless it might be the case that this rigor was one of the chief reasons for the survival of Jainism in India whereas the more tolerant and benevolent Buddhist systems did not survive.

The *Pramāṇamīmāṃsā*, which remained unfinished and was his last work, is Hemacandra's most important contribution to Jaina philosophical literature. It is primarily valued as a textbook which presents Jaina logic and epistemology with conciseness and clarity in spite of the Jaina penchant for systematic detail and genius for classification which continues almost endlessly and is unrivalled in any literature. Mookerjee writes:

> It is a standard textbook on Jaina logic and epistemology which every student of Jaina philosophy has got to study.... It is an ideal textbook and in spite of its truncated character all the relevant problems of logic and epistemology have received an adequate treatment in it. It is absolutely clear that a student of Jaina logic and epistemology will derive a

comprehensive knowledge of the subject from the study of this work. The popularity of this book is due to its comprehensive character alone. It is no doubt a difficult book but considering the range of topics dealt with within the limits, it is idle to expect that it should be easy to follow. Hemacandra's purpose was to write a standard textbook and he did not condescend to cater for men of dull understanding.[4]

Hemacandra was a scholar and teacher working within a long-established philosophical tradition so that pedagogy was a bigger problem than the philosophy itself. Hemacandra was not interested in presenting any "new" philosophy and cannot be said to be "original". But to think that this in any way diminishes Hemacandra's importance is, according to Mookerjee, to misunderstand the Indian perspective on such matters:

Indian writers do not make a fetish of originality either of thought or of language and they make no scruple of inserting the arguments of predecessors even in their own language provided the views expressed therein accord with their philosophical position. The writings of predecessors are looked upon as public property and they are used with perfect freedom and impunity....

As regards the originality of thought which is so highly praised in Europe and in the modern universities of India, our ancient writers did not set an inordinate value on it. It was as much a matter of minor importance with them as originality of verbal expression. A serious work on a philosophical topic did not hold an isolated position in India. It was rather a link in the expanding chain of philosophical speculations and what was the object of serious concern was fidelity to the fundamentals of the school, and originality was more or less suspect with the adherents of the system as rather furnishing a pitfall for error or misconception. We must not therefore expect either originality of expression or of thought in the sense of an abrupt departure from the fundamental tenets which give the school a stamp of distinctive individuality.[5]

Mookerjee argues that Hemacandra and other Indian writers

were not interested in attaining personal triumph by being original even though they were certainly skilful enough to do so. He points to Jayanta Bhaṭṭa as another important philosopher who explicitly declared that he had no original theory of his own to offer but only wanted to present a rounded exposition of his subject.

Jaina logic remains the heart-core of Hemacandra's work. Jaina multi-valued logic has its curve, as it were, between degrees of affirmation and negation instead of the more traditional and curiously more universal two-valued logic of absolute yes and no. Jaina logic has a constant factor of resiliency, a "perhaps", hence the classical term *syādvāda* or "maybe-maybe". All through the centuries the Jaina logicians had to defend their logic, at least when they came out of their evidently self-imposed isolation and, like Hemacandra, began to write in Sanskrit in order to get into communication if not controversy with the other schools of Indian logic. The *vyāvahārika* level is here the primary field of operation rather than the *pāramārthika* which the Mahāyāna Buddhists and the Advaitins claim as the only locus of ultimates. For with them it is either ultimate or not-at-all, whereas the Jaina logic stresses elasticity not only of affirmation and negation but implicitly of the varying degrees of excellence that a few reach but most only strive after.

Hemacandra's contemporary Vādi Devasūri (1086-1169) was acknowledged by him and others as one of the greatest debaters of his time, one of his most famous victories being an affirmative on the question of the female's capacity for attaining emancipation (*mokṣa*). Bhattacharya writes of his best known work: "The *Pramāṇa-naya-tattvā-lokālaṃkāra* is a standard work on the Jaina mediaeval logic, psychology and epistemology. It is naturally a stiff treatise; and its commentary is stiffer still. The book and particularly the commentary contain and develop at first the views of the opponent schools and then set them aside and finally establish the theories of the Jaina Śvetāmbara school."[6] The thirteenth century Jaina Malliṣeṇa wrote an important commentary called *Syādvādamañjarī* on Hemacandra's *An Examination in Thirty-two Stanzas of the Doctrines of Other Systems* in which Hemacandra criticizes Hindu and Buddhist philosophical systems. "The *Syādvādamañjarī* has come to be regarded as one of the most celebrated works on Jaina metaphysics and logic. By virtue of its systematic presentation of thought and its lucidity of style, though technically only a commentary, the book has been ranked almost as an original piece of work."[7]

Mookerjee makes the point that Hemacandra had little opportunity to make any new contributions on Jaina logic and epistemology since he was preceded by some of the very greatest Jaina writers such as Akalaṅka, Vidyānanda and Prabhācandra of the Digambara school and Siddhasena Divākara, Haribhadra, Siddharṣi, and Abhayadeva of the Śvetāmbara school. But Hemacandra avoids the formidable abstruseness of these writers with their unremitting elaboration of arguments and prolixity of expression. As Mookerjee puts it: "It would take years of extraordinary labour to make a study of these works and there again is every possibility for missing the forest in the trees."[8] Thus the importance of Hemacandra's *Pramāṇamīmāṃsā* as a textbook to guide the student through the compendious manuals and forbidding language characteristic of many Jaina savants.

5. Nimbārka

Nimbārka (c. 1175) is known as the "middle ground" philosopher between the extremes of the Advaitins on the one hand and Madhva on the other. The same has been claimed to a great extent for Rāmānuja also, so one must distinguish between these two with considerable care. It is fairly certain that Nimbārka did have access to something by and/or about Rāmānuja but it is not easy to discern just how much. The basic difference is that whereas Rāmānuja considers that the Fundamental *Unity* (not just sheer Identity) is inclusive of, but over-encompasses, the multiplicity of Reality, Nimbārka believes that that is still claiming perhaps too much. We experience difference sometimes, and we experience unity or unities sometimes, and it is unfaithful to experience to claim that one is inclusive or exclusive of the other. Nimbārka's intention all through his expositions is evidently to avoid extremes of all sorts, and to be not so distinctive but moderate in finding the most workable *middle ground* between all the various possibilities.

On the whole, Nimbārka stands in Indian tradition in a position very much analogous to that of Duns Scotus in Christian tradition. There is the background of Śaṅkara and of Aristotle respectively to which they cannot avoid making some concessions even though they are for the most part concerned to fabricate something better, more complete and well-rounded, and less extreme in stressing the knowledge aspect of the Being of God while yet not compromising the ontological implications of the supremely "intellectual". Both aim at comprehensiveness more than a single theory to explain everything. In spite of great skill in making close logical distinctions, both risk ambiguities in order to achieve this comprehensiveness. Nevertheless both are quite clear as to their basic purpose, which is the establishment of the right balance, not so much between *māyā* and Brahman, phenomenal and noumenal, as between the human soul and God. Both will acknowledge that Being in the highest sense of Reality (that which *is*) *is* God; but this definition is inadequate because it like any definition puts limitations on the Defined, even though Brahman/God not only allows those definitions for the sake of our understanding but sanctions and enjoins the way of definition as a major effort in approaching the 'problems' of both faith and practice. They both stand in sharp contrast with their Japanese Buddhist and Sūfī friends who have surrendered the rational almost altogether in favor of faith and devotion, as well as in contrast with such as Eckhardt and Rāmādvaya who adhere to the strict monist tradition.

Almost of necessity one takes the school of Nimbārka pretty much as a whole rather than giving reports individually of its members. With other traditions this would be a defect; but one gets the impression that the Nimbārkas differ very little among themselves, perhaps for structural reasons more than by circumstance since their position calls for less trimming of fine points and puts the focus in the opposite direction—rather healthily, one might assert, since of the trimming of fine points there is certainly no end. Nevertheless refutations remain a primary focus as is the case with virtually all commentators on the *Brahma*

Sūtras after Śaṅkara. But again it might be said of the school of Nimbārka that rather than indulge in fancy gymnastics of the mind, in spirit they tend to appeal back to the basics, even in their refutations.

Proofs for the existence of God are not normally stressed in any of the Indian systems, and the Nimbārkas are no exception to that rule. However over against the Advaita manner of relegating theism to the 'lower' *saguṇa*-Brahman, Nimbārka joins in with the other Vaiṣṇavas in not allowing that distinction. For if God be all that He must be, He cannot be relegated to a "second fiddle" role in the grand symphony of reality. The sharp distinction between *nirguṇa* and *saguṇa*-Brahman which receives so much emphasis by the Advaitins is considered as really unnecessary by the Nimbārka school. Dasgupta writes:

> The world is thus not an illusory imposition on the pure Brahman, but a real transformation of the varied powers of God. The difference of this view from that of Sāṃkhya is that while the Sāṃkhya believes in the transformation of certain primary entities in their entirety, the Nimbārkists believe in the transformation of the various powers of God. God Himself remains unchanged and unmodified, and it is only His powers that suffer modification and thereby produce the visible world.
>
> The explanation that the world is produced through the reflection of Brahman in *māyā* or by its limitation through it is invalid, for since the *māyā* is an entity of an entirely different order, there cannot be any reflection of Brahman in it or a limitation by it. It is not possible to bind down a thief with a dream-rope.[1]

Nimbārka's formula of difference-with-nondifference does not exclude the sense of hierarchy but rather is applicable to it. To a great extent the collapse of hierarchy into a more adamant dualism typifies the next period in Campanella, Vallabha, and Baladeva; but so far it is still preserved in Nimbārka as it is in Duns Scotus.

The Nimbārkas are concerned that the Rāmānujas have been too free in letting their Realm of Spirit be inclusive of non-spiritual things, at the risk almost that two Brahmans must be involved in such a broad-sweep view, one associated with matter and finitude and the other transcendental, the relation between these two not being sufficiently clarified. But on the topic of the Reality of World the differences between Viśiṣṭādvaita and Nimbārka's *Bhedābheda* are less large and more common ground can easily be found, as is often the case when there is a common opponent. The refutation is of strict Advaita's dogged insistence on the 'indefinability' of Brahman. This had virtually become a dogma even though it might be that Śaṅkara's original intention was to eliminate all grounds for dogmatism. The refuge into indefinability by the Advaitins is far too open, for utter indefinability leaves room, as it were, for all the demons as well as the angels to enter without any passport or admission fee. Indefinability, in short, is far too amorphous as a description of anything. Being a purely negative concept it must have something presupposed to deny or attempt to negate. It is necessary to presuppose some reality, indeed some *knowable* reality, before any denial can be asserted. In short, assertion of ignorance is impossible without some notion of what it is that one is ignorant of.

Rāmānuja is the most complete on the philosophy of embodiment, showing more difference from the Advaitins than Thomas from Bernard of Clairvaux or Nichiren from Kūkai. To a great extent Nimbārka is only following Rāmānuja here, although he is not so precise in defining what is meant by embodiment since this is not so much his concern as the right discernment of the relation of the soul in its essence with the existence of Brahman as a supremely Personal Deity. To a great extent the same might be said of the transition between St. Thomas and Duns Scotus. Dasgupta writes:

> As a part cannot be different from the whole, so the individual soul can never be different from God. But, in the state of bondage the individuals are apt to forget their aspects of unity with God and feel themselves independent in all their actions and experiences. When by absolute self-abnegation springing from love the individual feels himself to be absolutely controlled and regulated by God and realizes himself

> to be a constituent of Him, he loses all his interests in his actions and is not affected by them. The ultimate ideal, therefore, is to realize the relation with God, to abnegate all actions, desires and motives, and to feel oneself as a constituent of Him. Such a being never again comes within the grasp of mundane bondage and lives in eternal bliss in his devotional contemplation of God. The devotee in the state of his emancipation feels himself to be one with God and abides in Him as a part of His energy. Thus, even in the state of emancipation, there is a difference between the emancipated beings and God, though in this state they are filled with the utmost bliss.[2]

Like Rāmānuja, and differing from Śaṅkara and most Advaitins who are inclined to be Śaivites although officially not associated with any particular cult, Nimbārka is a Vaiṣṇava to whom *devotion* to the Lord as Brahman is the better and more natural attitude than assertion of complete identity. But there is already a shift of emphasis in the pattern of popular devotion in the Nimbārka school from Viṣṇu to Kṛṣṇa, which trend will later become much more prominent in the Vallabha and the Caitanya schools. Though the *bhakti* aspect prevails, the Nimbārkas tend to be slightly more restrained than the Śrī Vaiṣṇavas, while the Caitanyites tend to let emotions prevail over reason in a way that the Nimbārkas would not approve.

Nimbārka follows the traditional division of all reality into the three-fold classification of sentient, non-sentient, and Brahman. It will be remembered that Śaṅkara and his followers had hedged around these different categories in order to maintain that 'somehow' they were all One without any difference, the supposed difference being only superimposition (*adhyāsa*), ignorance (*avidyā*), etc. Duns Scotus and Madhva, the latter following the original realistic classification in the Vaiśeṣika, had taken these differences as irreducibly and unalterably and distinctly and eternally real.

Omniscience, omnipotence, and omnipresence are the necessary minimum attributes that must be ascribed to God. Even the Advaitins cannot get around the triad of *sat*, *cit* and *ānanda* although they mostly would like to squeeze that triad into the *jñāna* mould. One of the most cogent supports for the *bhedābheda* position is the recognition of the difference between, but the very intimate inter-relationalities of, the basic attributes of God. Again, the great merit of the Nimbārka school is the sense of due proportion and good judgment, avoiding all extremes. Admittedly Rāmānuja does tend to become almost excessively diffused in his zealous enthusiasm when it comes to the attributes. One cannot deny the plurality of the attributes even though they are intimately related, even organically so. The basic attributes are not indistinguishable, even though they are so intimately interrelated that to compromise any of them would be as bad as asserting their plurality without any common locus of reference.

Concerning the aspect of Mind, we may recall the debate over the higher Active Intellect in relation to the Passive Intellect among the Aristotelians, and the typical Buddhist way of stressing consciousness or, in the Theravāda, 'awareness' rather than mind in the sense of being a faculty or agency wherein the subject-object relationship is made. Here the Buddhists are not, when they are true to their own genre, ontologists. To them mind (*manas, buddhi, citta*) is not an entity or a faculty but a process, an operation, a continuum, whereas the rest identify, by varying degrees of equation, Mind with Being, so that knowledge is really something and is about something; it is not just the seeming localization of a continuum of causal process to be extinguished along with all the rest of the causal order. There is thus a sharp distinction, very difficult to reconcile, between this interpretation of enlightenment of the Vedānta and the Aristotelians where a greater degree of inclusive knowing is the end, not the cultivation of any sort of 'unknowing' as found also in the successors of Eckhardt, Tauler and Suso, for example, and in the Japanese adaptation of Zen, and in a few extremists among the Sūfīs.

Being of the nature of Mind, however, is only one of several principal characteristics which mark the Brahman. Invisibility and imperishability, for example, are also very important. Indeed they are not evidently subordinate to the others and the same problem is encountered, namely the relation of the related to the Relationless. The positive attributes include greatness, grandeur and glory, and exaltedness, but what about the infinitely small?

What does 'unlimited' really mean? Is it a limitation to suppose that God can be as wholly present in the most infinitessimal 'point' imaginable as well as beyond the ultimate possible conceivable magnitude? Here, by the way, may be a fault in Anselm's argument, for the *greater* than which anything can be conceived is much less paradoxical than the *less* than which nothing could be conceived. Perhaps the human intellect is too fond of thinking in terms of vast things, ambitiously ascribing to God all that it can possibly imagine; but to think of God as unlimited by anything entails equally the non-limitation at the other end of the continuum.

Concerning the *pramāṇas,* the basic argument is that knowledge is always individuated to a certain extent, at the first level at least. Knowledge, in short, is necessarily *about* or pointing to something besides itself. However, it must not be thought that this is asserted in a naive sort of realism, but with considered possibilities of the extremes that others can and have taken; for example, by no means is naive empiricism the necessary opposite of *māyāvāda.* Inference is just as important as perception. Negation in most if not all forms is rejected as a separate *pramāṇa* by this school. Negation must be negation or denial of something about a really existing something, so knowledge deals with what *is* known about the object (or subject) at hand. Negation cannot stand on its own feet, so to speak, like perception, or use its arms like inference. Dasgupta writes that "it is unnecessary to admit *abhāva* or *anupalabdhi* as a separate *pramāṇa*, for according to the Nimbārkas negation is not admitted as a separate category. The perception of negation is nothing but the perception of the locus of the object of negation as unassociated with it."[3]

The Trinitarian structure in Nimbārka is very vivid at times. The inconceivability is equatable to the Christian Father, the attributes of mind, etc., appropriate to the Eternal Word, the Son, and the Inner Controller appropriate to the Holy Spirit. Paradoxically these are irreducibly one-and-three in both difference and identity. There is tranquility and serenity for the very basic reason that therein alone is the foundation for Harmony. Any attempt to rise into a hyperstatic reduction of this to some 'nothing' above it is hybris; any compromise with the multiplicity less than this is metaphysical blindness. Knowledge, faith and grace, epistemology, ethics and aesthetics, the I-mode, the Thou-mode, and the That-mode by consequence must go together; any playing of favorites will only breed fanaticism. However, the key to comprehension of all this remains in the *Antaryāmī*, the Inner Controller, the Holy Spirit.

It would seem that there is no reason why all men should not acknowledge the Unicity of the one God, the Single Principle, Jahwe, Allah, Brahman, Tao, or whatever name one uses by dent of tradition. Differences are not necessarily to be abrogated but can remain in the local custom as long as it is understood that the intention is really the same. There must be a manner of meditation which is not exclusivistic and which does not engender fanaticism. We need not, as some think, abandon religion because the religions divide mankind. Instead, through an application of this difference-and-nondifference in togetherness rather than according to either/or it should be possible for each tradition to continue its path of Unity in its own terms. This does not mean a syncretistic muddle, however, as a wrong application of Advaita might entail, for difference is not denied. For that matter, even within any one tradition this logistic is highly commendable since, for example, a meditation on one Person of the Blessed Trinity for Christians, or on Allah and His attributes and His Prophet for Muslims, or on the *Trikāya* for Mahāyāna Buddhists, need not entail that one is not meditating on the other aspects in the same act. It is not necessary to strain at the whole of the Encompassing every time since if one adequately has a grasp of one aspect in its identity-and-difference one has a key to understanding the whole immediately. But some sort of trilogistic structure seems unavoidable. If so it might be argued that both St. Thomas and Śaṅkara (or rather Śrīharṣa) dichotomize too much and are not on such sound ground as Duns Scotus and Nimbārka. Whether one prefers to leave the nature of this trilogizing unexplicated or risk losing one's identity in 'entering' it in mystical contemplation beyond the ontologizing meditation may depend on one's temperament, type or vocation. The latter is the way of Rāmānuja, Bonaventure, and Dōgen; the former, Nimbārka, Scotus and Shinran.

In Nimbārka we find a systematic approach to reality which is not only representative of a realistic attitude but based on recognition of the necessity of positive assertions rather than the mere 'logic' of denial that characterizes most of the Advaita expositions. The most basic orientation of the system is to not risk subordination of either identity or difference one to the other but to leave that relation completely open, resiliently, we might say, without risking imbalance by reason of excessive emphasis on either.

6. Ibn Ṭufayl

The Neo-Platonic literary mystic Ibn Ṭufayl (d. 1185) is a noteworthy figure in the history of philosophy in Islamic Spain. Born near Granada, he held a high position in the court and was responsible for introducing no less than Ibn Rushd to the caliph. Ibn Ṭufayl was court physician and probably a political advisor as well, and certainly the chief influence in securing patronage for Ibn Rushd, who was by some accounts also his student. It was Ibn Rushd who succeeded Ibn Ṭufayl as court physician. Unfortunately we know very little about Ibn Ṭufayl as a personality, so little that Goodman writes: "Those searching for a figure into which they may breathe again the colors of sentiment and passion had best be warned to find another. Ibn Ṭufayl will not respond to their efforts at resuscitation."[1]

Although Ibn Ṭufayl wrote widely on medicine, science and philosophy, only one of his philosophical works is extant: *Ḥayy b. Yaqẓān* (*Living*, *Son of Wakeful*, or *The Living One Son of the Waking One*). This little classic is an allegory about a solitary on an uninhabited island who through natural growth discovers the true nature of himself, the world, and God. Though a parallel with Defoe's *Robinson Crusoe* suggests itself the two works actually have little in common besides the literary format. Siddiqi gives the following summary of *Ḥayy b. Yaqẓan*:

> The treatise dramatically opens with the spontaneous birth of Ḥayy in an uninhabitated island.... Unalloyed by social conventions, he is nourished there by a roe and taught by

natural reason or common sense, which ... equips him with inductive intellect to probe into the secret of things. Unlike the lower animals, he becomes conscious of his being naked and unarmed with physical weapons of defence. He reflects over the situation and covers the lower parts of his body with leaves, arms himself with a stick, and thus comes to realize the superiority of his hands over the feet of animals. The death of the mother-roe leads him to the discovery of the animal soul which uses the body as an instrument, like the stick in his hands, shares light and warmth with fire, and thus bears resemblance to the heavenly bodies. He then turns to the analysis of the phenomena of nature, compares the objects around him, and discriminates between them, and classifies them into minerals, plants, and animals. Observation shows him that body is a common factor in all the objects, but they belong to different classes because of the functions peculiar to them. This leads him to assume a specific form or soul for each class of objects. But the soul being imperceptible, his dialectical ingenuity at last brings him to the idea of an ultimate, eternal, incorporeal, and necessary Being which is the efficient cause of the peculiar behaviour of bodies. This makes him conscious of his own immaterial essence; and acting upon a three-point code of ascetic discipline. . .he is finally absorbed in the unrestrained contemplation of the Ultimate Being.

At this stage, Asāl, a contemplative and meditative soul from the neighbouring inhabited island, appears on the scene in quest of attaining perfection in solitude. He informs Ḥayy, the child of nature, about the Qur'ānic conceptions of God, His angels, prophets, the Day of Judgment, etc., which he by his self-developed intellect immediately recognizes as truths. He, however, in the first instance, fails to see the wisdom implicit in the figurative languages of the Qur'ān about God and the hereafter, and in the permission that it gives one to lead a worldly life—a permission which is likely to turn one away from the truth. Full of ambition and hope, he sets out in the company of Asāl to the said inhabited island ruled by Salāmān and begins to reform its convention-ridden people. He endeavours hard to enlighten the masses through pure concepts, but, in the end, finds these concepts far above

> their heads. He then realizes the wisdom of the Prophet in giving them sensuous forms instead of full light, returns to his lonely island, and is absorbed in contemplation.[2]

In its natural state, untainted by society and human conventions, the soul is predisposed to seek knowledge of the world and ultimately "illumination" by the divine. The final goal of mystical union is attained only after the intellect is perfected and the soul is purified through ascetic discipline. Ecstasy, which is the highest knowledge attainable, is superior to mere rational contemplation or "scientific understanding, yet these are prerequisites for attaining the beatific vision. As Siddiqi writes: "Not mere discipline of spirit, but the education of the senses and the intellect, too, is essential for such a vision. The harmony of experience with reason (Kant), on the one hand, and that of reason with intuition (Bergson and Iqbāl), on the other, constitutes the very essence of Ibn Ṭufayl's epistemology."[3]

In the manner of al-Junayd, Ibn Ṭufayl teaches a mystic state of utter annihilation of the self and absorption in God (*fanā*). Intellectual contemplation alone is deficient and falls short of the goal because the sense of self is never entirely overcome, and thus there is always "another" vis-à-vis the One. In his initial inquiry Ḥayy turns toward the world for understanding, but in the final states he turns away from the world which has become a hindrance to the higher reaches of the soul. The evolution of natural knowledge leads to a mystical knowledge of pantheism and the Oneness of Being. Ibn Ṭufayl, according to Siddiqi, "maintains in a mystic strain that the world is not something other than God....Ibn Ṭufayl accepts the principle that from one nothing can proceed except one. The manifestation of the existing plurality from unity is explained in the monotonous Neo-Platonic fashion, as successive stages of emanation proceeding from the divine light."[4] The final state of illumination for the soul is ecstasy, supreme bliss, divine intoxication, in which there is no other identity excepting the ineffable Identity of the True One.

In Ibn Ṭufayl we find a strong presentation of the two-truth theory which through Ibn Rushd became common among European scholastics. Ḥayy fails to make any impression upon the inhabitants of the nearby island when he attempts to teach them higher wisdom. Philosophy is for the few who are capable of enlightenment, while the figurative approach of religion is for the ignorant masses who are incapable of anything more than formal obedience. Nevertheless, philosophy and religion, dogma, and revelation are not in conflict at all, for Ḥayy is able to acknowledge the truths of religion as they are presented to him by Asāl, and later accepts the wisdom of giving the illiterate masses an "inferior salvation" since they are not capable of coming into full light.

Ibn Ṭufayl took the tittle and the names of the characters from Ibn Sīnā, and he says in the introduction that his intent is to present the illuminative philosophy of Ibn Sīnā. As a result some have thought that *Ḥayy b. Yaqzan* was little more than a repetition of Ibn Sīnā's ideas, and the work itself had even been attributed to Ibn Sīnā. However, Hawi argues that Ibn Sīnā was not the main influence on Ibn Ṭufayl, and that he owes as much or more to the influences of al-Junayd, al-Basṭāmī, al-Ḥallāj, Ibn Bājjah, al-Ghazālī, and al-Fārābī. But Ibn Ṭufayl also criticizes his predecessors, and thought, according to Hawi, that Ibn Sīnā was "not and 'Arif (one who experienced intimacy). His superior intellect permitted him to depict and discuss mystical gnosis as an 'imitator,' not as one who experienced it or belonged to the order."[5] Hawi continues:

> What distinguishes Ibn Ṭufayl's philosophy from al-Fārābī's, Avicenna's, and Ibn Bājjah's is his denial that the highest stage of felicity is achieved through union with the active intellect. His is a direct union with God, *excluding all intermediaries*. What distinguishes his mysticism from al-Ghazālī's is his insistence on complete union with God and all Being, a view that was attacked by al-Ghazālī. . . .Al-Ghazālī "destroyed" reason to reach mysticism; whereas Ibn Ṭufayl's Ḥayy reached his highest degrees of felicity through the aid of rational elevation from which he then rose to immediate experience.[6]

Meanwhile Siddiqi emphasizes the influence of Ibn Bājjah on Ibn Ṭufayl's *Ḥayy*:

> By far the most marked, deep, and saturating influence which

> seems to have coloured the basic structure of Ibn Ṭufayl's romance is that of Ibn Bājjah, his arch-rationalist predecessor. His lonely, metaphysically minded Ḥayy is only an extreme form of the "solitary man" of Ibn Bājjah's *Tadbīr al-Mutawaḥḥid.* Nevertheless, in spite of his recognition of the necessity of solitude for the improvement of theoretical reason, Ibn Ṭufayl feels rather unhappy over Ibn Bājjah's one-sided emphasis on the role of reason in arriving at the ultimate truth. . . . And it is the influence of Ghazālī and perhaps also of Suhrawardi Maqtūl, his Persian contemporary, that made him supplement reason with ecstasy in its flight to the celestial world.[7]

Ibn Ṭufayl presents the challenge and bespeaks the potential for those of the highest ability to attain an unqualified perfection. His basic criticism of such as al-Fārābī, Ibn Sīnā, Ibn Bājjah, and others is that they were content to stop short of the goal of full illumination. Still the themes in *Ḥayy b. Yaqẓān* are mostly the standard Neo-Platonic ones, and it is rather the unique literary quality of Ibn Ṭufayl which assures his continuing influence through post-Neo-Platonic ages.

7. Suhrawardī

Shihāb al-Dīn Yaḥiā al-Suhrawardī (1153-1191), also called al-Maqtūl (the Murdered), al-Shahīd (the Martyr), and Shaikh al-Ishrāq, is the founder of the illumination (*ishrāq*) school of Islamic philosophy. It is not surprising to learn, given the typical pattern of constant conflict between recalcitrant orthodoxies and innovations of genius throughout human history, that Suhrawardī was executed, thanks in part to a change in patronage and other external developments, in which the "Christian" Crusades may have been a factor. Although Suhrawardī's brilliance and boldness in exposition and other signs of uninhibited genius got him in trouble with the orthodox clergy who made a martyr of him at an early age, it might be remarked that it was not just his particular contribution that met with censorship but all varieties of Ṣūfism, as was too often the case in many periods of Islamic history. There seems to be two types of charismatic persons, those who suffer martyrdom at a relatively early age and those who by contrast acquire charisma like Rāmānuja by virtue of a very long and peaceful life. A third type would be such as Gandhi who indeed suffered martyrdom but at a relatively advanced age. Certainly the study of the dynamics of charisma needs to be widened and deepened much beyond what Max Weber and Sorokin were able to do. At any rate, Suhrawardī's charisma is remarkably like that of al-Ḥallāj.

Suhrawardī did not happen "out of the blue" but as a further development of Ṣūfī trends which had had a goodly five centuries or so to grow and to produce some strange fruits (from the orthodox point of view) following after some enticingly fragrant flowers. The basic concern of Suhrawardī is simply that of clarifying the spiritual path, no matter how far distant seems to be the goal. His *Ḥikmat al-Ishrāq* (*The Wisdom of Illumination*) was no doubt written with the motive of making it possible for others also to come into the Divine Light on which all else depends. For especially with the Ishrāqi tradition, mere information about it is not enough. Ṣūfī emphasis on experience even more than theory pervades the *Ḥikmat al-Ishrāq*, which is a synthesis of theory and practice as well as a synthesis of several traditions. Whatever his sources the actual synthesis was Suhrawardī's own, which is shown rather vividly in his eschatology where although the appeal is to the Qur'ān the interpretation is not so traditional but quite original. (Of course modern secularists would regard eschatology as no longer relevant for philosophy as such, and really even from the perspectives of systematic theology, it is generally considered as a little too esoteric to deserve very serious consideration—futurology being the result of that secularization. On the other hand, in the modern world at large we also have the work of Teilhard de Chardin and of Śrī Aurobindo, who have re-established a field of hope of a deeper sort.)

Although he had the good fortune of being translated into both Sanskrit and Hebrew, Suhrawardī is yet another of those major figures in the Islamic world east of the Mediterranean who never got Latinized and hence have not been known by Eurameri-cans until quite recently. His genius was quickly recognized in the Islamic world and he came to exercise tremendous influence. Indeed, according to Nasr, "the influence of Suhrawardī has been as great in the Islamic world, particularly in Shī'ism, as it has been small in the West."[1] Just as Aristotelianism was beginning to become a dominant factor in European philosophy it was declining as a major force in Islamic philosophy, and it was the Ishrāqī wisdom of Suhrawardī along with the Ṣūfism of Ibn 'Arabī which replaced Aristotelianism as the dominant force in intellectual Islam. Thus Suhrawardī has been almost as influential as Ibn Sīnā, for example, and Corbin writes that "it was only because his work was ignored for so long a time in the West (where one was accustomed to assessing Islamic philosophy from the viewpoint of what was known of it by Latin Scholastics) that an exaggerated importance was attached to Averroës."[2]

For Suhrawardī philosophy is not an exercise in analysis or criticism, nor merely aesthetic, nor only metaphysical map-making without there being a corresponding 'journey' to be undertaken. Like most philosophers until quite recently, Suhrawardī has a definite view of the true identity of man and his condition in this world. Man is a divine being by nature who has "fallen" from perfect light into obscuring matter. "Suhrawardī is essentially interested in demonstrating the celestial origin of the soul and the misery of its present state, and consequently in seeking a way by which the soul can escape from its terrestrial prison or its 'Occidental exile' and return once again to its original abode, where alone it can find felicity and peace."[3] It might be interesting to ask whether philosophy today still accepts this challenge of knowing and helping man to his true identity and destiny, or whether it has become perhaps too much self-absorbed, and perhaps too much enchanted by the fascinations of language, technique, and science. For Suhrawardī as for Neo-Platonists generally and indeed for most of the great thinkers-about-man in the world history of philosophy, man is a spiritual being in an essentially spiritual reality with a corresponding and destiny. Therefore spirituality, theosophy, esoterics, and logic are all part of the quest for release from worldly bondage and the attainment of enlightenment. As Corbin writes: "Suhrawardī did not separate philosophy and spirituality: a philosophy that does not terminate in or at least tend toward a mystical and spiritual experience is a vain undertaking."[4]

Suhrawardī found philosophy and spirituality united in the old Persian sages and in the pre-Aristotelian period in the West. He relies upon such teachers of the science of light as Jamasp, Farashaustra, Zoroaster, and others in the East, and Asclepius, Pythagoras, Empedocles, and Plato in the West. Corbin writes:

> A guiding thought dominates Suhrawardī's work: to restore the philosophy and theosophy of the sages of ancient Persia. Three centuries before it was effected in the works of the great Byzantine philosopher Georgius Gemistus Pletho, the conjunction of the names of Plato and Zoroaster was realized in the works of this thinker of Islamic Persia. Broadly outlined, this work (where the influence of Hermeticism and late Neo-Platonism was also joined) brought forth an interpretation of the theory of Platonic Ideas in terms of Zoroastrian angelology.[5]

However, Suhrawardī is not motivated by patriotism in his desire to restore the Persian sages but rather by his view of the history of philosophy according to which "wisdom, or theosophy, was revealed by God to man through the prophet Idrīs, or Hermes, who was thus considered... as the founder of philosophy and the sciences." Nasr continues to explain:

> This wisdom then divided into two branches, one of which came to Persia and the other to Egypt. From Egypt it went to Greece and finally from these two sources, namely Persia and Greece, it entered into Islamic civilization....
>
> The Master of *Ishrāq* (Suhrawardī) therefore considered himself as the focal point at which the two traditions of wisdom that at one time issued forth from the same source were once again unified.[6]

Suhrawardī also looked to such Ṣufīs as al-Basṭāmī and al-Ḥallāj as transmitters of this wisdom to himself.

Even as some in the twentieth century may find contemporary philosophy too non-spiritual and even anti-spiritual and not enough concerned with wisdom (a word of seemingly little philosophical significance today), so Suhrawardī already in the twelfth century felt he had to look back to pre-Aristotelian philosophy to find the correct balance between intellectual and intuitive understanding. The Greeks for Suhrawardī had displaced true wisdom by an over-emphasis on rationalism. In their hands wisdom had been too much reduced to intellect, intuition too much limited in its capacity for enlightenment. As Nasr writes of Ishrāqī illuminationism: "This school identifies philosophy with wisdom rather than with rational systematization. Philosophy for it does not begin with Plato and Aristotle; rather, it ends with them. Aristotle, by putting wisdom in a rationalistic dress, limited its perspective and separated it from the unitive wisdom of the earlier sages."[7]

If Peripeticism went to an extreme in its emphasis on discursive thought, it was not Suhrawardī's intention to go to the other extreme in his insistence on illuminative wisdom. Rather, they complement each other. The mind must be rationally trained, but the training must lead on to spiritual experience. Aristotelian philosophy is simply the necessary preparation for illuminative wisdom. As Nasr says of the *Ḥikmat al-Ishrāq*, "Beginning with logic, it ends in spiritual union and ecstasy."[8] Suhrawardī was a recognized master of both discursive wisdom and mystical wisdom. "Some Ṣūfīs, like al-Basṭāmī and al-Ḥallāj, may have attained an equal standing in the practical ways of mysticism, but none was able to combine the two ways, the theoretical and practical, with such consummate skill."[9]

Suhrawardī's Aristotelian teachings are based on Ibn Sīnā (Avicenna), who himself had planned to move from "the well-trodden Peripatetic path in the direction of a mystical and experiential approach to truth, which he designated illumination (*ishrāq*)." However, Ibn Sīnā never carried out this plan, but Suhrawardī did in his *Ḥikmat al-Ishrāq*, of which Fakhry writes:

> Apart from the mystical or experiential element which pervades this philosophy, its cosmological and metaphysical groundwork is not altogether unfamiliar. It is essentially an

> Avicennian, Neo-Platonic groundwork to which certain mystical and religious elements from Zoroastrian and other Oriental sources have been added. What sets it apart from the traditional Neo-Platonism of Islam is primarily its attempt to exploit to the full the light imagery, which as we have seen, Ibn Sīnā had first adumbrated and Zoroastrianism fully incorporated in its religious and metaphysical world-view.
>
> ... The metaphysical outlook of al-Suhrawardī remains essentially Avicennian or Neo-Platonic. This is perhaps nowhere better illustrated than in a short treatise entitled *The Philosophers' Creed*, in which he seeks to defend the "theosophists" against the strictures and slanders of the masses, who accuse them of godlessness or irreligion. Al-Suhrawardī argues that the theosophists believe in the unity of God, the creation of the world, and the inevitability of judgment. The first entity created by God is the first intellect, which in turn gives rise, through emanation, to another intellect, from which the Soul and the body of the first heaven emanate. The process goes on in downward progression until we come to the last intellect and the world of generation and corruption, which it governs. This lowest intellect is called by them the "giver of forms" or the "holy spirit".[10]

In the Ishrāqī system Light and Being are virtually synonymous. Darkness is not an opposing force in itself but simply a deprivation, an absence (*abhāva*) of Light, or in Suhrawardi's terms, an obscuration or obscurity. Suhrawardī is not exclusively interested only in the highest but also in the whole hierarchy of descending manifestations such that each individual existent still bears the 'signature' of its identity in relation to the other lights and ultimately to the "Light of lights" that is never obscured or subject to change. Nasr writes:

> According to Suhrawardī, all of reality is nothing but light which possesses various degrees of intensity. It needs no definition, for one always defines the obscure by the evident and there is nothing more evident and clear than light, so that there is nothing in terms of which it can be defined. In fact, all things are made evident by it and thus should be

> defined with reference to it. The Pure Light, which Suhrawardī calls the Light of lights (*nūr al-anwār*), is the Divine Essence whose light is blinding because of its luminosity and intensity. The Supreme Light is the source of all existence, since the Universe in all its planes of reality consists in nothing more than degrees of light and darkness....
>
> The ontological status of all beings, therefore, depends on the degree in which they approach the Supreme Light and are themselves illuminated.[11]

When Suhrawardī writes about the "Light of lights" he is dealing with that Undefinable Superfactor by which all other phenomena are defined or identified. This is, then, another way of expressing the 'That by which all else is known' as found in the Upaniṣads, the Tao of all lesser *tao's* the *Dharmakāya* or *Buddhatathatā* of Mahāyāna, and perhaps the *Haecitas* of Duns Scotus, not to mention the Light motif in the Fourth Gospel of the New Testament.

The concept of Angels is not so popular these days in secular Euramerica as once it was, especially among Protestants with their tendency to collapse the marvellous hierarchies into a radical dualism of God and devil, salvation and sin, body and soul. But given the principle of graduated hierarchies throughout existence as far as we know, admittedly it is a pretty great leap, so to speak, from the human soul to the Divine Light of the pure Being of God, and the concept of the Angels in monotheistic systems tends to fill that gap in a way the hierarchy of Gods does in a polytheistic system or the *vyūhas* in Rāmānuja's philosophy. Nasr writes:

> Angelology, which concerns itself with this vast hierarchy of lights, or angelic substances standing between this world of shadows and the Supreme Light, occupies a central position in *Ishrāqī* doctrine. The angel is at once the sustainer of this world, the instrument of knowledge, and that which man seeks to become and after whom he searches in his earthly life. Suhrawardī relies heavily on Mazdean angelology in describing the various orders of angels and uses its terminology... to name various angelic lights, while making use also of the

> traditional Islamic terminology derived from the Quran. It is always the beauty and the dominion of the angel which glitter most in the *Ishrāqī* cosmos and which most dazzles the sight of the one who undertakes the task of gaining a vision of it.[12]

Each angel and archangel is given his proper place in accordance with the particular realm of light assigned, including of course Gabriel who has the function of communicator to Man of God's messages. It is of some interest that Suhrawardī also accentuated the concept of the guardian angels and enlarged that theme. Nasr writes:

> Besides having this guardian angel (Gabriel) for the whole of his species, man has also his own guardian angel residing in the angelic world. Suhrawardī considers each soul to have had a previous existence in the angelic domain before descending to the realm of the body. Upon entering the body, the soul, or its inner center which is its immortal, angelic core, divided into two parts, one remaining in heaven and the other descending into the prison or "fort" of the body. That is why the human soul is always unhappy in this world; it is actually searching for its other half, for its celestial "alter ego," and will not gain ultimate felicity and happiness until it has become united with its angelic half and has regained its celestial abode. Man's entelechy is therefore to become once again unified with his spiritual "self," with his angelic prototype which is his real "self" and which he must "become" in order to "be"; that is, he must become what he really "is" and cannot attain peace and bring to an end this wandering as a lost child in the maze of the cosmic labyrinth until he has reunited with his guardian angel which is his real "self".[13]

Aristotle did not adequately account for the misery of the soul in this *saṃsāra-māyā valle lacrimarum* condition whereas the Neo-Platonist scheme came closer, and of course the doctrine of the 'fall' of Adam in the Abrahamic heritages also comes closer to satisfying that obvious observation in all of us.

Certainly the masters in this field had experiences beyond our present bourgeois university battleground of ideas. This is especially true when we consider the esoteric aspects of Suhrawardī's illuminationist philosophy. The problem is still with us as to how much esoterics can be included or even should be in any higher more all-inclusive synthesis. This question has recently become freshly vital since possibly as a reaction to the prevailing domination of the 'analytic' school in the English-speaking world there is a revival of interest in the Neo-Platonist heritage. However for Suhrawardī systematic logic is not to be abandoned but cultivated as a necessary tool for thinking—although today he would probably remind those who have got stuck with this craft of tool-making that although results of their labor are very useful that does not necessarily mean that everyone should drop everything else and join the tool-makers union, as it were, nor should it become an exclusive closed club. It is much more likely that some hunch or spontaneous notion may spark off new developments in that craft rather than mere technique; for just as in the fine arts and other fields, in philosophy also talent and technique have to be constantly harmonized. At any rate, we shall risk the generaliz ation that this illuminationist heritage may be distinguished from esoterics in the unphilosophical sense in that it retains a sense of system whereas anti-intellectual types of mysticism and esoterics often claim, whether successfully or not, to transcend systems altogether in their mystical immediacy or even in their magical control. Perhaps Suhrawardī was not yet able to 'reduce' everything to systematics, but he did have a vital concern that the Great Vision of the Prophet should be expanded by way of interpretation to become virtually all-inclusive.

It can well be argued that Suhrawardī's search for primordial origins and for ultimate ends is well in keeping with even orthodox Qur'ānic Islam, for hints about the primordiality of Light are there though not emphasized by other interpretations. The same themes can be found in Zoroastrianism, Hermetic Christian and Manichaean sources and others, and it was Suhrawardī's broad-minded affirmation of such universal perspectives, denying exclusive rights to orthodoxy, that got him into trouble. Although Suhrawardian all-inclusiveness incorporated the Hellenic and Hellenistic elements, some of which had been rejected by the ultra-orthodox Ash'arites and other Kalām specialists as well as by al-Ghazālī, still Suhrawardī considered the Greek heritage as only a purificatory discipline and not as a final end in itself, for no one faithful to the Abrahamic Revelation could dare to claim that, since it would be tantamount to denying revelation altogether.

8. Lu Hsiang-shan

Lu Hsiang-shan (1139-1193) insisted against the realist interpretation of Chu Hsi (1130-1200) that *li* and *ch'i* are identical, and therefore offered a monistic interpretation of the Diagram of the Supreme Ultimate inherited by both philosophers from Chou Tun-i. Cady suggests "ethical mentalism" as a descriptive epithet, along with "idealist monism" for Lu's general philosophy.[1] Lu Hsiang-shan and Chu Hsi characterize two basic streams of Confucian thought which can be traced back even to the difference between Mencius and Hsün-tzu. This difference becomes actively manifest with Han Yü and Li Ao in the late T'ang Dynasty after having been less apparent during the Buddhist ascendency, and continues on through the likeness and difference between the Ch'eng brothers. We see essentially the same type of polarizations occurring everywhere and in almost every century. As we have frequently put it, philosophies, like hands, appear in pairs. Thus, with only a few details neglected in favor of clarity in terms of basics, in this Great Summas period we have typically the following pairs: Chu Hsi and Lu Hsiang-shan, Nichiren and Dōgen, Madhva and Śrīharṣa, Ibn Rushd and Suhrawardī, Aquinas and Bonaventure, Psellos and the Hesychasts.

The contrast and comparison between Chu Hsi and Lu Hsiang-shan is inevitable. Lu insisted that the *ko wu* ("investigation of things") meant introspective ethical self-cultivation, while Chu was more 'objective' if not outright 'scientific' in his interpretation, believing that the objective study of nature and history was the way to true wisdom and enlightenment. Lu denied levels of reality for the most part, insisting that all is mind without essential distinction or differentiation, whereas Chu Hsi acknowledged at least two levels, parallel to Ibn Rushd or perhaps the School of Chartres or even Aquinas. According to Lu there is no distinction to be made between the undifferentiated Tao-as-such and the Tao as operative in and through the *yin/yang* polarization of the Supreme Ultimate; and thus by corollary the Supreme Ultimate and the metaphysical *li* are identical with the Tao. We might say that between Lu and Chu there is the distinction between the undifferentiated infinity of transcendence and the inexhaustibility of the infinity of differentiations and mediations. At any rate Cady gives us this summary contrast of Lu and Chu:

(1) As to metaphysics, Lu is an Idealist Monist. There is but one Ultimate in his universe, that of Li, Principle. Chu Hsi is Neo-Realistic. He has a concrete Universe of Li and Ch'i, Law and Ether, coexistent but with the primacy accorded to Li. Ultimately then we cannot deny a monistic solution to an otherwise complete dualism.

(2) As to mind, for Lu there is but one Mind throughout the universe; and it is identical with Li. Mind and the nature are not differentiated. Chu Hsi differentiates the Tao mind from the "human mind". Concrete mind in man is the embodiment of both of these. Mind contains the "nature" which is identical with "Li", pure ethical law, by which the Tao mind operates within man.

(3) Further with Lu there is no split between Divine Principle (Heaven's Li) and human desire. Normal human desire (only excess is evil) is a functioning of Mind which is Principle. These are put in opposition by Chu Hsi carrying his dualism into psychology.

(4) On the method in "study", personal development of character and understanding, Lu contended that its object, the understanding of Li, should be pursued "within the mind". His method was deductive, subjective and stressed the illumination of intuition. Chu on the contrary stressed ordered investigation of the phenomena of life and the survey of

literature and was inductive and more objective in his method.

(5) In the major stresses of their teaching, Lu gave the prime importance to practical moral development, while Chu Hsi felt the major importance of sound theory and intellectual thoroughness.[2]

Both Lu and Chu accepted rather responsible positions in public life, but then in China philosophers and scholars were expected to hold public office.

Lu Hsiang-shan is a systematic monist, and it may therefore be a mistake to call him a mystic if by that term we intend supra-systematic or para-systematic intuitive union. Nevertheless at times Lu appears as it were to be more of an Advaitin than the Advaitins themselves; or like the more extreme Ṣūfīs, he does not allow us to depart from the Supreme Unity—duality is out! Lu writes: "Mind is one Mind, and Law is one Law. Oneness (*i*) pertains to them throughout, and even in their most subtle meaning they contain no duality (*erh*). (In other words,) this Mind and this Law truly do not admit of any dualism."[3]

Lu takes advantage of the wide ambiguity of the term Mind, and as usual goes back to Mencius, interpreting him as claiming virtually complete identity between Mind (*hsin*), Law or Principle (*li*), and Nature (*hsing*), as well as 'Capacity'. (*ts'ai*). Lu's motive in coalescing these terms into a single identity is in order to emphasize the ethical rather than the epistemological implications. Whether some modern philosopher such as Karl Popper would accuse him of psychologism might be mooted as a telling question, though of course we do not have to resort to a modern Euramerican critique since that in essence was Chu Hsi's criticism. Lu writes:

> The ten thousand things are profusely contained within a square inch of space (i.e., the Mind). Filling the Mind, and, pouring forth, filling the entire universe, there is nothing that is not this Law....
>
> How can this Law not exist in us? If we cause our Will (*chih*) not to waver (in its pursuit of Law), then it (Law) will daily become clearer and brighter, like a stream which daily grows

> more luxuriant. If one seeks to infuse it (this Law into oneself) from without, this is to choke oneself off from its source and cut oneself off from its origin....
>
> If in the Eastern Sea there were to appear a sage, he would have this same Mind and this same Law. If in the Western Sea there were to appear a sage, he would have this same Mind and this same Law. If in the Southern or Northern Seas there were to appear sages, they (too) would have this same Mind and this same Law. If a hundred or a thousand generations ago, or a hundred or a thousand generations hence, sages were to appear, they (likewise) would have this same Mind and this same Law.[4]

According to Lu we need not look so much to the external universe but should apply the *ko wu* to self-knowledge since the same *li* is inherent in our own human nature. Whoever understands this can become complete master over himself, and therefore need not be bothered by the manyness of the externalia of the world. According to Siu-chi Huang:

> Lu Hsiang-shan adopts the traditional interpretation of Law as developed by the Sung Neo-Confucianists: (a) that it is the orderly principle underlying the universe as well as each individual thing, and (b) that it is a purely moral criterion for human conduct. Unlike Chu Hsi, however, he is not greatly interested in meaning (a), but greatly stresses meaning (b). He therefore unhesitatingly declares that the so-called "investigation of things," originally cited in the *Great Learning* as the starting point for virtue, and emphasized by the Ch'eng-Chu school, is, in reality, not fundamental. A conversation between Lu Hsiang-shan and his pupil, Li Po-min, touches on this point:
>
> "Po-min asked: 'How is one to investigate things (*ko wu*)?'
>
> "The teacher (Lu Hsiang-shan) said: 'Investigate the Law of things '
>
> "Po-min said: 'The ten thousand things (*wan wu*) under Heaven are extremely multitudinous; how, then, can we investigate all of them exhaustively?'
>
> "The teacher replied: 'The ten thousand things are already

> complete in us. It is only necessary to apprehend their Law.'" Evidently the assertion of the Neo-realists of Western philosophy that there is a world independent of the knowing conscious self would not interest Lu Hsiang-shan. What primarily concerns him is the single proposition that there exists one Law which is perfectly good and hence is to be regarded as the purely ethical standard for all men throughout all ages.[5]

One of Lu's disciples asked where to begin with the *ko wu.* The reply is the classical Confucian formula of beginning with self-cultivation before presuming to govern family or public affairs in a hierarchical framework of progressive control according to the Will of Heaven. But Lu also interprets this as "recovery of the original mind", cultivated spontaneously rather than systematically. This teaching was often difficult for his students, and it is reported that his answers to questions were often too vague to be of much definitive benefit. Hence another reason for the accusation that Lu was really a Ch'an Buddhist in Confucian guise.

According to Lu and Chu Hsi, but with greater emphasis in Lu, the goodness of the Original Mind is not just a subjective or merely personal, much less sentimental, attachment to naive piety but is profoundly rooted in the microcosm/macrocosm metaphysics:

> The universe (*yü chou*) has never limited and separated itself from man, but it is man who limits and separates himself from the universe.
>
> The Truth (*tao*) permeates all under Heaven; there is not even the smallest space (where it does not permeate). The four 'fundamental principles' (*ssu tuan*) and 'ten thousand virtues' (*wan shan*) are all conferred upon us by Heaven. They do not impose upon men the labor of adding any adornment. But it is men themselves who have vices, and (therefore) separate themselves (from them).[6]

For Lu there is a primordial harmony between the natural events of the world and the moral order such that one must assume that nature is moral, and that therefore one's destiny lies in that harmony. Thus the regular variability of the seasons furnishes the basic model for ethical theorizing according to the Diagram of the Supreme Ultimate in the classical microcosm/macrocosm philosophy. Incidentally, one corollary of this is that one should not engage in controversy merely to gain a victory over an opponent but only for the sake of getting more into harmony with the total pattern of reality.

Lu's monist tendency carries with it agreement with Mencius rather than Hsün-tzu in believing that human nature is inherently good. Of course this view was shared by most of the other Sung Neo-Confucians; but for Lu as later on for Wang Yang-ming (whom he influenced) this entails a profound confidence also in intuition, even to the extent of allowing some suspicion of the merely rational faculties. Lu agrees with Mencius' doctrine that compassion as well as reverence, righteousness, sincerity and such virtues are inherent in human nature; and that, moreover, all of these are summarized and brought back to their primordial unity, as it were, in the practice of restoration of the Original Mind (*pen hsin*). Lu wrote in one of his letters:

> Mencius said: "To know without any cognition is intuitive knowledge (*liang chih*). To be capable of knowing without the exercise of study is intuitive capacity (*liang neng*)." These are given to us by Heaven; they are innate (*ku yu*), and not infused into us from without. It is therefore said: "All things are complete within us. There is no greater joy than to find Sincerity (*ch'eng*) when one examines oneself." Such is my Original Mind (*pen hsin*).[7]

But was this doctrine of the Original Mind really Confucian or was it not, whether consciously or unconsciously with Lu, already deeply rooted in Buddhism? The Hua-yen school of Buddhism, for example, was very similar to Lu's interpretation. Of course we could even ask whether this was truly Buddhistic or really Taoist historically. Also comparison with speculations about the nature of Adam before the Fall in both Islam and Christianity might make a parallel study. Lu writes:

> Our Original Mind is not infused into us from without. At the

> present time, (in its original state) is it not peaceful and harmonious, and furthermore, without impediment? If we do not follow it with care and guard over it with stern attention, wicked influences and bad habits may take advantage of our negligence to assault us, and will thus destroy our Original Mind.
>
> ...(The question was asked:) "What is the Original Mind?" The teacher (Lu Hsiang-shan) replied: "The feeling of commiseration is the basis of Human-heartedness. The feeling of shame and dislike is the basis of Righteousness. The feeling of modesty and complaisance is the basis of Propriety. The feeling of right and wrong is the basis of Wisdom. All these are the Original Mind."[8]

According to Lu, in spite of the great diversity of views manifest in the ancient sages, behind and inclusive of all the many manifestations of wisdom the one Supreme *Li* still prevails; and Lu quotes the *I Ching* and Mencius insisting the Mind therein operative is the same as that *Li*: "For the mind is one mind, the principle (or truth) *Li* is one principle....This mind, this principle, in fact does not permit of any dualism."[9] Even though some sort of subjective idealism can be read into the text even of Mencius, again its prime source may rather be in the Hua-yen Buddhist school whose roots stem back to Vijñānavāda. Lu, however, tries hard to demonstrate that this doctrine is indigenous to non-Buddhist sources.

It is almost axiomatic that any consistent monism has difficulties with the problem of evil. It is not true for Lu as with some more extreme monists that the question just does not arise; nor does Lu assert that at the *pāramārthika* level the duality between good and evil, like all other dualities, is transcended and left behind in the realm of *māyā*. Lu is not a *māyāvādin* in that sense. Evil is real to him. Nevertheless, following Mencius as usual, Lu does not allow any really metaphysical doctrine of radical evil. Evil is only an external influence on the Original Mind. Mencius himself said that it was education that would allow us to minimize these external influences or corruptions, but Lu seems to put as much emphasis on meditation. Actually Lu seems not so much concerned with the nature of evil, which he tends to take as mere externalization and turning away from recollection of the Original Mind, as with the remedy for it. He writes:

> Mind should not be contaminated with anything; it should stand alone and independent. In its original state, the Mind of Man contains no disorder, (but gradually and) confusedly it is led astray by (external) things. If one has the proper spirit, he will immediately rise (above things), and will (attain the original) good. But if one continuously moves away (from the Original Mind), he will then become corrupted.
>
> . . .Where there is good there must be evil. (The transition from one to the other) is truly (like) the turning over of one's hand. Goodness, however, is so from the very beginning, whereas evil comes into existence only as a result of such a 'turning over'.[10]

Lu admits that there is such a thing as human evil desire (*wu yü*), whereas Chu Hsi and Aquinas assert that desires as such are not evil but can be if focussed on the wrong things. Lu does not think that evil desire is bound down by materiality as such, as some extreme Neo-Platonists and some Advaitins tended to believe. Again, perhaps almost like a crypto-Buddhist, he says that desire itself is the source of evil if not evil as such itself. Lu writes:

> What is it that will injure your Mind? It is Desire (*yü*). When Desires are many, what we can preserve of our (Original) Mind is inevitably little; and (conversely), when the Desires are few, what we can preserve of our (Original) Mind is inevitably much. Therefore, the Superior Man does not worry that his Mind is not preserved, but rather worries that his Desires are not made few. For if the Desires were eliminated, the Mind would automatically be preserved. Thus, then, does not the preserving of what is good in our Mind depend upon the elimination of what does it injury?[11]

All varieties of Buddhism teach that craving/desire is the chief source of suffering and in that sense evil. And when to this Lu adds that ignorance is also a source of evil, again we marvel how adroitly he has captured and adapted such teachings to Confucian terminology. Lu writes:

> Those who follow Material Desires (*wu yü*) gallop (after them) without knowing (where) to stop. Those who follow (superficial) opinions also gallop (after them) without knowing (where) to stop. Therefore, "although the Way (*taò*) is near, yet they seek for it afar; although a thing is easy (to deal with), yet they seek for it in its difficult (aspects)." But is the Truth (really) remote or the things (really) difficult? (It is because) their opinions are unsound, that they make difficulties for themselves. If one fully realizes one's error, then one's becloudings and doubts will be dissipated and one will reach the place in which to stop.[12]

Here it is not radical ignorance in the *māyāvādin* sense, but emphasis rather on the 'right opinions' as in Buddhist practice. Lu's emphasis is not on puzzling over the nature and origin of evil but constantly on the positive practice of cultivation of *jen* (human-heartedness) and of the Original Mind so that the elimination of the evil tendencies is the method rather than confronting the evil, battle style, with opposing force.

In Lu Hsiang-shan we find the usual themes of seriousness in study. If we translate the following into modern secular parlance, what Lu is counselling is allowing the subconscious mind to do most of the work in maturing thought and working out solutions to problems which elude conscious effort. Lu writes:

> ...When you are studying why do you need to agonize and sweat over the places you do not understand?...For anyone with your native gifts, when you think about it to the limit, naturally there is a way of solving the problem. But what is to be feared is lest within the mind there is obscurity so that one does not get the right solution. So it would be better to drop it temporarily and for a while let the question sink into the depths of the mind and work itself out.[13]

This is fairly typical; and while we do miss some of the technicalities of Nyāya and Aristotelian logic and categories, it must be acknowledged that as a psychologist Lu does make an excellent guide. However, was this characteristic more prominent in him than in the Ch'an Buddhist masters? This question was raised more than once by his friends as well as his opponents, and he was rather constantly on the defensive. His defense is almost always the same: "Re-examine the way of self-cultivation in Mencius, and you will find there all you need, i.e., 'extensive study, judicious inquiry, clear differentiation, careful reflection, and earnest performance'."[14]

Lu voices the opinion (common, by the way, with Thomas Aquinas) that if one is completely sincere in cultivating even one single virtue the other virtues will fall in line. He also counsels cultivating the fine arts as ancillary to the cultivation of the spirit of the Confucian gentleman. In his dwelling on excellence and perfection Lu is perhaps attempting to read into Confucian terminology something equivalent or rivaling the Mahāyāna *Prajñāpāramitā* literature. But it is here applied to the social realm insofar as he reiterates the classical Confucian teaching that the right to rule is totally dependent on the Will of Heaven, and that in turn on the virtue of the candidate.

Lu constantly complains about neglect of the ancients and the classics and the consequent danger that the Tao will be lost completely even as it had been in eclipse during the Buddhist ascendency. Nevertheless Lu records his objection to writing extensive commentaries as others were in the habit of doing since such activity was only an unnecessary burden on the mind, whereas he considered it his mission to unburden his students instead of piling still further bibliography and commentaries and erudite citations from the classics. But Lu does explicitly exhort his readers to extensive study, and more study, and still more study. Certainly he was not anti-intellectual as some of his Ch'an contemporaries were. Mencius remains Lu's chief authority throughout, even though interpreted according to the discipline derived from Han Yü and Li Ao of "quieting the mind" as the remedy for getting excessively entangled in rules and regulations as well as distractions from the senses and bodily functions. Lu carried on polemics against heresies and heterodoxies, even within the Confucian fold, not to mention Buddhist and Taoist ways. He even attempts a sort of apostolic succession from Mencius himself to Han Yü, which no doubt he is proposing as a counter-claim to historical authority over against the claim that the Ch'an patriarchs make about their "transmission of the Dharma".

Lu's attitude toward Buddhism is especially crucial since some opponents had virtually accused him of being a crypto-Buddhist. Along with the other Neo-Confucians Lu does make refutations of Buddhism, although they are not as severe as those of Chang Ts'ai or Cheng I. His criticism follows what had by then become virtually stereotypes: Confucianism was humanistic and positive in its emphasis, practical and healthily this-worldly, whereas Buddhism was too quietistic, selfish and other-worldly. Lu also seems to echo in spirit the old opinion that Buddhism was very un-Chinese, being a foreign importation and really incompatible with Chinese civilization. Lu writes in a letter to a friend whom he is trying to win away from his Buddhist leanings and bring back into the Confucian fold:

> The Confucianists although going to the length of speaking of that which is 'without sound or smell,' 'without location or substance,'...all place their prime emphasis on regulating the world. The Buddhists, although they are entirely given to saving men from the torment in a future period, all give the prime importance to escaping from the world.

And again:

> ...I only said (of Buddhism) that it does not give prime importance to regulating the world and that it is not the Tao of the Three Ultimates (Heaven, Earth and Man). Also, you say that Confucianism and Buddhism are the same. I am afraid that cannot be so. You are going to reckon all that exists to be empty unrealities.

And finally:

> Further the world is as it is. Suddenly you produce something that goes by the name of 'Meditation' (Ch'an). There is nothing else but waves rising without a wind, mounds of earth starting up on level ground.[15]

The Neo-Confucian criticism of Buddhism may seem strange in

view of the fact that the Buddhist system of contemplation was primarily designed for transcending selfishness or eliminating it by showing dialectically that ego as such is substanceless; the exercise of compassion is thereby unhindered and becomes the major remedy for the deliverance of mankind and all living things from suffering. The Bodhisattva Vow should have included all that Lu and his fellows intended. But then there seems to be some organic law governing the development of traditions both within cultures and provoking syntheses of cultures. Buddhism had had its day in China, just as Augustine had had full sway over Western Europe and Śaṅkara in India. With the demand for greater objectivity in the twelfth and thirteenth centuries, Aristotle, brought out of hiding by the Islamic rationalists, took over in Europe; and the dialectical swing back to the Confucian basis in China is in a remarkably similar manner, while Madhva seems to fit into this pattern likewise in India.

There is very little evidence that Lu knew very much about the Buddhist *sūtras*, perhaps for the simple reason that understanding depended on personal transmission and not on the *sūtras* themselves. Although Chu Hsi had seriously tried Buddhism at one time he rejected it more completely than did Lu. Lu's subjectivistic emphasis on meditative contemplation more than on objective investigation left him open to being accused of Buddhist influences, but he had never actually had any immediate association with any Buddhists as far as we know. Nevertheless he did adopt outright the *zazen* practice of meditation: "I request you, respected brother, to establish yourself immediately, sit straight, fold your hands, collect your spiritual forces (*ching shen*), and become lord over yourself. For when 'all things are already complete within us,' what can we then lack?"[16] Although Lu's doctrine of cultivation of the Original Mind is remarkably similar to its Buddhist counterpart, there is no conclusive evidence of direct influence. Nevertheless it seems to us the indirect evidence is rather strong, and in Lu's case we leave it open whether the dragon trampled on the lotus or whether the lotus had grown large enough to allow the dragon to play around in its petals.

In general we might say that, by contrast with the old orthodox Confucianism with its traditional hesitance in the face of change, the Neo-Confucians overall had accepted the Buddhist challenge to change, perhaps even more fully than a restudy of Heraclitus might have provoked in Western Europe. One may risk the generalization that although Aristotle's critique of Heraclitus was no doubt available and the whole dialectic of generation and decay was easily incorporated under the Biblical doctrine of creation, nevertheless the flexibility that more openness to change might have brought into the Christian scholastic systems was lacking. The hierarchical structures were stronger than the power to ascend them, and the anagogical path remained steep and severe. One might see in this the seeds of disintegration of the mediaeval synthesis already sown, germinating but not yet bursting the old forms, and a possible reason why China remained more stable until the violence of the European ego in the nineteenth century.

There are some things that we miss in both Chu Hsi and Lu Hsiang-shan. For example, the expertise in logic and epistemology always present in their Indian contemporaries. Likewise we miss any system of categories such as may be found in both the Aristotelians and the Vaiśeṣikas. And although the systematic Buddhist texts did have a very explicit theory of causation, and although in both Chu and Lu something like that is always implicit, we have nothing like the distinctions about the various kinds of causation found in the Aristotelians and in both Vaiśeṣika and Mīmāṃsā. The absence of an explicit systematic theism in both Chu and Lu may be a defect or an asset according to one's disposition. Though some studies have been able to point to close approximations, the Jesuits and the Dominicans as late as the sixteenth and seventeenth centuries could not quite agree whether the term *T'ien* could be used to translate the Biblical word(s) for God.

9. Ch'en Liang

Chu Hsi is reported to have said of Ch'en Liang (1143-1194) that "he got stuck in the varnish pot of profit and desire", and that his teachings were "heresies".[1] However, this word "heresies" may be a superimposition on the textual materials since generally heresy was not such a serious thing in China as it was in the Christian world, both Byzantine and Latin. At least heretics were not persecuted; indeed, too often intrigue at court rather than excellence of thinking was the determining factor as to who was considered orthodox and who would be demoted. At any rate, Ch'en Liang was very much concerned about the external weakness of the Southern Sung Dynasty which existed alongside the internal refinement and excellence, and expressed the wounded pride of those who had fled from the North after the victory of the Chin. Repeatedly Ch'en memoralized the emperor, advising him to be more aggressive against the Chin. Ch'en came from a family or rural landed aristocracy most of the members of which had had a military career and had not been very successful in climbing the usual intellectual ladder to officialdom because of failure to pass the required examinations. Thus we infer that Ch'en himself may have inherited a sort of resentment against the Establishment, or at least a large measure of frustration. We might speculatively infer that his identification with a minority tradition was one of the reasons that he failed the highest examination several times, though he finally succeeded in 1193 when he was already fifty-one years old.

Maoists such as Hou Wai-lu exalt Ch'en Liang as giving them full support and, *pari passu*, interpret him as a radical materialist. Hou links Ch'en Liang with Yen Shih (1150-1223), stating that they waged a common struggle against Chu Hsi and Lu Hsiang-shan. Hou cites Ch'en Liang as stating very forcefully that his own philosophy was a "philosophy of action"; and, "Act according to the principles of both righteousness and profit, benevolence and power; listen to the dictates of both reason and expediency"; and, "A man must serve his country and fellow countrymen with deeds and not words." Likewise Yen Shih is quoted as objecting to the Neo-Confucian attempt to elevate "reason above the world of reality"; and again, "To understand the general laws of the universe we must study and examine carefully the things of the objective world." Hou Wai-lu adds that in both cases their philosophy was "derived from their profound knowledge of history, science and technology, which enriched their philosophy and provided them with strong weapons in their fight against Neo-Confucianism."[2]

Ch'en Liang stresses what might be called a radical humanism, arguing against effete and unnecessary mysticism and pseudo-metaphysics and the tendency to decadence in scholarly commentaries as exercises in themselves or for the sake of display of literary style. He advocated a realistic and applicable study of factual history and the 'existential' position of man in the world.

> Quoting Wang T'ung, he said: "Between Heaven and Earth there is nothing but Man; because Man can glorify the Tao but Tao cannot glorify Man."
>
> Or at another place: "The direction of great events of the world cannot be changed by Heaven and Earth, nor by the genii and the spirits; the one who changes it is Man."
>
> Or more extensively: "The function of the human mind might be defective, but it can never be truly destroyed. The form of the law might be incomplete, but it can never be utterly abolished. That Man forms the great triad together with Heaven and Earth is not because Heaven and Earth move in their eternal orbits independently and thus provide Man with his power. If man did not have this position, Heaven and Earth could not move independently; and if Heaven and Earth were discarded, then there would be nothing to be considered the Tao."
>
> ..."In the world there are no lawless and cunning villains who cannot be restrained. The robbers (the Chin) do not have a power that is constantly on the rise and will not decline."[3]

Ch'en uses the traditional vocabulary about the Tao and the Confucian virtues, but he uses them to puncture stereotypes, trying almost desperately to arouse the intelligentsia and to get them to look at their actual situation in the world instead of poring over their books and worrying about their ceremonial propriety.

> The Confucianists of today, convinced of having grasped the teachings of rectifying the mind and sincerity of thought, are

> all paralyzed to a degree that they do not feel pain or itches. In a situation where the peace of the world depends on taking the great revenge for lord and father, they just raise their eyebrows and, hands in sleeves, talk about human nature and destiny, and they do not even know what human nature and destiny are really like. . . . The talented officials of today, convinced of having grasped the craft of making the nation rich and the army strong, are all wildly deluded and recklessly shouting; they do not take time out to investigate the essentials of establishing a state but just raise their eyebrows and with all their force discuss wealth and strength, and they do not even know what wealth and strength really mean.[4]

No doubt one major reason for Ch'en's unpopularity was his enthusiasm about Wang An-shih, whose attempts at reform had by this time fallen out of favor, even though if they had been successful they might have prevented the fall of the Northern Sung. Chu Hsi attacked Ch'en by accusing him of hegemonism; but ironically Ch'en turned the criticism into a compliment, saying in effect that that is exactly what he was trying to get across.

The key term in Ch'en Liang's philosophy is *kung-li*, which Wilhelm interprets as "pragmatism", that is, achievement for merit or profit in a down-to-earth practical way, instead of dreamily cuitivating one's 'virtue' in vague hopes that that will achieve results in other ways even if it does not do so in this all too-real world. Ch'en pointed out that the reason the dreaded Chin had been so successful was simply that they had not cultivated elitism but had attended to practical affairs; in other words, their scholar-advisers had "cultivated the Tao" for the benefit of society and not for their own sake alone.

Ch'en's attitude toward the classics was somewhat like those in the modern world who demand reading the Bible or the Qur'ān or the Vedas in modern vernacular translations in order to find out what is really there, instead of chanting them with great emotional fervor without paying any attention to the challenging and even revolutionary nature of their contents. Ch'en wrote:

> There is nothing in the book *Lun-yü* that does not concern practical learning. Scholars, in a vain search of what is called transcendence, select those of its sayings which sound subtle and mysterious, distort them until in their own minds they appear superior, and based on this they pass sentence saying: this is the essence, the others just specialize on dregs. Alas, this is the reason why they read and reread the book all their lives, get entangled in thorns and brambles, and still pretend to have grasped (its import). Now, the Tao which acts in this world does not have roots and ramifications. It does not have a within and a without; how then could the Sage in his sayings raise up the one and disregard the other? If he had done so, the Sage would have split the Tao in two; what good then would come from the rending of the book *Lun-yü*? I say: apply your intelligence (clarity) within, exert efforts in practical learning and strive for accordance in your own mind: profound merit will then be arrived at in force. Thus the transcendence of tomorrow will be nothing but the practical learning of today.[5]

According to Ch'en, Mencius advocates rectification not only of one's own mind but the mind of the people, so that selfish motivation may be uprooted. In Mencius he also found a basis for hope coupled with determination. For Mencius was not a fatalist passively waiting for Heaven to act. Man can change his own condition-in-the-world, and indeed he is not truly human in the best sense who does not cultivate his 'original mind' with that firm intention. There is no value in tradition as such, Ch'en seems to believe, but rather each idea must be measured against the time and place where it had been or ought to be applied; moreover, what might be thought to be deviant now may in the future prove to be the most valuable advice, and later on even become the official teaching.

All that Ch'en was really advocating was simply the best of Confucian teachings: That government has the "blessing of Heaven" and the right to rule only if it has the welfare of the people as its basic concern; and when that ceases to be true of any regime, it is doomed to be replaced by a revolutionary change that does have the welfare of the people at heart—as he could well demonstrate from a realistic study of history. One corollary of this is that no regime should presume to become permanent, since it is obvious that empires and dynasties rise and fall. Further, rule by inborn compassion according to Mencius's ideal pattern of motivation based on faith in the inherent goodness of human nature is not enough. Executive aptitudes in terms of concrete human institutions and organizations are necessary. Proper means are absolutely essential as well as admirable ends. Ch'en insists that no matter how sagely a person becomes, if the rest of society is not well ordered his saintliness and wisdom are really useless since he cannot be effective historically.

According to Chu Hsi, the true Tao ceased to exist on earth during the Han and T'ang Dynasties, although it continued to exist in some 'heavenly' realm. Behind this is Chu Hsi's view of human nature, which Carsun Chang characterizes as somewhat like Kant's, i.e., that we are indeed "citizens of two worlds", the bodily and the 'heavenly'. As a traditionalist Chu Hsi rebuked Ch'en Liang for arguing in terms of the actual history of the Han and T'ang Dynasties and advised him to go back to the ideal pre-Confucian eras of Yao and Shun for his models. But Ch'en was not satisfied with these legendary, semi-mythological models. Instead Ch'en indicates a very realistic approach to history and attempts to penetrate if not to debunk some hoary mythologizing of a dreamy idealist sort of antiquity. Ch'en may have been on firmer ground as far as philosophy of history is concerned than his famous critic Chu Hsi in a way that reminds us, for example, of Ibn Khaldūn over against some of his Ṣūfī contemporaries.

Like Mencius' correction of Mo Tzu's utilitarianism, Chu Hsi's correction of Ch'en Liang's utilitarianism indicates that orthodoxy put a higher value on knowledge for its own sake than on the practical spirit, even though that practical spirit had characterized so much of Chinese civilization. G.K. Chesterton is reported to have once said, "Heresy is a good thing—for orthodoxy!" So Ch'en Liang may be welcomed possibly as a Socratic gadfly to keep the more traditional establishment in philosophy from becoming prematurely drowsy. With the possible exception of the great Michael Psellos in the previous century, it might be difficult to find anyone in the rest of Eurasia so zealous for political and social reform until we get to Roger Bacon or even William of Ockham.

10. Ibn Rushd

Ibn Rushd (Averröes) was born in Cordoba, Spain in 1126 and died in Morocco in 1198. Up to the present he has been known almost entirely through his influence on the Christian and, to a lesser extent, the Jewish philosophers of the high and later Middle Ages; but fortunately we are beginning now to have more direct access to his own works in their proper Islamic setting. The net result no doubt will be that he will be appreciated more as a philosopher in his own right and not merely limited to his title of "Commentator" on Aristotle and Plato. He is one of the world's really supreme rationalists of all time, as also one of the greatest, if not the greatest, polymath of his era, rivalling even his contemporary Chu Hsi. Like Leibniz in Europe later, it might be said that Ibn Rushd in his own time "knew everything".

> The philosophical output of Ibn Rushd was as voluminous and varied as that of any of the greater philosophers of the East. Two characteristic features set his work apart from that of the two Eastern masters, al-Fārābī and Ibn Sīnā, his only two equals in the world of Islam: his meticulousness in commenting on the texts of Aristotle and his conscientiousness in grappling with the perennial question of the relation of philosophy and dogma. A third feature must also be mentioned: no other philosopher of note had either exercised the functions of canonical judge or composed systematic treatises on jurisprudence (*fiqh*). At least two such treatises are attributed to him, one of which, *Bidāyat al-Mujtahid*, is still extant. His medical writings, although they lie outside the scope of this study, may also be mentioned....
>
> ...All together, fifteen out of the thirty-eight commentaries

of Averroes were translated into Latin directly from Arabic during the thirteenth century.

Thereafter Ibn Rushd's commentaries may be said to have become part of the Aristotelian heritage of Western Europe. Ibn Rushd had scarcely any disciples or successors in the Muslim empire. Even his critics are of little consequence. With the possible exception of Ibn Taymiyah (d. 1327), none of them was of the stature of Ibn Sīnā's major critic, al-Ghazālī. His followers and critics in the West form a brilliant galaxy, however: Maimonides, Siger de Brabant, Moses ben Tibbon, Levi ben Gerson, Albert the Great, St. Thomas Aquinas.[1]

Ibn Rushd's method of dealing with the relation of faith and reason, of science and religion, of nature and the supernatural (and that distinction does not really take its sharp and systematic formulation until his work) has made him famous for beginning the history of the "double truth" theory, which states that since we cannot avoid recognizing both revelation and reason we must acknowledge both; and even though there may appear to be some discrepancy between them, we must nevertheless leave each field uninvaded by the other. Fakhry writes:

> ... The intermittent dialectical warfare between the theologians and the philosophers had seriously compromised philosophy in the Muslim world and brought it to the verge of bankruptcy following al-Ghazālī's classic onslaught. The rehabilitation of philosophy, Ibn Rushd felt, could be achieved only once it is demonstrated that no genuine conflict between philosophy and religion could arise, and that Scripture properly interpreted is in complete harmony with philosophy properly understood.[2]

Since within Islam there was considerable opposition to this sort of proceeding, his influence there was perhaps not so great as in Western Europe, particularly through Siger de Brabant and others such as John of Jardin.

At the beginning of his *Faṣl al-Maqāl fi ma bain al-Ḥikmah w-al-Sharī'ah min al-Ittiṣāl* (*Relation of Philosophy and Religion*) Ibn Rushd says:

> The purpose of the following treatise is to enquire through sacred Law whether the learning of philosophy and other sciences appertaining thereto is permitted, or called dangerous, or commended by the Law, and if commended, is it only approved or made obligatory.
>
> ...We maintain that the business of philosophy is nothing other than to look into creation and to ponder over it in order to be guided to the Creator,—in other words, to look into the meaning of existence or the knowledge of creation leads to the cognisance of the Creator through the knowledge of the created. The more perfect becomes the knowledge of creation, the more perfect becomes the knowledge of the Creator.[3]

This is quite typical of almost all his contemporaries and sets them somewhat apart from their predecessors who had for the most part claimed some immediate knowledge of God and not merely indirect knowledge through the study of nature. What has happened? Is this merely the exteriorization or objectification of Spirit that is almost always the *sine qua non* of scientific investigation? Is it some new liberation of the human mind, or a failure of theological nerve? Is it a retreat from the rigors of mystical discipline, or is it a deliverance from pseudo-mysticism? It is a challenging question why China and to some extent Japan and India did not precede the Mediterranean region in making vast scientific advances, for the same tendency to bring nature out of the field of piety and make it subject to rational investigation had also begun there. But this new foundation is not really so new, for al-Fārābī and Ibn Sīnā, as Ibn Rushd is quick to point out, had certainly done much to prepare the way, and no one can begin *de novo* and get very far.

When in the *Faṣl* Ibn Rushd comes to the question of the relation of faith and reason, he says:

> It is upon this point that the difference of opinion arises. Some say that the first principle is of reason, while others allege that it is of faith. That is to say they have thought that faith, even before knowing the methods common to all and to which the Law has made a call on all, is the only

> method of arriving at the truth. Thus they have mistaken the real purpose of the Law-giver, and being themselves in the wrong they have led others astray.[4]

Ibn Rushd advises returning to the Book as authority, yet not abandoning reason in its interpretation. He says that God "has led the many to good, especially the people who have walked in the path of scholasticism, and have a liking for the knowledge of the Truth."

Then follows a little section on the problem of the nature of God's knowledge. The basic problem is the degree to which there is a valid analogy between our knowledge and God's knowledge, since ours is subject to change without notice and is dependent both on the condition of the mind and on the condition of the things known. But God's knowledge, since He cannot change, cannot change; His omniscience must be completely commensurate with His eternity. The correlative question is that of God's knowledge of particulars. This question had already begun to trouble Christian philosophers also, and much more so than the Hindus to whom there was not such a hiatus between this knowledge that God must *have* and the consciousness that God must *be*. The absence of the *tat tvam asi* in the Aristotelian canon leaves a limited range of operation which always runs the risk of making God march to the tune of a man-made syllogism! Nevertheless the Averroists will always reply that mere human subjectivity is insufficient. Reason is in itself true, so God must be considered in *at least* rational terms. Excessive rationality means less of a risk than excessive irrationality and degeneration into mere sentiment and willful ignorance.

In his criticism of the Ṣūfīs Ibn Rushd says that their method is perhaps all right for themselves, but it is by no means fitted for the masses, who need rational and definable methods and principles. Even the Qur'ān, he says, always invites us to theorizing, judging, and admonishing by way of philosophy. This concern for the masses is in much of his work and in a way that very nearly anticipates Ibn Khaldūn's sociology of civilization. His objective concern for the whole of society is also not too different from the manner of his contemporary Chu Hsi.

As for the atheists, he says that they "are like men who can see and feel the created things, but would not acknowledge any Creator for them but would attribute all to chance alone, and that they come into being by themselves."

Then there follows in the *Faṣl* a little section on the Unity of God. Ibn Rushd follows the Qur'ān quite faithfully, especially in denying Sonship (against the Christians) and denying any possibility of any form of valid polytheism or dytheism (perhaps a remnant of Zoroastrianism still to be refuted). But his concept of Unity does not exclude, as it still does for the later interpreters of Śaṅkara, relationality within that Unity. In other words, the comprehensiveness which we find in Ibn Sīnā and others is more than continued and brought into even greater precision in Ibn Rushd. While the mythological consciousness is retained, it is brought under the thumb of systematization. Though the masses have this only, there remains the common bond that any man can still grasp the argument for the existence of God as One from the fact that, howsoever symbolically conceived, the unity of creation betokens the Unity of the Creator.

Ibn Rushd writes in considerable detail about each of the divine attributes: knowledge, life, power, volition, hearing, seeing and talking. Concerning the first, there is not the least intimation that, even though God's knowledge is co-eternal with Him, this eternal knowledge should be integral with His nature as is the case with the Vedānta. In the next section on the Divine Perfection there is a continued acknowledgment of the needs of the masses and attention to the dictates of the Qur'ān, with primary emphasis on the Creator-creation relationship that so sharply characterizes all of Islamic philosophy and theology. Quite contrary to the view of Rāmānuja, there is explicit denial that God may in any sense have a body; but the emphasis lies more in a denial of imperfection to God than a positive ascription of perfection to Him, for human frailty has difficulty indeed in conceiving of real perfection in itself. He goes on to a rather rigorous treatment of the problem of anthropomorphism, refuting the notion that because God must be a Self, He must have a body. He says that God is best conceived in terms of light, for thus He can be "felt" and yet is not a body; and the Qur'ān says, "God is the light of heaven and earth" (xxiv:35).

The problem of instruction of the masses comes to the fore

in the next section. After some consideration about the angels and their relation to God within the purely spiritual realm, and some acknowledgment of the importance of consideration of the Day of Judgment, he becomes quite explicit: "The law should be taken literally; and the conformity of religion to philosophy should not be told to the common people."

> For teaching philosophy to one who is not fit for it, will either falsify philosophy or religion absolutely or will show conformity between them by accident only. The right thing would have been not to disclose philosophy to the common people at all. But if teaching of it was absolutely necessary, then only that section of the people should have been taught who saw that religion was opposed to philosophy, in order to show that it was not so. And also it might have been taught to those people who thought that philosophy is opposed to religion. . . . Moreover they would know that the opinion about religion, that it was opposed to philosophy, was one which was either about some innovation in religion, and not about its principles, or is an error in understanding that is a wrong interpretation of it. . . .[5]

And again:

> . . .The Law first refused to disclose this secret to them and described God, for their sake, in terms which they can imagine, ascribing to Him the attributes of hearing, seeing, having a face, etc., at the same time telling them that He is not like anything that can be imagined. Had the intention of the Law been to make clear to the masses the fact of His having no body, it would not have mentioned these things in detail. But as light was the highest of imaginable things, it was given to them as an illustration of God, for it is the best known of the things to the senses and the imagination.[6]

What we see here is really the "two-truth" theory at work. Reason seeks to eliminate the mythological consciousness. And in order to avoid too much censure from the ultra-orthodox who have not come into the enlightenment of purely rational methods, one still allows that their mode of receiving and communicating truth is also valid; or else, being convinced of revelation oneself, one adjusts that as rationally as possible with the deductions of logical procedure based on the observation of nature. Hence it is better not to mix philosophy and religion, but rather one should leave each in its proper realm. Ibn Rushd carries on a long simile about a physician who discovers a new drug and tries it out on every sort of patient until he learns, all too painfully, that it is not a cure for all ills. Philosophy likewise is suited only to a few. "So it is necessary to bear in mind the limits which the Law has set about the instruction of every class of men, and not to mix them together....He who tries to instruct all people in the matter of religion, in one and the same way, is like a man who wants to make them alike in actions too, which is quite against the apparent laws and reason."[7]

In the next section on the acts of God there is again for the most part a reiteration of considerations about the Creator-creation relation, some mention of predestination, an observation that some things are made directly by God and that other things come about through mediating causes, that is, by causes which are placed inherently within the thing as in the case of the soul. Then there is a discussion of the point whether the actions of God are eternally or temporally caused. He resolves this by the doctrine of intention: God *intends* eternally, although He may be said (even though the Qur'ān is not explicit here) to *act* temporally. Nevertheless, many difficulties remain for the later scholastics to work still further on.

The second issue raised in this section is that of the role of a prophet. Here again we see reason in a wider range. Ibn Rushd must, of course, acknowledge the orthodox tradition and its basic role; but tacitly throughout he is using reason for the criterion of judgment (almost in the sense that Kant's third critique intends) even over the supernatural aspects of the prophet's role. Miracles besides not being the only requirement of the prophet, are subject to the scrutiny of reason, at least to the extent of determining whether they are genuine and historical or only reputed miracles. Ibn Rushd points out that although miracles may be the chief sign that a man is a prophet, this does not mean that everyone who can perform a miracle is a prophet for the magicians also are capable of that. The prophet is one who has a direct revelation from God, and as such his relation to the philosopher becomes sharply problematic. For there is always the possibility of a false claim to this gift, and the philosopher's role must be to distinguish between the true and the false prophet. Nevertheless, when the genuine is recognized its superiority must be acknowledged.

Ibn Rushd believes in the superiority of Islam, although with good reasons, for in the case of other dispensations, he says, there had not been such a clear call to the unity of the whole race. "So the dispensations before our own were meant for some particular peoples, ignoring all others, but our religion was meant for the whole human race."[8] Here is a challenge to the nationalisms that most of the modern secular world has gotten parcelled up into. Here also is a marked contrast with Chu Hsi and his continuing assumption that China was the center of the universe and that non-Chinese was incurably barbarian.

On the topic of predestination Ibn Rushd again shows himself to be the rationalist supreme. He is quite open in acknowledging that both the Qur'ān and reason itself admit discrepancies, and here he again invokes his doctrine of intention:

> ...The deeds attributed to us are done by our intention, and by the fitness of the causes which are called the Predestination of God, which He has furnished for us from outside. They neither complete the works which we intend nor hinder them, but certainly become the cause of our intending them —one of the two things. For intention is produced in us by our imagination, or for the verification of a thing, which in itself is not in our power, but comes into being by causes outside us....
>
> ...God's knowledge of these causes, and that which pertains to them, is the cause of their existence. So no one can have a full knowledge of these things except God, and hence He is the only Knower of secrets, which is quite true....A knowledge of the causes as a whole is the knowledge of what things would be found or not found at a certain moment of time. Praised be He Who has a complete knowledge of creation and of all its causes. This is what is meant by the "keys of the

> secret" in the following words of God, "With Him are the keys of secret things; none knoweth them besides Himself" (VI, 59).[9]

Thus predestination is put into a different light than that in which it is usually examined. It is not a question between determinism and free will but rather a pushing of the limit of human ignorance back to the ultimate point of human comprehension. How can man, finite as he is, have any notion of whether he is free or not. For even his freedom would be established by God. Reason must operate in terms of causes, and therefore reason, cause, and freedom all must find a reconciliation beyond themselves, which can be only in God. Those who assume that rationalism necessarily carries with it the basis of freedom should think again. Freedom must go according to chance which "knows no reason", unless it be some Reason that is inclusive of both chance and necessity. Almost by definition this must be in God.

In this as well as in the next section on the Justice of God, Ibn Rushd is dealing largely with the old Ash'arite-Mu'tazilite controversy. His resolution of the dilemma is contrary to the older one since he cannot accept in his rationalism the view that God should be blamed for the existence of evil. He seems to take the view that evil, or supposed evil, can be taken as medicine is taken: bitter medicine sometimes, but therapeutic. He also uses fire as an analogy since it is not evil or good in itself but good or evil according to its use. Thus, just as God could not be blamed for the creation of fire, so He should not be blamed for the creation of evil. According to Ibn Rushd, "Man is just because he gains something good by being so, which he cannot gain otherwise. God is just, not that he may become more perfect by His justice, but because His perfection requires Him to be just."[10]

The next section deals with the conditions of man at the Day of Judgment. Modern secular rationalism tends to neglect this heritage, and the question never arises in Chinese rationalism; but Islamic rationalism leaves no discrepancy between this eschatological perspective and the Greek heritage. It remains on top, as a matter of fact, and gives the Faith its great prophetic power. In Ibn Rushd we find the tendency, which becomes very complete in Ibn Khaldūn's philosophy of history, for the doctrine to be applied to whole blocks of society as well. The different Faiths are all subject to this Judgment. There is little possibility of any merely humanist interpretation here. It is no projection of a human moral code into a metaphysical superstructure but the bold *fact* that God has actually *revealed* that this is the standard set from beyond the range of normal human speculation. In passing Ibn Rushd quotes the Qur'ān (LXXV, 36) against the tneory (like that of the Rāmānuja school) that God created the world and men in sport or play; and he makes quite a point that since God has created man as a rational being, man will be judged as to how he has used both his theoretical reason and his practical reason. Both quantity and quality of deeds must be considered when it comes to the evaluation of the degree of virtue to which a man has attained.

Ibn Rushd surveys several views ranging around the different notions about the condition of embodied or disembodied existence after death. He gives some observations on the Islamic version of the doctrine of the glorified body or the resurrection body (which must not be confused, as is easily done, with the *liṅga śarīra* or subtle body of the Vedānta). It is conceived that the present bodies at the Day of Resurrection will be transformed into actual bodies that will be capable of, well, everything that the resurrection body of Christ was capable of. The tract closes with a consideration of the Law, which is supposed to govern all things and the problem is only how these things are to be classified.

Ibn Rushd's chief work, *Tahāfut al-Tahāfut* (*Incoherence of the Incoherence*) is primarily an attempt at refuting al-Ghazālī's *Tahāfut al-Falāsifah* (*Incoherence of the Philosophers*). Ibn Rushd takes reason into an expanded field of operation, namely that which includes the mystical, the prophetic and the legalistic without seeking to supplant any of them. Reason at once determines the proper field and function of them individually and collectively, and also its own limitations in acknowledging the sovereignty of God as above all that any human faculty can manage to reach. The two-truth theory thus becomes quite vivid. Al-Ghazālī for the most part represents the area of the mystical and the prophetic combined, and over against this the legal and the rational formulae, the 'second truth' (reason with a small *r*), comes into effect.

For Ibn Rushd arguments and counter-arguments are not useless; far from it! There is no other way of proceeding. And Ibn Rushd is very expert at it. The great patience and precision which he shows in the minute ordering not only of single views but of whole series of refutations and counter-refutations, marks the true beginning of the scholastic method. Abelard had begun the dialectical manner afresh in his *Sic et Non*; but whereas Abelard had only taken simple opposing views in a sort of sudden awakening to the fact that all scriptures and all philosophers did not agree, Ibn Rushd comes into the realization that reason in its comprehensive function must be capable of a very large measure of what we might call 'feedback'. Thus he proceeds through the arguments and counter-arguments concerning the eternity of the world, which constitutes the first section of the *Tahāfut*. This dialectical method had proved inadequate for al-Ghazālī, and from the scepticism into which it had led him he found refuge in the mysticism of the Ṣūfīs. Ibn Rushd refuses to allow this so easily. It does become quite evident that even he also tires of the arguments somewhat, but for a different reason. He still hopes for the opening of a new field of wider and more all-inclusive universals that will be objectively and inherently valid—even more valid than the subjective dangers of the mystical way, howsoever true its claims may be—and applicable without qualification after the dialectical process has cancelled out all false views.

In the middle of the fourth discussion on the proofs for the existence of God as Creator of the world—even though the Aristotelian view of the eternity of the world be granted in some carefully qualified manner, the *art of proper qualification* being his chief dialectical weapon—he says that it is the existence of an infinite series of causes and effects which demands the necessity of an Eternal Cause. Is the jump from the field of infinitude of causes and effects (which later was enough to satisfy Giordano Bruno) to the One Cause of this infinity valid? For there are many modes and manners and methods by which this shift may and/or must be made. Or, for that matter, is it necessary to make it anyway? Is it not already "there"? For a Vijñānavādin or even a Zen Buddhist contemporary such as Dōgen, it is not substantial causes that we are dealing with but modulational transitions from one plane of consciousness to another, divisions into distinguishable entities and individuated factors of causation being purely arbitrary. There is a constant continuum which God is, and it is fallacious to assert that in 'causing' anything 'finite' —for can we really find anything that is not in some sense or other infinite, at least infinitely divisible and infinitely multipliable, at least theoretically?—the 'Creator' is 'producing' anything outside of His own Infinity. Are we not really dealing simply with different orders or aspects of infinity, and with something that may be beyond (our conception of) infinity? Why should there be this field of the three-fold infinities between God and us and things? May not God/Allah deal directly with the whole and the part and with Himself in equal weight?

But these are not essentially objections. To a great extent they are precisely the gist of al-Ghazālī's argument against the Aristotelians. Without the vivid realization of the immediacy of God, nothing makes sense, no matter how long you argue; but with it, you need nothing else! The Aristotelian's answer to this is as forceful as it is simple: even this immediacy is of the nature of a universal. Such a universal is objective in the sense that it runs no risk of misconstruction, objectively or subjectively. Without this order of *super*-objectivity we have no locus of reference of judgment whereby anything else can be properly ordered in reference to the necessarily actual existence of God, or in reference to the relation of God to creation, which relation must of necessity be at once potential and actual, both subjective and objective. The *descending* hierarchy, in other words, may include the mystical; but lest certainty be sacrificed in the *ascending* order, there we must assert the way of universals.

Ibn Rushd's method is quite commensurate with his principle; in fact it is rather arbitrary to separate them. For the *way of universals* very soon converges on the *principle of perfection*, which is also in a sense another universal, yet in another sense is that by which a true (perfect) universal may be distinguished from an imperfect one. Any other less astute dialectician might be caught in a whirlpool in which the notion of perfection (or any other ultimate) begins to spin, so to speak, and suck the enquirer in, so that the enquirer disappears in that which he is seeking to investigate—this is essentially what the Mādhyamika had done. But the Aristotelian or the followers of Madhva or the Chu Hsi Neo-Confucianist cannot allow this. The *tat tvam asi* is not there. I observe a spiral nebula; I observe that there are others like it; I generalize: there is a genus which I call "spiral nebulae". But to say that in so far as I know these spiral nebulae I *become* them, this is not true because it is simply absurd! Nevertheless, since God's knowing cannot be outside of Himself or above Himself, then all knowing on His part (but not necessarily on *our* part) must be some sort of self-knowledge, even though there is or must be a mode of existence which we still do not understand whereby these things exist apart from His essence but not apart from His knowledge. Perfection, therefore, as one of His principle attributes is the link in His nature whereby this is possible: He both *is* perfect and *has* perfection which, because of this perfection itself, He must be able to impart by virtue of His omnipresence, whether He does so completely or not. From our human point of view it is necessary to make these distinctions, not merely because of our imperfection, but because in spite of this, through the resemblance of our intellect to His, we *must* come into some notion of His perfection as the entelechy of our very existence.

The fulcrum of the problem stands on the delicately balanced issue of the degree or mode of plurality which we must acknowledge to exist within the divine nature—we scarcely dare to say within the divine essence for that would compromise the necessary Simplicity; but then again we cannot admit a disparity between the divine Nature and the divine Being unless we admit some mode of necessary distinctions therein which nevertheless do not compromise the Unicity. Many like Bonaventura will follow al-Ghazālī's argument in this, while Aquinas will follow Ibn Rushd. Others will continue to say that this is simply beyond our ken and that we wrongly attribute these distinctions to God whereas they cannot really be His own. While admitting that our intellection is limited, Ibn Rushd as an Aristotelian cannot admit that what is universally applicable will not apply also to God, for God would not have constituted any supreme universality of truth that would not apply to Himself also. Madhva tends in the same direction. Padmapāda, Sureśvara and Vācaspati Miśra and other Advaitins try to avoid the fulcrum altogether, appealing to a sort of monism in which the weakness of the human understanding is simply ignored. Chu Hsi takes a rather middle position. The difficulty, nevertheless, cannot be easily handled, and Ibn Rushd seems to struggle with it considerably.

In spite of all his rationalism, at the most critical points Ibn Rushd takes refuge again in the Qur'ān. Revelation in some mode or form becomes for most men the ultimate appeal. Nevertheless, it is necessary to use reason in reconciling the discrepancies of revelation both within and with the field of reason itself. And this is precisely what the scholastics of all brands did. They took Aristotle into the sanctuary and to the minaret—it was Aristotle who said mass and called the people to prayer! Though the God of revelation cannot be explained in rational terms, still He must be at least a God of Reason also since reason is the highest thing we know; and thus it must be from Him, and we must use it even in our attempts at understanding Him. Hence the two-truths. In other words, even though God may not actually be a genus or a species or allow Himself to be confined within the categories, nevertheless we should be able to understand Him if only we could treat Him as though, being the Source of this mode of ratiocination, He willed us to do so.

Can Ibn Rushd be consistently an Aristotelian with all of the form-matter, substance-essence dichotomizing of the external world, etc., without admitting some form of *embodiment* of God? Officially as a Muslim he cannot admit embodiment; but for a Christian, Vaiṣṇava, or Neo-Confucianist would not that be a necessary corollary? Though Ibn Rushd could not go quite so far on literal embodiment, in regard to the operation of the causes there is not such a great difference between Him and the Viśiṣṭādvaitin panentheists. The greatest difference seems to be in the operation of the method of abstraction, the Rāmānuja school being, so to speak, more 'existentialist'. It seems that between these extremes Chu Hsi and Ibn Rushd steer as nearly as possible a middle course, while the Victorines, Hugh and Richard, veer back again toward a monism not unlike Śrīharṣa's, while Albertus Magnus is perhaps more of an Aristotelian (if that were possible) than Ibn Rushd to whom he was indebted considerably.

Alexander of Hales, the teacher of Bonaventura, is probably nearer in type to Veṅkaṭanātha. The pity is that communications were not quite adequate for these great minds to know each other face to face, even though they were definitely sufficiently open to account for a complex but real chain of possible if not definitely probable *indirect* influences. Thus the parallels between them are probably not accidental; and (Hegelian) *Weltgeist* or not, it had to use human instruments and inventions for trans-Eurasian communications.

The question of the quiddity also seems to vex Ibn Rushd, although it would seem that his universalism should lead him to put particular emphasis on it—unless, of course, he rather prefers to claim that the universals introduce nothing else than what already *is* and that the quiddity is that sort of a 'thing'. We have seen previously that the Buddhist concept of the *Tathatā* is not so closely comparable to the scholastic *quidditas*, for the former is a *je ne sais quoi* equatable with the *Śūnyatā*, whereas the scholastic *quidditas* is an attempt to designate something—God, logical category, abstract idea, universal-as-such—as existence, a *that* it is without designating *what* precisely it may be, and that as abstracted logically out of the existential situation, not as an intuitive apperception soaring over and around the particular in question as is the case with the *Tathatā*. Whereas al-Ghazālī affirmed this sort of quiddity, probably as the nearest possible rationalization of his intuitive mystical way, the stricter Aristotelians denied this as still too ambiguous.

On the question of God's self-knowledge, which was extremely crucial for al-Ghazālī, Ibn Rushd is less enthusiastic. He really leaves these higher 'knowings' in the realm of faith, the two-truth theory dichotomizing again, emphasizing difference more than identity and arguing only according to a weak reasoning by analogy. He also thinks that Ibn Sīnā's manner of commuting the problem into a proper discernment of the function of God's will is inadequate. Since we have no other way of proceeding except by substance and accident, universal and particular, matter and form, etc., we must trust revelation and not try to exceed the provisions of the revealed sacred Law, which emphasizes more the attributes and the transcendence than any particular doctrine about the modes of God's knowing, willing, existing, etc. Moreover, there is a grave danger of confusing man's manner of self-knowing with that of God's, and the analogy is not by any means self-proved. The self-knowing, so-called, of God is not the same as the Active Intellect, although indeed it must be affirmed that God is (also) *Intellectus Purus*; but even the highest reaches of human intellection cannot penetrate this mysterious realm. And since mysticism must not be allowed because of its emotional excesses and fantastic irrational claims, it is better to acknowledge simply the attributes of God, and acknowledge that these have a very close connection with His will, which nevertheless is really another attribute; and above all, affirm that God's knowing as all-knowing cannot be divided into self-knowing, knowledge of particulars and universals, or knowledge of the opposites.

Finally, after his refutation of Ibn Sīnā's version of voluntarism, which runs the risk of admitting too much pluralism by its multiplication of distinctions, Ibn Rushd concludes on this point:

> God's knowledge connot be divided into the opposites of true and false in which human knowledge is divided; for instance, it may be said that either he knows or he does not know other things, because these two propositions are contradictory, and when the one is true the other is false; but in the case of God both propositions, that He knows whom He knows and that He does not know it, are true for He does not know it through a knowledge which determines an imperfection, namely human knowledge, but knows it through a knowledge which does not carry with it any imperfection, and this is a knowledge the quality of which nobody but God Himself can understand. And concerning both universals and individuals it is true of Him that He knows them and does not know them. This is the conclusion to which the principles of the ancient philosophers led; but those who make a distinction, and say that God knows universals but does not know particulars have not fully grasped their theory, and this is not a consequence of their principles. For all human sciences are passivities and impressions from the existents, and the existents operate on them. But the knowledge of the Creator

operates on existents and the existents receive the activities of His knowledge.[11]

Here he is closer to Śrīharṣa, who is by no means less astute in dialectical skill and whose chief method in this respect (even though other differences are very wide indeed) is not so different from that of Ibn Rushd, namely the clearing away of all ambiguity concerning the singularity of the Divine Ground.

One wonders if Chu Hsi would not also accuse Ibn Rushd of being a '*Buddhist*', confusing the First Principle with mind or knowledge. His intellectualism made him somewhat unpopular among the ultra-orthodox even in Islam, and of course the Christian Averroists suffered somewhat the same accusation. However, Ibn Rushd's mode of arguing is closely guarded, and one must not read him carelessly, discrediting his use of the Qur'ān or misconstruing his reasons for not trying to explicate the doctrine of the modes of God's knowledge, since he knows full well that these things can only be a matter of the wildest speculation. Otherwise one may well be accused of spiritual pride.

The problem of God's knowledge of particulars is one that vexed all the scholastics. And the question of whether God's own nature *is* of the order of knowledge or whether knowledge is something He *has* divided them rather sharply. Al-Ghazāllī had inclined perhaps further than any Islamic philosopher towards the homogenous view of God's knowledge; he did not conceive of God's knowledge as knowledges, as distinct, but considered God's own nature as a homogenous luminous body of knowledge, an unbroken continuum. But Ibn Rushd, while not overlooking this possibility, does not think it entails the elimination of the other also.

One can see the force of a manner of arguing such as Śrīharṣa uses (or Dōgen for that matter): all these arguments and questions are only superficial waves on the surface—and why make more waves! From the standpoint of the Vedānta, whether of the Rāmānuja school or the Advaita school (but not from the Madhva point of view), there is in these scholastics the implicit assertion that truth or knowledge must itself be proved to be valid. This is really as unnecessary as it is vain, for unless we assume that truth is self-validating we have no ground whatsoever to stand upon and must admit nihilism of the most devastating sort. And this validity must be of such an order as to embrace both its subject and its object, its unity and plurality (although Śrīharṣa will deny that there is any valid plurality whereas Rāmānuja's interpreters will say that there is).

Honen, the Japanese Buddhist, and Hugh of St. Victor, the Christian mystic, take another way by seeking to obliterate both subject and object in attaining an ecstatic state which is purely spiritual non-intellectual, "above the mind". But neither a Neo-Confucianist nor an Aristotelian of any sort could ever allow such, for there is always the devastating question. But how did you know that that was "above the mind"? Moreover, an undue emphasis on these ecstatic ways destroys interest in the natural sciences, which must go on under penalty of disobedience to divine commands in the Qur'ān and the *ḥadīth*, which explicitly enjoin the scientific study of nature. The contribution of Ibn Rushd to the advancement of the natural sciences as well as, realistically, to administration of public affairs was probably superior to that of Ibn Sīnā or Albertus Magnus, and perhaps not inferior to that of Chu Hsi. The purpose of science is not the mere accumulation of facts but the arrival at a more immediate grasp of first principles, and to see their operation in all subordinate things. Thus there cannot be unnecessary knowledge; there must be a way of integrating every new discovery into the whole body of knowledge so that it is recognized as still only one fact of this vast universe and its Creator's operation and/or Being therein and thereupon.

There are the rudiments of the beginnings of what might be called the social sciences in Ibn Rushd, although not so clearly developed as in Ibn Khaldūn (d. 1406). Religion does not necessarily constitute a special case; it too must be subjected to rational scrutiny, and the views of members of different religions must be reconciled and brought into an ordered organon, even though this may prove to be the other side of the coin of the necessity of a two-truth orientation for the whole of mankind.

Though there is a high degree of eclecticism in Ibn Rushd, this does not preclude originality (although it must not be forgotten that originality is not necessarily a virtue). Ibn Rushd remains one of the greatest Aristotelians of all times and it would be quite mistaken to stretch him into another mould. But his interpretations of Aristotle do not remain slavish commentaries, only. Aristotle is only the basis upon which a system is built in which nothing remains unexamined *de novo* by dialectical reason.

Ibn Rushd should not be considered only in the light of European tradition. True enough he lived in Spain and even complains that he is not able to get sufficient moterials from the East; but it should be obvious that his indebtedness is much wider than merely the Byzantine sources for Aristotle and Plato. Moreover, it is difficult to believe, for example, that the Ṣūfīs, whom he so frequently criticizes, were not influenced considerably by Hindu and perhaps by Buddhistic belief and practice. It is doubtful that he had any direct knowledge of the Chinese systems, although conditions were such that within the century following him Nestorian Christians could go on pilgrimage all the way from China to the Pope and to France and return.

11. Chu Hsi

Chu Hsi (1130-1200) stands in Chinese tradition in a way comparable to Ibn Rushd in Islamic tradition, Thomas Aquinas in Christian tradition, or Śaṅkara in Hindu tradition. According to Chan, Chu Hsi's thought constituted the "completion" of Neo-Confucianism both in the historical sense and in the sense of systematic re-evaluations and reconstructions in an amazingly comprehensive synthesis. Chu Hsi's synthesis not only included the best of both Taoist and Confucian heritages, but he "saved Neo-Confucianism from the danger of falling into Taoism,"[1] which had too much turned to esoterics and magic. Chan writes:

> Chu Hsi was in a strategic position to promote the Buddhist and Taoist tendencies or to check them. He took the latter course. In the case of Chou Tun-i, he took trouble to inter-

pret the clearly Taoist concept of the Ultimate of Non-being in the Diagram of the Great Ultimate in Confucian terms.... In this way he purged Taoism from Chou. In the case of Shao Yung, he simply overlooked him altogether. The best evidence of his rejection of Shao Yung is found in his compilation of the *Chin-ssu lu* (Reflections on things at hand). In 1175 he and his collaborator, Lü Tsu-ch'ien (1173-1181), selected 622 passages from the works of Chou Tun-i, the Ch'eng brothers, and Chang Tsai to represent the total body of Neo-Confucian teachings. It is the first Neo-Confucian collection and the model for the *Hsing-li ta-ch'üan* (Great collection of Neo-Confucianism) which was the basis of civil service examinations from 1415 to 1905 and influenced and controlled Chinese thought for some 500 years. The anthology also inspired and set the pattern for many anthologies of Confucian thought from Chu Hsi's own time to the 19th century.

Shao Yung is completely absent from the anthology.[2]

The reason for the rejection of Shao Yung was that his esoterics of numbers was too extreme to merit serious consideration for systematic synthesis with such as Chang Tsai's views about the *ch'i* (material force) which Chu Hsi admired.

It might seem strange that Chu Hsi should bother about the transmission of the 'way' since if any philosopher, whatever his heritage, has *jen* then his authenticity should be self-validating intrinsically without regard to apostolic succession or even questions about orthodoxy or heresy. But Chu Hsi did indeed have to justify his return to the Four Books instead of the Five Classics, for thus he could be accused of 'innovation', which then with Confucianism (almost as much as with Marxism today) was regarded with profound suspicion. But one wonders whether there might be a Buddhist background to this since it might well be the case that the Confucians also had to vindicate their own "apostolic succession" as a counterfoil to the Buddhist claims.

According to Chu Hsi's pupil Huang Kan, "the transmission of the correct orthodox tradition of the Way required the

> proper men. From the Chou Dynasty on, there have been only several people capable of inheriting the correct tradition and transmitting the Way and only one or two could enable the Way to become prominent. After Confucius, Tseng Tzu (505-c. 436 B.C.) and Tzu-ssu perpetuated it in its subtlety but it was not prominent until Mencius. After Mencius, Chou Tun-i, the two Ch'engs, and Chang Tsai continued the interrupted tradition, but only with our Master did it become prominent." This view was accepted in the *History of Sung* and by practically all Neo-Confucianists.[3]

Chan claims that rather than any Buddhist influence Chu Hsi was simply following and applying his own philosophy of *li* in guaranteeing the authenticity of his interpretation of the Confucian tradition as such; and if we look back to the accounts of all the opposition he had to encounter in the court from rivals who also claimed historical validity for their varying interpretations and recommendations to the emperor in their mutual vying for high position, perhaps it is enough, aside from any reference to Buddhist ways. Chan writes:

> ...While the Buddhist classifications are syncretic in nature, the Neo-Confucian development is a logical scheme. It was not a resolution of conflicts of various schools but the evolution of a single system. In short, on the surface Chu Hsi's fixing of the tradition of transmission seems to be based on authority but actually it is an essentially philosophical matter.[4]

All across Eurasia in Chu Hsi's epoch such claims were quite universal. Chu Hsi's century, in short was an era of neo-orthodoxies everywhere, and the motif of return to the classics necessitated some vindication for their "correct" interpretation over against the accumulation of deviations and heresies.

The basic problem in interpreting Chu Hsi's metaphysics is the interrelations between *li* and *ch'i*. We are not involved merely in a philological difficulty in finding English equivalents for these terms, but rather we are involved in a long controversy of a major metaphysical problem that is universal. The problem as exposited by Chu Hsi can scarcely be understood except in the historical context. Others for centuries had used these terms, but Chu Hsi infused into them a new and profounder and much more vital meaningfulness and found in them a much more universal significance than his predecessors. In his views about the *li/ch'i* dialectic as in much if not most of his system, Chu Hsi's genius is not manifested so much in his originality as such, for in form his writings are quite traditional, most of them being commentaries on the classics and on the works of his immediate predecessors. The content of these commentaries often reveals very great dialectical skill in balancing opinions one against the other until a mature judgment can be made.

In seeking the history of these concepts and their interrelatedness with other key Chinese concepts, Needham says that it is really only with Hsi Khang in the third century A.D. that there begins to be somewhat of a mystical twist to the *li* concept. Then the Buddhist monk Chih-tun (314-366) of the T'ien T'ai school identified *li* with *prajñā*, while another Buddhist, Chu Tao-seng (d. 434) identified *li* with *Buddhatā* and Seng-chao (d. 414) used it to translate the Four Noble Truths. This presents a sharp contrast with the original Confucian intention which was a completely affirmative, naturalistic explanation of the order in nature or the world and not anything beyond it to be achieved by negation. Chu Hsi demystified the concept of *li*, removing the unnecessary superstructure that the Buddhist metaphysicians had built upon it—or more likely they had used the term for their own purposes, finding no other equivalent for their metaphysical Sanskrit terms in the Chinese language, and, as in the famous *ko i* period of adaptation, infused these naturalistic Chinese terms with meanings never originally intended for them.

The basic trend in Chinese thinking is to stress becoming over being, and becoming moreover (as the *yang* principle) counterbalanced by 'de-becoming' (to use Needham's word). In other words, Chinese thinking tends towards relations in ascendency over entities or substances. Thus *li* is perhaps best rendered as the "organizing principle" in the dynamism of cosmic processes of evolution and involution within the grand harmony of the Supreme Ultimate or Tao. To this generalization Chu Hsi is by no means an exception. One might even point to his interpretations of Chou Tun-i as full confirmation of this point. Needham criticizes interpretations which too sharply distinguish between the metaphysical and the physical since that does not conform to the organicism which is the core of Chu Hsi's system as of most Neo-Confucian thought. According to Needham, "*Li* might be a non-material principle, but it was part of the natural physical universe and certainly not subjective."[5] Thus it seems that Chu Hsi was trying to steer a middle course between idealism and materialism. Needham says of *li*:

> *Li*, then, is rather the order and pattern in Nature, not formulated law. But it is not a pattern thought of as something dead, like a mosaic; it is dynamic pattern as embodied in all living things, and in human relationships and in the highest human values. Such dynamic pattern can only be expressed by the term 'organism', and...Neo-Confucian philosophy was in fact a scheme of thought striving to be philosophy of organism.[6]

Needham claims that Chu Hsi came very close to anticipating developments in the European schools of philosophy between Leibniz and Whitehead. Needham also adds a note comparing some aspects of this organicism with Hegel's dialectics, especially in its role as the official philosophy of the Prussian State, since Chu Hsi's philosophy also became, and that quite dogmatically, the official state philosophy—but the comparison needs to be carefully qualified since Chu Hsi's system was banned at first and made into dogma later; hence the comparison is more apt in reference to the fate of Thomas Aquinas' system, which also was condemned at first and only later made into dogma.

According to Chan, Chu Hsi's predecessors did not make sufficiently clear the relation between *ch'i* (material force) and *li*; therefore he spent considerable effort in giving a critique of the views of each of his already-famous predecessors, the Ch'eng brothers in particular, contrasting their views in an effort at reconciling them. Thus in basic method, although by no means in particular details of doctrine, Çhu Hsi might also be considered a scholastic philosopher. Chan writes:

> Like the Ch'eng brothers, he said that "in the universe there has never been any material force without principle or principle without material force." However, he also said: "What are called principle and material force are certainly two different entities. But considered from the standpoint of things, the two entities are merged one with the other and cannot be separated with each in a different place. However, this does not destroy the fact that two entities are each an entity in itself." He sharply contrasts them. According to him, principle is necessary to explain the reality and universality of things. It is incorporeal, one, eternal and unchanging, uniform constituting the essence of things, indestructible, the reason for creation, and always good. On the other hand, material force is necessary to explain physical form, individuality, and the transformation of things. It is physical, many, transitory and changeable, unequal in things, constituting their physical substance, destructible, the vehicle and material for creation, involving both good and evil. "Principle refers to the Way," he said, "which existed before physical form (and is without it) and is the root from which all things are produced. Material force refers to material objects, which exists after physical form (and is with it); it is the instrument by which things are produced." It may be said that in all these differentiations, he is basically following Ch'eng I but the picture has now become clean-cut.[7]

In his explication of what we prefer to term "polarization" according to the famous Diagram of the Supreme Ultimate, Chu Hsi balances opinions against each other in the same way that he balances his conception of how *li* and *ch'i* operate reciprocally. However, Chu Hsi's "was not merely a structural reorganization or synthesis, as it has been often asserted. Instead, his was an organic reconstruction. This is his own version of Neo-Confucian philosophy. Perhaps it is more accurate to say that it is his own philosophy."[8]

Thus after balancing the opinions of Chang Tsai and Shao Yung against each other:

> According to Chu Hsi, the Great Ultimate is at once the one universal principle and the sum-total of all principles. This is not to be understood as a static condition. As Chu Hsi saw it, principle is inexhaustible. As there is a thing there is its principle. By the Great Ultimate is not meant that there is a definite terminating point. Rather the Great Ultimate means the reservoir of infinite potentiality. Thus new things are not only possible but even inevitable. The identification of the Great Ultimate with principle also means that principle is not abstract but concrete (*shih* (*at*) substantial). Chu Hsi always saw the Great Ultimate, or principle in its ultimate state, as embodying *yin* and *yang*, that is, the operation of the myriad things. He directly opposed the Great Ultimate to the Buddhist Emptiness which is devoid of things.[9]

One would like to see a detailed comparison and/or contrast to the cosmogenesis theories of the scholastics in Judaism, Islam and Christianity. Certainly there is no room whatsoever for the *ex nihilo* controversy here, or even the theory of the impossibility of infinite regress in terms of sequences of causation of an exterior sort; on the other hand, much closer perhaps to the Neo-Platonist concept of emanation, this cosmogeny of Chu Hsi's is much more close at hand in terms of possible empirical verification, in an 'organic' manner. As to comparisons and/or contrasts with his Indian contemporaries, certainly Chu Hsi has less emphasis on differences than Madhva, and it would be difficult to see him as an Advaitin such as Citsukha or Śrīharṣa; but whether his organicism is closer to Veṅkaṭanātha or to Nimbārka might be debated considerably.

In Chu Hsi's views of the function of *yin* and *yang*, again balanced judgment seems to prevail just as it has with the *li/ch'i* dialectic and with the classical and universal problem of the One and the Many or whole-and-part problem. Thus Chan summarizes Chu Hsi's view following after consideration of Chou Tun-i, Chang Tsai and the Ch'eng brothers:

> Chu Hsi's answer about activity and tranquillity is simply

> that because there are the principles of activity and tranquillity, material force becomes active or tranquil. It is because of these principles that there is activity which produces the material force of *yang* and there is tranquillity that produces the material force of *yin*. This does not mean that the Great Ultimate itself is active or tranquil, as in the case of Chang Tsai, or that the Great Ultimate itself can be active or tranquil, as in the case of Chou Tun-i, but because the Great Ultimate embodies the principles of activity and tranquillity so that the material forces of *yang* and *yin* naturally ensue. Here Chu Hsi carries his philosophy of principle to its logical conclusion and explains existence itself and its process of becoming in terms of principle.
>
> ...It is because there is the principle of creation that production and reproduction are natural. Once more, the concept of principle as the ultimate explanation is affirmed.[10]

Chu Hsi's organicism, wherein he explicitly states that the principle of creativity is inexhaustible and embraces reproduction in nature, would seem to have some advantages over his contemporaries' views which seem to be relatively sterile when it comes to the realization of creativity *in* nature. Most of them are so concerned, often almost exclusively, with the supernatural creativity of God, theologically considered rather than philosophically (and that complicated with the problem of attributes), that they fail to account metaphysically for creativity *within* nature. That concept at least in Western Europe did not gain much support until very late historically. Chu Hsi did not explicitly propose that creativity as such be included in any minimal system of categories as characteristic intrinsically of reality as such, but this concept that the material force of nature "reproduces without end" is important to the dynamism of his whole system.

Chu Hsi's work entitled "Explanation for Beginners of the Lore of Divination" which he wrote at the age of fifty-seven has been called the most pivotal of his works since it contains his basic ontology as he had developed it through many years of research and thinking. Chu Hsi emphatically stated, almost aphoristically: "Between heaven and earth there is only one Spirit (*ch'i*)."[11] But in accordance with the Diagram of the

Supreme Ultimate this single *ch'i* is known only through its self-polarization. The initial polarization is the source for the further proliferation, the first of these being the five elements (*wu hsin*). But it is still the one single *ch'i* operating through the multiplicity—or perhaps we should call it rather the multiplexity, since through the *ch'i* the organic Unity is never lost. But it is quite clear that the multiplexity is that of matter, as the eventual 'evolute' of the Supreme Ultimate, or more precisely, of the one *ch'i* pervading everything.

Chu Hsi does not allow us merely to contemplate that One Spirit in isolation mystically or even idealistically, for, as Goto puts it, the composite whole of this One Spirit is made up of the "commingling" or "conglomerating" of the many individualized *ch'i-s* as individual entities existing in limited time and definable, limited space. It occurs to us that perhaps the influence of Chang Tsai on Chu Hsi has been inadequately appreciated; nevertheless, perhaps the better judgment is that Chu Hsi was not allowing any extreme but was struggling for a middle-ground synthesis between Chang Tsai and the Ch'eng brothers. The English terms "matter" and "spirit" are so antithetical that it is difficult to think of them being the same thing in any sense at all. In metaphysical structuring—dynamically and not merely architectonically—Chu Hsi may have been closer to the Einsteinian formula $E=MC^2$: matter, as it were, being congealed or conglomerated or 'frozen' spirit; and energy, actually being spirit is simply 'thawed' matter.

If Chu Hsi's system could be recast into a theological mould (although the best interpreters warn against this extreme) he might have been described as a panentheist rather than a pantheist or a pluralist. Actually we need a different term for such a view analogous to panentheism in theology, perhaps something like pan-en-ontological. One may find apposite comparisons in the Mahāyāna schools, even in Nichiren, Shinran and Honen, based on the teaching of the *Lotus Sūtra* that the Buddha-nature is in everything. Whether or not Chu Hsi, consciously, or unconsciously derived this from Buddhist metaphysics remains a matter of specialized scholarship; but the metaphor he uses in explaining Chou Tun-i's Diagram is familiar to those steeped in the history of Buddhism in all its varieties in Japan during these centuries: Just as there is only one moon but it is reflected in many pools of water, so it is with the One Spirit that retains its identity but nevertheless influences or inheres in everything. Goto summarizes Chu Hsi's explanation of the Diagram of the Supreme Ultimate as follows:

> We have to remember that the One Spirit is the unifier of all the spirits (*ch'i*) as matter which goes to make up the shapes of all things. The Great Ultimate as the creative principle is the Logos, embracing and unifying all the logoi which manifest themselves in forms. In other words, the Great Ultimate is the ultimate cause, producing all different forms. It limits and objectifies the potential content inherent in it. At the same time it limits and objectifies the potential content of the One Spirit which is matter itself. Therefore the One Spirit as the source of matter can be assumed to comprehend within itself the spirit that dwells in each individual thing and to unify the spirits that are thus inherent in all things. Thus the One Spirit is the ultimate Source of matter.[12]

In the geometry of the solid cone the Great Ultimate is the point (whether it truly exists or is really a sort of infinity) and the many things emerging out of it are at once both an extension of itself and individualized entities within it. Indeed, the doubt whether it truly 'exists' is an even more difficult point than the manner of its relation to the plurality of existence. For some texts evidently allow an open ontologizing of the Supreme Ultimate (*T'ai Ch'i*) while others use the term *Wu-Ch'i* or the Extreme Nothing or Nothingness—a concept which could have its roots equally in Taoism and Buddhism. One view is that Nothing has no generative power and that the Many come out of the One on their own momentum, while the other view is that Nothing has the power of eliciting all things into existence and that therefore there must be a sort of 'something' that this 'nothing' is. Since this controversy exists in Greek, Arabic, Persian and Sanskrit texts as well as in Chinese and Latin, it is not just a linguistic problem but a genuine and unavoidable metaphysical one.

Quite axiomatically Chu Hsi explicitly taught that the *T'ai*

Ch'i (the Great Ultimate) is the *Wu-Ch'i*. One can readily see the analogies here to the very lively debate continuing between the Advaitins like Citsukha and the others concerning the relation between *nirguṇa* and *saguṇa*-Brahman. Though it is not clear whether he would have taken Madhva's side in that debate or whether he would have been more favorable, say, to the Bhedābheda position of Nimbārka or Bhaskara, or maybe even the Viśiṣṭādvaita position, it is definitely clear that he was not an Advaitin, as Goto makes quite clear as he summarizes this pivotal point:

> He holds that the *T'ai-ch'i* (Great Ultimate) is not of our world of realities but is "the extremity that transcends all shapes," hence its other name *Wu-ch'i* (Extreme Nothing). But nevertheless the *T'ai-ch'i* was conceived by Chu Hsi to be inseparable from the world of realities and the world of appearances. If indeed the world of the *T'ai-ch'i* were conceived by him to be an utter void that world of nothing would never become the source of all changes. Some people who hear the name *Wu-ch'i* (Extreme Nothing) would fancy that a nothing were an absolute nothing. The Chinese scholar Lu Hsiang-shan was one of these men. Chu Hsi conceived the Great Ultimate to be neither a virtual nothing nor an actual reality. But it is to be noted that Chu Hsi's conception of the Great Ultimate as an entity beyond our comprehension had something in common with a similar kind of notion current in Confucianism. Chu Hsi's theory that the Great Ultimate is a nothing transcending all relative entities does not imply that it is an absolute nothing and in that respect it is rather akin to the Taoist idea on the same subject.[13]

The *T'ai-ch'i*, the *I ch'i* and the *Wu-ch'i* are all going on simultaneously, perhaps in the same way that the Mahāyāna Trikāya and the Brahmā-Śiva-Viṣṇu and the Christian Trinity also act in a sort of timeless simultaneity.

Concerning *Chung*, Goto writes:

> The supreme central body of potential consciousnesses,

> which Chu-hsi called the *Chung*, was conceived by him to be the highest functioning body existing *a priori*, an active unity in itself working ceaselessly, thriving and endlessly evolving itself, "pure in its consistency, and endowed with all the *logoi*," the latter being constituted by *T'ai-ch'i* (Great Ultimate) itself, and ever ready to respond to all stimuluses and internal stirrings. When actual stimuli and impulses arise the *Chung* starts into action and sets the inferior bodies of potential consciousnesses in motion. These subordinate bodies of potential consciousnesses are represented by Chu-hsi to be four in number. It is to be noted further that these four subordinate bodies of potential consciousnesses are conceived to consist of innumerable indivisible bodies of potential consciousnesses which are destined to respond to innumerable individual stimuli and impulses.[14]

This suggests a much more extended study of the philosophy of motion among Chu Hsi's contemporaries including not only the Aristotelian scholastics but also Madhva and other thirteenth century Indian *ācāryas*. We may at least pose the question as to how this resembles and how it differs from the Unmoved Mover concept of Aquinas and his Islamic and Jewish predecessors and contemporaries. Or is Chu Hsi's view more like that of the Renaissance anti-Aristotelians who minimized this interpretation and posited the basic hypothesis that matter does not need to be "pushed around" but is internally as well as externally motivated. Of course if we take as basic the attitude that Chu Hsi's views were more like Whitehead's, then we must opt for a very dynamic, organic interpretation rather than a more Aristotelian view that depends on a Prime Mover. And what we have seems to point to the dynamic interpretation. Goto writes:

> The *Chung*'s movement by which individual consciousnesses are thus brought forth was otherwise described by Chu-hsi as the *Chung*'s limitation of its own content, whereby the content thus limited is clearly objectified as individual consciousnesses. After the individual consciousnesses are thus brought forth they are then according to Chu-hsi objectified by the *Chung* itself. Moreover, in Chu-hsi's conception the

> *Chung*, while thus working, particularizes itself in individual consciousnesses. Chu-hsi goes on to argue that when those stimuli or impulses disappear the *Chung* will recover its former state of quiescence. . . .
>
> Here we may recall that while the *Chung* is working in that way the *T'ai-ch'i* (Great Ultimate) which constitutes the essential part of the *Chung*, . . . is really actuating the *Chung* by virtue of its own nature of endlessly repeating the alternation of its movement and pause.[15]

Even though the Aristotelians and perhaps the Vaiśeṣikas of Chu Hsi's time likewise may have had a rather clear notion of the Prime Mover concept they seem not to have adequately taken into account the phenomenon of polarization, which Chu Hsi inherited from Chou Tun-i and the Ch'eng brothers and others. The Aristotelians do of course have their 'dialectic' of motion and rest, substance and accident, beginning and ending, etc., but these schematizations seems to be only descriptive manners of ordering or classifying mostly rather commonplace aspects of reality and seldom if ever in a truly organic, dynamic, growing sense, whereas these realist Neo-Confucians really did expect to find in nature itself that *li*, that principle, operating universally. The comparison might better be made in terms of the Neo-Platonic evolution and involution of the hypostases, especially since here we are dealing with 'consciousnesses' rather than with things; and indeed when Chu Hsi starts thinking in terms of the individual consciousnesses retaining their identity even when they sink back into the unity of the *Chung*, perhaps we do have a close analogy to the manner by which Plotinus expected individual souls to return through the *Psyché* and *Nous* to the One. The *T'ai-ch'i* resembles the One and *Chung* evidently resembles *Nous* or perhaps a sort of amalgam of *Nous* and *Psyché*. As Goto describes Chu Hsi's views the parallel seems rather remarkably close:

> Let us recall here that Chu-hsi emphasized the movement and pause of the *Chung*. In this connexion we may take him to imply, in making such an assertion, that when the *Chung* particularizes itself in individual consciousnesses and puts

> itself into self-differentiation, according to those individual consciousnesses the *Chung* is causing its activities. Again as to Chu-hsi's definition of the *Chung*'s state of quiescence we may take him to mean that when the individual consciousnesses that have been called into being by the *Chung* have sunk into the unity of the *Chung* upon the cessation of the stimuli or impulses the *Chung* is seen to be in a state of quiescence. The return of the *Chung* to its state of quiescence is in a way a pause of the *Chung*'s development. Thus the *Chung*'s movement and pause should both ... be considered to indicate its ceaseless development.[16]

Actually we need not go all the way back to Plotinus since something of the sort can be found in Ibn 'Arabī or Suhrawardī or perhaps even in Ibn Rushd's interpretation of the Higher Intellect in the Aristotelian system. Nevertheless for that comparison we might better take Chu Hsi's distinction of the three functions of the individual human mind, namely volition, emotion and wisdom, these roughly perhaps paralleling the vegetable, animal and rational souls in the Aristotelian tradition. That basis of comparison might be more rewarding since it is more in conformity with Chu Hsi's realist metaphysics. Also that comparison allows more room for Chu Hsi's philosophy of individuation, for he believes that each intellect has its own individual *li* (or *logos*, as Goto suggests) just as the great *Chung* accords with the Great *Li* whereby it emerges, as it were from the *T'ai-ch'i* and seems to return to it.

This leads us directly into what many moderns might consider as a sort of psychologism, since Chu Hsi does not separate his psychology from his metaphysics or his philosophy of nature, and correspondingly he does not leave any gap between those and his ethics. But in this he is typically Confucian Chinese, and that in a way that is not easy for the non-Chinese to empathize. One might even state that it is especially typical for the Neo-Confucians, both of the realist and the idealist types, to ontologize the virtues. For they are forces operative not only in human affairs but, as the harmony of the microcosm and macrocosm is achieved, in the universe at large. Of course these virtues are the classic four, *jen* (human-heartedness), *i* (righteousness), *li* (humility), and *chi* (wisdom). The relation of *Chung* to these four virtues is one of the basic problems in Chu Hsi interpretation since on the one hand he says that *Chung* is the Great Unifier of the *li*'s (principles) governing these virtues if not the virtues themselves; but it is evidently also the source from which they emerge and within which they are operative. Hence some interpreters see him as virtually a monist after all; but probably the better interpretation is that which puts more emphasis on his metaphysics of individuation, which he derived as much from Chang Tsai as from Chou Tun-i or the Ch'eng brothers.

This metaphysics of individuation whereby each individual thing and/or each individual virtue has its own individuated *li* as well as comparticipation within the Great *Li* associated with the *T'ai-ch'i* and/or the *Chung* is carried over into his philosophy of nature and the elements. Schematically the four ethical norms can be correlated with the four elements (or five, as one should include wood). These in turn are correlated with the four feelings, which must be distinguished from the virtues. These feelings are commiseration, shame, respectfulness, and discreteness. Of course such attempts at correlations were not new. It might be remembered that even Tung-chung Shu had done something like this many centuries earlier; and when Goto suggests that what is involved is a pattern of an ever-expanding circle, we could well look to the cosmological diagrams that often accompany expositions of the metaphysics of al-Bīrunī and/or the Ikhwān al-Ṣafā.

One difficulty in interpreting Chu Hsi is that our own modern post-Cartesian orientation has no footing at all in most Chinese systems, since if anything they are nearer to Whiteheadian 'organicism' which does not recognize any dichotomy between 'spirit' and 'matter'. Goto writes:

> But if we can break through the subjective world and penetrate deep into the objective world, then for the first time a bright world of essential truths embracing the two worlds, subjective and objective and at the same time surmounting both worlds, bursts upon our inner eyes. The attainment of this final status will give us a truly objective unprejudicedness

> an absolute liberty, a true creative power in the concrete sense of the word. Here then man reaches the absolute liberty of himself and returns to the true source of his being.[17]

In these ultimates Chu Hsi is actually not so far after all from his Śūnyavādin confreres or even from Citsukha. Ultimately there is even an identity between *saṃsara* and *nirvāṇa*—but only ultimately; for the most of us for all practical purposes that radical difference remains. It is a matter of levels perhaps. Goto concludes:

> When man finds himself in the position which allows the attainment of the absolute unity of the subjective and objective world, then the objective world of mutual conflict and convenient compromises and reconciliations will vanish. A world of complete unity of man's self and the visible things evolves. This reminds us of the ideal position in which Chuang-chou became a butterfly and at the same time the butterfly became Chuang-chou himself, as interpreted in its deepest implications. This position is also the position in which the body enveloped in burning flames is not injured thereby, nor the drowning man in the water drowned at all. Indeed, Cheng-tzu has said, "The benevolent man (namely, the man who has attained the attitude of his mind attuned to the *Chung*, represented by the absolute liberty of the self) sees heaven and earth and all things as one." This position is physically realized through the man's concrete experiences which are beyond the bounds of reasoning. In this position one's own mind and other people's minds melt and are fused together, and the self can freely pass through its own world and other people's worlds.
>
> He can then sympathize with the hearts of all things by the operation of his own heart, and can take the hearts of all things into his own heart. The sage's heart, as conceived by Confucianists, is realized then.[18]

Chu Hsi had the problem of incorporating the best of Buddhism, critically, into the Confucian structure, the issue being the adjustment of a metaphysics of total process and change to an ethical structure which was as unchanging and adamant as it was considered to be ordained by Heaven. It seems that this gap is bridged as much by Chu Hsi as by Ibn Rushd in his philosophy of mind (*hsin*). It should readily be seen how this should be possible since both Mādhyamika and Vijñānavāda had put much emphasis on *manas, buddhi, citta,* etc. Although it could scarcely be claimed that the strict Confucians before Chu Hsi had quite the equivalent of this with its claim of cosmic extension, they did have the concept of the Will or the Decree of Heaven and man's capacity to conform to it, and the capacity of learning as the chief factor that distinguishes man from the beasts. According to Chu Hsi:

> The Mind that is perfected is like a clear mirror which is free from blemishes. If you look into a mirror with patches... the effect will be that of your own person appears as blotchy. In the present day the conduct of many is marred by a number of follies and blemishes because their vision of themselves is imperfect. The Mind is essentially formless Spirit; all laws are complete within it, and all phenomena come within the sphere of complete knowledge. In these days people are for the most part perverted by their physical nature, and beclouded by creaturely desire. Thus their minds are darkened and they are unable to perfect knowledge. This is why the saints and sages placed such emphasis on the exhaustive investigation of principles.[19]

However, with perhaps a keener appreciation than is the case with the Aristotelian and more comparable perhaps to the Upaniṣadic tradition, the subtlety as well as the vastness and all-embracingness of the mind is kept in sharp focus:

> The mind is most spiritual. So fine is it that it penetrates the very point of a hair, or the smallest blade of grass, and I become conscious of them. So great is it that there is not a single place from nadir to zenith, or within the four points of the compass, where it is not present. Back through the countless ages of the past, or forward through the unknown periods of the future time, my thought reaches to the end

> of them at the very moment it proceeds from my Mind. It is unfathomable in its spiritual intelligence, most intangible, most spiritual and marvellous in its orderliness! And yet, though there is no one who does not possess this Mind, most men know only the desire for gain, till the Mind becomes completely submerged in it. At home and abroad, all that they seek is pleasure and self-indulgence; their every thought, the moment it is born, is of these things.[20]

This entails in a way that is not so clearly possible under an Aristotelian structure the possibility of spiritual cultivation which is integral with both being and morality. For whereas in the Aristotelian system the mind like everything else is taken to be a fixed entity with definite and well-defined function, to the Neo-Confucian, although there may be and indeed are fixed entities within the range of experience, the range of experience is definitely not fixed but is a matter of cultivation. The mind can be enlarged. True enough to a certain degree the individual mind within the personal psycho-physical organism seems to be limited; for example, my mind is not your mind or his mind. But this does not by any means entail non-relatedness. The fact that any mind, like the Aristotelian Passive Intellect, is capable of entering into relation with the structure, function and purpose of things, into their Tao, shows that what is supposed to be limitation is really not so. Hence the importance of expanding the mind, of identifying it even with, or as, the Cosmic Mind which keeps the Great Harmony in proper balance.

Scarcely any other philosopher has so keenly designated the bounds, or rather the boundlessness, of selfless love. Chu Hsi is quite open that all other virtues are only specializations of this. The aesthetic embellishments are there, the delight in spring, and all the lyrical tradition which is as ancient as the classical odes; but this never completely takes over (as often it does in Japanese tradition) without ethical considerations also. Extreme statements about mystical union are to be guarded rather closely, although it must not be denied that love has its role in imparting at least a sense of oneness with the universe. In his typical spirit of good judgment, moreover, Chu Hsi makes a very clear distinction between genuine love and mere shallow altruism:

> In saying that altruism is Love, altruism must not be regarded as parallel to Love. Altruism is simply the absence of selfishness. When there is no selfishness Love has free course. When the Master Ch'eng said "altruism is near to it", he did not mean near in the sense of being like it, but when there is altruism Love is present, therefore he used the word "near".... Just as you remove the dam the water flows freely, but the flow of water is not made by the removal of the dam. The water is there originally, but damned up; as soon as the dam is removed it flows. Love is there originally, but is cut off by selfishness; when one's selfishness is conquered and removed that which then acts is Love.[21]

Strange indeed that the politics of most of the Caucasian segment of humanity, in spite of its supposed adoption of Christianity, has not operated according to this assumption.

It was by interpretation rather than by innovation that the Neo-Confucians and Chu Hsi in particular were able to revitalize the ancient ideal of *jen* over against the more definite codes of the Buddhist *pāramitās*, for example, which were much more explicit and also which assumed a metaphysical rooting in the concept of constant change and impermanency, which was diametrically opposite to the Confucian emphasis on permanence and stability. By putting together Ch'eng Hao's emphasis on creativity and Ch'eng I's emphasis on orderliness, Chu Hsi was able to bring virtually the whole of reality into focus by viewing it through the virtue of *jen*. *Jen* is not treated as a merely human virtue but as a cosmic principle, almost equatable with *li*. As Chan epitomizes the matter:

> In emphasizing this creative character of *jen*, Chu Hsi was strictly following Ch'eng I. However, he also defined *jen* as "the character of the mind and the principle of love". He understood this principle to be the mind of Heaven and Earth to produce things. In other words, he put Ch'eng I's interpretation of *jen* as creation on the basis of principle. Only because of the principle of the mind of Heaven and

> Earth to produce can love grow. The upshot is to provide a metaphysical basis for Confucian ethics. This is an important way in which Confucianism became new, and this is an important way Neo-Confucianism was completed.
> ... It is clear that Chu Hsi owed much debt to Chou, Chang, and the Ch'engs, particularly Ch'eng I, but he was not strictly following a tradition. On the contrary, he remade it.[22]

Almost as transparently as in the Christian mystics where it is the bond of union between the Persons of the Blessed Trinity, love (*jen*) is the most all-pervasive of all possibilities which the human soul can reach.

Chu Hsi disagreed systematically with the idealism of the Buddhists. He evidently did not know anything about the original Sarvāstivāda texts which had been brought from India, much less the realist schools of Abhidharma Buddhism and the later development of Theravāda. Of course the refutation of this Buddhist idealism was necessarily much more subtle with Lu Hsiang-shan and his predecessors and successors since with them it was a matter of making distinctions between different kinds of idealism rather than, as with Chu Hsi, insisting on the reality of the external world. Chu Hsi would have found Madhva's criticism of *māyāvāda* very compatible, perhaps even more so than that of the Viśiṣṭādvaitins. We might find corresponding parallels in Ibn Rushd over against al-Ghazālī, and Thomas Aquinas against the Augustinian idealists.

Chu Hsi considered Buddhism as a religion rather than as a philosophy or a group of differing philosophies, whereas he considered Confucianism as an ethical system of philosophy. According to Chan:

> Chu Hsi's knowledge of Buddhism was very superficial and in saying that Buddhist ideas came from the *Chuang Tzu* and the *Lieh Tzu*, for example, he revealed both his prejudice and ignorance. But his attack on Buddhism was more comprehensive than his predecessors', for he criticized Buddhism from all points of view—ethical, theoretical, practical, historical, and textual.[23]

Since Chu Hsi had not studied the systematics of the Buddhist systems it is left open for speculation what his considerations might have been if, for example, he had had access to the systematic epistemology and logic of Dignāga and Dharmakīrti and a full appreciation of the Mādhyamika and Yogācāra systems such as Hsüan Tsang must have brought back to China, but which, for reasons that are still not clear, had fallen into neglect.

One reason for the decline of Buddhism during the Sung Dynasty was the popularity of the Ch'an and Pure Land schools both of which were anti-intellectual in character. Ch'an furnished an 'escape' for the upper classes while the Pure Land sects made room for all sorts of semi-superstitious cultic devotional practices and became popular religions of salvation for the masses, but with very little content as far as systematic philosophy is concerned.

> It therefore comes as no surprise that with the supremacy of these two schools, with their antitextual and antischolastic tendencies, there has not emerged any writer or thinker within Buddhism since the Sung Dynasty comparable in stature to such figures as Tao-sheng and Hsüan-tsang. For, after all, the strength and vigor of Buddhism rested on the principle of equal emphasis on all three aspects of the Buddhist discipline—moral conduct, concentration, and wisdom. Special attention to one, to the neglect of the other two, would certainly result in the deterioration of the dharma.[24]

Obviously Chu Hsi was attacking Buddhism at its worst, and for that no doubt the more intelligent Buddhists themselves would thank him. Actually Chu Hsi could have taunted the Buddhists of his time for having allowed a confusion in their own systematics between the *pāramārthika* level and the lower levels of reality. The saying that *saṃsāra* is the same as *nirvāṇa* had been used, or misused, in the extreme and had allowed a pretext for almost every kind of abuse if not outright vice such as the original Śākyamuni Buddha would never for a moment have allowed.

As for the Buddhist method of meditation, which Chu Hsi closely associates with Taoist "yoga", his objection is somewhat typical of modern objections: all they want is tranquillity. And moreover this is not necessarily attained by their method since as soon as they come out of their yoga there they are involved in the external world again as though they had not been meditating. Although he agrees that tranquility of mind is a good thing, it can be cultivated by other means, chiefly by assiduous study. To make a full time job of such practice (as with Bodhidharma) meant neglect of the normal human responsibilities in the external world.

> The Buddhists are fundamentally afraid of life and death and are selfish. Is theirs the way for all? They devote themselves only to penetration on the transcendental level, not to learning on the empirical level. This being the case, can their penetration on the transcendental level be right? Their two levels are basically disconnected. Whatever is separated is not the Way.[25]

It might be argued that Chu Hsi ignores the Bodhisattva ideal and in general the criticism by the Mahāyāna schools that the "Hīnayāna" is justly called the "lesser way" because it has forgotten the Buddha's own doctrine of Compassion. This may be because he was not so familiar with the T'ien T'ai, Pure Land and other varieties of Buddhism which did emphasize that aspect of Buddhism and even themselves tended to share Chu Hsi's criticism of Ch'an.

Chu Hsi was historically responsible for establishing the "Four Books" (of Confucius and Mencius) as the authentic recension rather than the "Five Classics" which most of his predecessors had accepted and worked on almost unquestioningly. Chan writes:

> The more important contribution he made with the Four Books is a new methodology, namely, the investigation of things. He put the *Great Learning* at the head, even ahead of what he considered as the foundation, namely the *Analects*, primarily because he saw in the *Great Learning* a pattern of

> life and learning....According to it, the beginning of the whole process of learning and living is the investigation of things. Only after this, will extension of knowledge, sincerity of the will, rectification of the mind, cultivation of the self, regulation of the family, ordering of the state, and bringing peace to the world be achieved step by step.[26]

Chu Hsi allowed a good measure to the practice of "allowing the mind to be empty", but he did not see that this was enough even though the Buddhists had claimed to arrive at genuine selflessness and altruism. This introspective tendency seems much better balanced in Chu Hsi than in the Buddhists by this discipline of objective observation and investigation of such a 'scientific' sort that one wonders that the scientific revolution which has given Western Europe a great heyday of world hegemony did not have even further development in Sung China before Europe came into the lead. It is often charged that the Chinese and Indic minds alike really tended more toward the feelings than to reason of the Aristotelian type. We have seen that this is by no means necessarily true. Certainly the Victorines and the followers of St. Bernard were past-masters at the cultivation of feelings of piety and the supra-rational field of mystical awareness; and certainly the Nyāya logic which continued to develop was in many respects more precise than that of Aristotle, and certainly we should take note of the many discoveries which later found their way to Europe from China (gunpowder, moveable type, magnetic compass, etc.).

The area of Aesthetics in comparative philosophy, though it is only beginning to be explored, is virtually unlimited, especially if one takes the classical triad of epistemology, ethics, and aesthetics (or in the Indian schools, *jñāna*, *karma* and *bhakti*). Through a prejudice among aestheticians dealing in Euramerican textbooks one nevertheless gets the impression that the scholastics had no aesthetics at all, and that prejudice tends to spill over into the comparative field in a very unhealthy way. The popular notion is that Taoism encourages aesthetics at the expense of ethics, whereas Confucianism stresses ethics at the expense of aesthetics, whereas Buddhism at its best stressed epistemology at the expense of both ethics and aesthetics. Of course it can be debated whether this impression is unjust even to the point of prejudice or whether in fact it does have an historical basis.

There are very few philosophers among Chu Hsi's contemporaries in Eurasia who did not also write poetry. Those who espoused the ascendence of *jñāna* or epistemology over ethics and/or aesthetics often wrote devotional poetry or other lyric forms that do not necessarily conform to their own systematics. This raises the classical question as to whether any one or two of the *jñāna-karma-bhakti* triad can or should be reduced to any other, so that it may be a radical mistake simply to seek for a 'definition' of the beautiful or of art instead of seeking to induce a sense of creative appreciation and participative creativity. Correspondingly, it may not be the best to reduce the cultivation of aesthetic refinement—as indeed some classical Confucians and even some Neo-Confucians insisted should be the case—to a subdivision of cultivation of one's ethical integrity. Also it may be observed that those whose philosophy systematically has a profound aesthetic or *bhakti* or devotional orientation seldom write poetry as a sideline from their systematics, the systematics being *ipso facto* expressed poetically. In the class of those whose poetry seems to lie outside their systematics we might point to Thomas Aquinas, Abelard, Śrīharṣa, Chu Hsi, Citsukha, Ibn Rushd, Madhva and perhaps Maimonides, Nichiren and Eisai. In the other class we might put Rūmī, Bonaventure, Bernard of Clairvaux, Suhrawardī, Lu Hsiang-shan, certainly Ippen, Rāmānuja, Pillai Lokācārya and perhaps Dōgen.

Chu Hsi's nature poems far outnumbered those which directly treat Neo-Confucian themes. He not only loved nature but was one of those fortunate men who almost always lived in places noted for natural beauty. The Chinese generally have always regarded nature with awe rather than fear; thus, attitudes of reverence, gratitude, and appreciation naturally induced a sense of harmony and a sort of *wu wei* attitude toward the activities of nature. Indeed perhaps this is why the *māyāvāda* aspect of Buddhist idealism never got an easy reception in Chinese cultural streams and if anything rather tended to be interpreted in terms of Taoist aestheticism instead of metaphysical reality.

Chu Hsi himself emphasized that even the contemplation of

natural phenomean involves the perception of the operation of *li* in all things. Such *ko wu*, investigation of things, improves virtue. We may well remember that Chu Hsi always counselled exhaustive study as much more rewarding than meditation or cultivation of 'emptiness'. It is humanness (*jen chi*) that is involved, not mere aesthetic enjoyment of any sort as an end in itself; and even achieving harmony of microcosm with macrocosm does not necessarily involve either extreme asceticism or abandoned indulgence, but simply and purely the completion of the rational potentialities inherent in human nature. Li Chi writes:

> The Taoists, then, wanted to break through human limitations; in the face of nature, they were full of longing and discontent. The Buddhists, on the other hand, wanted to break down those limitations in order to attain transcendental wisdom in a recognition of *śūnyatā*. The Neo-Confucians accepted nature in a purely human way, attending to the way they found it and trying to learn from it by bending themselves to its ways.[26]

According to Li Chi, aestheticism even of a refined sort was directly antithetical to the Neo-Confucian cultivation of moral excellence. Poetry was, especially with Chu Hsi, *allowed* rather than deliberately worked on as a major pursuit. It might almost be said of Chu Hsi if not also of several other Neo-Confucians that they were poets in spite of themselves, not because they wanted to be known for literary excellence as an end in itself. Relatively frequently Chu Hsi would vow not to indulge in poetry writing any more; and then, another poem would be written.[27]

Li Chi relates what may seem a curious paradox in Chu Hsi's character: his love of fine tea overpassed, almost, by his love of wine. This certainly corrects the impression, if anyone has it, that Chu Hsi was nothing but an old strict Puritan. Whether he had a real sense of humor or not we have little evidence; but where he did not sanction abandon to sensuous pleasure, neither did he condemn desire as such. Rather, rectification of all extremes seems to be his norm, and that applied in such a way that "moderate extremes" were not excluded. Li Chi concludes, "This paradoxical man seems to have set up barriers all around himself and then searched for ways to avoid them for short periods of freedom."[28] Perhaps it should also be said of Chu Hsi that he was not only a complete, profound and versatile philosopher but a complete and completely human person.

As for what is absent, by comparison, from Chu Hsi's system we might mention a definite system of categories, distinction of varieties of causation such as may be found among the various Aristotelian scholastics, distinctly syllogistic logic such as may be found in both the Indian and European scholastic systems, and for good or for ill it is very difficult to superimpose a truly theistic construction on Chu Hsi's metaphysics. He is a philosopher through and through, and not a theologian; and from his refutations of what he knew of Buddhism we certainly become aware that he was not a mystic or illuminationist. The method of balanced judgment is no doubt Chu Hsi's best claim to fame—in addition to being the fundamental characteristic that he shares with virtually all of the constellation of great minds in this Great Summas period in the world history of philosophy.

12. Maimonides

Moses Maimonides (1135-1204) is at least of the same importance as Chu Hsi and Ibn Rushd, and follows after a long line of other great minds such as Bahya Ibn Pakuda, Joseph Ibn Zaddik, Judah Halevi, Abraham Ibn Ezra and Abraham Ibn Daud. Maimonides' *Guide of the Perplexed* has become such a classic that no educated person East or West could remain entirely ignorant of it. It was published in 1190 and has been a great source of spiritual strength to many ever since, including even the great Spinoza. Critically read it will be found to be as sound in logical acumen as in spiritual consolation. Perhaps Maimonides does not engage in such extreme or subtle dialectics as Śrīharṣa, but his insistence on consistency is unexcelled by anyone before Spinoza. Perhaps he does not achieve the serene simplicity of Chu Hsi, but his logical approach to the Simplicity of God is as exact as it is rigorous. Compact, brief and precise, Maimonides combines learning at least as wide as that of Aquinas with a skill for condensation that has seldom been equalled anywhere.

> Moses Maimonides (son of Maimon), the most distinguished Jewish philosopher of the middle ages, was born in Córdoba (Spain) in 1135. He received his earliest education from his learned father. In addition to a solid grounding in rabbinical studies, Maimonides profited from the Greco-Arabic learning then available in Islamic Spain and North Africa. When Córdoba fell into the hands of the Almohads in 1148, his family was forced to flee because of the religious intolerance of the new conquerors. After a long period of wandering through Spain, they sought refuge in Fez, Morocco. Religious persecution threatened them there as well, and it was only through the aid of a friendly Muslim poet-theologian that they managed to escape. In 1165 they departed for Palestine and eventually settled in Egypt. The family then suffered a severe financial reverse. In order to cope with these new difficulties, Maimonides began to practice medicine, and he eventually became court physician. He was appointed *nāgīd* or chief of the Jewish communities in Egypt, and apparently was held in high regard both by Jew and by Muslim. He died in 1204. . . .
>
> Interestingly, Maimonides did not regard his *Guide of the Perplexed* as a philosophical work. He rather addressed it to Jewish believers who were well grounded in their own religious heritage and who had some acquaintance with Greek learning. They might easily be led into a state of "perplexity" before apparently conflicting claims of philosophy and religion. His purpose seems to be to guide such "perplexed" individuals to a deeper insight into philosophical truths without compromising their religious commitment and, at the same time, to increase their appreciation of Scripture itself. In so doing he displays vast philosophical erudition and a great debt to Aristotle and certain classical commentators such as Alexander of Aphrodisias (ca. 200) and Themistius

(Ca. 317-ca. 387). At times he agrees with Avicenna and at times he differs with him.[1]

Before examining the *Guide* itself it might be helpful to note the following by Husik on Maimonides' method and rationalism:

> His method, in general, of quieting the doubts of the "perplexed" is the old one—as old as Philo and beyond—of regarding Biblical phrases as metaphors and allegories, containing an esoteric meaning beside or opposed to the literal. Accordingly he lays the greatest stress on the explanation of Scriptural "homonyms," as he calls them, borrowing an Aristotelian term. A homonym is a word which has more than one meaning; a word which denotes several things having nothing in common. Thus when I apply the word dog to the domestic animal we know by that name, as well as to Sirius, known as the dog-star, I use dog as a homonym. The star and the animal have nothing in common. So the word "merciful," one of the attributes of God in the Bible, is a homonym. That is, we denote by the same word also a quality in a human being; but this quality and that which is denoted by the same word when applied to God have nothing in common. They are not merely different in degree but in kind. In fact, Maimonides insists, there is really nothing *in* God corresponding to the word merciful....
>
> There is really nothing new in this, and Philo apart, whom Maimonides did not know, Ibn Daud anticipated Maimonides here also in making use of the term "homonym" as the basis of this method of interpretation. But whereas Ibn Daud relegates the chapter treating of this principle to a subordinate place, his interest being as he tells us primarily ethical—to solve the problem of free will; Maimonides places it in the very centre of his system. The doctrine of attributes as leading to a true conception of God—of God as absolutely incorporeal and without any resemblance or relation whatsoever to anything else—is the very keystone of Maimonides' philosophical structure. His purpose is to teach a spiritual conception of God. Anything short of this is worse than idolatry. He cannot reconcile the Bible to such a view without this "homonymic" tool.[2]

It is in line with Maimonides' general rationalistic and intellectualistic point of view when he undertakes to find a reason for every commandment, where no reason is given in the Law. He shows himself in this an opponent of all mysticism, sentimentality and arbitrariness. Reason is paramount. The intellect determines the will, and not even God's will may be arbitrary. His will is identical with his reason, hence there is a reason in everything that he wills. We may not in every case succeed in finding the reason where he himself did not choose to tell us, but a reason there always is, and the endeavor on our part to discover it should be commended rather than condemned.[3]

Maimonides' chief concern is with the Unicity of God. Drawing heavily from the Islamic sources, in the first chapter of his *Guide* he goes to great pains to select the best arguments between the Mutakallimūn and the Ash'arites; but he advances some considerations that are valid in themselves, thus combining the best of the revelation to Moses and the best of strict logic inherited from the Greek sources. Besides the question of God's attributes, in the following he also expresses his view on the problem, which had become common all across Eurasia, of the gap between the common people and the enlightened which had become so wide and so universal:

> ...We have stressed the fact that metaphysics is a dangerous and subtle subject which few can understand and which must not be divulged to the mass of people. It must on no account be imagined that these strictures apply to our denial of anthropomorphism and divine affections...all must clearly realize that our knowledge and His knowledge, or our power and His power, are not different merely in quantity or intensity.... Everything that is attributed to God Almighty, however, is so completely different from any of our own attributes that no common definition can ever be found for the two. In the same way one applies to His existence and the existence of other things the term 'existence' by way of homonymy, as I shall explain later. So much is enough for children and common people to fix in their minds the notion that there is a

> Perfect Being which is neither a body nor a force within a body, that He is God, that no manner of imperfection attaches to Him, and that therefore He is not subject to aflections.[4]

Although he will not compromise on the difference between God and man (wherein he most resembles Madhva), Maimonides must still account for the way whereby this is known.

One can scarcely accuse Maimonides of fanaticism because of his astuteness in logic and his excellence in virtue, but one wonders whether his zeal for consistency has not led him into further difficulties. For he virtually denies that God may have any attributes lest His Unicity be compromised. He does not clearly see, as the followers of Rāmānuja and the best of Christian philosophers and to some extent the Neo-Confucianists did, that the admission of this one attribute of "unicity" itself entails a field of relationality within that Unity. If one says that God is the One as the Neo-Platonists and the strict Advaitins do, then one must risk pantheism. But if one asserts, as Maimonides does, that God, as One, is *different* from anything else, then one has more than Unity. Is there a possible concept of "surplus of unity" which is valid which will account for difference as well as unicity? Maimonides writes:

> If, however, you are one of those high-minded people who strive to reach a higher stage, that of speculation, and to believe with absolute certainty that God is truly One, His Unity being true Unity without any trace of compositeness whatsoever, you must know that God has no essential attribute whatever in any form or any manner. As we cannot admit that He is a body so we cannot admit that He has any essential attribute.
>
> If one believes Him to be One and to possess a number of attributes, one in fact says that He is One and thinks that He is many. This is the same as what the Christians say: He is One but He is Three, and Three are One. There is no difference between this and saying: He is One but has many attributes, and He and His attributes are One....
>
> Furthermore, if the attributes are many, then many things must have existed eternally. Belief in Unity cannot mean

> essentially anything but the belief in one single homogeneous uncompounded essence: not in a plurality of ideas but in a single idea. Whichever way you look at it, and howsoever you examine it, you must find it to be one, not dividing itself in any manner or for any reason into two ideas. No plurality must be discoverable in it either in fact or in thought, as will be proven in the course of this treatise.[5]

Nevertheless, tradition and the weight of other philosophical arguments force him to admit other attributes in some sense or other. Like the Muslim scholastics before him, he divides these primarily into essential and negative, i.e., into those which are inseparable from God's existence and those which can be known to us only negatively because of our limitations.

The problem of God's will and His wisdom lead yet further into that area where scarcely man dare to tread without danger of what St. Bernard and Hugo of St. Victor had called inept "curiosity", which has been nevertheless the bane of the prophetic tradition. Rather than seeking to reflect the Will of Heaven such as we find in Chu Hsi, too many, blinded by what they thought to be the will of the Lord, have led the people into battle chanting the Psalms of Vengeance—unless, of course, it be true that many really *should* die in the Crusades for the greater glory of God. But this is not what Maimonides means by the will of God. If the Unity of God is sufficiently stressed, how can it be asserted that God has a Will at all without risking anthropomorphism? Revelation (the Scriptures) by itself does not give an adequate answer; reason must be called in to gain consistency and coherency. Maimonides writes:

> Thus the consistent investigation of every purpose will lead us to His will or His wisdom—according to which opinion we accept. Both of these have proved, according to our system, to be identical with His essence. Neither His will or intention nor His wisdom are things in any way separable from His essence. God is, therefore, the ultimate purpose of everything. Moreover, the purpose of all things is to resemble as far as possible His perfection, and that is what we mean by His will, i.e., His essence, as will be shown later. For this

reason we say of Him that He is the Purpose of Purposes. I have now made clear why one says of God that He is Maker, Form and Purpose, and that this is why the philosophers call Him Cause and not merely Maker. . . .Since God, however, is also the Form of the world, as we have explained before, and supports its continued existence and permanence, it is absurd to believe that the supporter could disappear, and yet the thing he supports continue to exist although it has no existence except by virtue of the support it receives. This is all that need be said concerning the error of the theory that God is only Maker and not also Purpose and Form.[6]

With any of the Jewish, Christian and Islamic scholastics the question up to now has been, not whether or how much, but how well they used Aristotle, who must be taken for granted. If they had not had Aristotle, could they have found an alternative in any of the other traditions, and if so, would that have altered their position very much? We would only suggest that there would not have been much difference as far as the positing of the Fundamental Unity is concerned, but there might have been some difference as to how to "get back" once one has seen the almost infinite range of possibilities of structures and processes and sustained cycles and epicycles and causes and effects, creations and emanations, combinations of opposites, etc., which must be accounted for either within, or in some other relation to, that Fundamental Unicity. Of course Śrīharṣa and Dōgen would insist that we never really got separated from Unity, which simply remains just that, One only and without a second, all these other things being not only superfluous but illusory superimpositions (*adhyāsa*). Honen would have us find the way back by devotional surrender to Amida; Hugo by ecstatic contemplation of the Trinity. But Maimonides seems to rely on the solid foundation of the sheer structure of logical necessity. Thus, in a form which only a Spinoza could imitate, the second book opens with twenty-six axiomatic propositions which Maimonides introduces as follows:

Twenty-five of the propositions which are employed in the proof for the existence of God, or in the arguments demons-

> trating that God is neither corporeal nor a force connected with a material being, or that He is One, have been fully established, and their correctness is beyond doubt. Aristotle and the Peripatetics who followed him have proved each of these propositions. There is, however, one proposition which we do not accept—namely, the proposition which affirms the Eternity of the Universe, but we will admit it for the present, because by doing so we shall be enabled clearly to demonstrate our own theory.[7]

The second book is for the most part a reiteration of the arguments seen in the Islamic scholastics, with perhaps a slightly greater emphasis on the *ex nihilo* argument for the creation of the world.

Maimonides seems to be bothered somewhat by Aristotle's levels of the intellect, although he cannot entirely reject this in favor of the more radical Biblical teaching concerning the exalted transcendence of God and the comparatively vague Biblical teaching about the Spirit of the Lord "that filleth the whole world" which provokes the pronouncements of the Prophets. Even here for the most part he follows Ibn Sīnā, whom he mentions explicitly—another demonstration of the fact that there was much more interchange between Islamic, Jewish and Christian philosophers in the medieval period than is generally supposed. Aristotle and Plato bind them all together so that it is strange that there was not more concord on the political and military levels. As to these levels of the intellect, Maimonides writes:

> After these prefatory remarks I shall deal with Aristotle's assertion that the first intelligence is the cause of the second and this is the cause of the third. In this way, even if their number came to thousands the last intelligence would still, without any doubt, be simple. Whence, then, does the composite character originate which is, on Aristotle's own assertion, found necessarily in the things existing around us? Let us concede to Aristotle his whole theory that the further the intelligences are removed from the first, the more compound their functions become, because of the greater number of

> intelligibles apprehended by them. Even if we concede to him this wild guess we still must ask how the intelligences came to be a cause from which the spheres resulted, and what relationship is there between matter and the incorporeal which contains no matter whatsoever.[8]

In other words, even though in the realm of nature Maimonides is willing to concede to Aristotle almost everything, in the realm of non-material spirit he sees more than Aristotle taught and exerts constant effort to keep this as the primary focus. This is equally true on the issue of the eternity of the world. He will not surrender his faith in the Special Revelation to the Jews and appeals to the Law of Moses as the final authority in any disputable case. On this doctrine he is especially insistent since the Old Testament is full of citations which promise that the "world will perish and vanish away" but "the Word of the Lord will abide forever".

The same applies for the most part to his treatment of prophecy as such, although here again he does not say much more than Ibn Sīnā had said. Grace alone is not enough. The prophet's intelligence must be *trained*:

> According to this view it is impossible for an ignorant person to become a prophet. Also a man cannot go to bed as an ordinary person and wake up as a prophet, as if he had found something, but the process takes place in the following way. If a man is virtuous and perfect in both logical and moral qualities, if his imaginative faculty is as perfect as can be, and he undertakes the preparations of which you will hear, he must necessarily become a prophet, since that perfection is natural to us. According to this view it is not possible that a man should be fit for prophecy and prepare himself for it and yet not become a prophet, any more than that a healthy man should eat wholesome food without it forming sound blood, or similar cases....This then is our dogma: nothing can be done without training and perfection.[9]

And perhaps more curiously than with Ibn Sīnā, he links the gift of prophecy thus defined with the Active Intellect of Aristotle:

> It must be understood that the true character of prophecy is that of an emanation flowing from God by means of the Active Intelligence first upon the rational faculty and then upon the imaginative faculty. This is the highest rank attainable by man and the utmost degree of perfection which can be found in his species. That state is the highest degree of perfection of the imaginative faculty. Such a process can by no means take place in every man. It cannot be achieved by perfection in the speculative sciences or by improvement of character to the highest pitch of goodness and nobility, unless there is added to these the perfection of the imaginative faculty in the very core of one's natural disposition to the highest possible degree.[10]

In other words the prophet is above the philosopher, but it does the prophet no harm to be well equiped with the philosopher's tools.

The third book goes on to cover the problems of theodicy, although there is nothing particularly unusual about his vindication of God's appointment of both good and evil, for which there are sufficiently numerous examples of citations in the Old Testament. God's will is simply inscrutable, and one must leave it at that. Then he proceeds to the knotty problem of God's knowledge of particulars. Here he takes the typical scholastic view:

> It is generally agreed that it would be incorrect to ascribe to God the acquisition of new knowledge, i.e., that He should now know something that He did not know before. It would be equally incorrect to ascribe to Him manifold and multiple acts of cognition, even according to the view of those who believe in divine attributes. Assuming this as proven, we, the believers in the Divine Law, say that He knows many and manifold things by the same act of knowledge and that His acts of cognition do not vary according to the variation of things known, as it would be the case with us. We further say that all things that emerge anew were known to Him before they existed, and He knew them continually. For this reason He does not acquire any new knowledge whatsoever. He knows

> that so-and-so does not exist now, but will exist at such-and-such a time and will remain alive for so-and-so much time and will then be non-existent. When that person comes into being, as God knew he would, no new piece of knowledge has been added. It was not as if something hitherto unknown to Him had occurred, but something occurred which He continually knew would occur in the way it did....
>
> The philosophers, however, declare without further ado that God's knowledge cannot extend to the non-existent or that any knowledge can encompass the infinite. Therefore, since He does not acquire new knowledge, it is absurd that He should know anything of those things that emerge anew, and thus God does not know anything except permanent things that do not change. Some of them have still another doubt. They say, even if God knows only the permanent things, this would still imply many acts of knowing, since the acts of knowing vary according to the things known, because to every knowable object belongs a particular act of knowing. Therefore God cannot know anything except His own substance.
>
> My own opinion is that the reason for falling into these errors is that they treat God's knowledge as something comparable to our own.[11]

He continues to elaborate on this answer, including the old question about the relation of God's knowledge to His essence, only reiterating the same point concerning our inadequacy without giving any explanation of that.

For the most part Maimonides is not aware of the positive alternative, as may be seen in the Japanese Buddhists in particular and to some extent in Śrīharṣa, that God's knowledge is not limited to propositional reasoning as ours is but must be immediate and not limited to the subject-object relationship. The answer therefore can be that God's knowledge is not a *having* as ours is but is inseparable from His Being. After all the various digressions and pilgrimages and permutations and perambulations, one seems to be reduced again to the irreducible formula of the *sat-cit-ānanda* according to the Viśiṣṭādvaita (Rāmānuja) interpretation, which is not far from the Christian doctrine of the Trinity rightly understood. For even the knowledge that

God's knowledge is different from ours entails some sort of panentheistic communicability within the nature of God so that we may somehow be co-participators in His knowledge even of our unknowing. Is Maimonides trying to force this richness of the *super*-abundance of God's knowing, willing, being, etc. back into an impossible monism even after that had been proven not so acceptable by the generation immediately preceding him? Sometimes one gets that impression. At the close of chapter twenty he says:

> The sum total of the idea that I am trying here briefly to explain is the following: we cannot apprehend the true nature of God's essence: yet we know that His existence is the most perfect, without any admixture of imperfection or change or affection in any way. Similarly, though we do not know the true nature of God's knowledge, because it is His substance, yet we know that He does not sometimes apprehend and at other times remain unaware, i.e., that He never acquires any new knowledge, also that His knowledge is not of a multiple nature nor finite, that nothing of all existing things is hidden from Him and that His knowledge of them does not change their nature, but the possible retains its nature as a possibility. Anything in this enumeration that appears contradictory, is so only owing to the structure of our knowledge, which has nothing in common with His knowledge except the name.[12]

The *Guide* proceeds on through more discussion of the Ash'arites and the Mu'tazilites and the interpretations of the *Torah* and *Talmud* to a consideration of the doctrine of divine providence.

> I believe that divine providence extends, in this lower sub-lunar world, only and alone to human individuals. The human species is the only one in which all conditions of individuals and the good and evil that befalls them are according to deserts, as it is said, 'For all His ways are justice' (Deuteronomy 32:4). With regard to other animals, and still more so to plants and other things, my view is

> identical with that of Aristotle; I do not believe in any manner whatsoever that this leaf has fallen because of any providential act, or that this spider has caught that fiy through the personal and actual decree of God, or that Jack's spittle, in moving so that it descended upon this particular gnat at a particular spot and killed it, was directed by decree or destiny, or that the fact that this fish snapped that worm from the surface of the water was due to an act of the personal will of God. All this I hold to be pure chance just as Aristotle does. Divine providence, in my opinion, follows in the wake of divine emanation. It is the species which is affected by this rational emanation, so that it possesses reason, and everything that is accessible to a rational being becomes accessible to it—it is that species, I say, which divine providence constantly attends, and whose every action it assesses for reward and punishment. Though the sinking of a ship and the death of its passengers, or the collapse of the roof upon those who are in the house, may be due to true chance, yet the fact that the ones travelled in that ship or the others sat in that house cannot in our opinion be anything but a result of divine will in accordance with their deserts, as dictated by His judgments, the principles of which our minds are insufficient to know.[13]

Which is better: (a) a way which, in fear of anthropomorphism, makes God so logically undefinable as to be almost a *Śūnyatā* after all, or a *nirguṇa*-Brahman; (b) a way which, in fear of excessive human "rationality", puts all faith in revelation and/or intuition, running the risk of superstitious credulity and/or sentimentality; (c) a way which insists that reason itself is a divine faculty and therefore must be cultivated in all things, even interpretation of revelation; (d) a way which, at the risk of inconsistency, seeks to combine all of these in an organic harmonious whole in order to penetrate barriers that dogmas and syllogisms too often exaggerate.

There is a sort of faith in providence not only in Jewish, Christian and Islamic scholasticism and some varieties of the Vedānta but even in Neo-Confucianist tradition wherein the Will of Heaven includes what man is and should do, and if it is contravened the wrong thereby incurred will in the course of the cosmic nature of things get balanced out in the succeeding cycles. There is thus at least this much in common to most members of our twelfth century conclave: the relation of man to the universe and to God (or the Supreme Principle) is basically that of microcosm/macrocosm although it might be conceded that Chu Hsi does not allow so much room to the personal factor. Ibn Rushd might criticize Maimonides in this regard in the same way as he did al-Ghazālī: piety of this sort is what may be expected of the masses, but for the philosopher and the sage the considerations that come in about one's own salvation and sanctification should have long since been left behind. The man who would be truly wise only considers this and all other things alike *sub specie universalitatis*. If God governs human affairs and is the creator-preserver-destroyer of the whole of the universe, there is no reason why either mediately or immediately He should not be the Cause of *everything* that happens therein, or else He would not be really omnipotent. Again, it is only our ignorance that hides this Cause from view. The importance is in, as the emphasis should be on, the Cause, not the caused. Is this not the better view of divine providence, or are we reading too much of Śrīharṣa into Maimonides' doctrine?

It might be argued that to abandon the doctrine of providence altogether is like abandoning the firm-footedness of earth and falling out into infinite space. But one may recall that the Chinese Zen masters used to say that salvation, far from being the "rock of ages" and the consolation of personal security which the nineteenth century hymns so widely celebrate, is like "having the bottom fall out". Clinging, that is the trouble. Let go, even of your cherished doctrines and traditions, and then you will be free. But Maimonides would rejoin an emphatic No! This would be disastrous to society as well as blasphemous. Virtue is necessary; personal merit must be gained. This is no matter of gnostic illumination. And therefore, whether we like it or not, every creature will vary in his worthiness of providence:

> This means that divine providence does not extend to all individuals of the human race in the same way, but to a degree varying in proportion to their share of human perfec-

tion. From this consideration it necessarily follows that God's providence for the prophets is particularly intensive, graded again according to their prophetic rank. His providence for the men of virtue and the pious will also correspond to the degree of virtue and piety they possess, since it is that quality of divine emanation which makes the prophets speak, and produces the good deeds of the pious and perfects the knowledge of the men of virtue. As for the ignorant and impious, the less they possess of this emanation, the less attention will they enjoy and the more will approach the order of individuals of animal species. 'He is like the beasts that perish' (Psalm 49:12).

For this reason killing them is considered a small matter. If it is to the public benefit it is even commanded.[14]

From this Maimonides goes on to reflections on Job. What should we say of Job from the global perspective? Self-commiserating wretch, why didn't he *do* something about his condition and the condition of those around him? (modern, secular). It was all *māyā* anyway; he needed more detachment in the first place (Buddhist or *māyāvāda* Hindu). He should observe the proper ceremonies and do something for the good of society and the moral order (Neo-Confucianist). He should have made his devotional surrender to God sooner than he did (*Ṣūfī*). He should have worked harder (Puritan Protestant). He should never have been duped by such superstition (Communist). His twelfth century would-be counselors and consolers would only have magnified the conclave that did their best in the authentic script. Maimonides simply says, "As soon as he obtained reliable knowledge of God he realized that true happiness, which consists in knowing God, is in store for all those who know Him, and none of those afflictions can dull it."[15] Then after a reference to the rather universal analogy of a prince who forgets or is kept ignorant of his true identity until he meets someone who awakens him to his true nature (a favorite metaphor with Rāmānuja), Maimonides states his conviction that above all logical and mathematical and other formal disciplines is the knowledge of God and His love.

> The stress is in every instance on intellectual apprehension, not on imaginations, for thinking about imaginations is not called 'knowing' but that which cometh into your mind (Ezekiel 20:32). It has also become clear that, after comprehending, the aim should be complete devotion to God and perpetual exercising of intellectual thought in His love. This succeeds mostly in a state of solitude and seclusion; which is why every man of virtue secludes himself as much as possible and keeps company with others only when this is unavoidable.[16]

Incidentally, what probably escapes the casual reader in the tradition of illustrative stories in the Talmudic heritage which, marvellous saint that he was, Maimonides probably used in *viva voce* instruction warm-heartedly balancing off his logical rigor in writing.

Not unlike Honen, for example, Maimonides does not escape from the necessity of a Quest which "has no earthly end", although he would probably insist that Hōnen did not have an adequate conception of God. Maimonides had perhaps a more purely non-anthropomorphic conception of Deity than any other Jewish or Islamic or Christian philosopher ever had. But this did not entail for him an abandonment of personal piety and solitary contemplation, although his contemplation was not that of cultivation of emptiness any more than that of the Neo-Confucianists, who criticized the Buddhists for overdoing this sort of thing. His ethical sense is too strong for this; God's ordinances are as definite as His nature is obscured to mortal view.

God's ordinances and His providence are very closely allied. The one lays down the provisions of the Covenant relation with man; the other, the Promises. Maimonides shows some prudence in this matter by teaching a graduated doctrine. God's providence may not be limited in any sense, but the human capacity to receive His bounties and to comprehend His ways varies considerably. In this light he treats the problem of theodicy. The man who is most favored of God will not necessarily be spared from evil and suffering but rather will be expected to be able to bear a much greater share of it. It will not affect him, however, and he will persevere to Beatitude with greater speed than the man who abandons ethical excellence or weakens in the face of suffering.

Finally, Maimonides lists four types of wisdom available to man. The first is the economic, although it is soon seen to be limited in duration and security. The perfection involved is strictly external to the self where the true perfection should lie. The second, perfection of physique and physical well-being, is more clearly related to the true self. However this too is seen as quite inadequate for even an ass can have it. Brawn is for carrying bricks and mortar, not for designing the building to be built. Spiritual benefit has little relation to its embodiment. The third is the ethical. It involves not only the self but relations with others, with society. But this is still inadequate as an end in itself and is only instrumental since the good of society and the good of the individual are both not only mutually dependent on a higher locus of the Good but also subject to change and alteration in different circumstances.

Maimonides argues that the fourth, the rational virtues, alone are good in themselves. Herein is the secret of eternal life as well as the characteristic that distinguishes man as man. Even the social insects may have some ethical order, but it is doubtful if they have means of investigating the heavens. The chief reason why the rational virtues are the most exalted is that they are most inalienable to the self. Even in solitude where no ethical problems are pressing, reason must hold sway. It is almost identical with one's own existence and the surest guarantee of God's sovereignty.

Husik gives us the following concerning Maimonides' influence:

> The *Guide of the Perplexed* was translated into Latin not long after its composition. Before Albertus Magnus, Alexander of Hales, the Franciscan leader, and William of Auvergne, the Bishop of Paris, had read and made use of Maimonides' philosophical masterpiece. Albertus Magnus was still more diligent in his adoption of Maimonidean views, or in taking account of them, where he is opposed to their adoption. But it remained for Thomas Aquinas, who made the most syste-

> matic attempt in the medieval schools to harmonize the philosophy of Aristotle with the doctrine of the Church, to use Maimonides as his guide and model. ... It is no doubt an exaggeration to say that there would have been no Aquinas if Maimonides had not preceded him.... But there is no doubt that the method of harmonizing Aristotelian doctrine with traditional teaching so far as the common elements of Judaism and Christianity were concerned was suggested to Aquinas by his Jewish predecessor. ... After Aquinas also, Duns Scotus, the head of the Franciscan school, had the "Guide" before him, and in comparatively modern times, such celebrities as Scaliger and Leibnitz speak of the Jewish philosopher with admiration and respect.
>
> That 'Maimonides' influence upon Jewish theology and thought was deep and lasting is a truism. ... What he said or wrote could not be ignored whether people liked it or not. They could afford to ignore a Gabirol even, or an Ibn Daud. But Maimonides must be reckoned with.[17]

One leaves Maimonides with the impression that here is a man—almost more than Spinoza whom he influenced, and equally with Śrīharṣa his Advaitin contemporary—whose being and thought are as nearly monolithic as one could ask. This does not mean, however, that he was a strict monist. The influences of both Aristotle and the Old Testament are too much in evidence to allow this sort of interpretation. But one finds in him little of duplicity or sense of conflict between the sacred and the secular, for the latter is simply found inadequate. One finds a person devoted to the pursuit, not of human happiness, but of Beatitude, with all things properly subordinated to this one end. He is wise because his wisdom which is not of this world guides him *through* the world in serenity, detachment, and good judgment. Maimonides finds not refuge *from* the duties of life in the pursuit of the Eternal, but finds, in the contemplation of the Unity of God, that by which all else is ordered and directed to its proper end, leading *through* these duties to their true purpose beyond the grave. If he constructed no great *Summa*, built no architecturally perfect system, contributed nothing essentially novel or unique, nevertheless he became a great soul, a *mahātma* from whom one may readily accept counsel in perplexity. Maimonides, rather unlike Ibn Rushd, sees no reason for abandoning piety, howsoever much it may demand the service of the intellect and all other faculties. Sanctity and wisdom are inseparable for him, as reason and the moral law are both only two sides of God's relation with man as microcosm—but microcosm which is by no means self-sufficient. The total dependence on God as well as the unquestioning obedience to His Law may not appeal either to the modern individualist or to the Vedāntic non-dualist who would remove the difference between God and man; but like the followers of the cult of Amida in some respects, Maimonides finds the sufficiency which is from purely spiritual resources more than adequate. Man's chief effort is not in his search for God, but in his response to God's Goodness and to the contemplation of His Being which He allows. This response demands the maximal use, not the negation, of all of man's faculties. The verse at the end of this edition of Maimonides' *Guide* summarizes much:

> To each who calls Him God is near indeed
> If he but call in truth nor turn away.
> By each who seeks Him He is found with ease,
> If straight to Him he strives and does not stray.

13. Honen

The *yin-yang* pattern, that where there is one great soul there will be his complement, applies in the case of Honen (1133-1212) also, for just as we have St. Francis and St. Dominic in Western Europe, al-Ghazāli and Ibn Rushd in Islam, Chu Hsi and Lu Hsiang-shan in China, so with Honen in Japan we have Eisai. Honen is perhaps really more comparable to St. Francis or St. Dominic than to the "philosophers" in the technical sense. Though we cannot here deal with his miracles and the hagiographical stories of his life, these might best express the unanalyzable factor in Honen's charisma.

Honen was born in 1133, in a province far from Miyako, as the only son of a local chief. When he was eight years old a sad fate befell his family. Bandits raided his home and the father died from a wound inflicted by them. The dying father asked, as his last request, that the son should never think of revenge, as was usual at that time among warriors, but should endeavour to become a virtuous monk....

After five years Honen was sent to Mount Hiei to be trained for an ecclesiastical career. An obedient novice and thereafter a studious monk, he passed nearly thirty years on Hiei and went through all the branches of learning and disciplinary training taught and practised there. He became renowned for his learning and virtue, and could have aimed at a high position in the hierarchic organization, but his soul sought after something more than erudition or fame. He had studied, meditated, and prayed in search of repose of the soul, until he was finally converted to a whole-hearted belief in Amita's grace. He had tasted, as he later stated, several rich and delicious foods, philosophical wisdom, moral discipline, mystic ceremonies; but his soul hungered until he found an everlasting satisfaction through the daily fare of rice which he secured in the all-saving grace of the Buddha Amita.[1]

Honen became the founder of the Jodo (Pure Land) school of Amida pietism. Along with the Shin school of Shinran and the Ji school of Ippen, the Jodo school teaches reliance on the grace of Buddha, not self-reliance or self-effort. "The Buddha of all other exoteric schools is Sakyamuni while the Buddha of these schools is Amita or Amitabha ('Infinite Light') or Amitayus ('Infinite Life') whose Land of Bliss (*Sukhāvatī*) is laid in the Western Quarter, often designated as the Pure Land (Jodo)."[2]

In the *Senjaku Hongan Nembutsushu*, by the very nature of its title, "Selection of the *Nembutsu* of the Original Vow", Honen set forth the *nembutsu* as the sole-practice for attaining the Pure Land. But in his personal life... he did engage in other practices, even Tantric rituals. He also allowed his disciples equal freedom to follow their own predilections. This tolerance plus the fact that Honen's principal disciples greatly varied in age, as well as theological training prior to and after their period of study with him, naturally led to divergent interpretations and ultimately even new religious movements.

While Honen was alive, disputes arose over issues such as 'the merits of faith versus practice' and 'one recitation of the nembutsu versus many.' These problems intensified after his death, and to make matters worse, nearly all of Honen's writings other than the *Senjakushu* were destroyed in the 1227 attack on his tomb....

...We can regard six principal disciples of Honen as influential in the transmission and development of the Jodo tradition, these consist of: Shōkōbō Benchō, Zennebō Shōkū, Ryūkan, Kakumyōbō Chōsai, Jōkakubō Kōsai, and Shinran.[3]

According to Anesaki, the last of Honen's teachings was "The Testament in One Piece of Paper", which Anesaki calls "the briefest confession of a pietist saint":

> Our practice of devotion does not consist in that of meditation as recommended and practised by sages of the past. Nor is our "Calling the Name" (*Nembutsu*) uttered in consequence of enlightenment in truths attained through learning and wisdom. When we invoke Buddha and say "Namu Amida Butsu," with the firm belief that we shall be born in Buddha's paradise, we shall surely be born there. There is no other mystery here than uttering His Name in this faith. Although the three kinds of thought and the four methods of training are recommended, all these are surely implicit in the faith that our birth in Buddha's Land is certain. If I knew anything more profound than this, I should be forsaken by the two Lords (the Buddhas Sākyamuni and Amita) and be cast outside the embracing vow (of Amita).
>
> However extensively one may have comprehended the teachings propounded during the lifetime of Sākya-muni, he should as soon as he has put faith in salvation, regard himself as an equal of the most ignorant, and thus should whole-heartedly practise *Nembutsu* in company with any simple folk, entirely giving up the demeanour of a wise man.[4]

Anesaki explains the "three kinds of thought" as "sincere thought, that there is nothing more important than birth in Buddha's land; the profound thought and belief, that all-embracing is the vow taken by Buddha to save all, even the sinful and depraved; the earnest desire to dedicate everything to the cause of faith." And the "four methods": "expression of reverence towards Buddha; exclusive faith in Him; uninterrupted repetition of his name; untiring devotion to Buddha throughout life."[5]

The constant repetition of the Holy Name was the heart of Honen's practice and teaching. Unfortunately this has become unpopular even among some monastic communities. It is strange indeed that the Protestant and secular orientations alone have neglected the rosary. If there is any one thing, elementary though it be, that symbolizes the basic difference between medieval and modern, perhaps it is the rosary. One might marvel: what a mechanical way to pray! What a ruse to avoid thinking ! But this is not true. The rosary is a practical device for keeping recollection, for "not departing from the Unity". The greatest of India's philosophers as well as Aquinas and many others of Europe's greatest minds are very often depicted in the popular iconography with the rosary as part of their expression. (The spread of the rosary, like that of the halo, throughout Eurasia, in Hinduism, Buddhism, Islam and Christianity, suggests, though it does not prove, that communications were much more open than has been supposed by philosophers heretofore).

Honen's learning was so wide that instead of going to the people the people came to him, evidently people of all ranks, breaking through the crust of Samurai artificiality. It was said of him, "What a pity such a man should be leading such a retired life!" What we find with Honen is a *bhakti* type of *marga* at least as intensive as that of the Rāmānuja school, and if not so systematically leading to ecstatic contemplation as what we find in Hugo of St. Victor, at least as intensive in zeal towards attainment of a transmundane Goal. Indeed, it was perhaps an overemphasis, which left itself open to a Shintō counter-reformation, which in turn led to the actual militarization of the monasteries under Kiyomori, an event scarcely paralleled anywhere else in the history of celibate communities in any culture.

Honen believed that it was very difficult to achieve Buddhist enlightenment through disciplined meditation in his age "because we are so far removed from the Great and Holy One (Shaka) and secondly because its doctrines are too hard for our little intellects".

> This age belongs to the latter days of the Law, and it is full of the five corruptions. It is through the one gate of the Jōdo alone that man can pass to salvation. For this reason it is said (by the Buddha) in the Larger Sukhāvatīvyūha Sūtra, "If there be one sentient being who has committed sin all through his life and who, when he comes to the end of his life, repeats my name over ten times in succession, without being born into the Pure Land, may I never obtain perfect knowledge."[6]

Thus, since it is so difficult to become a saint who has really achieved the levels of consciousness claimed in the texts, it is better to follow the path of surrender to Amida, relying solely on Amida's Vow. Has Honen over-simplified the path, or has he validly opened an existential simplification? In the following, Honen sees the *nembutsu* not only as a simplification but as a definitely superior way:

> It is hard to understand and interpret the holy mind of the Buddha, but I shall try to explain it under two aspects, first, from the standpoint of superiority and inferiority, and secondly, from that of ease and difficulty. In regard to the first, the *Nembutsu* is superior and all other practices are inferior, because all virtues are wrapt up in the one sacred name. These are the four wisdoms, the three bodies, the ten faculties, external signs, light rays, the sermons, the benefitting of others—indeed all outward activities. These, I say, are inherent in the sacred name of the Buddha. For these reasons do we regard the *Nembutsu* as having merits surpassing all others. Not so is it with the other practices, which are all limited to some one aspect. The sacred name is like a house which comprises within it all its constituents—the beams, rafters, pillars, veranda, and everything else used in the building.... We may learn from this the lesson that the

> merit of calling upon the sacred name surpasses that of all other practices....[7]

Partially reminiscent of the revived controversy in the Neo-Confucianists concerning the goodness or badness of human nature, but perhaps closer to the counsel we find in St. Bonaventura if not already in Hugo of St. Victor (quite in contrast with Guido the Carthusian and Pope Gregory), Honen counsels us *not* to dwell on sins unduly (or even at all!) but on God's mercies and His will that *all* should achieve salvation.

> Do not be troubled about whether your heart is good or bad, or your sin light or grievous. Only determine in your heart that you will be born in the Pure Land, and so repeat the *Namu Amida Butsu*, and let the conviction accompany the sound of your voice, that you will of a certainty be born into the Pure Land. Then, according to your determined faith, that *Karṃa* will certainly be produced which will result in your birth in that land. ...It all depends on your own mental, act, which makes everything easy. If in your mind you waver, you will end in wavering. But if you make up your mind to it, that settles your destiny to be born into the Pure Land.[8]

Although the capabilities of different classes and the levels of attainment of different saints may vary considerably, the attainment of the Pure Land as a common goal lends a remarkably democratic touch to Honen's teaching. Like Rāmānuja before, he seems to have been very lenient towards women and 'outcastes' in regard to eligibility for the higher spiritual attainments. He even claims that the most unlettered may receive the same degree of salvation as the most learned if only he/she adopts the simple practice of constant repetition of the Holy Name, provided, of course, that one practices with sincerity and purity of heart. The cult of the Sacred Heart of Jesus had not yet historically gained the popularity in Christianity that it enjoys today, although it was not unknown; and we can see in al-Ghazālī and Ibn Gabirol an emphasis on purification of the heart, and we may well remember the traditional Confucian emphasis on sincerity. So it is not surprising to find Honen, as a *bhakta par excellence*, stressing this considerably.

Three of Honen's disciples once asked him, "Can the likes of us who cannot strictly keep the ten cardinal commandments, but who are always giving way to our illusive thoughts, and lack in moral courage and diligence, can we, in spite of the evil in us, if we but look to Amida's Original Vow and think that we shall be sure of attaining Ōjō, thereby actually attain it?" Honen replied, "Of course you can. The common man does not know to what extent all his evil passions and sins hinder him from attaining Ōjō. But if one repeats the Nembutsu in harmony with the Original Vow, there is no sin great enough to nullify it or to hinder one from attaining it. It entirely depends on our faith, and not on whether we have sin or not, for all common mortals may attain it. What has the presence or absence of illusory thoughts to do with it?"

Although he later de-emphasized this in favor of the *nembutsu* only, Honen's meditation on the glories of the Pure Land is amazingly like the Vaikuṇṭha meditation of the Śrī-Vaiṣṇavas, even more so than like the depictions of Heaven in the Latin West. In India the descriptions of Vaikuṇṭha, the Vaiṣṇava Heaven, had become such a popular theme of poets and artists that even today at Tiruchinopoly one may see a little model of that 'place' in the massive temple. In Islam there is perhaps considerably more emphasis on fear of Judgment, but the dreams of Heaven, especially (oddly enough) in the Cult of the Assassins, take a very prominent place indeed. The intensive aesthetic aspect of Japanese tradition may be a forming factor in Honen's adaptation of Buddhist teaching. Without acceding overmuch to Northrop's famous phrase "the undifferentiated aesthetic continuum", we may acknowledge that there is something here which Northrop was trying to indicate, something that is beyond the realm of ordinary description. Resort to metaphor is often not considered good philosophy, but there do remain regions of the mind and of human experience which stubbornly defy "philosophical" treatment and yet yield as gracefully as the bamboo in an evening breeze to the artistically chosen phrase (the *meaning* is not in the bomboo but in the wind!). This aestheticism, however, does not allow any softness in other matters. The Shintō spirit of hard, even militaristic discipline tempered Japanese Buddhism at least as much as Confucianism had altered it in China. Any vow, once taken, must be kept at any cost. This was promulgated by Amida's own example, whose Vow for the liberation of all sentient beings must remain unquestioned.

After meditating with images, after the phantasia has been purged of these, there should be clear (if not clairvoyant) perception of everything from one's own motives for any decision to the nature of the transitions from gross to subtle to absolute and beyond. In this, in short, or is it not, a retreat from logic in an attempt to circumvent logic altogether? That is not easy to answer from the outside, for the training of the very person himself and not merely his faculties is at stake. This is perhaps what the Aristotelians were grappling with in dealing with the active intellect and speculative intellect; but over and over again it seems that they stop short of the Goal (even though they do not stumble as far as they do go), not willing to abandon the subject object relation, the transivity between the active and the potential, and the insistence that the quiddity of anything whatsoever must be the quiddity of *something*, be it word or work or wave-length of some hypothetical *X*. And it would seem that the Mādhyamika attempt to meditate on 'emptiness' has resulted in simply a parallel set of images which is just as inadequate as the conundrums of logical operations. So, even if the intellectual component is not so strong in Honen, perhaps this is counterbalanced by the ethical, the devotional, and the aesthetic.

In their study *Honen the Buddhist Saint*, Coates and Ishizuka include an appendix with the title "Things That Honen Was Always Saying" from which we have taken the following few selections:

> If you think there is uncertainty as to the efficacy of calling upon the sacred name once, then it means that there is doubt about it every time you call upon the sacred name. The Buddha's Vow was to give birth into the Pure Land to those who would call upon his name even once, and so there is efficacy in every repetition of the sacred name.
>
> Even though you may be doing something else, let that be done while you go on with the main work of life, which

consists in the practice of *Nembutsu*, and do not let it be a sort of side work to anything else.

The countenance of a man who longs for Paradise, and fixes his whole mind upon the one object of teaching it, will always appear as if he had a hatred and abhorrence of the world.

I am a man who wears no official head-dress. I am nothing but the foolish Honen, weighed down by the ten evils, and I say that the only way for me to attain Ojō is by calling upon the sacred name.

If one becomes a learned man, there is danger of losing the disposition to practice the *Nembutsu*.

A man who cannot make up his mind, but is always thinking himself unfit in this way or that, will not be sure of attaining birth into Pure Land.

When a deer is being pursued by the hunters, it does not stop even to look around for its fellows or look back at its pursuers, but with all eagerness hastens straight forward, and no matter how many may be following it escapes in safety. It is with the same determination that a man fully entrusts himself to the Buddha's power, and without regard to anything else steadfastly sets his mind upon being born into the Pure Land.

Where one is to receive something from another, which is better, to have already received, or not to have received? I, Genku, repeat the *Nembutsu* as if I have already received.

Birth into the Pure Land is certain, when you think it so, but also uncertain when you think it so.

A man who plans to jump over a moat ten feet wide must make every effort to jump fifteen feet. And a man who would be born into the Pure Land must concentrate his energy upon believing that he will of a certainty be so born.

In life I pile up merit by the practice of the *Nembutsu*, and at death I go to the Pure Land. Whatever befalls, I have made up my mind not to be anxious about myself, and so come life, come death, nothing troubles me.

When someone once said to Honen that his repetition of the *Nembutsu* must be very acceptable to the Buddha, he asked "Why?" "Because you are a wise man, and know in depth

> what merit there is in the repetition of the sacred name, clearly understanding the meaning of the Buddha's Original Vow." At this Honen replied, "You have not yet really come to believe in the Original Vow at all. As to calling upon the sacred name of the Original Vow of the Buddha Amida, it makes no difference whether the man be a woodcutter, a gatherer of grass or greens, or a drawer of water or the like, whether he be utterly unlettered in Buddhism or other religions, it makes no difference, I say, so long as he calls upon the sacred name."
>
> After Honen's death, Jushimbo, a priest of the Mii Temple, dreamt that he asked Honen about the way of the *Nembutsu*, when Honen replied, "There is nothing special to be said about it at all except that it be repeated."

Certainly this is not philosophical if we limit philosophy to logic, epistemology, formal ethics, definitional aesthetics, and ontology. But whether it could be called anti-philosophical or not is another matter. It is rather simply piety trying to take the place of systematic considerations, as is almost always the case when a cult is of such a character that it can have common appeal to all and sundry.

Mediaeval man throughout Eurasia and also in Japan was a *homo viator*, a pilgrim on a path, a follower of a Way. It might be said that Honen was simply a simple saint; but he knew the schools, understood the arguments and the differences between the different interpretations of the Buddhist classics (many of which contain some very rigorous logic and dialectics), and he found them all unsatisfactory. Thus out of 'knowledge' Honen chose the Pure Land sect whose *bhakti* to Amida was the key to everything, in spite of the fact that the Buddha himself had inculcated not so much devotional fervor as rational conduct and motivation by the great virtue of compassion.

14. Eisai

Rinzai Zen has become popular virtually the whole world over, and the cultic perspective has engulfed Eisai in a legendary halo almost as much as the mythologized Bodhidharma so that it is difficult to find what can be called thinking rather than some uncanny relation with 'reality'. Eisai (1141-1215) was the founder of the Rinzai School of Zen as Dōgen was the founder of the Sōtō, which together constitute the two most important branches of Japanese Zen. Eisai started his religious life on Mt. Hiei where he studied esoteric Buddhism, but he soon decided to deepen his understanding by visiting China and even eventually India, the birthplace of Buddhism. Though the Chinese authorities never permitted his departure from their coasts for India, he did complete two trips to China at a time when communication with the mainland was considered all but impossible. Zen was the only form of Buddhism which Eisai found still flourishing in China. He returned to Japan as a fully approved master carrying the *inka*, a seal which formally permitted him to teach Zen of the Rinzai variety. But he also carried with him something which has caused him to be even more generally appreciated by posterity: tea. This he introduced to Japan to help keep his fellow monks awake and healthy, and in 1211 he wrote a two-volume work called *Kissa Yojoki* (*Drinking Tea for Health*) in which he gave an esoteric interpretation of the organs of the human body.

In Kyoto, Eisai urged the adoption of both Zen and tea but soon met opposition from the already established religious groups So he moved to Kamakura where he met with greater acceptance. When Eisai returned to Kyoto he encountered opposition again, and he is said to have compromised Zen in order to make it acceptable. But the spirit of Zen, like the Taoism which influenced its development in China, is a flowing, flexible spirit, so perhaps Eisai's "compromise" was really a manifestation of its natural functioning. However that may be, the Matsunagas write: "Although Eisai is considered to be the founder of Japanese Zen and legitimate transmitter of the Rinzai school, his teachings are generally regarded as impure Zen", due not only to his own interests but the necessity during his age of presenting Zen in a mixed form involving Tendai (which itself was a Chinese and Japanese effort to accommodate all points of view), esoteric matters, Zen meditation and Buddhist rules of learning. "The question is", the Matsunagas continue, "with his own personal background and inclinations whether Eisai would have introduced pure Zen practice if the nation had been prepared to receive it?"[1] The answer to this question is somewhat unclear, though one sees evidence that Eisai would have been eclectic and esoteric under the best circumstances. However, in detailing Eisai's introduction of Zen to Kyoto in 1202, the Matsunagas say that he was "forced" to teach the mixed tradition rather than the pure single-practice he had studied in China. If Eisai had to cloud the purity of his teaching to suit otherwise hostile audiences, then his true beliefs may ironically be seen more clearly in Dōgen than in his own writings. Saunders writes: "If compromise characterizes Eisai's Zen, that of Dōgen...is typified by its intransigent and uncompromising attitude toward all that is not Zen."[2] But if Zen is judged too severely on the basis of "purity" it may become a distortion rather than representation of the Buddha (or the *satori*) it would serve; and yet if any form of Zen is too isolated from other forms of Buddhism there is a fair question whether it is any longer Zen, pure or otherwise. Significantly, Dōgen was briefly associated as a disciple with Eisai when the latter was over seventy and Dōgen was about fourteen, and Dōgen admired Eisai even after developing his own way of interpreting Zen.

The followers of Eisai used the *kōan* as an aid in meditation whereas the followers of Dōgen did not, regarding *zazen* (seated meditation) as more or less an end in itself, the incarnation, so to speak, of enlightenment. The most distinctive feature of Rinzai as opposed to Sōtō is this use of the *kōan*, and the nature and function of the *kōan* provides us with the vital and dynamic substance of Rinzai. The Matsunagas write:

> The *kōan* checks the intellect by its logical absurdity. It is impossible to solve the problem presented by reason, i.e., Koa-fen Yuan-miao's famous: "All things return to the One, where does the One return?" and Chao-chou's reply: "When I was in the district of Ch'ing, I had a robe that weighed

> seven *chin*," is nonsensical, yet it is capable of producing an inner realization that years of study and reflection might easily fail to achieve...
>
> Thus the *kōan*, in an attempt to impede the growth of intellectualism and at the same time prevent the individual from being submerged in quietism, functioned in a two fold manner: 1) ideally to check the intellect either by allowing it to realize its bounds or ideally to shipwreck it, and 2) to affect the maturity of the Zen consciousness.

That Zen consciousness is indescribable but at least can be hinted at by words such as these from the Matsunagas:

> With the mind engaged upon a seeming object (the *kōan*), self-reflection can be internalized until the self virtually disappears—the mind and body obliterated in existence—and when the object is experienced in fact as one's own fundamental nature, the individual is engulfed in the flood of liberation, while at the same time made aware of his unity with existence—almost as though plunging into the waters of a southern ocean and feeling its all embracing boundless warmth.

The spontaneity and liberation implied in the above and in the admonition to "destroy the Buddha" by Lin-chi (d. 867, from whose name Rinzai is derived) were not intended for beginners but for experienced monks who had mastered the techniques but were becoming dull or complacent. Liberation presupposes arduous discipline, which does not *earn* enlightenment but somehow opens one to it. Instead of validating objective knowledge or a logical solution to a *kōan*, the master validates the new consciousness manifested by the disciple's answer to his assigned *kōan*—or his style of answering it.

For readers of English it is easier to have a clear idea of the teaching of the Rinzai school of Zen than of the thought of its founder. Of coure this clear idea represents a bit of averaging and generalizing from the complex and varied forms of Chinese Zen (Ch'an) before Eisai's time as well as the plethora of varieties and sub-varieties of Zen after Eisai. D.T. Suzuki gives us some hints about Zen which are not to be read directly into Eisai but neither are they to be entirely disregarded in interpreting his thought. Rather they apply to the Zen which developed after the time of Eisai, sometimes with his more or less direct influence and sometimes without. According to Suzuki, attunement to life is attained by means of a state of mind known in Japanese as *mushin* (*wuhsin* in Chinese). *Mushin* means "no-mind", "going beyond the dualism of all forms of life and death, good and evil, being and non-being. This is where all art merges into Zen." *Mushin*, Suzuki writes, "may be regarded in a way as corresponding to the concept of the unconscious."[3]

The immovable state of Zen consciousness is extremely fluid. This "absolute fluidity of the mind (*kokoro*)," as Suzuki terms it, seems self-contradictory but is really the touchstone of life which cannot be captured by logical words or phrases. From one point of view the concept of "immovable fluidity" is quite consistent with an important development in modern logic, the discovery or rediscovery of the "universe of discourse". In a typical Venn diagram a circle is inscribed in a rectangle. When speaking in a commonsense way we see a given thing as either in the circle or out of it. The function of Zen and the rectangle is to keep us aware that there may be significant realities that are outside the range of such judgments entirely, that is, outside our immediately surrounding "rectangle" of discourse. *Satori* may be seen as the state of consciousness associated with the removal of all rectangles rather than any kind of objective inventory of exactly what is in or outside our circles or rectangles of human discourse.

The way to remove the restrictions of ordinary discourse, the way to achieve immovable fluidity, is known as *kufū*. Suzuki writes:

> The *kufū* is altogether personal and individualistic, it is to develop out of oneself, within one's own inner life. *Kufū* literally means "to strive", "to wrestle", "to try to find the way out", or, in Christian terms, "to pray incessantly for God's help". Psychologically speaking, it is to remove all the inhibitions there are, intellectual as well as affective or emotional, and to bring out what is stored in the unconscious

> and let it work itself out quite independently of any kind of interfering consciousness.

In explaining the concept of "the mind of no-mind" (*mushin no shin*), Suzuki says, "A mind unconscious of itself is a mind that is not at all disturbed by affects of any kind. It is the original mind and not the delusive one that is chockful of affects. It is always flowing, it never halts, nor does it turn into a solid."

Eisai's major work, *Kōzen Gokokuron* (*Treatise on the Propagation of Zen for the Protection of the Nation*), was written to answer criticisms and misunderstandings of Zen. As one might infer from the title Eisai was particularly concerned to refute the notion that Zen would somehow be bad for Japan. With his book Eisai hoped to gain political acceptance for Zen and to show its relevance to the degenerate times in which he lived, known in Japanese Buddhism as *mappō*. Here we present our own translation of the first part of the introduction to that work (translated by Hideo Murakami):

> Introduction to the Argument that to Promote Zen Is to Protect the Nation, by Eisai, the *ācārya* (one who knows and teaches the rules) who has returned to Japan after studying on Mt. T'ien T'ai in the Country of the Great Sung; who holds the priestly rank of the Great Dharma Teacher for the Propagation of the Light, and who outlines the following:
>
> How encompassingly great is the mind and heart of man! It is not possible to measure the heights of heaven, but the mind and heart of man transcend those heights. The depths of the earth are impossible to fathom, but the mind and heart of man reach deeper than the bottom of such depths. The light of the sun and moon cannot be excelled; and yet the mind and heart of man excel the light of sun and moon.
>
> The Universe contemplated by Buddhism is immeasurably vast, but the mind and heart of man are larger yet than this macrocosm. Mind and heart envelop the Great Space and are pregnant with Primal Energy.
>
> Heaven and earth are at the behest of the mind and heart of man; heaven encompassing the myriad things above, and earth supporting the myriad things below. The sun and moon

move by means of me who have this mind and heart; the four seasons of Spring, Summer, Autumn and Winter change through me; the myriad things are generated through me.

There is nothing that is not founded through the operation of mind and heart. We cannot help but extol how great is this mind and heart of man! It is impossible to put a name on such a giant of a thing, but if we have to, we can call it *Kokoro*. The teaching that expresses this *Kokoro* is called the most superior and incomparably great teaching; it is also called the teaching that clarifies the First Principle. It is called True Characteristic of *Prajñā* (Wisdom) and again the Primal Truth *Dharmadhātu*; again, it is the Highest *Bodhi*; again, the Way to Enlightenment as seen in the teaching of *Śūramgama-Samādhi*; again, the teaching of the Wonderful Mind and Heart of Non-arising Non-annihilation. Accordingly, the Buddha's lifetime teaching is explained through the three types of Dharma Wheel and the Eight Treasuries of Scriptures, as well as the Four Schools and Four Denominations of Zen, or explained through the Five Yanas (vehicles), but all these Teachings boil down to the Teaching of the *Kokoro*.

The powers attributed to *kokoro* almost remind us of God in Jewish and Christian scriptures and thought. See, for example, the 139th Psalms:

> Whither shall I go from thy Spirit?
> Or whither shall I go from thy presence?
> If I ascend to heaven, thou art there!
> If I make my bed in Sheol, thou art there!

But *kokoro* is *ningen no mono* (human). It is not God but egoless human consciousness which can be achieved by arduous human discipline. As Eisai himself explains a little later in his introduction, the Zen vision of the Law or *Dharma* outwardly "favors discipline over doctrine" and inwardly brings the Highest Inner Wisdom." Instead of attributing magical or supernatural powers to enlightened *kokoro*, Eisai's praise was no doubt a signifying of the tearing away of mind's small egoistic boxes, those restrictive universes of discourse. Eisai seems to imply to his disciples that if they cultivate right *kokoro* they can be in charge of everything since *kokoro* encompasses the universe. But would the Buddha have encouraged control of anything except selfish desire, and is there anything to be controlled in a sea of impermanence (no substance), or anyone to do the controlling (no soul)?

Dharmakāya is the Mahāyāna Buddhist term for the transcendental Buddha in the Buddhist *Trikāya* or Trinity. Robert Aitken writes: "Mind as used by Eisai is the *Dharmakāya*. It is completely empty, yet charged with potential. It has many names as Eisai says. Another name is Buddha nature....The denominator of the universe is empty infinity—infinite emptiness—which is full of possibilities. It is called the unborn, because it is not born and also does not die." And this empty yet infinitely charged potential seems to be exactly what Suzuki called *mushin*, no-mind or "mind of no-mind". Aitken concludes suggestively: "For the last sixty years or so, physicists have been uncovering the fact of mind. For example, back in 1920 or so, Arthur Eddington said, 'The universe is mind stuff.' Nowadays people like David Bohm are conjecturing that not only is the universe mind, but each element of the universe, even a blade of grass, contains within it all that intelligence."[4]

Some of Eisai's quality of life and thought is certainly to be found in Dōgen, who frequently eulogized the purity and simplicity of Eisai's life style. The kind of thinker and teacher Eisai was is perhaps captured in the following story which Dōgen is telling to his disciples:

> When the late Abbot (Eisai) was still at Kenniniji monastery, a poor man once came and said, "My family is so destitute that they have had nothing to cook for several days. Myself, my wife, and our three childern are on the verge of starvation. For pity's sake, please help us!" At the time there was in the Abbot's quarters nothing whatever—no food, no clothing, no money—for him to give away, and he was almost at the end of his wits. There was, however, some beaten copper which was to be used in making a halo for the statue of the Lord of Healing. He took it and broke it up in his hands. Then, tying it in a little package, he gave the copper to the poor

man. "Exchange this for food and save your family from starvation." The man went away overjoyed.

But some of the Abbot's disciples criticized his action, saying, "This was no less than the halo of the Buddha statue. Giving it to a layman constitutes the crime of using what belongs to the Buddha for one's own private purposes. Isn't that wrong?"

"You are right," the Abbot replied, "but just consider the will of Buddha. He sacrificed his very flesh and limbs for the sake of all mankind. If some men are about to die of starvation, would he not want us to give the whole Buddha figure to save them? Even if I should go to Hell for this crime, I would want to save people from starvation." Such loftiness of purpose is well worth reflecting upon. You students should keep this in mind.[5]

For too many, Eisai has become a mere bookmark in the history of Zen. Most historians deal with the life and times of Eisai without saying much about his thought, perhaps because his thought can never be exactly recovered and the 'pure' thinker may be mostly lost to us. While more and more of Dōgen's work has been appearing in English in recent years, only small portions of Eisai's major work have as yet been translated even though Eisai is certainly worthy of more general intellectual attention.

For conclusion, the Matsunagas write: "To attempt to view the development of Zen historically is a near hopeless task, for in the Buddhist tradition Zen followers tend to deny the validity of chronological history, but more than any other sect they treat historical facts with a certain vengeance". It is almost as though the Zen scrambling of history were a perverse *kōan* designed specifically to awaken the would-be historian to an ahistorical level of consciousness.

15. Śrīharṣa

Śrīharṣa (c. 1225) is among the post-Śaṅkara Advaitins most ardently studied in the old unwesternized tradition. Certainly there is scarcely any representative of that tradition who deserves more attention, though until recently very few materials were available even about him much less translations of his famous classic, the *Khaṇḍanakhaṇḍakhādya*. And it is only very recently that his effort at poetics and dramatics has become available in translation, namely the *Naiṣadhacarita*. Śrīharṣa and Citsukha, who are virtually inseparable in the old tradition, are the standard filters through which virtually all students of Advaita in the unwesternized tradition learn the standard interpretation—perhaps too much divorced from historical considerations. But then with Śrīharṣa and Citsukha the brilliance of their dialectical skill demands so much that historical perspectives are often forgotten, even when the intention is to keep them well in mind. Citsukha is Śrīharṣa's chief interpreter while Śrīharṣa follows in the heritage primarily of Vācaspati Miśra. What provoked Śrīharsa's further "patchwork" dialectics—as *historically* it can be regarded, and in admiration that he could do such a truly brilliant job of it—was that Bhāskara, Rāmānuja and several others had done some rather devastating criticism of Śaṅkara, and Vācaspati also had been exhaustively refuted and criticized.

With the "exfoliation and elaboration" following the original ninth century "monism in many moods", even those claiming to be monistic at heart had been becoming much more complex in their manifold dialectical defense of metaphysical unity. This trend may be said to have affected not only Śrīharṣa but even Dōgen, Ibn 'Arabī, Suhrawardī, the Victorines and the School of Chartres. It was really not until Śriharṣa that Advaitic dialectic finally took on its full systematic shape after several centuries of ironing out the inconsistencies left behind by Śaṅkara due in part to his early death. Śrīharṣa was especially anxious to defend Advaita against the "technical intricacies" of such writers as Udayana of the Nyāya school. And he shares with Gangeśa the genius for exhaustive analysis of details, leaving no possibility, or impossibility, unexplored. Those who are not Advaitins will not necessarily agree that Śrīharṣa "destroyed the imposing edifice of the Nyāya-Vaiṣeśika system"; nor will they be satisfied with his method of letting opposing systems cancel each other out without supplying some positive alternative, for it still may not necessarily be true that mere cancellation of falsehood will allow Truth to shine forth. One can see how Śrīharṣa's heritage was most likely rigorous Śaiva rather than Vaiṣṇava, Śiva being the Great Destroyer delivering us from false enfatuations, while the Vaiṣṇava theist focuses on all the marvellous attributes of the Deity as existentially operative in the world and not only as a matter of abstraction.

The *Khaṇḍanakhaṇḍakhādya* is specifically directed against the Nyāya system, which holds that the categories of experience are real and definable. Śrīharṣa, on the other hand, holds that only the non-dual Brahman is real while the world and world-experience are phenomenal only, unreal, and indefinable. The concept of indefinability (*anirvacanīya*) is at the centre of Śrī-harṣa's refutations, for his technique is to take the Nyāya definitions and show that they are untenable. Though Śrīharṣa is concerned with the Nyāya, his refutations could equally apply to any other system which offers definitions of categories of reality, for Śrīharṣa wants to refute *all definitions*, reality being indefinable from the Advaita point of view. Theoretically he is not holding any position of his own, his criticisms being, like Nāgārjuna's, of a destructive nature, after which, the obstacles being removed, the light of truth is supposed to shine through. Dasgupta writes:

> This indefinableness is in the nature of all things in the world and all experiences...and no amount of ingenuity or scholarship can succeed in defining the nature of that which has no definable nature or existence. Śrīharṣa undertakes to show that all definitions of things or categories put forward by the Nyāya writers are absolutely hollow and faulty even according to the canons of logical discussions and definitions accepted by the Naiyāyika; and, if no definition can stand or be supported, it necessarily follows that there can be no definitions, or, in other words, that no definitions of the phenomenal world are possible and that the world of phenomena and all our so-called experiences of it are indefinable....It is useless for

> any one to attempt to find out what is true by resorting to arguments; for the arguments can be proved to be false even by the canons on which they are based. If anyone, however, says that the arguments of Śrīharṣa are open to the same objection and are not true, then that would only establish his own contention. For Śrīharṣa does not believe in the reality of his arguments and enters into them without any assumption of their reality or unreality.[1]

As for the possible demand that Śrīharṣa should prove the idea of the ultimate oneness of Brahman, he says that such a demand would show that the idea already exists, else such a demand could not be made. Furthermore, the Upaniṣadic texts present that reality.

Thus in typical Advaitic style Śrīharṣa refutes false positions but offers no position of his own which could be refuted in turn. Here is how Dasgupta summarizes one of Śrīharṣa's refutations:

> Turning now to Śrīharṣa's refutation of the Nyāya categories, we note that he begins with the refutation of "being" or positivity (*bhāvatva*). He says that being cannot be defined as being existent in itself, since non-being is also existent in itself; we can with as much right speak of being as existing as of non-being as existing; both non-being and being may stand as grammatical nominatives of the verb "exists." Again, each existing thing being unique in itself, there is no common quality, such as "existence" or "being," which is possessed by them all. Again, "being" is as much a negation of "non-being" as "non-being" of "being"; hence "being cannot be defined as that which is not a negation of anything. Negation is a mere form of speech, and both being and non-being may be expressed in a negative form.
>
> Turning to the category of non-being (*abhāva*), Śrīharṣa says that it cannot be defined as negation of anything; for being may as well be interpreted as a negation of non-being as non-being of being....Nor again can non-being be defined as that which opposes being; for not all non-being is opposed to all being (e.g. in "there is no jug on the ground" the

> absence of jug does not oppose the ground in respect of which the jug is denied): if non-being opposes some existent things, then that does not differentiate negation; for there are many existent things which are opposed to one another (e.g. the horse and the bull).[2]

Dasgupta remarks that Śrīharṣa's technique often leads him to "verbal sophisms", and often he does not do justice to the general philosophical ideas which the system is attempting to present, howbeit via definitions. Furthermore, the refutation of existing definitions does not necessarily mean that better definitions could not be found, nor did he prove that the concepts were inherently so self-contradictory that never could a valid definition be found; rather, he attempted to refute the actual existing definitions which had been put forth by the Nyāya and sometimes by Prabhākara. To refute a definition of a thing does not necessarily prove the thing to be false; to refute a particular presentation of a concept does not necessarily prove the concept itself to be false.[3] As for the effect of Śrīharṣa's criticism on Nyāya, Dasgupta writes:

> In one sense the criticisms of Śrīharṣa and some of his followers had done a great disservice to the development of later Nyāya thought; for, unlike the older Nyāya thinkers, later Nyāya writers, like Gaṅgeśa, Raghunātha and others, were mainly occupied in inventing suitable qualificatory adjuncts and phrases by which they could define their categories in such a way that the undesirable applications and issues of their definitions, as pointed out by the criticisms of their opponents, could be avoided. If these criticisms had mainly been directed towards the defects of Nyāya thought, later writers would not have been forced to take the course of developing verbal expressions at the expense of philosophical profundity and acuteness. Śrīharṣa may therefore be said to be the first great writer who is responsible indirectly for the growth of verbalism in later Nyāya thought.[4]

Another major objection that has been given ever since Śaṅkara himself is that Advaita is really a sort of Śūnyavāda Buddhism in disguise, or rather some undefined and by its own profession undefinable merging of Vijñānavāda and Śūnyavāda. One wonders specifically whether Śrīharṣa had not been influenced by the split between the Prasangika and the Svatantra branches of the Śūnyavāda. As for his citing the *śruti* (scripture) as the final authority, his opponents (Madhva vividly, for example) can easily cite other *śruti* to refute his eclectic use of them.

With Śrīharṣa *method* seems to have assumed a new and important if not strategic position and role in the history of Indian philosophy. The *Khaṇḍanakhaṇḍakhādya* might be said to be basically a phenomenology of technique of refutation. Few have dared to carry the matter back into itself as far as Śrīharṣa, questioning dialectical method along with every other method of arriving at some glimpse of valid irrefutable truth. He carries the Advaitic aspect of *counter*-assertions as far, perhaps, as it possibly could be done by any merely human mind, the assumption being evidently that complete scepticism is the prelude to enlightenment. Of course total scepticism does not necessarily lead to mysticism, but the trained mystic may use it as a device for unhooking the neophyte. This sort of reductionism may be used in order to deliver the *upāsaka* from false confidence in inadequate 'gods' or theories—as was the habit, for example, of Aurobindo and Nishida Kitaro, whether or not this may be said of Wittgenstein. But again we may not *assert* anything. Advaita (theoretically never asserts anything; it only carries 'Socratic' method as far as humanly possible, and that is its glory and its provocativeness ever and always. As with Kant many centuries later in a different culture, only after reason has exhausted itself can faith validly take over. Of course all of this is nothing more, or less, than an elaborate extension of the *via negativa*.

Śrīharṣa's literary masterpiece, the *Naiṣadhacarita*, is a sort of "other side of the coin" work to balance off the extremes of the *Khaṇḍanakhaṇḍakhādya*. These two masterpieces are of rather equal importance. Indeed, the literary works of Śaṅkara himself show that after all he was also somewhat of a *bhakta* (in spite of himself, one might say). In Islam the Ṣūfīs seldom tried to philosophize in systematic form but wrote beautiful poetry for the most part instead, and it is well known that Thomas Aquinas' hymns show a different side to his character, as was true also of the great Chu Hsi, whose poetry has only belatedly begun to receive the attention it deserves—and so on all across Eurasia, raising the question of an intrinsic defect of philosophizing only as *jñānīs* and leaving the *bhakti*-poetic forms outside. Admittedly the ideal is seldom realized, namely balance and harmony in completeness between *bhakti* (aesthetic), *karma* (ethics), and *jñāna* (epistemology).

16. Ibn 'Arabī

Compared to the simplicity of the monistic and/or pantheistic tendencies of the ninth century, as for example with al-Ḥallāj, Ibn 'Arabī's monism is much more systematic and developed; thus he fits into our basic overview theme of "elaboration and diversification". A strong charge of heterodoxy by opponents and apologists has been associated with Ibn 'Arabī. The controversy ranges around the various interpretations that can be made—largely perhaps according to the interpreter's degree of spiritual advancement rather than to Ibn 'Arabī's own philosophy—concerning his teachings about the inadequacy of unaided human reason to reach beyond itself into the realms of divine illumination and intuition. But Ibn 'Arabī's thought is not an amorphous romantic mysticism like that often associated with the more extreme forms of Ṣūfī mysticism, as well as with Rinzai Zen for the most part, but is philosophical mysticism in the fullest systematic sense of that term.

Ibn 'Arabī (1165-1240) was born in Spain at Mercia. At the age of eight he left his native place and went to Lisbon where he received his early Qur'anic education. Later on he shifted to Seville, which was then a Ṣūfī centre and where he stayed for thirty years. Ibn 'Arabī, who travelled throughout the Muslim world

> with a keenness for knowledge unsurpassed by that of many others and a strong determination to get at the naked truth, could have easily gathered a full idea of all the schools of

> Muslim and non-Muslim pantheism. He himself says that he travelled over all parts of the Muslim world in search of knowledge and met leaders of all shades of opinion. The Muslim world of Ibn 'Arabī's days stretched from China to Spain and Cape Comorin to Lake Aral and was the meeting-place of all the civilizations and religions. This immense amount of knowledge which Ibn 'Arabī was able to get was not an unmixed blessing. It bewildered him to some extent, rather distracted his energies and rendered his system less pointed than one would wish it to be.[1]

Ibn 'Arabī was in the fullest sense of the word a searcher and anything but a dogmatist, unlike many of his opponents after his death and even during his lifetime. We cannot trace all of his desperations in his search for an adequate teacher, but it is quite clear that that was the motive behind his wanderings which took him from Spain across the Maghrib to Baghdad, Egypt and of course to Meccah. His extended pilgrimage took him also to Anatolia, for which reason he remains even today very popular with the Turkish people as well as with Turkish scholars. It is not clear whether he had direct contact with Byzantine Neo-Platonists or even perhaps with some Hesychasts, but it is quite certain that he did learn Greek.

By Ibn 'Arabī's own time we have not only Marco Polo but Ibn Būṭṭūṭah and many other records besides Ibn 'Arabī's own wanderings from Spain to Baghdad, where Indian science and Indian philosophy, both Hindu and Buddhist, were pretty well known; and communications with China were sufficiently open that the Chinese had tried to make an alliance with the Muslim world against the Turkish and Mongol peoples in the in-between areas. Certainly interpretation of Ibn 'Arabi's philosophy outside of its historical milieu makes even less sense than similar efforts at interpreting Zen or Advaita as though they never occurred as a very real current in a very real world. Though they all portend to deal in eternal verities (and perhaps they do), it can still be demonstrated that the manner of dealing with these eternities does have a pattern of historical development as far as interpretation is concerned. These factors are, nevertheless, in the background and should not be taken as a substitute for heeding the actual philosophical thinking that Ibn 'Arabī challenges us to do alongside the necessary ascetic discipline in order to reach up into the more ultimate ranges of—no, not just Spirit in a merely religious sentimentality, but Being itself.

The label of "pantheism" is sometimes used as though it were a disease to be ashamed of, in spite of its universality in world history and its persistence against constant censure and opposition. One could present a long review of pantheism in the Greek, Jewish and Alexandrian heritages—which, although some do not like to admit it for some strange reason or other, is just plain Neo-Platonism—as well as Hindu and Buddhist pantheisms (which may also have some Neo-Platonist roots), the Avataṃsaka or (in Japan) Kegon variety of Mahāyāna being the most likely candidate in this respect by virtue of its All-in-One and One-in-All teachings—not to mention pantheism in Islam at large before Ibn 'Arabī's own pantheism.

Neo-Platonic pantheism had reached Arabia long before the Prophet Muḥammad's time, probably in both its 'pagan' and its Christian and Jewish forms (derived from Philo for the most part). The teachings and examples of al-Basṭāmī and Rābi'ah are important relatively early examples of Ṣūfī 'pantheism'; and of course we cannot forget al-Ḥallāj. Though a terribly; sensitive point, we might risk the statement that generally Shī'a Islam has been less intolerant of pantheism than Sunni orthodoxy among the Shī'as this is especially true of the Ismā'īlīs. By the beginning of the eleventh century pantheism in some form or other had really become quite common in the Islamic world, even though it was also not uncommon for those who held to such teachings to suffer censorship and even persecution.

According to Husaini, up to perhaps the time of Ibn Bājjah (Avempace, d. 1138) Spanish Muslims had been "the most conservative of all". Even Ibn Bājjah "was not an original philosopher of any note"; although his philosophy does contain "germs" of Neo-Platonism somewhat after the manner of al-Kindī and Ibn Sīnā, it "was not a fully developed pantheism".[2] Likewise, although many have made quite a fuss about Ibn Ṭufayl (d. 1185) because of his "Robinson Cruso" manner of presenting his thinking in literary form, Husaini is of the opinion that he, unlike Ibn 'Arabī, did not leave behind him a system of his philosophy, even though what he did write does contain Neo-Platonist "Scholasticism in its most mystical form". As for Ibn Rushd (1126-98), Husaini is of the opinion that it was not his Aristotelianism that caused his being censured but the Neo-Platonist elements in his system. "His conception springing from the Neo-Platonic view of Material Reason is peculiar. The Material Reason is eternal, imperishable Spirit, as eternal and imperishable as the Pure Reason or the Active Spirit over us. His system when consistently carried out yields a pantheistic view."[3] Others of course might disagree with this for it is indeed a matter of emphasis as to what aspect of that intellectual giant one prefers to stress the most since he is the most comprehensive Islamic philosopher before Ibn Khaldūn or Mulla Ṣadrā al-Shīrāzī.

In his work *The Pantheistic Monism of Ibn al-'Arabī,* Husaini explains:

> The philosophy of Ibn al-'Arabī is known as the theory of *Waḥdat al-Wujūd*, or Unity of Existence, and the one English word which can best represent this theory is "monism" which holds that "reality is just one self-existing thing or system and that all things and events of daily experience are but part or modification of this ultimate thing". I could have named my work The Monism of Ibn al-'Arabī, but since there are many kinds of monism—substantial, attributive, Materialistic, Agnostic, Atheistic, etc., I thought it advisable to qualify the word "monism" with the word "pantheistic".[4]

Husaini gives this interpretation of *Waḥdat al-Wujūd* as Ibn 'Arabī used it:

> *Waḥdat al-Wujūd* is the theory which regards all finite things as mere aspects, modifications, or parts of one eternal self-existing Being and views all material objects and all particular minds as necessarily derived from a single infinite substance. The one absolute substance, the all-comprehensive being is called God....In *Waḥdat al-Wujūd*, monism and determinism are combined, so that the All of Nature is believed to be co-extensive with God and the Divine Being is supposed to be fully and exhaustively expressed in the divine manifestations.

> ...Since there is only one being, if we assert God, the Universe must vanish; and if we assert the Universe, God must vanish.[5]

That the whole system can be built on the foundation of just that term *Waḥdat al-Wujūd* rather than being an exaggeration seems from our wider perspective to be almost an understatement. For this term could be extended to include the semantical implications and connotations of technical terms in the full range of comparative philosophy and history of religions, such as Brahman, Tao, and Tathatā. Husaini points out that the *Waḥdat al-Wujūd* is remarkably similar to the Advaita Vedānta as well as very much like Neo-Platonism and modern pantheism. However, given the strong theistic strain in Ibn 'Arabī's interpretations, it might be that he is closer to panentheism than to strict Advaita. At any rate, Ibn 'Arabī's "advaita" is certainly not the extreme variety like Gauḍapāda's and not even so much like Śaṅkara's as like that of his contemporaries Śrīharṣa and Citsukha.

In dealing with the theme of Being and non-Being, Ibn 'Arabī's very keen logic suggests some possible influence from the Nyāya-Vaiśeṣika or even perhaps more likely from the heritage of Dignāga, Dharmakīrti, Śāntarakṣita, Dharmapāla, et al, who had been active in Kaśmīr and whose influence probably had spread well into Central Asia. It is in his paradigm examples that we sense the likelihood of Indian rather than Greek sources, the term translated as non-existence, for example, evidently being close to the Sanskrit *abhāva*, which we are prone to translate as absence rather than negation, although even by Ibn 'Arabī's time the Latin Scholastics (not to mention the Byzantines, who are not yet that well known) were making the distinction between what they termed *privation* as distinct from *denial.* Ibn 'Arabī's rigorously systematic way is indeed far closer, in spite of his mysticism, to the Aristotelian and Navya Nyāya logicians than to any variety of Zen or what we thus far have even from Chu Hsi and his immediate disciples. Or again, in some ways his logic seems to have some resemblance even to his Jaina contemporary Malliṣena in that he seems to stay away from any sort of absolutism, pointing out that at least within the Great-Con tingency of human experience and aspiration (not to say desperation) everything is so interrelated with everything else that the safer way is always to distinguish in what respect *each* thing is like or unlike *each* other thing, and in what respect each and every one of these innumerable things partakes of Being or even may be said to *be* Being. His penchant for classification is also very Jainistic. Or again, although as far as basic types of philosophy is concerned he is poles apart from Madhva who is certainly anything but a pantheist, nevertheless insofar as he is always explicit in making distinctions, i.e., in pointing out *differences*, there is a resemblance to Madhva.

Much of Ibn 'Arabī's philosophy, in spite of the Neo-Platonist aspects, is still basically Aristotelian, although no doubt filtered through Porphyry, John Philopon and others. He always makes the most of the usual Aristotelian categories: essence, property, space, condition, time, quantity, relation, accident, activity, passivity. Thus we should be reminded that at least in the case of Ibn 'Arabī mysticism need not be extra-logical, even though it might ultimately be supra-logical or even super-logical. More specifically, this probably should be taken as a reminder that just as al-Ghazālī had not been satisfied with Ibn Sīnā's Aristotelianism but sought to transcend it, but by using it, so Suhrawardī, Sabziwāri and Ibn 'Arabī were using Ibn Rushd's Aristotelianism as a means to higher ends.

Having given first the negative-privation-absence side, Ibn 'Arabī then gives the corresponding positive classification of existing things as varieties of Being, which Husaini has schematized as follows:

- Existence
  - Real
    - Existing by it self
      - Spiritual
        - Necessary—God
        - Contingent—Spirit
      - Material
        - Compound—Body
        - Simple—Atom[6]
    - Existing by another
      - Inseparable—Property
      - Separable—Accidence
  - Ideal
    - Absurd

Each of these in turn is explicated with full awareness that distinctions involve both similarities and differentiae, universals and particulars, as well as relations like the Nyāya-Vaiśeṣika *samavāya* and *saṃyoga*. This series of distinctions climbs through the hierarchy of existences to the problem of the Universal of universals or Being of beings quite logically. This culminates in statements like the following:

> God has created us from an eternal being so that eternity is attributed to us....On the other hand this reality is the root of all existing things in general. It is the root of atom and the sphere of life....
>
> Similarly, with regard to man we say that he has life and knowledge, and so he is living and knowing. The reality of life is one, and the reality of knowledge is one. Their attribution to the living and the knowing is a single attribution. But with reference to the knowledge of God we say that it is eternal and with reference to the knowledge of man that it is temporal.[7]

Ibn 'Arabī reminds us that we are necessarily always dealing in contingencies—or, as one might say, if not with *māyā* in the sense of *upādhi*, nevertheless in the sense of what we might call "dialectics at the second level". Thus we are reminded once again of the constantly present doctrine of levels of Mahāyāna and Advaita Vedānta, at least in its later forms as found in Śrīharṣa and Citsukha, the latter being exactly Ibn 'Arabī's contemporary.

In his structured schematic formula what Ibn 'Arabī has intended for us to understand primarily is that the core of true philosophizing lies at the *pāramārthika* level beyond all possible and actual schematizations; but this does not entail, as some Rinzai Zen buffs seem to attempt, abandoning all schematizations altogether, lest instead of transcending them we fall for beneath them into anti-thinking. There is a parallel or almost direct correlation between Ibn 'Arabī's distinction between *al-Ḥaqq*, or the Real, and *khalq*, or the phenomenal, and the classical distinction between the *pāramārthika* and the *vyāvahārika* 'levels' of reality. For Ibn 'Arabī both of these are aspects of the One, and that One is God, Allah. Affifi quotes Ibn 'Arabī as recording this relation in the following words: "If you regard Him through Him...then He regards Himself through Himself, which is the state of unity; but if you regard Him through yourself (i.e., from your point of view as a form) then the unity vanishes."[8] One is immediately reminded of the Vaiṣṇava poet Nammaḷwar who exclaimed, "Thou singest of Thyself through me!", or Bernard of Clairvaux's 'reduction' of reasons for devotion to God until there is no longer any desire, even the desire for God, but only adoration, not for His benefits or even for His attributes, but for His own intrinsic Being. Ibn 'Arabī further writes: "Unity has no other meaning than two (or more) things being actually identical but conceptually distinguishable the one from the other; so in one sense the one is the other; in another it is not.... Multiplicity is due to different points of view, not to an actual division in the One Essence."[9]

In his treatment of the universal problem of the relation between immanence and transcendence, Ibn 'Arabī distinguishes between two fundamentally different kinds of transcendence:

(1) That which belongs to the divine Essence *per se* and *a se*—the absolute simplicity and unity of the One—the state of the *Aḥadiyyah*.

(2) Transcendence asserted by the intellect, which must be always coupled with immanence and which may assume the following forms:

(a) God may be called transcendent in the sense of being absolute; or

(b) He may be called transcendent in the sense of being a necessary being, self-begotten, self-caused, etc., in contradistinction to the contingent, created or caused beings of the Phenomenal World; or

(c) He may be called transcendent in the sense that He is unknowable and incommunicable and beyond all proof.

This second kind of transcendence Ibnul 'Arabī condemns if

> taken by itself (i.e. without immanence) to be an explanation of the whole truth about Reality. Reality as Ibnul 'Arabī understands it has both aspects: transcendence and immanence.[10]

This being the case, again it seems that Ibn 'Arabī might better be called a panentheist rather than simply a pantheist. At any rate, unity is maintained by starting with pure transcendence and then including immanence; if one starts with immanence, it becomes more difficult to avoid a duality.

Ibn 'Arabī is not unaware of the problem which the Advaitin Vedāntists also had to face, namely whether or in what sense knowledge of finite things (qualities, as Ibn 'Arabī puts it) and knowledge of spiritual reality (God, Brahman, Tao, Allah) involve the same *pramāṇas*; or whether the *pramāṇas* can be applied analogously, as in some places the Latin Christian Scholastics argued (or applied 'obliquely' as others more cautiously affirmed); or whether applied only dialectically, such that whatever is affirmed of finitude must be denied of ultimacy. Ibn 'Arabī opts for the last position, un-equivocally; and in doing so perhaps he is closer to his Byzantine sources and contemporaries than to others, even though one can find traces of something remotely similar even in Dōgen's Sōtō Zen. Ibn 'Arabī writes:

> As regards the knowledge of God as an incorporeal essence capable of admitting qualities, we say that we do not know Him. Therefore, it is not allowed to think about God, for not a single truth about Him can be inferred. We fear lest one who thinks about God should think or contemplate through semblance and comparison.
>
> It is known that, to know a thing, it is necessary that we should know previously something connected with it, so that the new piece of knowledge may be put in its proper place. It is also known that we do not know any such connection between God and His creation as exists between one thing and another, i.e., connection as genus, species, individual of a species, etc. We do not have the previous knowledge of anything by establishing a relation between which and the Self of God we can know Him....[11]

It has become almost axiomatically clear that the borderline between mysticism and skepticism is a very thin one, since after the *via negativa* is rigorously applied to all empirically knowable or analogically knowable reality, as Ibn 'Arabī boldly states, "None shall know God either directly or through reason."

Whether or not, as some have argued, such a theism leaves God "out there" and man therefore free of inhibitions in his investigation of natural phenomena, Ibn 'Arabī is quite clear in his classification of the *pramāṇas* as far as finite definite things are concerned. Each *pramāṇa* is valid in its own realm of operation and we know different types of things in accordance with the different types of *pramāṇas*. His classification includes: (1) sense perception, (2) imagination (very much dependent on the senses), (3) cogitation (correspondences and absence of them), (4) reason (which includes not only inference but dialectical negation, so that he quotes one al-Ṣadīq who says that "The admission of inability to know God is the real knowledge of God."), (5) memory (also dependent on the other *pramāṇas*). Ibn 'Arabī concludes:

> I have described all the methods through which a man knows in his capacity as man through human faculties and endeavour. Reason can only receive what God grants it of His knowledge. Through reason we cannot know except that there is an existence and that it is one and is the worshipped. We cannot know more than that.[12]

Finding parallels and comparisons and differences with the Neo-Confucian contemporaries of Ibn 'Arabī is not such an obvious matter; but when we re-examine the distinction between the "things above shapes" and the "things within shapes", we might find him again in a middle position between the realism of Chang Ts'ai and the idealism of Lu Hsiang-shan. This becomes more clear where Ibn 'Arabī compensates his rigorous application of the *via negativa* and what might appear to be a rather orthodox transcendent theism with emphasis on what Husaini translates quite openly as the Holy Ghost. Indeed, again we wonder whether in the final analysis Ibn 'Arabī is not more of a panentheist than a pantheist as most commentators claim. Perhaps it is a matter of emphasis, but certainly when he records that "there are grades in it" it might appear that he is much closer to a panentheist position, or even to Chang Ts'ai and Chu Hsi than to Ḍōgen or Citsukha. Ibn 'Arabī writes:

> When it is established that one should follow something to know God, it is better to follow God Himself. If you know God through God and know all the affairs through Him, you shall have no ignorance, no suspense, no wavering, no doubt. ...One who follows one other than God follows one who is capable of mistake. If he happens to be correct, it is by chance.
>
> Know, may God help us and you with His Holy Ghost, that every knowledge, inferential, practical, intuitive, etc. is based on following something. Yet there are grades in it.[13]

There is almost what might be characterized as a "leap of faith" in his emphatic stress on distrust of unaided reason when it comes to speculation about the nature of God. Technically, of course, the Obedience he enjoins is based on the revelation of the Qur'ān; but this is compensated with the emphasis on the Holy Spirit or God-within-us. He is all too aware that 'rationality' leads only to disagreements and controversies. Although he sometimes seems to make a large concession to anti-intellectualism, we must be quite aware that here he is writing in the context of philosophical theology. Elsewhere, especially in his glorification of the cosmic possibilities of human nature, one almost senses a "down-going" like that of Nietzsche or Dōgen. But in the present context his meaning is clear: Although reason may be fit and proper as far as the *vyāvahārika* level is concerned, it is not adequate where the *pāramārthika* level or the theological level is concerned.

Even Citsukha finally appeals to revelation, though of course his scripture is the Vedas rather than the Qur'ān; but the basic attitude is very similar. In the Neo-Confucian or Buddhist context there is not quite the same emphasis since the concept of revelation is lacking in both cases. Even so, it must not be forgotten, for example, that Chu Hsi got into serious trouble because of his altering what had been for many centuries regarded as the indispensible and not-to-be-questioned Confucian classics; and as for the Buddhists, each sect or subsect took this or that sūtra as its "scripture". (It is certain that Ibn 'Arabī is not unaware of Indian philosophy, though how much of it he had actually studied would be a topic to be researched by specialists. But at least in the present context he does list the "Brahmins" along with the other "rationalists".)

One might well recall the classical Islamic distinction between the position of the prophet and the mystic, the latter being only in the mode of seeking in the ascending order, while the former is a "down-goer" in that he has a Message from God and is proclaiming it authentically to the world. In the face of the mystic one also becomes enraptured, or at least bitten, as it were, by the Socratic fly and, leaving all else, begins his Enquiry into Brahman; but in the face of the prophet—and it could be argued that Ibn 'Arabī still takes this position rather than that of the "flight of the alone to the Alone" (to use the Plotinian classical formula)—one is compelled to Obedience to the Prophet's Revelation.

Generally there is a tendency to ignore the problems of causation when dealing with mystical or pantheistic thinkers since it might seem that all that one could say about such a system is that God is the only true cause and the world in its entirety is no more than the contingent manifestation of this causal power. Such a position does not involve causation in the usual sense but is really only another aspect of the *pāramārthika/vyāvahārika* relation, or the paradox of the *āvaraṇa/vikṣepa* revealing-and-concealing mystery. Affifi reports that at least in one context Ibn 'Arabī actually regarded "cause" and "effect" as mere words, as two subjective categories; indeed, it has become fashionable to interpret Ibn 'Arabī as even denying causation altogether. But on more careful investigation we can distinguish two different senses of causality:

(i) Causality as applied to the universe *as a whole*, i.e., the question whether the universe *as a whole* is caused and if so what is the cause?

(ii) Causality as applied to some parts *in* the universe, i.e., the causal connection between the various parts of the uni-

> verse as we usually know it, i.e., the question of causality as applied to the universe as an organic whole, some parts in which stand in a definite causal relation to others.[14]

Affifi notes than Ibn 'Arabī has no objection to the latter kind of causality,

> ...although he regards it, like multiplicity itself, as merely relative and apparent...(since) it is causality in which (both) the cause and effect belong to one and the same continuant, the divine Essence....All that Ibnul 'Arabī is anxious to do is not to admit the reality of particular causes in the Phenomenal World, for such admission would commit him to polytheism.[15]

Now such a position in the face of a strict Aristotelian or a Vaiśeṣika position does seem extreme. But the similarity with Citsukha is such that we begin to wonder whether when Ibn 'Arabī was in Baghdad he might not have come in contact with some form or other of the *satkāryavāda* doctrine as interpreted by the Advaitins. Certainly he could have had access to al-Bīrūnī, whose cosmology was very similar to that of the Ikhwān al-Ṣafā, and who not only knew Sanskrit but was not uninformed about the doctrine of *māyā* and related topics. Among the Japanese contemporaries of Ibn 'Arabī it would be difficult to find anyone who bothered about causation or logic at all, except perhaps some Hossō scholar-thinkers like Zōshun or his disciple Kakuken. Although one can find a rather definite philosophy of causation in Chu Hsi, the Lu Hsiang-shan heritage tended to neglect it.

As for the notion of the "end of the world" or the concept of the "next world", Ibn 'Arabī insists (almost as though he were a Buddhist) that both this present world and the next world are always in the process of being created and destroyed. Affifi points out that there is a contrast here between Ibn Rushd and Ibn 'Arabī, claiming that the latter is the "more profound thinker of the two" since Ibn Rushd asserted the eternity of two beings, God and the universe, "while, for Ibnul 'Arabī, there is only one eternal being which he calls now God, now the Universe. The distinction he draws between what he calls the contingent and the necessary is but a formal one. In reality the contingent and the necessary are one."[16] Of course this reminds us of those varieties of Mahāyāna Buddhism which make the claim that ultimately *saṃsāra* and *nirvāṇa* are one.

In dealing with the traditional problem of the proper interpretation of the Divine Names and their relation to the problem of the attributes of God, Ibn 'Arabī says that an attribute is a divine name manifested in the external world. The attributes in general and in their grand ensemble constitute what he calls the "Theatre of manifestation, a field of operation for the divine substance to manifest itself in different degrees".[17] In that regard he might be closer to the disciples of Rāmānuja rather than to the Advaitin 'monists' who were his contemporaries—although on the point of dogged insistence on the *nirguṇa*, attributeless Brahman the thirteenth century Advaitins moderated somewhat from Gauḍapāda's and Śaṅkara's original extreme assertions. Ibn 'Arabī is much closer to the sort of Advaita that one finds in the heritage of Vācaspati Miśra in that rationality remains completely not only valid but obligatory at its own level; even though ultimately it can be transcended, without it one simply falls into the abyss of unreason or outright irrationality of an even subhuman sort.

According to Affifi, Ibn 'Arabī is too much like Hegel, even to the compromising of his theism, in that ethical propositions are ranked as completely subordinate to logical relations. Being and the Good are identical, evil being only a sort of negative foil without ontological roots. Even good and evil are attributive, not substantive, and are quite on par with any of the other attributes that are (merely) ascribed to Allah but are not necessary as are Being and Unity. However, Affifi explains that Ibn 'Arabī is fully aware of the "grave inconsistency of holding a notion of an Ethical God side by side with a pantheistic ONE. At the same time he is eager to preserve in his writings an apparent picture of the Personal God of Islam—a merely verbal mask behind which his pantheistic God can be easily detected."[18]

Ibn 'Arabī's ethics is very much involved in his ontology since he is never willing to compromise his emphasis on the One, even though he does allow for more plurality within that One than some of his Ṣūfī predecessors. With Ibn 'Arabī "we are always moving in a closed circle of thought. . .(since all the phenomena of manifestation within the Many are subjective). . . .From whatever point we start on this circle we always come back to where we started, and nothing more is gained than the bare assertion that there is but One Reality."[19] Indeed, it is like multiplying the number one by the number one an infinite number of times; one will always come out with one as the answer. Such monistic trends of course were not very welcome within orthodox Islam. We should constantly remind ourselves that Ibn 'Arabī was by no means unique in this trend within his own time since essentially the same problems can readily be found among his Zen and Advaita contemporaries and in the school of Lu Hsiang-shan among the Neo-Confucianists.

One cannot but wish that more scholar-thinkers familiar with both Zen and with Ṣūfism would guide us in the right channels through the ocean of possible comparisons and contrasts, for the following might apply equally to Dōgen and many others, even if once again we overlook the Hesychasts of Byzantium who were Ibn 'Arabī's contemporaries:

> The pivot around which (his ethics) all turns is *self-realization*. Everything and every action has one ultimate aim which it is bound to achieve, and this is to realize itself and in so doing it realizes one or other of God's infinite perfections which include the so-called imperfections according to Ethics and Religion.
>
> Ibnul 'Arabī does not give us an ethical *system* with some definite ideal to strive after, but rather a metaphysical account of an ethical theory of Determinism. His is not a normative Ethics; it does not teach us what we *ought* to do, but *how* we come to do what we do, and *who* is the actual doer of actions.[20]

According to Affifi, Ibn 'Arabī attempts to balance off the extreme determinists (with most of whom in the Islamic past he was completely familiar) with the 'libertarians' (some of them more or less heretical) in a position not dissimilar from that of Leibniz's "pre-established Harmony". As a monist he must affirm that ultimately God is the only doer of all actions; but on the other hand these actions cannot countervene the laws of nature and of human behaviour, which God has determined to the extent of implanting in each of us a potentiality for fulfilling the vocation or destiny for which each of us is responsible. The determinism, insofar as it is that, is typically from within and not by compulsion from without. This internal determination, then, is a sort of self-determination in that man is "determined" from eternity to fulfil his destiny, even though he is responsible proximately.

Ibn 'Arabī's philosophical anthropology or philosophy of man is especially important from the modern humanist perspective which has become so vital as the necessary commonground for world peace and the nonviolent unification of mankind. Ibn 'Arabī's text on man's nature virtually anticipates everything that later can be found in Pico della Mirandola's all-time classic on the dignity of man. Indeed, what Pico later had to offer was only an echo of what had been virtually commonplace in Byzantium and Islam for several centuries. Ibn 'Arabī's little essay on man may sound exaggerated to some moderns just as it did to the ultra-orthodox theologians of his own time. But was it not almost, as it were, prophetic? In our entrance into the Space Age, mankind has actually taken on a new dimension of responsibility such as this mystical insight into man's true nature could intuit only poetically and in the perspective of theoretical metaphysics. But it has been the faith in this perspective rather than in that of the "fall" of man and the gloominess of the Augustinian doctrine of "original sin" that has made these recent scientific openings possible. The following is only the first part of Ibn 'Arabī's essay:

> What about the saying that He created Adam after His own image? The answer is this:
>
> Know that every form taken by a thing is its own substance and not other than it, for, verily, it is not outside it. It is necessary that the Universe should be the form of God so far as it manifests His substance. The man Adam is to be interpreted as the whole of the Universe, for he is the Microcosm which is but the miniature of the Macrocosm.
>
> What is the explanation of the term "Adam"? If you choose,

he may be explained as Divinity itself, or, if you so choose, he may be explained as the totality of Divine names. Or, he may be explained as in the saying of the Prophet, "Verily, God created Adam after His own form." This is the explanation. When God says that He created Man with His two hands, we understand that He gave him perfection and created him as perfect and comprehensive. On this account he is called the compendium of the names, for he is the totality of the Universe with reference to its realities. ... The Universe is Adam in its details. He in his turn is the comprehensive book. He is for the Universe what the soul is for the body. Man is the soul of the Universe and the Universe is the body. The total is the whole of existence which is the Macrocosm, and Man is contained in it. If you look at the Universe alone apart from Man, you shall find it like a body without life. The perfection of the Universe is through Man, just as the perfection of the body is through life. Man is infused into the body of the Universe. In the Universe it is Man who is intended....

So, in our opinion, it is established that Man has two aspects—external and internal. The external aspect resembles the Universe in its entirety,...and the internal aspect resembles Divinity. The whole, in an absolute sense, is Man.[21]

In the history of Latino-Gothic philosophy formerly, one did not consider humanism as such as significant until the Italian Renaissance; but more recently there have been some reconsiderations of this view to the effect that really much of the same motif was already beginning to be manifest, especially at Paris and Oxford but also at Padua and other medieval universities even in the thirteenth century. By then, for example, there was a valiant contest between the Seculars and the Friars over the running of the university; and certainly in Aquinas and Roger Bacon there is a humanism (theistic of course) that is a sort of presupposition over against the more rigorously theological Augustinianism of the previous centuries; and even Bonaventura Franciscan that he was, definitely emphasized the untarnishable *Imago Dei* as the core of human nature over and above the doctrine of the fall of Adam and the intrinsic evil nature of man by virtue of original sin. Even Aquinas seems to soften this fallen nature of man (which, alas, Calvin and Luther later revived) and to stress rather man's God-given rationality.

But has there not been a parallel transition in the rest of Eurasia also? For in India, if not in Southeast Asia also, over against Śaṅkara's rigorism already Rāmānuja, Śrīkanṭha, and Nimbārka tend to stress the goodness of man, minimizing caste restrictions and giving women more freedom for the higher pursuits; and instead of cultivating the utter transcendence of the Divine Ultimate in the rigorous application of the *via negativa* they tend to worship the Avatars of Viṣṇu, especially Rāmā and Kṛṣṇa. Likewise is there not a parallel transition from the rigor of Kumārajīva's Śūnyavāda to Chu Hsi's revival of Confucianist humanism? As for Japan, in spite of Dōgen's attempt at returning to stricter monastic discipline and rigorous *ascesis*, Honen, Shinran, Nichiren, Ippen and a host of others definitely (largely by emphasizing the *Lotus Sūtra* over and above the *Prajñāpāramitā* and other more ascetic sūtras) put man in a more warm-hearted and dignified position in the universe, teaching that all people (even women and criminals) can easily be saved whether by self-effort or by the "other-power" grace of Amida or the Mercy of Kannon or other interceding Bodhisattvas.

Then behind Ibn 'Arabī himself there seems to have been something similar transpiring ever since the beginning of Hellenic and Hellenistic influence on Islam. By his time the Ash'arite censorship of the Mu'tazilites had almost been forgotten; the sciences had flourished from astronomy to agriculture; and, not to retrace the thought currents in the *Falsafah* or the basic theme of man's capacity for *theosis* among Ṣūfīs, even the Qur'ān was being reinterpreted as stressing the dignity and perfectibility of man. Ibn 'Arabī had been heavily influenced by the Ikhwān al-Ṣafā who had put special stress on the cosmic nature of man and therefore on man's perfectibility. Ibn 'Arabī's own mysticism is by no means a retrenchment back away from the *Falsafah* humanism of such as al-Ṭūsī in the East and Ibn Rushd in Spain but rather a further working out of its implications.

As might be expected, Ibn 'Arabī's aesthetics is closely linked with his pantheism and with the varieties of love, for the simple reason that the One can be approached equally in terms of *bhakti*, *karma*, and *jñāna*, or aesthetics, ethics and epistemology. Affifi reminds us that even the great Ḥallāj had speculated that love was a cosmic force constantly operating throughout the universe and not merely in human psycho-physical organisms. This is based on the by then ancient and rich tradition of the microcosm/macrocosm harmony, which had been refined to a very high degree by the 'idealist' Chinese Taoists and Neo-Confucianists and even by the Han syncretistic Confucianists like Yang Hsiung (53 B.C.-A.D. 18), even if we do not specify the rich heritage of Neo-Platonism in this regard. Therefore to find *Eros* still hovering over the Holy Qur'ān in Ibn 'Arabī's time should not surprise us.

Basically Ibn 'Arabī distinguishes three kinds of love, e.g., natural love, spiritual love and divine love, the first two being no more and no less than species of the latter except on a lower scale.

> By divine love he means the essential love of the One—the eternal love which is the source of all other kinds. Before any form of modalisation, the One, in His supreme "isolation" and simplicity, loved Himself for and in Himself, and loved to be known and to be manifested. This was the cause of creation. In loving Himself, the One loved all the things latent in His Essence and hence they are impregnated with the love they now manifest in different ways. "The love of the a'yān began," Ibnul 'Arabī says, "when they were still in the Blindness (*al-'amā'*) when they first heard God's creative Word (Be).[22]

If we did not know that this has roots in Neo-Platonism we could easily read into it the sort of cosmology that one finds even in the Upaniṣads, not to mention many varieties of the Vedānta. Nimbārka specifically emphasizes the *bhakti* 'erotic' aspect, whereas the Advaitins place their emphasis on *jñāna*, which is not self-creative. Thus the *jñāna* aspect imposes even greater problems than the lover-love-loved triad involved in the *bhakti* aspect, since the knower-knowledge-known triad has no inherent creative power whereas love does, inherently, and not in an ancillary way.

Ibn 'Arabī takes Divine Love as the Whole *a priori* primordially, so that other kinds of love are only parts of that Primordial Eros that not only undergirds all reality but is identical with it:

> Love is the working principle in all manifestations of the One, from the highest to the lowest. It reaches the zenith in Man, the perfect Man. who above all creation experiences all the three kinds of Love. Through Love the Whole is bound together and through it the object of creation is realized.[23]

Ibn 'Arabī did not treat love of any kind as an end in itself; it has no intrinsic value. The basis and cause of all love is Beauty. Such a view had already been held even by Ibn Sīnā, who also had equated the concept of the Beautiful with the concept of Perfection, and that in such a way that of course only God could be called truly Beautiful without qualification, and therefore only God could be loved without any reservations. Thus, in sum, Affifi says that according to Ibn 'Arabī:

> We love God. . .because God is Beautiful, and He loves us and all His creation because He loves the Beautiful. God's Beauty is the source of all types of beauty. It is the source of all spiritual and intellectual beauty as well as the beauty of form, although God's Beauty is above all form and shape. God loves beauty of form because form reflects His own Beauty as it reflects His Being. In abstract beauty as well as in beauty of form therefore God ought to be loved and worshipped, and this is how a perfect Gnostic knows Him, loves Him and worships Him.[24]

Like many philosophers, especially those rooted in disciplined mysticism, Ibn 'Arabī also expresses his intention or his vision in his poetry. Jalāl al-Dīn Rūmi is most famous for his Ṣūfī poetry and only occasionally appreciated for his systematic metaphysics, which is expressed in prose; whereas Ibn 'Arabī is known most for his metaphysics and only occasionally for his poetry. The following is representative of this aspect of his expression in that form:

He praises me and I praise Him,
And he worships me and I worship Him.
In one state I acknowledge Him,
And in the A'yān I deny Him.
He knows me and I know Ḥim not,
And I know Him and behold Him.
How can He be independent
When I help Him and assist Him?
In my knowing Him, I create Him.
Thus we are informed in the Tradition,
And in me His object is realized.[25]

Ibn 'Arabī's intuitive reflections on the holy visions of the Prophet, being the result of illuminative experience, should help to bring the reader into the same divine illumination or enlightenment. Even after a study of the great Ibn Sīnā and al-Ghazālī or even Ibn Rushd, one finds a degree of excellence in Ibn 'Arabī not equalled elsewhere as far as the illuminative tradition is concerned. Indeed, Aynī[26] is willing to assert that Ibn 'Arabī surpasses completely all of the Greek philosophers before him, and, rightly interpreted, is by no means inferior to modern European philosophers like Descartes, Spinoza, Leibniz and Kant. Spinoza should be mentioned especially as perhaps the nearest among modern European philosophers to what Ibn 'Arabī has to offer.

17. Citsukha

The view is supported almost universally that as far as dialectics is concerned Citsukha (fl.c. 1250), along with Śrīharṣa to whom he is primarily indebted, is virtually unexcelled by anyone after Śaṅkara, not only in terms of refutation of rival systems but in terms of positive doctrinal developments. As far as refinement of method is concerned, Citsukha is very closely parallel to the developments between Ibn Sīnā, al-Ghazālī and Ibn Rushd in

Islam, between Abelard and Duns Scotus in Latin Europe, between Ibn Gabirol and Maimonides in the Jewish scholastic heritage, and even to some extent between Han Yü/Li Ao and Chu Hsi/Lu Hsiang-shan. In all cases the basic problem is the right use of reason in relation to what might generally be called (à la Jaspers, for example) transcendence, or the problem of contingency, more often phrased in terms of faith and reason. Dōgen and Citsukha have very much in common as far as *type* of philosophy is concerned, but they are radically different in their modes of expression since Dōgen prefers metaphors and anecdotes comparable to those used in Ṣūfī literature while Citsukha is a master dialectician. Nevertheless Dōgen in dealing with what classically we still call the *via negativa* also has to use argumentations in order supposedly to remove the obstacles to non-argumentative contemplation. If Citsukha cannot necessarily be said to excel his Eurasian contemporaries, he certainly is their match, so that one can only regret that then a world conference of philosophers could not have been held to see how they might operate in *viva voce* encounters with each other. Even so perhaps it is not impossible that there will be such "dialogues in limbo" someday when philosophers specializing in these various thirteenth century *ācāryas* re-enact such a seance. For they are being studied and restudied intensively as being in most respects still very relevant to present day problems.

Śrīharṣa was the seminal formulator while Citsukha is his commentator. "The dialectical campaign begun by Śrīharṣa, and which revolutionized the philosophical thought of India, was continued by Citsukha in an equally brilliant way with a more comprehensive approach. The pioneering work of Śrīharṣa found its technical perfection in Citsukha's *Tattva-pradīpikā* which is a beautiful reflection of the Advaita tradition that had flourished before him.[1] Śrīharṣa had definitely been challenged by what Sarma explicitly states had been "the vigorous growth of the pluralistic systems like the Nyāyavaiśeṣika" which he admits had "dimmed the vitality" of Śaṅkara's original efforts. Śrīharṣa therefore had had to sharpen considerably his dialectics in *defense* of the system.

Citsukha's contribution over and above Śrīharṣa's work was chiefly in terms of reconciling the differences "that existed in the subschools and various other noted writers of his own system."[2] Vācaspati Miśra, Prakāśātman, Śaṅkara himself, Sureśvara and Ānandabodha are among those in the Advaita tradition whose works are used by Citsukha. Controversies had been continuing ever since the ninth century among these and other Advaitins; nevertheless, it is difficult to believe that the very greatly extended subdivisions of the Advaita school came about except in response to the challenges of those like Rāmanuja, Śrīkaṇṭha and Bhāskara and their followers and predecessors. At any rate by Citsukha's time the sub-schools of Advaita were evidently drifting apart too much, and the chief intention of Citsukha was to reconcile them.

Thus the *Tattva-pradīpikā* is heavily syncretistic, but then syncretism has always more or less characterized Advaitic philosophers of all ages. This assertion might be extended to Eurasian monisms in general, and because of the increase in dialectical skill everywhere there had been an increase in points to syncretize. The enlargement of the complexities to be reconciled had already been established, according to Sarma, by virtue of Śaṅkara's own method which is quinticized in the term *ṣaṇmatasthāpanācārya*, "which means that what is good in all other systems is accepted and complemented by him in Advaita and that his criticism of other systems is only constructive and not destructive"—as has been the method of orthodox *prāsaṅgika* Mādhyamika.

Citsukha's work was of sufficient weight that not only later Advaitins like Ānandajñāna, Nṛsiṃhāśrama and Madhusūdana Sarasvatī are indebted to him but the Advaita that is refuted by such as Veṅkaṭanātha of the Viśiṣṭādvaita school and Jayatīrtha of the Dvaita school is his and not only that of Gauḍapāda and Śaṅkara. As Sharma puts it, "The significance of his contribution can be understood from the influence he wielded on succeeding writers on Advaita and the opposition he invited from writers on rival systems"—as manifested in the commentaries on Citsukha's work, including for example that by Sukhaprakāśa, and in the sub-commentaries such as those by Pratyagrūpa, Ānandajñāna, Amalānanda, and on down into the sixteenth century with Madhusūdana Sarasvatī's defense against the Madhva Dvaita Vyāsatīrtha, and even Appayadīkṣita, all of whom are deeply indebted to Citsukha. The list could continue into the present, including K. C. Bhattacharya, for example. This is very important for understanding the historical interplay of the various Indian systems, though thus far very little work has been done on this topic, even within the perspective of the history of Indian philosophy quite aside from the global perspective. In that perspective one could ask whether there was any dialogue between Citsukha and the Jainas such as Hemachandra who was virtually his contemporary. And in the larger framework one likewise wonders whether his works were known in the Hinduized states of Southwest Asia; and whether indeed there was any interchange at all between him and other Hindu philosophers and the Muslims, who were by this time fairly well established in the north and on the west coast of India. Communications in general were very open all across Eurasia before the Mongol 'conquest', but alas communications among traders and armies does not necessarily entail exchange among pundits, either then or now!

Citsukha's chief disciple was Sukhaprakāśa, who was in turn a teacher of Amalānanda. Those accustomed in Zen circles to trace the lines of transmission may rejoice that they can find very similar records in India, for guruship in India continued (and still continues within the non-alienated tradition) to be of crucial importance, in fact no less so than with the Zen patriarchs.

By common consent, especially among the commentators, the *Tattvapradīpikā* is Citsukha's magnum opus. In his treatment Sarma condenses the principle themes as follows:

> The full name of the work is *Pratyak-tattva-pradīpikā*. Its commentator Pratyagrūpa interprets the title in a significant way: It is a lamp (*pradīpikā*) which throws light on the true nature (*tattva*) of the *jīva* or individual self (*pratyak*) that is not different from Brahman. The chief purpose of the work is to refute the objections to the *advaitaśrutis* raised by modern writers of rival systems. That is to say, it is more dialectical in character. It is divided into four chapters called *paricchedas*, touching, like the *Vedāntasūtra*, on the four

points *samanvaya* (synthesis), *avirodha* (non-contradiction), *sādhana* (means) and *phala* (end).

The first chapter treats of the Advaita concepts like the self-luminosity of Ātman, and its import is to show that the non-dual Ātman is synthetically and unanimously conveyed by the essential *Śrutis,* which are of the most valid means of knowledge. The second chapter contains the refutation of the concept of difference held by the systems like the Nyāya, Mīmāṃsā and Buddhism. Thus it is shown in this chapter that the *advaitaśrutis* pointing to the absolute Brahman stand uncontradicted by the ontological and epistemological systems of other philosophies which are in themselves self-contradictory. The third chapter deals with the means to *mokṣa* or Self-realization, *śabda* as a direct means of spiritual knowledge and *jñāna* as the sole means of the realization. *Jñāna-karma-samuccaya* is in a sense accepted. Karma stops with giving rise to *jñāna* which alone leads to *mokṣa* ultimately. Thus *karma* is a means of the means to *mokṣa.* This view is meant to show the individuality of the Advaita doctrine as distinct from that of the Naiyāyikas who hold that *śabda* is an indirect means and the Mīmāṃsakas who hold that *karma* is the means to the highest good. Citsukha synthesizes the pre-Śaṅkara and post-Śaṅkara phases of Advaita in accepting this sort of combination of knowledge and work. The fourth chapter treats of the Advaita conception of *mokṣa.* The Buddhists, the Naiyāyikas and the Sāṅkhyas are criticized in this context. *Mokṣa* is not a negative state of being free from misery but is of the nature of positive bliss, realized through the destruction of *avidyā,* which conceals it. Besides a few more theories of Advaita like the locus of *avidya* are discussed.[3]

In his refutations of Nyāya-Vaiśeṣika Cituskha refers specifically to Udayana, Śrīvallabha and Vādivāgīśvara as well as Bhāsarvajña. Definite representatives of the other systems also come under the genius of his critique, including Kumārila, Prabhākara, Śālikanātha and Bhavanātha, as well as Dignāga and Dharmakīrti. Not only Śaṅkara but also Gauḍapāda is not forgotten. Needless to say, he uses the scholastic method of *pūrvapakṣa* and *siddhānta*. One may indeed wonder whether Citsukha is, after all, "only just another Advaitin," all of whom still sound very similar to each other. But Sarma claims that his merit lies especially in his adroitness and profundity in handling the doctrine of the self-luminosity of Brahman.

Citsukha follows Sureśvara mostly in regard to the intention of *śabda*, which had long since acquired a very rich and heavy semantical burden virtually parallel with that of the *Logos* concept, the Stoic version of which had infiltrated Islam and the Neo-Platonic version of which had become the basis of Christian Trinitarian theology. He also follows Sureśvara in regard to *manas*, which is loosely the equivalent to *Nous* in the Greek heritage or *mens* in Latin, although much richer in its function as the meditative as distinct from the merely ratiocinative faculty. The chief *pūrvapakṣa* argues that no immediate knowledge comes from *śabda* because *śabda* must deal with canonical *śruti* or at least be based on such. In the global perspective *śruti* may well include not only the Upaniṣads but the Mahāyāna sūtras, the Bible and the Qur'ān, for the same difficulty persists universally and the technicalities are treated with very similar methods everywhere. At any rate, *śruti* is often inconsistent or even contradictory so that one has to be either eclectic or syncretistic. Hence *śabda* cannot give us immediate gnosis or esoteric knowledge much less enlightenment or salvation unaided by reason (inference, dialectic, and the whole range of possible *pramāṇas*). Citsukha's little *siddhānta* here is that although the letter-of-the-law words themselves cannot impart the necessary *direct* knowledge, nevertheless *śruti* can lead to the direct insight that is beyond the ferial functioning of the senses and of the lower reaches of the cursory-thinking mind.

In short, Citsukha was not a Hindu 'fundamentalist' such as some Mīmāṃsakas indeed had been—just as Ibn 'Arabī, for example, is sometimes accused of misuse of the Qur'ān and Rūmī even of neglect of it over and against some of their orthodox 'fundamentalist' inheritors of Ash'arite views, not to mention similar treatments of scripture among the Latin scholastics from Peter Damian to such as the Victorines and Bonaventura's glorious allegories. Perhaps what has really happened in the modern secularized world is not a discarding of *śabda*—for that would be impossible in the extreme!—but simply enlargement of the range of the *śruti* from which to select or syncretize what we hope will become more adequate global bases for complete *dhyāna*.

Within Citsukha's own context Sarma concludes that "salvation is attained through direct knowledge arising out of verbal testimony....This knowledge is not a mental or sensory perception."[4] In popular presentations it has been usual to add after such a statement that intuitive experience 'dawns' as an awakening to a new level of Awareness as different from ordinary knowledge as sleep is from ordinary waking consciousness. In other words, it is really not "knowledge" in any ordinary sense of the English word but a different type or level of consciousness. The real issue here is not the type of knowledge or consciousness but what provokes or evokes it, and what fruition comes from it; also, whether once reached it becomes a permanent state with the yogi then exempt from the usual distinctions of right and wrong, this being the *a-dvaitic* state which supposedly transcends all dualities and polarizations (which is after all a very universal problem with any monism, including most of Zen and some Ṣūfī *mārgas*).

Much difference had developed historically on the issue of whether mere removal of *avidyā* automatically allows *Brahma-vidyā* to "shine forth" unhindered, or whether something else is involved such as *karma yoga*, i.e., ritual duties. Whereas Bhāskara had held that *jñāna* is even subordinate to *karma*, most Advaitins insist that *karma* really does not count at all. Sarma writes: "Some Advaitins do not have objection to the view that *karma* is *subordinate* to *jñāna*, the goal of freedom being achieved only through *jñāna* finally. Writers like Maṇḍana and Ānandabodha accept such a view....Citsukha, too, accepts such a reconciliation of *jñāna* and *karma*."[5] Nevertheless, even though *karma* is asserted to be subordinate to *jñāna*, the sādhaka is obligated to observe the karmic duties until full *Brahma-vidyā* "dawns" lest he fall down into incapacity to reach the goal.

The situation might be expressed in a logical dilemma: Either we admit that both *karma* and *jñāna* (or any of the other pairs that tend to get polarized) are necessary; or we subordinate *jñāna* to *karma* and risk anti-intellectualism and blind action; or else, denying the reality of difference between good and evil, we risk doing nothing and thus inadvertently promoting conflict. This problem may sometimes seem a bit technical and all too similar to the relatively petty endless theological squabbles that have led to anathemas and 'holy' wars and caused much suffering instead of curing it; but, on the other hand, once one realizes that a very basic issue is involved and a very universal one at that, then one realizes how serious the problem really is. For example, this is very similar to the differences between Honen and Shinran on the one hand, and Nichiren on the other; or between the Hesychasts and their opponents in Byzantium; not to mention the perpetual controversy in Latin Christianity between faith and works and similar controversies in Islam.

Citsukha's view on *vidyā* and *avidyā* entails two interpretations: "In the first, *avidyā* and *vidyā* are related as means (*upāya*) and end (*upeya*). This *avidyā* which is the means has two aspects, the bad...is removed by the good aspect in the form of *śravaṇa*, etc., as crystal shows its natural whiteness when the color of the object placed near it is taken away."[6] The question here is in what sense does the good aspect take on a positive force against the bad; or, the bad being removed by any means whatsoever, the good, which has no active karmic force but is simply *svabhāva*, self-subsistent, eternal, undifferentiated and needing to be neither active nor passive nor both, then "shines forth" unhindered. Following Maṇḍana, Citsukha then adds the other interpretation to the effect that *vidyā* and *avidyā* "are never separated". As Sarma words it: "The *vidyā* or Ātman *always* shines, as even for the knowledge of difference and plurality of its shining is essential. But it shines sometimes as tinged (*anubaddha*) by *avidyā*. When this *avidyā* or experience of difference is removed by another *vidyā*, i.e., *śravaṇa*, etc., the *vidyā* or Ātman shines pure."[7] Such differences, in spite of the logic of non-difference that all Advaitins supposedly affirm, are, moreover, still different from Śaṅkara's own explanation. Śaṅkara himself not only allowed but even counselled mental or psychic *upāsanā* of a particular deity in the place of the old sacrificial rites, since true *upāsanā* leads to union with that deity and this union is one with the One non-dual *nirguṇa*-Brahman. Hence Śaṅkara taught that "both *avidyā* and *vidyā* are to be performed by one and the same person and that both together yield (the same) desired fruit."

Citsukha develops the typical Advaita theme of the *refutation of difference*. Although his method is different, the ultimate "realization" involved puts him closer in type of philosophy to such as Ibn 'Arabī, Suhrawardī, Lu Hsiang-shan and Dōgen in that basically he is still valiantly trying to defend a type of monism, although one with considerably greater complexity than what we found in the ninth century. The Advaita tradition all through the centuries since Śaṅkara tried to eliminate discrepancies, not to say contradictions, in their denial of the reality of *difference*. This very denial of difference remained the most basic problem. Before going into this topic Citsukha, following tradition, has already treated the other typical posits and proofs for other major aspects of his Advaita Vedānta, such as the self-luminosity (*svayaṃprakāśa*) of Brahman/*ātman*, the 'contingency' of the world, the problem of radical ignorance (*avidyā*), the indescribability (*anirvacanīya*) of Brahman, and the claim that all the Upaniṣadic scriptures can and must be interpreted as referring directly to *nirguṇa*-Brahman. Needless to say, this entails a lot of logical manipulation of the texts, and Citsukha, no less than his predecessors among post-Śaṅkara Advaitins, is quite capable of handling these logical matters. But when it comes to what is considered to be the undivided unity of all the Upaniṣadic scriptures, he has to go into a very complex chain of arguments, since very obviously there are contradictory statements, in the whole corpus. Others openly acknowledge and adjust the discrepancies as intelligently as possible, whereas ever since Śaṅkara all Advaitins are duty-bound, as it were, to deny that there are any discrepancies whatsoever, what appear to be discrepancies being only due to our ignorance of *avidyā*. Much of this manner of dealing also involves the marvellous attempt to purge the *Tat Tvam Asi* (That Thou Art) of all sense of otherness by minimizing to meaninglessness the *Tvam* aspect.

In all of these points Citsukha studied the positions of his predecessors very carefully before adding his own supplementary definitions and expositions, usually taking each point through the various *pramāṇas*. But this is especially critical in the case of *svataḥ-prāmāṇya* and *śakti*. Although Śaṅkara himself had taken the *śakti* concept into consideration, he had left it without much enlargement. But in the other systems, especially in the Śaiva tradition but even pivotally in the Tantric system which had become extremely popular by Citsukha's time, Śakti is even elevated above Śiva and in a sense becomes equivalent to *saguṇa*-Brahman, if not even to *nirguṇa*-Brahman. Hence again, *historically* Citsukha has a different task to face than that which Śaṅkara of his immediate interpreters had.

The *svataḥ-prāmāṇya* is simply the purely logical concept that sooner or later the locus of irreducibility of any argument has to be acknowledged in some necessary axioms and postulates, as in Geometry. Citsukha reviews the traditional manner in which both the Mīmāṃsā and the Nyāya logicians deal with it, and there is nothing essentially new here. But the *śakti* concept whereby it becomes self-evident that necessary axioms and postulates are irreducible, poses a real problem for the strict Advaitin who does not like any 'otherness' at all and, as it were, would like to see his coins with the same stamp on both sides. The Sanskrit language being very flexible for philosophical concepts, basically Citsukha simply posits the parallel concept of *sva-śakti* or self-manifesting of the self-validity of intrinsically necessary propositions. Since the only truly irreducible concept is *nirguṇa*-Brahman, automatically the *sva-śakti* makes it possible for every logical proposition concerning every possible concept or Upaniṣadic scripture to refer back to that *nirguṇa*-Brahman.

Citsukha must qualify the *śakti* concept as being inherently plural. There is no one *śakti* but many *śaktis*, whose function is to make various interpretations of the *śrutis* not only possible but activated. Indeed, each inference in a logical operation is, as it were, the result of the operation of its own *śakti*. As is likewise true of the relation between Tao and *teh* or between *stasis* and *dynamis* in Aristotle, without any activating *śakti* the original proposition would not yield any possible inference at all and therefore each proposition would simply remain in its own unrelated isolation, since it is the *śakti* of concepts and propositions to bring them into activated relationships. Hence, since relationships are never single-ended, the *śaktis* that bring them into play must be plural. Thus, not only with logical propositions but even with words themselves, their *śaktis* are what makes them communicative, through mutual connections between them. Thus a logical chain has been established whereby all *śabda*, all words, as part of the nature of the All-encompassing Brahman, ultimately, through their *śaktis*, lead to the concept of Brahman. Hence Citsukha can round out his argument by saying that the *śaktis* are admittedly within *māyā* but have the capacity to lead us beyond *māyā* to Brahman, somewhat like the classical metaphor of removing a thorn by using another thorn.

On the theme of refutation of difference one can find much in terms of both contrasts and comparisons. Dōgen, for example, through his system of *sādhana* attempts as most authentic Zen patriarchs to get beyond the dualities to the Supreme Immediacy of the Suchness, Tathatā, or Dharmakāya Buddha; but, on the other hand, there is radical contrast and even vehement open hostility on the part of Madhva and the Islamic and Christian scholastics in the Aristotelian tradition. Indeed, if enlarged sufficiently this theme could involve the whole range of the Great Summas Period.

Citsukha uses the age-old method known as *virodha-parihāra* or removal of contradictions, which attempts to demonstrate that without the basic stance of non-difference his opponents will sooner or later refute themselves, or at least prove inconsistent with themselves. In his refutation of the Buddhist position that "difference is the very nature of things" Citsukha is evidently not referring to the Yogācāra or the Mādhyamika schools but to the Sarvāstivādins or the even earlier classical realist schools of Buddhist philosophy which emphasized the *kṣaṇavāda* over virtually everything. In short, where is the locus of the difference? If it is in the thing itself that would be contradictory, since nothing can be different from itself in its own nature. But if it be in the relation between itself and what it is becoming, then what will guarantee its continuity. For if there even be an unlimited continuity of things-in-difference or differences-in-things, the situation of dependency on that-from-which-it-is-different implies an underlying non-difference; for otherwise there would be utter chaos, confusion and general disorder, if indeed there would 'be' anything at all. For difference would in that case even prevent anything from coming into existence; therefore, Advaita!

Citsukha then goes on to examine the situation with attributes. Here the difficulty lies not with the Buddhists but with the Bhaṭṭas: "The perception of difference between the qualifying attribute and qualified is possible only when both of them and their mutual relation are cognized at a time."[8] What is involved here is the centuries-long controversy about *savikalpa pratyakṣa* and *nirvikalpa pratyakṣa* which had been debated ever since the seventh century at least. Citsukha's basic stance is in the infinite regress fallacy. As Sarma words it: "...For in order to differentiate the difference of a thing and its attribute another difference is required, for that another, and so on."[9] Since there is so much confusion about whether we indeterminately perceive a determinate object, and/or determinately perceive an indeterminate object without further theorizing about it, difference either way must be under suspicion as not very reliable.

An important theme for any Advaitin is whether we perceive dyads as such; and even if so, does such a perception then contradict the Advaita non-dualistic metaphysics. The Advaitin *non*-dualists emphasize this negative way of putting the matter and object to being called "monists" as asserting too much. Their *Brahma-vidyā* or *Brahma-sākṣātkāratva* is a *darśan*, a *vidyā*, and not a *tattva*; it is a vision, not a principle; and it is rather on the order of insights and inspirations rather than expostulations and argumentations. It is a matter of the logic of reduction rather than of induction or deduction, so that where dualities occur or dyads emerge or conflicts and polarizations come into play, one should rather seek the background milieu or the Tao in which these phenomena are operative.

According to Citsukha, we really do not perceive two's as such at first. The notion is superimposed by our minds and by habitual association of the individualities involved. As for the objection that this does not prove his ultimate non-duality, the reply is simply that that would be premature since he is only refuting false views, not asserting any others, in confidence that falsehoods being removed the Truth will shine forth. Citsukha argues, we never make simultaneous inferences any more than we make simultaneous perceptions. Even though there may be only a momentary subconscious difference between these different functions, the mind only performs one function at a time, and only later on integrates them into *gestalten*. Hence the notion that inferences give us two-ness is unsound.

The problem of size as Citsukha treated it is actually the same problem that troubles us more than ever now that we have electronic microscopes and radio telescopes. The extent of sizes large and small has in recent times been dramatically enlarged, stretched indeed in a mind-boggling way; but philosophically does the problem just remain the same? Concerning Citsukha's view of space (*dik*), the bold-faced assertion is that it is not an intelligible concept. This might seem blindly dogmatic if not preposterous, not only from the broader perspective of the history of science in any civilization and the full wide-ranging field of comparative philosophy, but from the standpoint of the history of Indian philosophy itself. But then Dignāga and his successors had done a rather devastating job of undermining time and other 'material' categories, reminding us that, even though at the pragmatic level we must deal with them as though they were real, they are after all at best only ideas. Further reflection would put us back into the long history of the treatment of Zeno's paradoxes, which were never forgotten, especially by the Muslim *Falsafah* and the Byzantine philosopher-humanist-classicists. The history of science in India is only slowly being mapped out; thus we cannot make any accusations against Advaita's supposed neglect or disparagement of science as merely *māyā* so that there is no worth in tinkering with the "facts of the world". Although it would seem that the Madhvas would make better scientists by virtue of their being realists, thus far we have little information about the extent to which such assertions could be justified historically.

One may ask whether Citsukha, by over-employing the *prāsaṅgika* method of exhaustive refutation of everybody else, had not refuted himself also so that he should have surrendered to the Śūnyavādins or Mādhyamika 'sceptics'. Needless to say the controversial nature of all these points was not ended once and for all by Citsukha any more than by the debate between Ibn 'Arabī or Suhrawardī and their opponents in the Muslim world, or between the Chu Hsi school of Neo-Confucianism and the Lu Hsiang-shan school, or between the followers of Dōgen and the followers of Nichiren. Perhaps it still remains frameable in terms of where one locates the 'somehows', whether at the practical level or the theoretical level—or even, Advaita style, to push them back and back until all 'somehows' disappear. But not all thinkers are convinced that they will or even can disappear, at least this side of some super-*nirvāṇa* that would be the Supremely Ultimate *Pralaya* from which would never again emerge all of this that we call *saṃsāra*.

18. Dōgen

Dōgen (1200-1253) is the First Patriarch of the Sōtō school of Zen Buddhism. However, he "objected to calling his school the Zen-shū or Sōtō-shū, since this intimated that it was merely one sect of Buddhism; he believed it *was* Buddhism."[1] Dōgen's variety of Zen shared the belief of other Kamakura sects of the thirteenth century that a single practice (for Dōgen, *zazen*) was the way to enlightenment or the Pure Land. In the Pure Land sects there was a tendency to include other practices in the one best practice; however, Dōgen tended to exclude all other practices from his way. He "saw no compromise and believed that his Dharma *alone* represented Absolute Truth. . . .Such an uncompromising attitude was unlikely to win Dōgen popularity."[2] And it did not. Sōtō became popular only after Dōgen.

Eight years before his birth the Kamakura shogunate was established by the Minamoto clan. Founders of parallel or rival sects were active in various ways throughout Dōgen's life: Eisai, Honen, Shinran, Nichiren and others. The government regulated or curtailed the sects at will. At the same time that new sects were arising, older forms of Buddhism were suffering decline in both discipline and morale as well as morality. Dōgen was greatly disturbed by the secular and religious corruptions in his native land. Indeed, Dōgen lived and died amidst a tangle of political, religious and natural changes, crises and catastrophes. Virtually any stability of thought, any right-mindfulness of conduct in

Dōgen's life, was purchased by this philosopher-monk out of very unpropitious and even harsh circumstances.

The time of Dōgen's birth was marred, according to some interpretations, by the refusal of the clan into which he was born to accept him as legitimate. When he was two, his father died; when he was seven, his mother died.

> As the greatly bereaved young boy watched the smoke drift from the incense during his mother's funeral he perceived the transitory nature of all things. It was at this time the resolve to find the true way awakened in him—both his parents were gone and he was now determined to overcome this ephemeral world of pain and pleasure, joy and sadness.[3]

As a Zen master, he said, "When I was quite young, the realization of the transiency of this world stirred my mind towards seeking the Way."[4] At age thirteen he was initiated into training as a Buddhist monk; but the very next year he experienced a fundamental doctrinal doubt and began to travel in search of the right master. The Jōkyu War occurred the same year he became the disciple of Myōzen (1217).

> This war was a result of an emperor's attempt, which failed, to regain some of the power taken from the emperors by shoguns and others. "Its miseries and sufferings—especially banishment of three ex-emperors (all were related to Dōgen's family), numberless bloody executions, and the involvement of armed monks—may have prompted Dōgen to decide to study in China."[5]

In 1225, at age twenty-five, he experienced enlightenment in China under master Ju-ching, from whom two years later he received the seal of the Sōtō sect which he introduced to Japan.

In 1230 when Dōgen moved to a temple in Fukakusa, famine and natural calamities rampaged all over the country, and two years later when he began his masterwork, *Shōbōgenzō* (*The Eye and Treasury of the True Law*), Kyoto was filled with the dead from starvation. Dōgen's neighbor-monks considered him and his followers too innovative. "They descended on his monastery and attempted to burn it down in the summer of 1243. . . .Consequently, Dōgen accepted the invitation of his lay disciple Hatanō Yoshishige, the daimyo of Echizen (present-day Fukui prefecture) to establish a monastery in his domain."[6] In 1253 he finished *Shōbōgenzō* (or was still perfecting it) and died on August 28 of that year.

"The Rinzai school was never to attain unity as an order and Dōgen's following would probably have shared the same fate if it had not become a popular mass movement with a necessity to focus upon the personality of the faunder,"[7] as well as on some of the lay-oriented, faith-emphasizing teachings. The shift toward a popular movement was made by the second successor of Dōgen, Tettsū Gikai. Tettsū and the disciple Gien had a complicated dispute which resulted in Tettsū and his group of "progressives", who were concerned with making Sōtō a mass movement, abandoning the headquarters at Echizen to Gien and his conservative monastic followers and setting up a new centre in Kaga.

Tettsū's disciple Keizen Jōkin (1268-1325), who is known to modern Sōtō followers as "the second patriarch", had been exposed to several Rinzai scholars as well as to the masters of his own sect, and had assimilated teachings from the older traditions. More important even than Keizan's ability to borrow and synthesize from diverse sources was his sense of people's needs. Although the older sects of Buddhism sometimes expanded into rural areas, they seemed less aware of basic problems of the masses such as funerals: "This was one area the followers of Keizan entered, assimilating popular exoteric rites of the older sects. . .and devising simple funeral and memorial services that featured sermons on Buddhist teachings for warriors and commoners alike."[8] Sōtō priests initiated social reforms, engaged in the building of roads, irrigation systems and bridges, and set up forms of medical treatment. The precedent for what they did existed in at least one of Dōgen's statements: "To row a boat, or to construct a bridge over a river is equally bodhisattva's practice of giving."[9] Eventually even Dōgen's quotations on faith became what the Matsunagas have termed "the nucleus of a mass movement". *Zazen* was not replaced but it was more than slightly displaced, so far as laymen were concerned, by faith. "By these means, the Sōtō sect was able to attract the masses, whereas Rinzai Zen failed to do so, largely because Sōtō followers were not restricted by the aristocratic (temple) framework. Isolated in the countryside, Sōtō priests felt a natural familiarity with the peasants."[10]

Dōgen must have been tempted to popularize his version of the *Dharma*, for popularization almost at any price was the current of the times as may be seen with Honen, Shinran and others. However, not only did some rivals oppose Dōgen at court powerfully and effectively, but one competitor, Bennen, set up a popular form of Zen almost in the shadow of Dōgen's monastery. "Dōgen's move to Echizen removed his school for the remainder of his lifetime from the mainstream of Kamakura Buddhism."[11] The intolerable pressures of opposition and competition explain Dōgen's move socially and psychologically, but is there any philosophical justification for his "retreat"?

In Hindu tradition even today—and one may well suppose that something of this came through to China in Buddhist guise—the expression straight from the *Gītā* is there: *sthita-prajñā* ("stability-wisdom") which means *staying put* in the North American idiom, the idea being that if a real yogi is worthy others will come to him and he does not need to go to them. Actually this is of considerable historic interest because the same typology between the wandering begging friars and the settled-in-one-place *sthita-prajñā* monks is definitely generalizable. The Benedictines and the Carthusians "stay put", whereas the friars (basically Franciscans, Dominicans and Carmelites) are supposed to wander and teach as they beg their way. Likewise among Ṣūfīs one may find both types. In Japan Ippen and Dōgen are examples of these types, each excellent in his own way rather than one being superior to the other.

Dōgen's guru Ju-ching gave him the parting admonition that he "should retire deep into the forests and educate only a few elect disciples."[12] Scholars are not all agreed evidently as to Dōgen's reason for establishing such strict discipline, even excluding women from his immediate following. Maybe in part it was not only his guru's salient advice but sad experience and disgust with all the corruption that prevailed in the so-called monasteries in both Japan and China.

As for the accusation that Dōgan was "aristocratic", this is probably both true and defensible. In the wider globel context there were very few commoners in any part of Eurasia who were literate enough to receive any more than the most menial role in any monastic community be it Basilian, Benedictine, Carthusian, Ṣūfī, Hindu, Buddhist or whatever; and as a matter of fact many in such conditions were slaves. Better to be a slave in a monastic community than a beggar on the streets, we might surmise. At least one would not go hungry. But the monastic life is necessarily a selective process. Not everyone is fitted for it, whereas "the elect who were chosen to join their ranks and attain Buddhahood would feel the call to come in search of the perfect master—as for the rest, they would merely hope to benefit from the virtues acquired by the monks."[13] Interestingly enough, just as in China Dōgen had received more spiritual help from a humble kitchen-monk than from most higher-placed monks, so in Japan it was a humble layman who was instrumental in inviting and serving as patron for Dōgen to establish his retreat-house monastery at Echizen.

Dōgen implied in "Bendōwa" that "women and layman were capable of Enlightenment, an idea he later seemingly set aside in his preoccupation with the monastic life."[14] The Matsunagas inform us that Nichiren and other Kamakura religious leaders made an important place for women in their respective sects. "And even Dōgen, who advocated the monastic life, was known to state that women were not necessarily inferior to men, since intrinsic worth was determined by the harmony of one's life with the way, and of one's body with the right law. His school, as it became a mass movement, received strong support from its female followers."[15] Although contradictory statements can be cited from Dōgen, Kim is correct when he says, "Thus Dōgen ridicules the Buddhist practice of no admittance to woman (*nyonin-kinzei*) as 'a laughable matter in Japan'."[16] Dōgen tells with approval of two nuns who achieved such status and recognition for their insight that monks sought their instruction. Even a master made prostration before one and became her disciple. Of sceptical monks, Dōgen asks, "What makes you noble just because you are a man?"[17]

Kim categorically states that "Dōgen's religion abolished the separation between monkhood and laity."[18] Nevertheless in other passages, as Kim hastens to point out, Dōgen argues for the clear superiority of monkhood. This inconsistency poses one of the thorniest problems in Dōgen studies, which may be illustrated by two quotations written about three years apart. In the first, Dōgen asserts that anyone who equates a layman with a Buddha or patriarch has "the mentality of criminals who have fallen into the darkest hell."[19] In the other Dōgen, writes:

> Anyone who practices and attains the Buddhist Dharma, even a girl of seven, will be the leader and compassionate father of all monks, nuns, lay people and sentient beings. In (the Lotus Sūtra) the daughter of a dragon king became Buddha. She should be venerated, honored and respected like all the Buddhas and tathagatas.... Those who do not know this and lack the right transmission are to be greatly pitied.[20]

One way to resolve this stunning contradiction is by assuming, as Dōgen did, that "renunciation is the seed of Buddhahood"[21] and that therefore any layman, even a woman or child, who displays Buddhahood must have renounced the world. Or we could simply follow Nakamura here and elsewhere: "Though it is doubtless true that Dōgen was a distinguished thinker as well as a high-minded spiritual leader, he was not the sort of thinker who developed a logically system of thought."[22]

Dōgen vacillated between seeing some value in secular literature (he wrote a volume of poetry) and considering it a waste of time. Sometimes he warned students away even from Buddhist literature, but he imported from China to his monastery a library as a functional part of monastic life. Nakamura says that Dōgen thought "Buddhism should be practiced for its own sake and not as literature, which has no value for genuine devotees of Buddhism"; nevertheless, he was a great poet: "His Chinese poems are lofty and elegent, while his *tankas* vibrate with warm sympathies for the beauties of nature."[23] Kim probably puts Dōgen's ascetic withdrawal from culture, the world, and especially the social order in the clearest light:

> (It) was Dōgen's method of coping with his sense of pessimism

> ...in the intractable secular context. He became entirely concerned with the education of a select few in order to exemplify his vision of an ideal community as a challenge to the world. In this regard, his and his followers' ascetic endeavors were as intensely and passionately social as they were personal. Indeed they were intended to transform the world as well as the self.[24]

When Dōgen was finally invited to the Kamakura court in the winter of 1247, he stayed for a few months, but unhappily, and was glad to return to his peaceful (world-transforming) solitude.

Dōgen's chief *kōan*, if he had chosen to use the *kōan*-method rather than *zazen* as the primary meditative discipline, might well have been, "Who certified the first Buddha?" The historical Buddha found enlightenment by vigorous self-reliance, self-reflection and self-effort. He had no teacher. Dōgen had masters but added creatively (if unconsciously) to what they and the Buddhist tradition conveyed to him. Though the enlightenment of the first Buddha would seem, like the First Cause in the systems of Aristotle and Aquinas, to need nothing and no one prior to it, Dōgen writes: "Only Buddhas transmit the Dharma to Buddhas, the partiarchs to patriarchs, this is the nature of attainment. This is the single transmission and therefore is Supreme Enlightenment. Unless one is a Buddha, he cannot certify another Buddha, and unless one obtains the certification of a Buddha, he cannot be a Buddha."[25] And in "Shisho" (the seal of transmission) Dōgen writes: "We have learned that Shakyamuni Buddha received the transmission after Kāśyapa entered parinirvana .... To think that Shakyamuni Buddha did not receive the transmission from Kāśyapa Buddha is the belief of nonbelievers."[26] Dōgen might explain this cyclically: the historical Śākyamuni inherited *Dharma* from Kāśyapa to whom he in turn (from the standpoint of enlightenment) transmits it! But this merely adds another paradox to the one we already have.

Actually, in Dōgen's highly personal but nevertheless authentically Buddhist perspective, enlightenment does not depend upon having a clear conception as to whether there was a first Buddha who needed to authentication. It is not useful to argue that there was or that there was not such a Buddha. Dōgen's point is that enlightened insight is not a mythological creature which has somehow been conceived and born apart from any nurturing womb of tradition or spiritual authority. Moreover, the practical "first cause" of enlightenment is the practice of *zazen* under disciplined obedience to a duly certified master.

If forced to make a doctrinal statement, Dōgen would probably appeal to two ideas to resolve the paradox. First, "If you are not a Buddha you cannot clarify the essence of this principle..."[27] And what is the principle? The "mutual pledge of enlightenment" by which Buddhas authenticate each other: "If you are not a Buddha, you cannot possess the seal of enlightenment; if you do not possess the seal of enlightenment, you cannot be a Buddha."[28] This sounds suspiciously like a Buddhist version of election of the saints or some kind of elitist exclusivism; and sometimes Dōgen does write very exclusivistically, as when he spends several pages showing that Sukō never achieved enlightenment and was not an authentic master but a kind of persistent blockhead.[29] Nevertheless, Dōgen's capacity for seeing Buddhahood everywhere is impressive—and credulous. In "Shiso", for example, he tells us that "there is no place where Buddhas are not" so that chrysanthemums and pine trees transmit the seal of enlightenment.[30] "Even soil, sand, and stones possess the ability to feel sincerity."[31]

Dōgen was confronted with the social-spiritual problem of how to conduct himself as monk and leader so as to be careful of the *Dharma* when, in the worst of times, even its guardians seemed most careless and uncaring. This breakdown of monastic discipline caused Dōgen to welcome his contact with the stricter Theravāda when he encountered it in China, though it was regarded as inferior in Japan (and he continued to repeat the deprecatory formulae concerning it). Nevertheless, Theravāda was a link to the authoritative past, as was also the secret transmission of the *Dharma* through the masters. Thus Dōgen's solution, in part, was to find the most severe master available and so restore the solid precedent in his monastic order (and to an extent in Japan) for right and disciplined practice of the *Dharma*.

Criticizing the practice of Tendai, Shingon and the Pure Land, Dōgen likened the constant chanting of the *nembutsu* "to the fruitless croaking of a frog day and night in the spring rice-field."[32] While Dōgen acutely satirized the sole reliance on the *nembutsu,* he advocated sole reliance on the practice of *zazen.* But is his one way really any better than "croaking" the *nembutsu*? Maybe a human being who insists on many hours of seated meditation (*zazen*) is like a sitting bullfrog which has lost his voice?

Writing in Chinese, Dōgen clarified and refined the actual procedure of *zazen* in a document which he entitled "Fukanzazengi" (Principles for the Promulgation of *Zazen*). Apparently the Tendai clerics for whom Dōgen wrote this treatise did not doubt that *zazen* was one legitimate practice among many. What they did doubt was that it was the one exclusive practice of Buddhism. For this astonishing claim they demanded doctrinal justification. Dōgen took up the challenge and in Japanese recorded an exchange concerning the matter entitled "Bendōwa" (Talk about Undertaking the Way) Careful reading, Kasulis argues, will show that it is record of a failure. Dōgen appealed to scriptural authority and to his own transmission. He was met with scepticism on both accounts. Somewhat in desperation he seems driven to argue that the ultimate source for the way is "not a historical transmission (but) rather the very things experienced in the world: the weeds, flowers, mountains, and water....This is a foreshadowing of the new approach that Dōgen would eventually take. In '*Bendōwa*' however, its significance is not yet recognized."[33] Failure of his appeal to scripture to win a crucial debate may have sent Dōgen "to the things themselves", as modern phenomenologists would say.

Whether indeed the story of the Buddha holding up a flower to his audience, the significance of which was grasped only by Mahākāśyapa who quietly smlied, is apocryphal or not is beside the point. The important thing for all varieties of Zen including Dōgen's is that nonverbal communication was takan as the key to the whole tradition. *Presence*, as Gabriel Marcel might say, is even more important than principle if peace is to be perfected and wisdom (*prajñā*) is to be effected. Or in Japanese terminology, the key to it all is *ishin denshin* (transmission from mind to mind) without the use of words (*furyū monji*).

So far even "pop Zen" is aware of the "Wordless Way". But

what gets overlooked at the currently popular level is that Dōgen is not as wordless or irrationalistic as some of his terminology in raw and undigested form would suggest. The Matsunagas explain his stance in the *Shōbōgenzō* in which he clarified both the intuitive experience and its transmission, communication, or perhaps we should say, evocation.

> As he reasoned, if it be possible for individuals to receive the intuitive experience of Enlightenment by observing the serenity of nature and thereby "hearing" the Buddha's preaching in the whispering of the wind or the bubbling of a mountain stream, then it also must be possible to penetrate the symbolic language of the scriptures and receive the same experience.[34]

Discounting for the moment Dōgen's use of hyperbole to make his points, the following statement at least shows he did not mean for his followers to take language lightly: "You should clearly understand that, because everyday language (*kajōgo*) is the whole universe, the whole universe is everyday language."[35]

As unconventional as Zen Buddhists have at times seemed to outsiders, Bardwell Smith reminds us of the dynamic balance that is working when he says: "The most characteristic tension or rhythm within Zen Buddhism may be its honouring of tradition on the one hand, and its insistence that tradition be transcended on the other."[36] The term "rhythm" may more accurately reflect the Zen reality than our perhaps heavier word "paradox". The "wordless way of Zen" is like the fading away to silence of the thunder before the next crash. But the Zen tradition "hears" the boom of the silence. Bodhidharma who brought Zen to China in 520 A.D. taught:

> A special transmission outside the scriptures.
> No dependence on words or letters.
> Direct pointing at the soul of man
> Seeing into one's nature and the attainment of Buddhahood.[37]

Because of Dōgen's time or temperament, the boom of silence

was receding relatively (but not permanently) into the quietness of sound teaching. "The blend of sounds and quietness are as basic as the flow of seasons into each other."[38] Or, in Dōgen's own exact words, "The emergence of our own body and mind is the appearance of all the elements in a unified whole" which "is beyond words, a wordless word, an echo of the absolute independence of saying or not-saying."[39]

The context in which the term "wordless word" is found shows that ultimate enlightenment brings with it the emergence of all the elements. Such enlightenment is "the elements experiencing their own existence with nothing extra. One form is composed of all elements and is body and mind. ... Time is completed and actualized by this underlying unity which exists everywhere."[40] The title of this chapter, "Kaiinzammai", says all this and also shows again Dōgen's indebtedness to Kegon. The Japanese title translates the Sanskrit *sāgara mudrā samādhi* which literally means "ocean-imprint *samādhi*" (the highest stage of enlightenment). "These supposedly is the meditation Shakyamuni entered before delivering the *Avataṃsaka* (*Kegon*) *Sūtra.* All truth is at once reflected in that state, just as all images are reflected in a quiet sea. It is the highest form of insight."[41] This is true for Dōgen, because enlightenment simply is this world just as it is, functioning perfectly as it does. One master stated that the great ocean (enlightenment) never contains any corpses (illusion). Dōgen goes much further than this, reflecting Kegon but outstripping it too.

> Even if a corpse is a corpse, when it functions harmoniously with the universe it is contained there. The past and future have their own functions and nothing can be said to stop breathing. All things are contained in one thing, one thing contains one thing, all things contain all things. When this occurs the meaning of "involves the entire universe" emerges. This is *Kaiinsammai.*[42]

The beginner may have some feeling of being dropped in the midst of a kind of Buddhist miscellany when he is first exposed to Dōgen. Little organic connectedness is at first apparent as it would be for example in his contemporary Thomas Aquinas.

"Genjō-kōan" (the opening chapter of the *Shōbōgenzō*, written in 1233), "Bendōwa" (first written chapter, 1231), and "Ikka-myōju" (One Bright Pearl, 1238)—each contains in compact form much of the rest of Dōgen's work and his overall philosophical contribution. A word about Dōgen's method in the *Shōbōgenzō* is in order before we proceed to the substance of his insights. Many chapters begin with a brief dialogue or anecdote usually involving a master and one or more disciples. Dōgen sometimes gives several responses to the *kōan* or question; or else several interpretations of the answer, which is characteristically more of an enigmatic response (another *kōan*?) than answer in a straightforward intellectual sense. These stories and their pnrases and sometimes their personae are held up for reflection, admiration or condemnation as seems appropriate to Dōgen. Contradictions are sometimes present between given chapters and even within them. Some chapters just stop without apparent conclusion. In some Dōgen poses a question and commands, "Answer quickly". In others he seems to recapitulate and encourage further deep thought on the matter at hand. Dōgen, like other thinkers of this period, "takes off" from a scriptural text or, even more commonly, a monastery tradition. Unlike many such thinkers he seems to be freed from as well as by his text to speak creatively, imaginatively, and at times fancifully.

Dōgen's philosophy is perhaps most tersely summarized by the three section-headings which the Matsunagas use to organize their treatment of Dōgen's thought (plus our suggested fourth heading): (1) Practice Equals Attainment, (2) The Manifestation of Ultimate Reality is Genjō Kōan (and, we add, it is "One Bright Pearl"), (3) All Existents Are the Buddha Nature (each moment is totality), (4) Life is Time, the Moment is All.

Practice Equals Attainment. Even after enlightenment, practice of *zazen* is important because there is no dichotomy between the discipline of means and the attainment of ends. "Zazen is not the means to enlightenment, zazen itself is the completed action of the Buddha. Zazen itself is pure, natural enlightenment."[43] Attainment is *in* the means so they can never be separate. According to Nakamura, Dōgen taught that contemplation should be realized in one's actions in everyday life. "So-called contemplations are everyday activities like sweeping the ground and the floor."[44] One of Dōgen's most important related ideas is "total exertion" (*gūjin*). This doctrine means in part that every thing or act is itself and nothing else; in part that every experience is somehow a reflection of all experience; in part that the meaning of a word is totally exerted so that there is only that one meaning throughout the entire universe at a single instant; and finally, that all dualism is empty and that "emptiness is emptiness". In Dōgen's own words, "He who knows a single object comprehends the entire universe."[45] Or, "A single total experience is a single thing in its totality. The total experience of a single thing is one with that of all things."[46]

A good comparative theological study might be an investigation of Dōgen's un-Zenlike emphasis on repentance and faith (and maybe even grace) as prerequisites for right practice:

> If you are physically or mentally lazy and lack faith you must repent before Buddha and show your earnest resolve. The virtue of repentance purifies the mind; it also increases our faith and improves our attitudes for practice. Once pure faith is manifested, discrimination of self and others ceases—there is equality and harmony. Buddha's great compassion also emerges and our virtue benefits and influences all beings, living and non-living.... If we repent, surely we will have Buddha's assistance (even if we cannot perceive it). ... The power of repentance removes all sins.[47]

According to Kim, "zazen-only cannot be fully understood apart from the consideration of faith."[48]

Ultimate Reality as Genjō Kōan (and One Bright Pearl). "Genjō-kōan" is the title of the first chapter of the *Shōbōgenzō*. The Matsunagas suggest that Dōgen may have chosen this title to contradict the famous *kōan* master Ta-hui who is known to have written a work with the same title. In it Ta-hui stressed the riddle-like *kōan* as the way to attain *satori*. "*Genzō* literally means 'to manifest and achieve,' while Dōgen considered *kōan*, as a 'public document' or 'standard of judgment,' to be synonymous with truth."[49] Dōgen writes in the *Shōbōgenzō*:

> The fish swims in water without ever mastering the water, the bird flies in the air without ever mastering the air. . . and if the bird is placed outside of air it will surely die, as the fish will surely die placed outside of water. One must realize that water is life and air is life. . . . Considering this fact, if there should be birds and fish who try to fly or swim only after they have mastered the air and water, then they will never find a path (to fly) nor a place (to swim) in either the air or water. When one realizes this in accord with his own actions, then that is *genjō kōan*.
>
> To master the Buddha way is to master oneself,
> To master oneself is to forget oneself,
> To forget oneself is to realize the myriads of dharmas,
> To realize the myriads of dharmas is to drop one's body and mind, and the body and mind of others.[50]

"To drop off the body and the mind" is one of Dōgen's favorite expressions and sometimes one of his most puzzling. Once in a talk to his monks he explained "dropping off the body" as willingness to endure pain and severe self-discipline without regard to one's health, and "dropping off the mind" as shedding one's preconceptions about Buddhism.[51]

One of the most important and difficult chapters of the *Shōbōgenzō* is "Ikkamyōju" (One Bright Pearl). The key to it is the Buddhist teaching, "The entire universe is one bright pearl." This teaching can be approached historically through a look at the sect of Kegon (Chinese, Hua-yen) which developed a philosophy of 'Totality', in the other words, a theory of the total interdependence of all things and all thoughts. In Kegon, the term *Dharmadhātu* (lit. Realm of the *dharmas*, or reality) "was used philosophically to denote the subjective essence of Enlightenment, Absolute truth and the all-embracing totality of the infinite universes (realms of experience) revealed within Enlightenment."[52] The Matsunagas further explain:

> Devotionally, the *Dharmadhātu* was equivalent to the *Dharmakāya*, symbolized in Kegon thought as the great Buddha Mahāvairocana, who manifests the infinite universe but yet is inherent within each and every existent. Certain problems

> do arise when the subjective nature of this concept is overlooked, since it then would appear to offer a speculative metaphysical world view very contrary to the teachings of the historical Buddha. But without a subjective experiential approach, Kegon thought is logically inconceivable, since it violates the basic principles of reasoning.
>
> Experientially in Kegon philosophy, the entire universe is embraced within a single thought.[53]

Artistically, the Kegon doctrine of totality was cast in bronze as the Great Buddha (Daibutsu) Mahāvairocana, "the centre of the universe", which is housed in the Todaiji in Nara and was reconstructed for the second time when Dōgen was six.

Philosophically, it may not be too bold to claim that Kegon teaching was incarnated fully in Dōgen's thought, especially in his exposition on One Bright Pearl. The Matsunagas further write concerning Kegon teachings: "all existents, while still preserving their individual identity, mutually interrelate and interpenetrate each other."[54] "Each individual dharma is subjectively viewed as equivalent to the totality of the universe." Adherents of Kegon believed, for instance, that "if a rock was equivalent to the totality of the universe (tathatā) and a rooftile likewise, then the rock and the rooftile must be experientially identical despite their completely different appearances."[55] The legend of Indra's Net brings us perhaps closest to the one bright pearl. According to the legend, "the great god Indra had a net woven with jewels tied into a mesh; in the brilliance of the light, each of these jewels reflected each other infinitely."[56]

Logically it seems impossible for one thought, tile, jewel or pearl to encompass all the rest, indeed the whole universe, for either the individuality of the individual or the apparent reality of the universe necessarily becomes an illusion. The whole universe cannot be completely in the one bright pearl (or atom or whatever) and at the same time not be completely in it. Commonsense realists gag at the suggestion that a thing or *dharma* is more than just that thing, but various kinds of idealists often insist that a thing has "depth" or self-transcendence and so may be constituted or defined by its "external" relations, especially to mind. Dōgen offends both idealists (with his nominalism) and realists (with his one bright pearl of universal enlightenment). Realization, Dōgen seems to believe, takes in or absorbs both the insights and illusions of the monk, and also somehow transcends all part/whole dichotomies. Dōgen writes in his chapter "One Bright Pearl":

> All the universe is the unceasing process of pursuing things and making them the self, pursuing the self and making it things. . . . Because of the pursuing of things and making them the self the universe in its entirety is unceasing. And because its own nature is prior to such activity, it is beyond grasp even through the essence of the activity.
>
> One bright pearl is able to express Reality without naming it, and we can recognize this pearl as its name. One bright pearl communicates directly through all time; being through all the past unexhausted, it arrives through all the present. While there is a body now, a mind now, they are the bright pearl. That stalk of grass, this tree, is not a stalk of grass, is not a tree; the mountains and rivers of this world are not the mountains and rivers of this world. They are the bright pearls. ... Perplexed thoughts, doubts, and man's accepting or rejecting are but passing, small-scale notions. Moreover, this is only (the pearl) appearing as small-scale notions.
>
> Should we not cherish such infinite colourations and brilliance? Each of the many facets of its radiant variegations are the merit of the entire universe—who could usurp it? Not a man in the marketplace could throw a tile away. . . . Even if there is perplexed or troubled thinking, it is not apart from the bright pearl. It is not a deed or thought produced by something that is not the bright pearl. Therefore, both coming and going in the Black Mountain's Cave of Demons are themselves nothing but the one bright pearl.[57]

The cave of demons (illusion) is usually rejected by Zen, but it is as real as enlightenment for Dōgen. Even the discarded tile is not useless. As Waddell and Abe explain, "The idea here seems to be that since all things—even the proverbially useless tile—are the bright pearl, they are beyond being accepted or rejected, picked up or thrown away. Man cannot usurp *or* throw away the bright pearl."[58] The one bright pearl is in time and temporal processes as well as in the spatial universe. The "Zenki" chapter of the *Shōbōgenzō* brings this out even more clearly. "Zenki" means "the total activity of life and death." "The ultimate goal is detachment from, that is total immersion in, life and death."[59]

All Existents Are the Buddha Nature. According to the Matsunagas, Dōgen deliberately misread the famous Buddhist saying, "Everywhere exists the Buddha nature", to mean, "All existents are the Buddha nature". His polemical interest in this change of emphasis was to refute as clearly as possible two misconceptions which had grown up among Buddhists who had fallen away from the *anātman* teaching (no soul, no substance) of the Buddha. There is a rather universal human pining for permanence which infests even Buddhism, the philosophy most dedicated to dispelling the mirage of permanence. Against this mirage Dōgen liked to quote Hui-neng's phrase "Impermanence is the Buddha nature". For, as the Matsunagas explain, Dōgen "believed that the mountains, trees, water, and all manifestations of Reality (*genjō kōan*), including human beings, were the Buddha nature."[60]

Another misconception which Dōgen wished to overcome was the idea that Buddhahood could be equated with all functions of the ignorant mind, even the most unworthy ones. If all existents are the Buddha nature, to exclude base functions of the mind from Buddhahood would seem a logically impossible task. How Dōgen accomplished this task—or, indeed, whether he did—is not clear. Maybe a monk without practice would be to Dōgen like a bird without air, a fish without water, or a man without life. Maybe, in short, a nonpracticing monk would be neither a monk nor an 'existent' but rather a logical anomaly if not an outright contradiction in terms.

The key technical term is *sokushinzebutsu* (Mind is the Buddha). Dōgen interprets this to mean not just any kind of mind or 'minding' but what we might call "high-mindedness" or "dedicated minding". Direct experience, with no splitting up of reality into experienced, experiencer, and experiencing, or appearances and their underlying metaphysical entities, or even illusion and reality—such non-discriminating experience, Dōgen seems to suggest, will overcome all artificial separations or divisions. So one thing really cannot (or need not) symbolize or somehow "stand in place of" another. But surprisingly enough, according to the Matsunagas' translation, an element of symbolism enters here. In Dōgen's own words: "Various Buddhas symbolize Śākyamuni Buddha, and Śākyamuni Buddha symbolizes the 'mind is the Buddha' (*sokushinzebutsu*). . . . When one becomes an Enlightened Buddha, together with the various Buddhas of the past, present and future, certainly one will become Śākyamuni Buddha, this is precisely *sokushinzebutsu*."[61]

Life Is Time, the Moment Is All. If *all* is contained or can be contained in each moment (the classical Buddhist *kṣaṇa*), we need no symbols to bridge the chasm between one moment and any previous or succeeding ones. Therefore, the need to let the Buddha's moment of enlightenment symbolize mine, or vice versa, is 'symbolic' only—that is, vanishes as any kind of literal statement.

In order to illuminate the plenary moment, the Matsunagas discuss "The Absolute Now or Totality of the Moment". We could also designate this as a discussion of "Time and the Law of Interdependent Origination" (*pratītya-samutpāda*), "wherein all existents are believed to rise and fall in accord with interrelated conditions."[62] While this is part of a very ancient Buddhist understanding, Dōgen gives it his distinctive imprint. The major source for his position is the chapter *U-ji* (Being-Time) in the *Shōbōgenzō* which is devoted to the contention that "existence is time".

One of the captions under which the Matsunagas treat Dōgen's notion of time is "Self-identity of Existence and Time". Evidently this is a sort of echo of what we encountered in Dignāga (c. 400-480 A.D.) who thought of time as ultimately unreal but pragmatically inescapable: like the rising and setting of the sun, the beating of biological hearts, the rhythm of music, or the still more homely examples the Matsunagas give when they remind us that watch or no watch, clock or no clock, time concerns finite, immediate happenings, like the crowing of the rooster, going to school or going to the office, or the smell of food that is cooking —or a breakfast that is burning, or a person getting wet in a cold rainstorm, or the many 'thing-events' which Japanese artists are fond of depicting. Illustrations aside, the general principle is clear enough (and perhaps Kantian enough): time does not deal with *Being* but with *Existence*. Kasulis helps us dig deeper into Dōgen's "existential" meaning of time:

> Dōgen then asks us to investigate our experience. Does time really fly away? If it did, there would be a gap between ourselves *as* time and things *as* time. Hence, the idea that time flies away must be based on self-delusion: misled by a metaphor that points to one small aspect of time-consciousness, we have convinced ourselves that we experience something that we have not really experienced at all. This does not imply that there is one and only one correct characterization of a particular thing. For example, as Dōgen points out in the "Genjō-kōan" fascicle, the ocean is a different thing-as-experienced to a fish swimming in it, to a deva looking at it from heaven and to a man in a boat. The occasion or situation is different in each case, so the "ocean" is legitimately characterized respectively as a "jeweled palace," a "necklace," and a "great circle." That is to say, the occasion determines the perspective that any given expression will take. In short, the meaning of an expression always has a contextual dimension. Consequently, Dōgen frequently analyzes the classical Zen *kōans* from the contextual point of view since the situation in which something is said is crucial to understanding what is being said.
>
> Can we talk at all about that which is independent of situation or perspective? For the fish, the deva, and the person, is there anything in common about ocean-as-experienced? Yes, for all of them, it is simply "the presencing" (*genjō*). To ground one's experience in this prereflective experience is the key to Zen practice and therefore the essence of enlightenment as well; to experience this presencing is to focus all of one's energies.[63]

In short, all time, or every time, is "Specific Time". "For example", the Matsunagas explain, "at this specific moment of time, a dog is strerched out on the study floor before the fire with its head resting upon a book."

—a few minutes from now the dog may be outside playing with its mates, the book back upon the shelf, the fire dying out and the lights off in an empty study. Each moment contains a similar multitude of relationships. Dōgen could even imagine the condition of the peak of a mountain or depth of an ocean in a moment of time—far from the far reaches of the stars to each individual spot on earth, the single isolated moment holds an infinite number of happenings and captures numberless existents.[64]

Would Dōgen, were he alive today, have difficulty believing in this kind of capturing, or strong mutual interrelationship of everything, in the light of the unimaginable distances of modern astronomy?

Dōgen, who is typically fond of paradoxes, often uses the phrase, "the continuity of non-continuity". As Dōgen himself explains it in the *Shōbōgenzō*:

> Firewood becomes ash and cannot revert back to firewood, however, one should not cling to the idea that firewood precedes and ash follows. We must realize that firewood is at the state of firewood existence, and even though we may consider its future and past, before and after, these are separate. Ash is at the state of ash existence, and has its own before and after. Just as once firewood becomes ash, it can never revert back to firewood, so after death, one can never revert back to birth. It is the tradition of Buddhist Dharma not to consider that birth becomes death, thus it is called non-birth. The fact that death will not become birth is due to the Buddha's non-extinction. Birth is a single state of existence and death is a single state of existence. It is like winter and spring, one should not think that winter can become spring nor does spring become winter.[65]

The Matsunagas' commentary on this reminds us of Meister Eckhart's Eternal Now. In fact they actually use the words "Absolute Eternal Now" and emphasize what they refer to as the "*existential* here and now". Though there is a discrepancy in wording between these ways of speaking and Nāgārjuna's denial of any absolute whatsoever, both agree that only when we stop absolutizing shall we be free to deal with the present moments as they come and go with increasing degrees of freedom.

The caption "Applied Time or Time in Practice" means an extension into practice of the realization of the necessity of non-absolutizing—not an easy way to live, no doubt, but at least for those who are suited to the way of *prajñā* it is the most rewarding since it does not seek for any reward. Dōgen writes:

> Merely considering birth and death are Nirvana, one should neither avoid birth and death nor seek Nirvana; only at such a moment can one become free of birth and death. It is improper to consider that birth leads to death, for birth is a temporary state separate from future and past, therefore in Buddhist Dharma birth is called non-birth. Extinction is also a temporary state separate from past and future, therefore extinction is called non-extinction. So when we speak of birth, there is nothing other than birth, and when we say extinction, there is nothing other than extinction.[66]

The Matsunagas offer this comment: "Since each moment is a totality within itself, the ultimate time becomes sitting-meditation (*shikantaza*). For although by itself the hour possesses no meaning—if the individual occupies it with meditation, he is capable of condensing the experience and wisdom of a hundred years within the moment."[67]

We suggest this metaphysical/pragmatic rule in interpreting Dōgen: The world of experience is as it is (but not quite) with nothing left over (that is, not much). If there is a logical problem with this rule, it is Dōgen's. Kasulis, one of the best interpreters of Dōgen, trips over a zeal for phenomenological rigour when he says, "There is nothing behind this world that is waiting to be manifested; there is just the presencing of what is."[68] This runs directly against Dōgen's own explicit statement in the *Shōbōgenzō*: "Here we must realize that the true forms of the mountains, rivers, and the earth in their original states differ from their existence as natural phenomena." In this same passage, in contrast to his statements locating enlightenment even in illusion Dōgen laments the scarcity of sincere truth-seekers: "It is pitiful that we are living in a treasure mountain but cannot see it. If we develop an enlightenment-seeking mind everything becomes the practice of enlightenment even if we are in the midst of the various worlds of samsara."[69]

In a similar vein, Dōgen is not mystical (that is, not very mystical). The textual proofs of a slight degree of mysticism, which we might term "a thimbleful of Buddha-traces", are scattered like ephemeral dewdrops throughout Dōgen's writings and will be unmistakable to everyone except the person whose soul is too heavy-booted to notice. Dōgen writes: "When you meet Buddha you will see Buddha in your self and others. Do not be amazed or frightened at the appearance of a Great Buddha or doubt the existence of a small one. These diverse forms of the Buddha are in the sound of a valley stream and in the colour of the mountains."[70] The valley stream is just the valley stream, the mountain is just the mountain—and yet a bit more. Joyously but without sentimentality Dōgen specifies what and who the "bit more" are: diverse forms and sizes of the Buddha. "The sound of the valley is His great tongue."[71]

Every reader who has struggled with Dōgen directly can concur wholeheartedly with Kim when he writes of this thinker: "His language and thought are forbiddingly difficult and subtle, yet irresistibly intriguing, and more often than not, exasperate the students of Dōgen, who alternate between hope and despair."[72] In fairness to Dōgen we need continually to remind ourselves that *zazen*/enlightenment is his "ultimate concern" and that logical or conceptual truth is at best a distant secondary concern (which is not to say it is no concern at all). Since enlightenment, not abstract truth, is the be-all and end-all of *zazen*-*zazen* yields nothing beyond itself, it *is* enlightenment—to the person interested in enlightenment more than logic Dōgen might say: If one of my statements shatters your complacency, well; if not, choose what I said in the opposite vein for your liberation. If one kind of statement encourages your total effort, accept it; if not, heed the opposite kind. If neither kind of statement alone cures attachment to body, mind and self, accept my mutually exclusive statements simultaneously and at face value. Then surely the paradox of self-contradiction (the essence of your "self") will bring *satori*. If not, remember that the not-bringing is *satori*. Do not worry that I who taught *zazen*-only speak to you in *kōans*. Those trapped in dualistic thinking imagine that *kōan*-

meditation is unimportant to my students and myself just because I *say* it is unimportant!

A case for Dōgen's Buddhist orthodoxy can be made socially, traditionally and doctrinally. Socially, Dōgen recognized the (sometimes) equal importance of lowly monks, Zen masters and women. The original Gautama Buddha had exemplified a democratic ideal as opposed to the spiritual hierarchy contained in the doctrines and caste system of Hinduism and so upholds our first argument for Dōgen's orthodoxy (or orthopraxy). Secondly, Dōgen placed great stress on the secret transmission of Buddha's enlightenment through a succession of masters. The practice of keeping lists of the succession of certified masters was unique to Zen in contrast to other schools of Buddhism. This concern for purity of doctrine and getting back to the original source or sources of a faith is a second characteristic of orthodoxy. (However, we should perhaps note the zigzag involved when Dōgen on the one hand insisted on a kind of apostolic succession and, on the other, on the fact of his having learned from a lowly kitchen monk.)

Dōgen's orthodoxy is perhaps hardest to prove in terms of his specific teachings. Certainly his emphasis on the primary or sole value of *zazen* in itself and not for anything else, not even *nirvāṇa*, seems impossible to square with Buddhist orthodoxy, or even with Dōgen himself at times. But the middle way of both Dōgen and the historical Buddha emphasized the need both for continued practice of meditation and for social interchange in the *saṅgha* even after enlightenment. Neither total absorption in the larger society nor total withdrawal from all social intercourse was the orthodox way. Dōgen did agree, then, in a most important respect with Gautama who is the norm of Buddhist orthodoxy: There is no substitute for either the *saṅgha* or the personal practice of meditation.

Tradition is never a substitute for either wisdom or compassion, but Dōgen reminds us once again that tradition can mediate precious human values. Zen, Dōgen makes clear, is not simply or even necessarily iconoclastic. Sōtō the sect and Dōgen the monk amply illustrate that there are fruitful traditions for the nature of *dharma* and for the embodiment of freedom and *satori* in the fleeting but all-encompassing moment.

Finally, only a lopsided account of Dōgen's philosophy would leave out his tooth cleaner. "Dōgen was very proud of adding the washroom (*goka*) to the monks' hall for the purpose of washing the face, and especially the teenth, which he greatly stressed."[73] Use of the wooden tooth cleaner had gone out of fashion in the Zen monasteries of China. Dōgen restored its place in Zen life, stating with obvious enthusiasm, "This is my new idea." Understanding "the meaning of the use or non-use of this tooth cleaner" shows that the monk is "the bodhisattva who understands the Buddha-dharma."[74] Dōgen provided the following little litany to be recited while cleaning one's teeth:

> Using the wooden tooth cleaner every morning,
> May I vow with sentient beings,
> To attain teeth strong enough
> To gnaw all the illusions.[75]

19. Shinran

The most famous statement of Shinran (1173-1262), the founder of the Jōdo Shinshū or *True* Pure Land sect, reverses the equally important assertion of his master Honen, the founder of Jōdo Buddhism or the Pure Land sect. While Honen said, "Even a bad man will be received in Buddha's Land, but how much more a good man !" Shinran taught, "Even a good man will be received in Buddha's Land, but how much more a bad man!"[1] Both Honen and Shinran seem to have anticipated Martin Luther's "faith alone" or "grace alone" by about three centuries. Other parallels have been made between Shinran and Luther, including that both were "married priests".

With Shinran faith is more important than knowledge. The evil in this life lies in doubt and disbelief in the merits of Amida, not in non-knowing (*avidyā*). Shinran says: "We go around the worlds, the circle of existences; 'tis in the main because of bondage of the doubtful mind." And as for Shinran's view of this existence: "All beings are illusory, transmigrating endlessly.... Like a silkworm they fetter themselves. Pitiful are they, who are bound in the Three Realms and thus have nothing pure and true."[2] But then the *valle lacrimarum* concept of life *in via* is presupposed in virtually all mediaeval *Weltanschauungen*—Bonaventure and all Franciscans distinguished *in via* (*saṃsāra*) from *in patria* ("pure land") sharply.

In the Pure Land sects there is emphasis on the conventional or phenomenal world in which human beings suffer and yearn for some form of release, and the Buddha is seen to adjust his teachings and mercies to the three levels of human capacity: superior, average, and inferior. Superior and average beings can gain the Pure Land by some kind of practice of virtues. But most people (as Shinran considered himself) are "inferior" in type and must benefit from the acts and mercies of the Bodhisattvas who stand just short of *nirvāṇa* and vow to forego it until all other beings find Enlightenment. According to the *Meditation Sūtra* "even the lowest individual guilty of the worst sins is capable of attaining the Pure Land on the eve of death if he recites the name of Amitayus up to ten times."[3]

The *nembutsu* (Praise to Amida) may actually receive more emphasis in the Pure Land sects than the Pure Land itself. The bridge between the Buddha's enlightenment (symbolized by the Pure Land) and the ordinary man's self-delusion is the compassionate vow of the Bodhisattva or the chanting of praise to Amida. The Matsunagas write that "the essence of Amida's role is the inherent potentiality existing within each sentient being for the attainment of Enlightenment." But this Potential is clouded by false egocentric illusions, much as brass is coated with tarnish. We may symbolize Amida outside ourselves but can discover him only within. "The link between the indwelling Amida"—and the Pure Land he opens up for us—"is the *nembutsu*. In the words *Namu Amida Butsu*, the subjective self (symbolized by *Namu*) and its core of being are inseparably united."[4] To praise Amida is to dissolve egocentric tarnishment and manifest the deepest potential of the self.

Reciting the *nembutsu* was an intrinsically valuable act for Shinran as *zazen* was for Dōgen. The difference is that effective recitation is a gift of Amida for the sake of the believer and his on her entrance into the Pure Land, while *zazen* is performed purely for itself and thoroughly rooted in time as a present process. As is true of seated meditation, the doer does not repeat the *nembutsu* to earn the Pure Land. Honen seems to have mixed works and grace in his theology or even wavered between them, for a person, according to Honen, can invite Amida's grace or cooperate with it by *nembutsu* recitation. Shinran, however, taught a "purer" gospel of grace in that man can do absolutely nothing for himself. Since Shinran believed that "salvation truly depended on nothing but the grace of Amida, it was needless and perhaps dangerous to act as if one's conduct, or one's state in life, could have any bearing on ultimate redemption."[5] When Amida effectualizes *nembutsu* recitation, the *nembutsu* thereafter becomes an act of gratitude, not a petition and certainly not a "good work" meriting admittance to the Pure Land. Amida, presumably, makes even the expression of gratitude possible. Dogen also refers to "the assistance of the Buddha," and advises trust in the "home" of the Buddha, promising that everything will be conducted by Buddha. Generally, however, Dōgen is closer to Honen than to Shinran because of the latter's belief that there is nothing we can do for ourselves: even *numbutsu* is prayed through and for us by Amida.

The Buddha admonished his followers to rely upon themselves. For Shinran the step of self-reliance is pedagogically necessary in order to learn that the self is unreliable, utterly helpless really to help itself. But were not the Buddha and his followers able to rely on themselves? If the answer is that they must have been we still must add, "at the time they lived", in order to be faithful to the world-view from which Shinran and his contemporaries worked. According to that view, the Buddha lived in the Age of Right Law, which was followed by the Age of Imitative Law, which in turn was followed by the Age of Degenerate Law (*Mappō*) "in which Dharma was entirely destroyed." In the Age of Degenerate Law normal remedies will simply not do and in fact may be dangerous because they induce false security. Something more powerful than normal self-confidence or ordinary medicine is needed when everything and everyone is fatally infected. Someone who somehow transcends the epidemic is needed. Only a compassionate Buddha or Bodhisattva will do.

According to Kim, Dōgen worked out a metaphysics of

impermanence whereas Shinran and other Japanese Buddhists of the time did not.[6] Perhaps Shinran merely presupposed impermanence without trying to explain it. What he knew he needed to face was the total spiritual inadequacy of human beings. In a writing in which Shinran, like Augustine, makes his confession, he tells us:

> Though I seek my refuge in the true faith of
> the Pure Land,
> Yet hath not mine heart been truly sincere.
> Deceit and untruth are in my flesh,
> And in my soul is no clear shining.[7]

Elsewhere in the same confession Shinran cries,

> There is no end of evil nature,
> Man's mind is as abominable as a viper.
> Therefore, no man should act wise or good,
> Since he inwardly embraces illusions.[8]

While Dōgen's religiousness concerned radical impermanence, Shinran's dealt with radical sinfulness, to use Kim's term. The following seems to be Shinran's most balanced and Buddhistic statement on sin: "Though sin hath no substance in itself, and is but the shadow of our illusion, and soul (literally, the essence of mind) is itself pure, yet, in all this world is there no sincere man."[9] Nakamura notes a similarity between Shinran's view of sin as devoid of reality in itself and that of the Christian thinker John Scotus Erigena.[10]

While Hōnen advocated that the *nembutsu* should be repeated sixty thousand times a day, Shinran believed that one repetition with a true, pure, and sincere heart would be enough. That one repetition of *Namuamidabutsu* (which Nakamura translates, "Oh save me, thou Amitabha!") is based on the effective grace of Amida, who shapes the faith of the single-hearted believer. Even a powerless sinner (or righteous man) living in a degenerate age can thus be saved. Then faith and work are merged by Amida in the act of repeating the *nembutsu*. *Nembutsu* is gratitude, not petition. Adoration and grace are not separate.[11]

Although the Chinese sources of Pure Land thought located

the Pure Land far away in space or after death in time, Honen and Shinran saw the Pure Land as available within this life. As Nakamura explains, "The practice of the most pious among the believers is to realize what is beyond this world within this very world."[12] What Nakamura calls the "secularism" of Pure Land theology is given its theoretical basis by Honen but carried to its extreme by Shinran. The Pure Land means the end of illusion, which comes not necessarily at death but at the moment of faith. The Pure Land does not literally begin in this life, but the moment of faith assures us that the Pure Land will follow as surely as sunrise follows sunset. The distinction between "secular" Shinran and "spiritual" Shinran may be the same as that between *nirvāṇa*, which the Buddha achieved within his lifetime and taught others how to approach, and the ineffable *Mahāparinirvāṇa*, which no one enters till death. Shinran, like the Gospel according to John, sees eternal life and light in the midst of suffering and darkness and not just at its end. Reality (even ultimate reality) encompasses error and illusion in Dōgen; *nirvāṇa* encompasses affliction for Shinran, who writes, "Without being delivered from afflictions, one attains *nirvāṇa*."[13]

The marriage of Buddhist monks had certainly occurred before Shinran, but wives were kept secret and the act, though regarded as a sin, was "merely one of the one hundred and eight hindrances to Enlightenment."[14] Shinran attributed his marriage both to revelation and principle, and grounded his marriage on religious experience and what we might call a "democratic principle". Amida's two attendant Bodhisattvas are Mahāsthāmaprāpta (Wisdom) and Avalokiteśvara (Compassion). Avalokiteśvara in his transmigration from India through China to Japan underwent a change of sex. In the female form of Kannon, Compassion came to Shinran. Shinran's vision of Kannon seems to call for an imaginative description such as that by Hyakuzo Kurata in his *Shinran* (a novel): "In the dream the Kannon Bodhisattva said: 'Reverend, if you are destined by your former Karma to come in contact with a woman, I shall become a beautiful woman and be your wife. I shall make an ideal home all my life, and in my last moments shall guide you to the Land of Bliss.'"[15] The Matsunagas write: "Shinran's dream of taking Kannon, the symbol of compassion, as a wife was a revelation of his personal role among the masses, as well as a promise of hope for every householder who aspired to reach the Pure Land—and directly after joining Honen's movement, Shinran began to make his interest in the plight of the commonman apparent."[16]

Saichō, the founder of the Tendai sect in Japan, put an end to discrimination in ordination, even so far as the semi-slave class (*nuhi*) was concerned; put by Shinran's time the Tendai itself had become aristocratic and had not remained true to Saichō's equalitarian ideals. The Matsunagas write: "To a certain degree Honen's movement was a fulfilment of Saichō's dream, but Shinran was to carry the ideal further by even abolishing the separation of the elite clergy from the laity in his concept of *hisō hizoku* (neither monk nor layman)."[17] Even though Shinran's marriage was very important as a symbol of the inclusion of the laity in the hope of the Pure Land, Pure Land sectarianism unfortunately was not so inclusive in its development. The fervent insistence on "one way" earned for Amidists the name "single-minded" (we might almost say, having a one-track mind). Shinran, a man who claimed to have no disciples, inaugurated a movement that ossified into an institution that not only excommunicated people but even warred with its adversaries. In the sixteenth century devotees of Amida defended their temple on Osaka with the cry: "The mercy of Buddha should be recompensed even by pounding flesh to pieces. One's obligation to the Teacher should be recompensed even by smashing bones to bits!"

Alfred Bloom, a not uncritical devotee of Shinran's teaching, states two points that stand out most clearly about Shinran: the hope he held out for even the meanest person, and the ground of that hope, grace. Bloom recognizes the principal difficulty in Shinran's ethical thought: "It tends to make compassionate action a matter of the future and not of this world." One almost has to have risen to Bodhisattva status to help anyone, including even one's self. "Hence the egolessness which Shinran inculcated often took the form of a passive quietism" and, after his death, "became an acquiescence to the reigning mores."[18] Sometimes the emphasis on the salvation of the wicked and even the righteous may also have led to antinomianism or the view that one may do anything since salvation is assured in any case.

The trend toward religiosity without regard to strict logical system may be a general characteristic of Japanese Buddhism throughout its history. The Japanese never really cultivated systematic logic or grammar whereas a whole discipline of the metaphysics of grammar had been in the Indian heritage since Patañjali if not before. Dōgen is one of the few exceptions as far as real metaphysical system is concerned. Nevertheless, in some form of interpretation or other, such doctrines as the *Trikāya* were known and taught; but it seems that the interest even here was not so much in the metaphysics out of which they were derived as in the practical application to daily life. The challenge always remains to keep faith and reliance on grace adequately balanced with effort and intelligence, for faith too easily degenerates into blind credulity just as intellect too easily degenerates into sophistry.

20. Rūmī

The Ṣūfī Jalalu'l-Dīn Rumī (1207-1273) is the greatest mystical poet of Persia, and, according to Nicholson, "every Sūfī after him capable of reading Persian has acknowledged his unchallenged leadership."[1] Rūmī is firmly in the *bhakti* tradition with emphasis on love rather than intellect, and his famous *Mathnawī* of about 25,000 rhyming couplets is not a systematic presentation of philosophical views; nevertheless, according to Hakim, "Writing systematically on all the problems dealt with by Rūmī... would be really equal to writing a whole history of philosophy and theology and mysticism in Islam"—furthermore, to study Rūmī is to study "*the best achievements of philosophical and religious life in Islam.*"[2] Actually the major content of Rūmī's thinking had already been developed by Suhrawardī and Ibn 'Arabī, but Rūmī had the art of presenting this content with an aesthetic and uncompromising passion. In his unrestricted emphasis on love Rūmī sometimes to be anti-philosophical, and he definitely rejects analysis and idle speculation in preference for an immediate experience which transcends logic and reason. Rūmī says: "I have tried far-thinking intellect; henceforth I will make myself mad." Although Rūmī sometimes seems to be completely eclectic, choosing doctrines from here and there as the spirit moves him, Hakim argues that there is method in his madness, "which is in some ways more consistent and methodical than many systems of scholastical and intellectual metaphysics."[3]

It was Rūmī's son who organized disciples into a regular order which in the course of time became famous as the "whirling dervishes"—the "whirling" is simply a dance form done to musical settings of Rūmī's poetry. Rūmī's father, who had been a Ṣūfī *pir* (guru), died while Rūmī was still very young. Henri Corbin describes the Ṣūfism of Rūmī's father as "aesthetic quietism", and sees in Rūmī's *Mathnawī* all that we today call metaphysics of the imagination and phenomenology of symbolic forms. The *pir* is very important in Islam in general and of course in Ṣūfism in particular, for just as in the Zen apostolic succession of patriarchs and in many if not all varieties of Hindu tradition but especially those like Kasmir Śaivism with a heavy emphasis on esoterics, the *personal transmission* from master to disciple is considered as absolutely essential. For many this is as true today as it ever was, and there are innumerable stories told of the ways that Ṣūfīs as well as yogis and Zen masters awaken super-consciousness or enlightenment in their disciples, often treating those they like best with the roughest tests or even insults. Undoubtedly Rūmī's most significant personal encounter was with Shams of Tabriz; as Nicholson writes, this encounter was

> marked by a mystical intimacy of the closest kind with a "Perfect Man," i.e. one of the saints in whom Divine attributes are mirrored, so that the lover, seeing himself by the light of God, realizes that he and his Beloved are not two, but One. These experiences lie at the very centre of Rūmī's theosophy and directly or indirectly inspire all his poetry....
>
> In 1244 a wandering dervish, known to posterity by the name of Shamsu'l-Dīn of Tabriz, arrived at Konia. Jalālu'l-Dīn found in the stranger that perfect image of the Divine Beloved which he had long been seeking. He took him away to

his house, and for a year or two they remained inseparable....

A Platonic type of mystical love had been cultivated by Sūfīs long before Rūmī declared that he and Shams-i Tabriz were "two bodies with one soul." In this union of loving souls all distinctions vanish; nothing remains but the essential Unity of Love, in which "lover" and "beloved" have merged their separate identities.[4]

Since Rūmī is in the Neo-Platonic heritage emanation is the theme quite overtly and of course Eros is the thrust of Return to Unity. At the culmination of the theme of the Return to the One, Rūmī reminds us that two finite material things cannot co-exist in the same space and time; but thanks to Love, two wills can!

Rūmī has been considered one of the most remarkable evolutionary thinkers in the entire history of philosophy. In the *Mathnawī* he offers a theory of creative evolutionism influenced in part by the Ikhwān al-Ṣafā and Ibn Miskawayh. As Hakim explains, an infinite number of egos emerge from the Cosmic Ego, and this in essence is the totality of existence. The infinite, self-existent, self-sufficient Spirit "drops egos" to the lowest level of sentience and consciousness; but spiritual reality is the only reality, so even matter is spiritual.[5] Hakim explains further:

> In the realm of appearance matter was the first form of existence, or one might put it like this, that the soul started its existence in the form of matter consisting of dimly conscious monads and for an immensely long period lived as that and was driven about without any choice of its will. It lived as fire and water, as wind and cloud until it entered the next higher stage, that of plant life.... He teaches us that there is only one way of rising from the lower to the higher stage and that is by assimilation of the lower into the higher. He untiringly repeats the instance of matter assuming organic life by getting assimilated by a plant and plant rising to animal life by getting assimilated into an animal organism.... He does not believe like Darwin in a passive and mechanical natural selection. He seems to have anticipated Bergson in

> the idea that Evolution is creative. The "Elan Vital," the will to live a higher and fuller life, creates new organs. For Rūmī too life is nothing but a product of the will to live and ever dissatisfied with the present equipment, life creates new desires. . . .
>
> As to what is the nature of the force that drives this process his reply is that it is *Love*. All the processes of assimilation, growth, and reproduction are manifestations of Love. Without Love there would have been no movement in the universe. The first Beloved, the Eternal Beauty, is the motive force in the process of Evolution.[6]

Following Rūmī we should never forget that Creation, thanks to the Love wherein and wherefrom it was and is being created, is *Beautiful*! We might make comparisons with Kasmir Śaivism more readily than with Śaṅkara's Advaita since in the heritage lift by Abeinavagupta and his disciples the aesthetic element plays such a predominating role. But then again as far as Love is concerned we could also make some comparison with the Rāmānuja school and others who put *bhakti* in a place more prominent than *jñāna*. The *Theia Mania* of Plato, the divine madness of creativity, takes its proper place in Rūmī's logic; reason, the intellect itself, is after all only a tool.

The final goal of evolution—and Rūmī is very much a teleological thinker—is the realization that there is really no true gap between the being or the soul of man and the being of the universe and ultimately even the Being of God. In reality the soul is the substance and the universe of phenomenal forms is a collection of the soul's attributes. According to Hakim, Rūmī "wants to convince man of the fact that his real self, far from being a product of nature, is the source of all nature. The physical body as well as the universe are the products and reflection of the transcendental self of man."[7] The *Telos* of creative evolution is the Ideal Man, which concept Hakim has summarized as follows:

> The Ideal Man is one who has realized his transcendental or eternal self which is uncreated and divine.
>
> It is possible for every individual to realize it; it is the end and goal of life.

The man who realizes it is clothed with the attributes of divinity and it is indifferent whether one calls him a saint or a prophet.

The Ideal Man is in immediate touch with God; neither prophets nor angels intervene between the two.

Different individuals having attained to this stage are united in a way that they are one as well as many; in the Realm of Spirit numerical plurality does not exist.

The Ideal Man can work miracles which do not mean the annihilation of causation but only bringing into play causes that are not within the reach of common experience.

The Ideal Man freely merges his own will in the will of God in the ultimate relation of love; so one can say that he exists and does not exist at the same time.

Life in God is not annihilation but transformation; therefore every soul that begins to live in God has his being in Him.

As the Ideal Man becomes emptied of his own self, it is God that lives in him and speaks through him and works through him.

His eye pierces every evil because he sees with the Light of God.

His assertion of his identity with God is justifiable because it is not he but God that speaks through him.

The Ideal Man is identical with Logos or the Universal Reason that creates and governs the Universe.

The Ideal Man being the Final Cause of Creation is the last of Creation in point of time but existed before the Creation as an idea.

The Adam of the Qur'ān represents the Ideal Man to whom the angels paid homage.

The Ideal Man is the embodiment of Universal Reason and is identical with the Universal Soul; therefore, no power is outside of him.

The Ideal Man does not represent only a possibility. In every age there is someone who has realised it.

It is not contemplation but thorough transformation of the self. The Ideal Man is absolutely dead to himself. He lives in God and God lives in him.

> No metaphor can explain the nature of this union of God and Man Incarnation as well as unification as conceptions derived from space are misleading when applied to non-spatial realities.[8]

The question of whether or to what extent the individual preserves his (or her) individuality after the experience of mystical union or enlightenment is a perpetual problem also in Mahāyāna Buddhism with its emphasis on non-ego and the selflessness of the Bodhisattva Vow, as well as with the *jīvan mukti* concept in Advaita and Kasmir Śaivism, even if we disregard some of the teachings of the Victorines, the Carthusians, and other mystics of the Latin world as well as the Hesychasts of Byzantium. Hakim states that Rūmī's view that the soul survives but its attributes are annihilated is unintelligible: "The essence of his being survives but his attributes are merged in the attributes of God, like the flame of a candle that in the presence of the sun exists, and does not exist. The flame of the candle *exists* because if you put cotton on it it is burnt away; it *does not exist* because it gives you no light: the light of the sun has annihilated it."[9]

Both Rūmī and al-Ghazālī experienced a radical conversion thanks to Ṣūfī influence and both were mystics with a heavy background in systematic philosophy. Both authors are indeed of virtually equal merit although al-Ghazālī is known mostly for his philosophy and scarcely at all for his poetry whereas the very opposite is true of Rūmī. Rūmī not only approved of al-Ḥallāj his famous saying *Ana'l-Haqq* ("I am God") but even imitated him and offered the following defence:

> When a fly is plunged in honey, all the members of its body are reduced to the same conditon, and it does not move. Similarly, the term *istighraq* (absorption in God) is applied to one who has no conscious existence or initiative or movement. Any action that proceeds from him is not his own. If he is still struggling in the water, or if he cries out, "Oh, I am drowning," he is not said to be in the state of "absorption". This is what is signified by the words *Ana'l-Haqq*, "I am God". People imagine that it is a presumptuous claim, whereas it is really a presumptous claim to say *Ana'l-'abd*, "I am

> the servant of God"; and *Ana'l-Haqq*, "I am God," is an expression of great humility. The man who says *Ana'l-'abd*, "I am the servant of God," affirms two existences, his own and God's, but he that says *Ana'l-Haqq*, "I am God," has made himself non-existent and has given himself up and says "I am God," i.e. "I am naught, He is all: there is no being but God's." This is the extreme of humility and self-abasement.[10]

As a poet Rūmī attempts to convey the ineffable through a profuse use of forms and analogies, but he is aware of the limitations of using any forms to express the Formless. The forms must be transcended; the analogies are useful. "Creating forms and then transcending them is the progress by which man can approach God."[11]

21. Naṣīr al-Dīn Ṭūsī

In separating those who may be classed as Great Summa writers (for architects, as it were) from their contemporaries who were much more individual thinkers and not synthesizers of tradition, Ṭūsī (1201-1224) fits into the latter category. Ṭūsī is an ethicist and a theologian, and a Shī'a rather than a Sunni—since communications were cut off between Shī'a Islam and Latin Europe unfortunately the stereotype still remains that Islamic philosophy as such is Sunni Islam, and that culminating and ending with Ibn Rushd (with something of the Ṣūfīs coming into the picture through Victorian translations of Ṣūfī poetry as literature rather than as philosophy).

We shall be following Ṭūsī's work on ethics, but first we may note this on his life:

> He was born in 597/1201 in Ṭūs (in N.E. Persia, the native area of Ghazālī and of many other Arabo-Persian scholars of mediaeval times, now a ruin); and he died in Baghdad, for five centuries the spiritual and political centre of Islam, in

672/1274. He was the contemporary within Islam of scores of eminent figures (e.g. two of Persia's greatest writers, Rūmī, d. 672/1273 and Sa'dī, d. 692/1292), with many of whom he was closely acquainted; and, outside Islam, of such unwitting fellow-labourers as Albert the Great, Thomas Aquinas and Roger Bacon, of whom he quite possibly never heard. (Since he allegedly amassed a vast library, containing many foreign books, and as the Mongol period was one of lively foreign contact, it is impossible to be absolutely certain of this.)

He early mastered all the various disciplines then constituting learning, but he showed a particular predilection for mathematics, astronomy and philosophy (it is important here that he was especially well-versed in the writings of Avicenna d. 429/1037). To dramatic notice he comes first in the service of an 'intellectual' Ismā'ilī Governor of Quhistān.... Willingly or unwillingly, Ṭūsī remained in Ismā'īlī employ at Quhistān, at the Alamūt headquarters, and elsewhere, until 645/1247, when he finally succeeded in defecting to the all-conquering Mongols under Hulagu. Perhaps the only certain fact about this period of twenty years or more is that it was one of the most productive of his career. For the next seventeen years, however, Ṭūsī is in the very van of momentous affairs, forming one of the remarkable band of Muslims who, so to say, stage-managed the Mongol take-over of many Islamic lands and the extinction of the Caliphate, but made possible thereby the continuance in new and flourishing forms of Islamic learning, law and civilization. During the last eight years of his life he resumed his scholarly publication, working particularly in the field of astronomy, at the great observatory in Marāgha (in Ādharbaijān) which Hulagu had encouraged him to build.[1]

And we have the following from Siddiqi:

Ṭūsī's chief claim to fame rests on his persuading Hulāgu to found the celebrated observatory (*raṣad khānah*) at Marāghah, Ādharbāijān, in 657/1259, which was equipped with the best instruments, "some of them constructed for the first

> time". Here he compiled the astronomical tables, called *Zīj al-fikhāni,* which "became popular throughout Asia, even in China"....
>
> Himself an accomplished scholar rather than a creative mind, Ṭūsī's position is mainly that of a revivalist and his works are largely eclectical in character. But even as a revivalist and eclectic, he is not lacking in originality, at least in the presentation of his material. His versatility is indeed astonishing. His manifold and varied interests extend to philosophy, mathematics, astronomy, physics, medicine, mineralogy, music, history, literature, and dogmatics.[2]

Ṭūsī's native city of Ṭūs was within the range of Buddhism's previous expansion into Central Asia, and Nestorian Christians had been present in that area also; in addition, it is well known that commerce between China and Byzantium passed that way. These things then were most likely present in his cultural background.

The *Nasirean Ethics* by Ṭūsī is divided into three discourses: ethics as such, economics, and politics. The first is in turn divided into "principles" and "ends", very rationally. Ṭūsī and Ṣūfī heritage also, which, like Zen, claimed to transcend reason, at least ultimately. And Ṭūsī is by no means merely a *Falsafah,* merely interpreting Aristotle as were some of his contemporary scholastics both in Islam and in Latin Europe.

In the first discourse Ṭūsī takes sides with those who advise correction of old faults as more important than espousing new virtues. This is a delicate matter which is not often discussed openly, although St. Bonaventure, Honen, Shinran, most of the disciples of Rāmānuja and generally those who depend heavily on grace more than effort advise to the contrary. After this quite systematically he classifies the virtues and vices, with justice as the noblest of all virtues. He concludes with a consideration of the relation between the degrees of true felicity or happiness. As for the second discourse, "On Economics", the original meaning of the word was simply the art of managing a household. Thus this includes such matters and considerations as regulation of property and provisions, regulation and proper upbringing of childern, rights of parents as well as regulation of wives and governance of servants and slaves (for of course no part of the world had yet thought of banishing the *institution* of slavery).

In his discourse "On Politics", no doubt being therein indebted to the philosophical historians before him who had in great measure already anticipated what later gets synthesized in Ibn Khaldūn, Ṭūsī puts heavy emphasis as a Muslim humanist on altruistic love as essential for the survival and flourishing of civilization. He goes on to a sort of sociological, scientific consideration of divisions in different types of societies, including social classes, castes and trades, coupled with a study of the conditions of cities. After considering these factors, he approaches the specifically political problems concerning regulation of kings and their appointees and retainers—the king's court, in other words, or bureaucracy. He then considers friendship, an ancient classical theme too often neglected in our modern computerized deontological calculations. Finally, as a sort of epilogue, he concludes the entire book with some considerations of Plato's "testaments".

At the outset Ṭūsī acknowledges indebtedness to Miskawayh (d. 1030); indeed Ṭūsī's work here is not much more than a Persian translation of Miskawayh's work on ethics. After acknowledging his indebtedness to al-Fārābī, Ṭūsī posits the basic metaphysical principle that every existence has a perfection, i.e., as its entelechy, whether it achieves it or not. With Aristotle's four causes in the background, he considers the material necessities, the plant and animal kingdoms. He does not assert man's right to exploit them unreservedly, but rather says man should treat his physical environment as he treats his body. Ṭūsī considers that the 'perfection' of these lower orders lies in their subserving man's needs in this way.

But man needs not only the lower orders but his fellow human beings too. The anarchistic ideal remains only a delusion. For Ṭūsī at least as much as for Chu Hsi and his immediate successors, human existence is social existence and from birth to death entails mutual aid rather than competition. (One could almost read into this text what Kropotkin and Sorokin tried to tell us in the just now passing-away generation of intellectual giants.) Ṭūsī emphasizes the need for cooperation for human survival. For civilized human societies to do well, what he calls "combination" (*ijtimā*) is necessary. Thus human cities take on cultural traits or characteristics over and above the mere numerical accumulation of people and equipment. He would certainly concur with the distinction between *gesellschaft* and *gemeinschaft* of the pre-Nazi German sociologists.

Having posited and briefly discussed the ideal situation, he then turns to the obstacles in the way of achieving it: man's greed and pride primarily, and from them his destructive tendencies and disregard for the rights of others. Hence government is necessary for the sake of restraint. Certainly Ṭūsī is no Taoist; but neither would he sanction the literalistic codes of rewards and punishments of the Legalists at the other extreme. Although he leans very heavily on Aristotle in these matters, he is also fully aware of the Islamic claim to prophetic revelation, although, perhaps more liberally than many of the Sunni orthodox theologians would like to allow, he associates this rather closely with Plato's institution of the guardians. Ṭūsī uses the classical metaphor derived from Plato that the good political administrator will be more like a good physician, prudently and skilfully applying his craft for the health of the society and of the individuals in it. Among his contemporaries one might find him more in accord with Chu Hsi and his immediate followers and interpreters than, say, with Nichiren; or again, having common roots, he would be more in accord with his Byzantine contemporaries such as were carrying on the work done by the great humanist Psellos in the generation just preceding him, than, for example, John of Paris (Jean Quidort, 1241-1306) who tried to bolster up the papacy over all other powers.

Ṭūsī warns against both extremes of anarchy and of tyranny; and in that we find some fascinating parallels to the Neo-Confucianists' arguments against the 'other-worldliness' of the Buddhists, who renounce the world to gain further merit than the common people which they then distribute in response to the support of the laity. In a sense Ṭūsī's criticism must be of the Ṣūfī monastic societies, which were quite similar in most respects to Christian and Buddhist monastic ways. It should not be overlooked, meanwhile, that Ṭūsī is in these things, as well as in his theory of the Imāmate, not only completely aligned with Shī'a theory but even manifests himself as an advocate of the Ismā'īlī doctrine, which (according to Marshall Hodgson's research) was much more democratic than the orthodox Sunni political polity in regard to the Califate. Indeed, he was so opposed to what he considered the extremes of autocracy of the Sunni Baghdad Califate that this was evidently one of his chief motives in siding with the Mongols against the hypocrisy and corruption that Baghdad by his time had fallen into.

According to Ṭūsī, the "dispositions" of man can be changed. "Disposition is a habit of the soul necessarily effecting the easy procession of an action therefrom, without need of any reflection or deliberation."[3] Disposition here might be compared to *saṃskāra* in Sanskrit terminology, perhaps especially as used among Buddhists. A lot of attention was given to this concept during the period when Sanskrit texts were being translated into Chinese; and the Japanese, Dōgen especially, mulled the concept over considerably, trying by introspective meditation to penetrate the karmic level of what might be called predispositions operating according to cause and effect. The Buddhists of Ṭūsī's time, such as Dōgen and certainly the less rigorous Shinran and Nichiren, all affirmed, in contrast to the Neo-Confucianists, that human nature can be changed, for it is basically good since we all share something of Buddhahood.

Ṭūsī further considers the age-old controversy about whether our temperaments are natural and unalterable or not. In this controversy he comes down very heavily against the determinists as well as those who believe that human nature is inherently evil. He argues rather forcefully, appealing to common sense, that otherwise education and training of youth would not be necessary. Moreover, he reiterates his philosophy of the entelechic perfectability of man. His goodness lies in his perfectibility as a process, or as an achievement, not as a fixed entity.

Ṭūsī gives his own interpretation of Aristotle's philosophical psychology, including the vegetable, animal and rational souls, the appetites, and the observation that in the acquisition of knowledge there is a sort of nonmaterial motion which nevertheless naturally tends towards equilibrium. Then his classification of the virtues and vices follows the Aristotelian "golden mean", the *meden agan*. In this his relation to Aristotle is somewhat parallel to Chu Hsi's relation to Confucius' (and perforce Mencius') avoidance of extremes, and perhaps to attempts at rediscovering the original Buddha's "middle way". Ṭūsī's basic classification scheme is simply that of Aristotle: wisdom, justice continence, and courage, each in dynamic balance harmoniously with the others if our training is correct. Evidently Ṭūsī feels, no need of reconciling these Greek virtues with some of the injunctions of the Qur'ān, whereas one often feels that Aquinas has to be cautious, especially in matters of secular ethics against the Biblical claim to be a New Dispensation higher than the pagan lack of one and superceding that given to Moses. In concluding this discussion, Ṭūsī writes:

> These virtues have further been defined as follows: 'Wisdom' means realizing the knowledge of whatever tends towards existence; but since existent things are either divine or human, wisdom is of two kinds, 'knowable' and 'do-able', i.e., speculative and practical. 'Courage' signifies that the irascible soul should submit to the rational soul, so as not to become agitated in perilous affairs; and it should proceed in accordance with the latter's opinion, so that the action it performs becomes fair, and the fortitude it displays, praiseworthy. 'Continence' signifies that the faculty of appetite is obedient to the rational soul, its controls being in accordance with the exigency of the latter's opinion; moreover, the operation of freedom should be apparent in it, and it should be quit of bondage to the soul's passion and of servitude of pleasures. 'Justice' signifies that all these faculties are in accord with each other, subordinate to the distinguishing faculty, so that the conflict of passions and the opposite attractions of the faculties cannot precipitate its possessor into the whirlpool of perplexity; and the operation of equity and impartiality should be apparent in it. God it is, who prospers and assists![14]

Nevertheless, one senses that there is something defective in this schematism, classical and weighted with tradition though it was already by this time. In that perspective one wonders what Ṭūsī would have said concerning the *Pratītyasamutpāda* or the *Prajñāpāramitā* literature or the discipline of complete detachment demanded by the Śūnyavāda heritage or even the Vedāntic interpretations of the *niṣkāma karma* of the *Gītā*. However, this only reflects what remains a pivotal problem *par excellence* all through the many places and periods of our world-wide survey: asceticism vs moderation, which is the better norm and how can they be reconciled.

Ṭūsī employs the typical metaphor that we should go after spiritual values and virtues with at least as much zeal as conquerors and adventurers go across deserts, oceans, and dangerous paths in search for material treasures; and having gained something of spiritual treasure, we should guard it with at least as much care as the merchant or the conquering monarch guards his wealth. Ṭūsī is not unaware that such things are doubly difficult for a young prince since he is exposed to many more temptations than the common lot of us and yet more is expected, even demanded, of him (compare the Confucian ideal). The prince is to be concerned and actively engaged in seeing to the intellectual and spiritual as well as the merely physical welfare of his subjects. And the prince is in another difficulty in that there is no one above him to check his excesses, except Allah. His responsibilities being greater, his temptations are also much greater, and the punishments for evil eventually likewise are greater, for even the Qur'ān quite plainly says, "Assuredly, kings are the ones who are deprived."

Following Galen, but guided by the many commentaries on Galen that were by then available to him, Ṭūsī takes us through the hierarchy of values again, counselling moderation in food and drink, correction of faults, strengthening friendships by removing occasions for strife or discord, and even learning to derive benefit from the attitude of enemies. He cites al-Kindī as instructing us to be living examples of what we teach. As the best of Taoism as well as the best of Mahāyāna teach, virtue is not truly virtue unless it has become such second nature that one is not conscious of practicing it. Ṭūsī says that one should not be like the whetstone that sharpens knives but itself remains dull; rather we should be "like the sun, diffusing light from our essence upon a moon, so as to lend it a likeness to ourselves, albeit its light falls short of the sun's own: this is exactly our state as regards the diffusion of virtues."[5]

From these considerations of the virtues, Ṭūsī then proceeds, continuing his analogy of the politician as a good physician, to make prescription for the vices. The faculty of judgment plays a major role. Ṭūsī's scheme is simple enough: diseases of the speculative faculty (matters of judgment) are three: perplexity, simple ignorance, and compound ignorance. "Perplexity is caused by the inability of the soul to distinguish truth from falsehood due to the conflicting evidence and confusing arguments for and against a controversial issue."[6] Though sophistical arguments can be as dangerous to the unaware as valid reasoning is necessary for right human conduct, Ṭūsī would not be in accord with those among some Ṣūfīs and not a few Rinzai Zen people who claim that logic is only so much bother and that what we really need is intuitive insight which is spontaneous. He insists that familiarity with the logical fallacies is helpful; such, in short, is the remedy for perplexity. "Simple ignorance consists in a man's lack of knowledge on a subject without his presuming that he knows it."[7] As for the treatment of simple ignorance, Ṭūsī prescribes "meditation on the state of man and other animals, so that one becomes aware that the virtue of the human being over other animals lies in reason and distinction, whereas the ignorant (who is lacking in this virtue) is to be numbered among the other animals not among the former (human) species."[8] Compound ignorance "is a man's lack of knowledge on a subject coupled with his presumption that he knows it. In spite of ignorance he does not know that he is ignorant."[9] Ṭūsī says this is the most dangerous vice because it can be the most destructive. He prescribes study of the mathematical sciences first, but it is philosophy itself that is the remedy for this disease—a matter evidently often overlooked in his milieu just as some modern psychiatrists have not come under the influence of Karl Jaspers and others who fully realize that human beings do have real philosophical problems and not merely psychological twirks that bother them.

Next Ṭūsī takes us through the faculty of repulsion, which deals with anger, cowardice, and fear, the first deriving from excess, the second from neglect, and the third from depravity. This theme is so universal that from Thomas Aquinas to Dōgen there is scarcely a philosopher worthy of the title who does not deal with it in some form or other. One might risk the generalization that there is less consideration of it as such among the Mahāyāna Buddhists for the simple reason that anger is supposedly already eliminated before the more serious *sādhana*, in terms of the *pāramitās* for example, is undertaken. In the Abrahamic heritages, perhaps from Zoroastrian influence, very often evil is something to be battled against in an eternal struggle with hope of final victory only in some eventual apocalypse; whereas with Buddhism in general the real problem of human existence (although admittedly evil is often personified as Mara, the Devil-tempter) is not evil or sin as such but ignorance and suffering. Hence if one reflects that getting angry will only increase suffering, one might reflect more profoundly on one's true motive and method. In the Psalms and in the Old Testament prophets there are vivid passages where the Lord Yahwe is depicted as a God of Anger—indeed, so much so that the other prophets and Jesus himself had great difficulty overriding this motif with the concept of God as all-merciful. The same problem obtains with varying passages in the Qur'ān and in the *hadīth*, and no doubt Ṭūsī was not unaware of these things though in this treatise he poses almost entirely as an interpreter of Galen, Isocrates and other Greek philosophers.

In short, whereas the rational approach to controlling the passions is what we have here as inherited from the Greeks, in Buddhism this is not enough. Rather one seeks by adequate meditation and application of the *pratītyasamutpāda* to eliminate the root-cause of the passions by "cooling them down" instead of fighting them or trying to control them in the middle of all sorts of frustrations. Meanwhile there are the *bhaktas* like Nimbārka and Shinran who are so much engaged in devotion to the Compassionate One in response to grace freely given that scarcely does the problem of anger arise. Certainly the (Neo-) Confucian Gentleman would loose face if he became angry in public, and if the disgrace were serious enough he might in the extreme even be honor-bound to commit suicide. Something of the same sort may likewise be found in the Bushido-Code of the Japanese Samurai, which was beginning to emerge in the thirteenth century. One must learn to use his sword for the defence of honor and enforcement of justice, even when revenge in feuds between rival clans is involved. But the emphasis should be on the duty to use his sword selflessly and dispassionately, perhaps even more so than the knights of the Crusades in Latin Europe. Actually something of the same teaching and training, once one peals off the more modern and moderated commentaries, is very plain in the *Bhagavad Gītā*.

Quite rationally Ṭūsī reminds us that the causes of anger may be scientifically classified and treated intelligently rather than emotionally: conceit, pride, contention, quarrelsomeness, jesting, arrogance, scorn, treachery, unfairness, and the quest for precious things. Likewise he discerns the results of anger to be classifiable:

> The consequences of anger, or the accidents of this disease, are seven categories: regret, the expectation of requital in this world and the next, the hatred of friends, the scorn of the ignoble, the rejoicing of enemies, disturbance of the constitution, and physical suffering—and these altogether. Anger is momentary madness; and the Prince of Believers, Alī has said, 'Vehemence is a species of madness, for its author has regrets, and if he does not regret, then is his madness firmly established.'[10]

Throughout Ṭūsī's approach is that of human rationality as the fulfilment of human nature at its best, this being equated directly with true spirituality rather than some unknowable supra-rational faculty as some intensively intuitional philosophies tend to teach.

Conceit is a matter of false presumption. The remedy is in finding the perfection which one claims for oneself in others. Pride, needless to say, deserves considerable space because of its pivotal importance in the Thomistic scheme of the vices and in other thirteenth century philosophers as well. At the pinnacle of his consideration Ṭūsī quotes a couplet which was evidently a folksy proverb: "If you take pride in ancestors who passed on long ago,/Men will say, 'You speak true, but hȯw poorly they begat!'" As for jesting, Islamic courts as those in mediaeval Europe had their court jesters (one wonders whether the reinstatement of this honorable profession is not badly needed today). Ṭūsī warns us that keeping the balance in jesting is not always as easy as it might seem. Laughter and jesting are good where there is laughing together instead of laughing at another. In that matter, alas, philosophers are often prone to take themselves more seriously than even politicians and theologians; and in treatises on aesthetics humor seldom takes its rightful place. Finally, meditation on the transiency of things, and even of life itself, remains the universal remedy for the universal vice of "quest for precious things".

Ṭūsī next takes us through faintheartedness to fear, these two being the classical pair in the Aristotelian scheme. But the emphasis here as ever is not on the structural framework as such so much as on practical consideration of the consequences and the cure. Incidentally, though often overlooked by interpreters who are looking for the more passive aspects of what they consider to be 'oriental mysticism', *vīrya* is one of the *pāramitās*. *Vīrya* means manliness, determination, steadfastness—a nexus of meanings that really is clearer in connection with the counterbalancing *kṣānti* (patience). It almost means perseverance in spite of difficulties. Perseverance becomes a major technical term in Christian monasticism also, meaning the will to continue in one's vocation steadfastly in spite of constant temptations to "return to the world". Similar considerations can be found in the Neo-Confucianists; in that case, however, the evil is the shirking of responsibility in the conduct of public duties rather than a merely private matter. There comes to mind also Arjuna's faintheartedness in the face of the Great Battle. As for the cure of this 'disease', again the advice is to remove the cause. In this case a little irascibility, in right measure, is not only allowed but encouraged.

Ṭūsī equates fear with apprehensiveness, noting that although most of the passions are focused on the past or immediately present experiences, fear is almost always focused on the future. Fear of death, Ṭūsī observes, is the most universal by far. Rational consideration of its universality should relieve us of some anxiety about it, although a prudent life will be lived in such a way that death will not find us unprepared for it. However, Ṭūsī is more concerned with the petty fears that surround the greater fear of death, such as worrying about whether it will hurt, fear of dying before one's task is done, fear of losing property and prestige. Fear of death considered in this light really amounts to scarcely more than a catalogue of things transitory and often as not trivial to which we become attached. Again reason, being the twin of detachment, should provide a very good remedy.

According to Ṭūsī, Plato himself is supposed to have said, "Die by will, and you will live by nature." The old Ṣūfī saying also comes to mind: "Die before you die!"—which reminds us of similar sayings in Meister Eckhardt and of the ancient Buddhist practice of meditating in graveyards. But again Ṭūsī would call us back to practicalities. He goes on to consider the more common causes of the fear of death, such as fear of punishment after death, for which the remedy is confession and absolution and restoration of innocence in a good conscience rather than any further worry about it at all. Likewise with worry about the welfare of one's family, business or whatever, they should simply be provided for within one's legitimate means without further worry about the rest. Ṭūsī concludes, "Death is not mean, as the common run of people suppose; on the contrary what is mean is the fear which is a necessary consequence of ignorance."[11]

Ṭūsī then considers the diseases of the faculty of attraction, which includes the appetites, love of idleness, grief and envy. Concerning excess of appetite, in our larger perspective by the thirteenth century we have considerably less emphasis on sheer asceticism and more emphasis on control and moderation, Chu-Hsi and Aquinas being prime examples of those who counsel moderation and control rather than ascetic denial, though we could also point to Honen and Shinran, Nimbārka, Madhva, and even more emphatically than Ṭūsī, Ibn Rushd. By way of *pūrvapakṣa* one could point to Dōgen, Lu Hsiang-shan, Citsukha or Ibn 'Arabī; nevertheless, even with them we scarcely find characters like Peter Damian, Bhartṛhari, Bodhidharma, al-Ḥallāj and other early Ṣūfīs, and some of those 'puritans' in Byzantium who were partisans of Iconoclasm. Ṭūsī appeals to al-Ghazālī, who had likened the appetitive faculty to a tyrannical revenue agent, for "if the latter have a hand to collect men's wealth, without any restraining or inhibiting force in the shape of punishment by the ruler or fear of God or a compassionate nature, he will seize all that the tenantry possess, afflicting everyone with destitution and poverty."[12]

Although Ṭūsī seems not to emphasize this, many of his contemporaries would also include intellectual and aesthetic appetite as needing similar discipline. Bernard of Clairvaux, for example, in the previous century had warned about idle curiosity that allows the mind to become fascinated with all sorts of miscellaneous information. Although Dōgen was not as extremely anti-intellectual as his Rinzai Zen contemporary and some-time teacher Eisai, and although he was himself quite an astute and even critical scholar, he did not put much store by it and denounced those who relished exhibitionism in display of learning. The Advaitins of the thirteenth century likewise, although intellectually brilliant, implicitly if not explicitly did not encourage 'secular' learning not connected with the "inquiry into Brahman". Bonaventure even went so far as to say that philosophy (meaning Aristotelianism with all its juggling of logical propositions as an end in itself) is the lowest descent the soul can reach. Finally, it was because of the temptations of the intellectual appetite in excess over real spiritual discipline that al-Ghazālī renounced his profession of logic professor to go off and associate himself with the Ṣūfīs and to write his refutation of Ibn Sīnā's Aristotelianism.

In his consideration of grief, if we did not know that it was in the perspective of Aristotle's *genesis* and *pthora* (coming-into-being and passing-away), we might even think that Ṭūsī was some sort of crypto-Buddhist. He quotes a typical didactic verse: "He who is rejoiced not to see what hurts him,/Let him not take up anything whose loss he fears!" Ṭūsī quotes an anonymous man of wisdom who said, "If the world had no further fault than the fact that it is on loan, it would still be proper that the man of noble purpose should pay it no heed." Finally he appeals to Socrates who is supposed to have said of happiness, "It is because I set my heart on no thing so as to become grief-stricken when it is lost."[13]

In conclusion, Siddiqi gives us this estimation of Ṭūsī and his importance:

> In an age of widespread political devastation followed by

> intellectual decline, Hulāgu's patronage to Ṭūsī is of singular importance in the history of Muslim thought. The revival and promotion of philosophical sciences in the late seventh/thirteenth century centered round Ṭūsī's personality....[14]
>
> Historically speaking, his position is mainly that of a revivalist. But from the standpoint of the history of culture, even the revival of the philosophical and scientific tradition, specially in an era of political and intellectual decline, though marked by tiresome erudition and repetition, is no less important than origination, inasmuch as it prepares the ground for the intellectual rebirth of a nation.[15]

Ṭūsī was equally prominent in mathematics and astronomy and the other sciences as well. Moreover he was no exception to the rule that mysticism and science were by no means at odds with each other in Islamic civilization: "Though not a mystic, he is an advocate of a rational treatment of mysticism."[16] In short, Ṭūsī was not merely a theologian in the limited sense, but all in all a well-rounded philosopher such as one typically finds in the Islamic tradition.

22. Bonaventure

St. Bonaventure (1221-1274) and St. Thomas (1225-1274) evidently met face to face only once or twice. But the way that their systems complement each other is another of those exemplifications of the *yin* and *yang* in history, as also in the case, for example, with Chu Hsi and Lu Hsiang-shan, and al-Ghazālī and Ibn Rushd. Bonaventure, like Rāmānuja and his school, is pimarily a *bhakta*, and indeed one of the few ecstatic souls who has had the patience to philosophize and administer a monastic society as well. The story is typical of this man that when the legate came from the Pope to offer him a cardinal's hat the legate was told to wait, for the dish washing must be finished first! It could never be said of Bonaventure that his learning compromised his humility.

Although after his rapture on Mount Alverno Bonaventure stayed on in the world until the *Itinerarium Mentis in Deum* and the *In Hexaemeron* were completed, it was with a certain patient impatience that he did so. If ever there was a Christian who reached the *jīvan mukti* or the Bodhisattva condition on earth, it was he. It is unfortunate that since the Roman Church has taken St. Thomas as its official philosopher much of the interpretation of St. Bonaventure has a Thomizing influence, a softening of his illuminationism and exemplarism and an attempt to crystallize the even and harmonious flow of piety, patience and perfection, of wit, wisdom and wonder. Like Plato he is an inveterate poet who nevertheless knows how to restrain from poetizing in order to distill another essence. And like al-Ghazālī, whom he admired, he was very much aware of the 'reduction' of everything to 'theology', by which he means not the theoretical disputations about God but the *immediate* operation of the Holy Spirit in rendering everything transparently referrable to its Source, Sustenance and End.

Bonaventure's exemplarism may be simply taken as closely allied to Rāmānuja's philosophy of embodiment whereby, by proportional analogy of Being, all things are at once other than God and yet are the embodiment of God: He is personally 'present' in them all—and in a sense doubly so in the soul—as their inner ruler, as their 'Soul of the soul' and as their 'end' in salvation. Love (*bhakti*) is this bond of intimacy made manifest. For both Bonaventure and Rāmānuja, in both the emanational order and in the causative order God provokes love because He is bliss, love, the end as well as the means of salvation.

Again and again Bonaventure stresses the importance of the affections as against the intellect. It was he who set the tradition of voluntarism which has been characteristic of Franciscan tradition ever since. The affections, not the intellect, set the will. But since voluntarism in the modern world means something slightly different, since there is a tendency to identify the affections more with aesthetics and the will with ethics, as the intellect with epistemology, it is good to keep in mind that for Bonaventure the will is not just a moral matter. It is also the seat of mystical devotion pure and simple, which includes also the aesthetic, and re-includes the intellect in the process: it is the will that effects mystical union. For, as with Rāmānuja, it is in affective devotion that the soul is freely under the inspiration of grace; and there is scarcely any philosopher in the history of all of western philosophy who lays more importance on grace. But grace in turn is primarily operative through meditation and contemplation; again, like Rāmānuja he is a *bhakta par excellence*, and not a *karma yogin* nor a *jñānī* as were Thomas Aquinas and Meister Eckhardt and the Dominicans in general.

In a little allegorical work entitled "The Six Wings of the Seraphim" Bonaventure suggests that the discipline of meditation is three-fold. First there is the constant memory of God. One should imitate the angels, who never depart from contemplation regardless of their mission. Although one cannot ordinarily be in a constant state of actual meditation, yet one can so direct the (subconscious) intuition of the heart by memory that whenever the opportunity arises the heart will surge up into actual prayer, just as a sculptor who, having always an image constantly in his imagination, will go to work on its embodiment in stone as soon as the opportunity arises. Secondly, in all actions and conversations one's continuous 'study' (i.e., focus of attention) should be toward pleasing God as though one were actually in His physical presence as before a judge in a tribunal who sees all that is going on. Thirdly, he counsels what is now called ejaculatory prayer: in everything one does, a quick effective leap of the mind in prayer should fortify the soul in such a way that the actions themselves will become expressions of prayer (as in the case also with *kaiṅkarya* for Śrī Vaiṣṇavas), the emphasis being on thanksgiving and praise. For this quick and secret prayer is more important than the actual work at hand.

Reason is only ancillary: by it we cannot 'prove' being, but by it we can distinguish grades of being, which are not to be considered as unreal. Being is essentially undifferentiated, but in such a way that it is structured by its capacity to produce relatedness. The first relatedness is simply that which prevents us—like Heidegger or Eckhardt or Śūnyavāda—from confusing Being with Nothing. The succeeding grades come in emanational order toward materialization in such a way that reason can follow back, by an *a posteriori* 'reduction', their inherent reality to the Prime Source, even though reason alone cannot embrace

That. In short, the relation of things and ideas to Being is that of qualified identity. Unlike the Advaitins, Bonaventure does not admit that *gnosis* in God is completely undifferentiated, but also, unlike the Aristotelians and Madhvas, he does not insist that there is no *unitive relation* which binds the world, ideas and souls to and within God. Thus his position is very close to that of Rāmānuja as far as ontology and ideation go.

Once one is inspired with Bonaventure's spirit it is not easy to settle down to careful analytical study of the details, for he himself saw the limitations of the analytical method. Rather, analysis, analogy and anagogy trilogize throughout his work. Indeed, he is so completely and consistently a trinitarian that it would seem that the Blessed Trinity had specially chosen him. Bonaventure is not a dialection, although like Rāmānuja when it is necessary he can dialecticize; for dialectic, like hierarchical principation and spiralling contemplation, is only one of three modes of ascent to the contuition (distinguished from intuition) of the Divine. The term *contuitus* seems to us to carry the connotation of repose, of the *established abiding* which is the same as Rāmānuja's fullness of connotation of the term *dhyāna*, wherein there is not merely recollection of the Lord as such, but also a peaceful, communing accord with the Lord because of His glorious and infinite qualities, which qualities are thereby, in their enjoyment, reflected participatively in the *jīva* also. *Plenitude in tranquillity*: intuition cannot possibly express this, nor the *mutuality of possession*, "My Beloved is mine and I am His": this is contuition, *dhyāna*, *bhakti* in every nuance of profundity and intimacy for both Rāmānuja and Bonaventure.

In his *Commentary on the Sentences* it is amazing how marvellously Bonaventure can take a traditional doctrine and infuse it with light and life. Especially important are the sections dealing with the *interincessiones* of the Blessed Trinity: the Three Persons are not interrelated in a simple triangular fashion but in such reciprocating, nine-fold interreciprocity that out of this can be explained every possible emanation, sustenance and 'reduction' leading back to the Divine Superabundance of Being. In many respects Bonaventure is closer to Padmapāda than to almost any other tradition. The image of the reflection in a mirror is one of his favorites, the whole of creation being the mirror. The soul of man, at least after he is led into the illuminative stage, is microcosm, the whole of the macrocosm in miniature. He makes much of the restoration of the *Imago Dei* as the ultimate end of salvation and sanctification and beatification: Christ restores man to the innocence he had before the fall of Adam. "It is only necessary to polish the mirror," he says in one place in a spirit quite different from that of Aquinas or even Augustine, who would rather emphasize the way of abstraction than risk the dangers of the borderfield between pantheism and panentheism. For Bonaventure the Truth is self-illuminating and therefore needs no exposition added to it, but rather needs only to be allowed a sufficient field of reflection in order to outshine all possible darkness. For Truth is not that whereby God and all else is known, but God *is* Truth.

The *Itinerarium Mentis in Deum* has rightly been described as the most marvellously carved jewel in the whole corpus of Christian mystical writings. The chapters on universal analogy and on intellectual illumination are in particular to be studied with care. There are others in whom this universal analogy becomes operative, particularly Abhinavagupta, the Kaśmir Śaiva philosopher, and Padmapāda, the interpreter of Śaṅkara. Concerning intellectual illumination, again the definition of *con*tuition as distinct from *in*tuition is to be carefully noted, for it is a term relatively unique in Bonaventure and seems to indicate very closely what the Rāmānuja school means by *parajñāna* and the Advaitins by *Brahma sākṣātkarātva*.

The *In Hexaemeron* is one of the most exalting and illuminating pieces of writing in any age or any language, even for its literary value, not to say its philosophical and religious value, embodying almost everything that may be found in Dante's *Divine Comedy*. In the *In Hexaemeron*, into the simple allegory of the six days of creation in Genesis Bonaventure weaves a whole tapestry of multidimensional considerations which *move* in a way that the structuralism of St. Thomas could scarcely allow. The non-Christian may find it difficult in some respects to see in Jesus of Nazareth all the things attributed to Him as the Eternal Word, but this is no more of a problem than with the mediaeval accretions around the Person of Kṛṣṇa, for example. One may find here something that is not just the traditional repetition of set formulae, for St. Bonaventure seems to achieve certainty in an area where others are still fumbling in the dark.

For Bonaventure it is more important to trace the emanational order of the eternal art, the work of the intellectual creature and of the sensible world, than it is to trace the sense impressions back through the logic of universals and particulars. Aristotelian syllogistic logic is not a principle but an instrument of the lowest level for gathering material for contemplation. Bonaventure does not condemn it but sees its function as merely ancillary. Christ's life is also the perfect syllogism: the major is the passion, the minor is death and the conclusion is the resurrection. Christ as dwelling in us is the *hegemōn* up the mountain of contemplation, whose base is the political virtues, whose middle is the purgative virtues, and whose summit is the cardinal virtues.

The division between the *status viatoris* and the *status patriae* then becomes vivid. Here the seven departments of wisdom which must come under this 'second level' of illuminative certainty (metaphysics, physics, mathematics, logic, ethics, politics, theology) are illumined only imperfectly, but in the Fatherland (Heaven) they are in complete illumination. But this is still only a beginning, for this illumination is only a preparation for the inflaming of the affections and the strengthening of the effects. This ardency of desire for wisdom—for which St. Bonaventure is called the Seraphic Doctor—is directed through discipline, delight, rectitude, custody of the laws, sanctification, incorruption, and 'deiformity'. It may already be seen how that Bonaventure has found a way of philosophizing which is more like the music of Brahms or César Franck than the pedantic semantic dead ends of positivists and the usual sort of sermon-vendors which fill too many of our universities and churches today. It is as though when he says Mass, the whole of the Heavenly Hierarchy becomes visible to the naked eye and, as it were, one peers through the whole panoply of the galaxies and constellations right into the immaterial sanctuary of the Supreme, where the act of worship becomes compellingly involuntary. The classical Greek *meden agan* has completely yielded to the *nihil satis* of the Gothic pointed arch. Bonaventure takes over where Boethius had left off: there is no longer a search for wisdom but a veritable explosion of certitude. The Johanine *idou erchou*, "come and see", becomes irresistible, and not minding the suffering for the glory that awaits at the summit, one climbs.

Thus Bonaventure does not believe in the extinction of desire nor even the moderation of desire, but counsels fanning it until it becomes an all-consuming flame of purgation leading through the difficult barriers of realizing God as the Author of Wisdom. This leading must penetrate the uniform, the multiform, the omniform, and the nulliform, the first manifesting itself in the rules of the divine law, the second in the mysteries of divine scripture, the third in the *vestigia* (in the full Platonic sense) of good works, and the last in a suspension of divine excess. In elaboration of the scheme he says of the first, the uniform, that it is thus that we know the modes by which a thing is its necessary being, and that this existential nature of things has so linked with the highest good as to promote intrinsically veneration and love. This existentialist orientation brings him to a typical criticism of Aristotle: things do not have their *ratio essendi* 'ad exterius'. Everything as bearing within itself its own God-infused law of intrinsic existence has its own *singularity of form*, which is really more than it needs for itself alone but whose certitude and necessity overflow back, as it were, into the Divine Mind. Thus every individuated existent, as an individuation of the Divine Light, is worthy, as revealing the fullness of the Lord's glorious qualities, of being the object of contemplation; and reciprocally, things are so seen only in a state of contemplation, of *dhyāna*, which itself is an intensification of that same Light and Love.

The second, the multiform, is best exemplified in the manyness of the modes of reparation: there is not just one sacrament, not just one Mystery, but many. This statement, which Bonaventure is emphatic in making, is much more akin to Jaspers' opinions about exclusiveness than to the dogmatism of modern scholasticism, and akin again to the spirit of toleration in Rāmānuja, who in the *Gītā Bhāṣya* notes that anyone who comes in sincere devotion to deity in any form (for God is not limited by any particularity of form) will be received as though the devotion were consciously to the highest Form. The only requirement is the exercise of the 'theological' virtues of faith, hope and love:

faith, which opens the way to the (hidden) allegorical meanings; hope, which opens up the anagogical way to the fullness of grace; and love, which takes the soul to the certitude and secrets of mystical union, as typified in the cry of the lover in the Song of Solomon, "How beautiful are Thy cheeks, O my Love!" Thus truth, when its mystery is unveiled, is found to be identical with beauty (and only then!); and hence the coy hiding behind the veil makes the multiplicity of the forms of wisdom meaningful: there are as many forms of wisdom as there are forms of truth, and only those who are pure and simple enough to see its beauty are allowed to look behind them. *Dhyāna*, then, is no less than a taking part in this *līlā*, this game, of love.

In dilating on the third 'face of wisdom', the omniform, Bonaventure urges that one should be always (meditatively, in a state of communion) looking deeper and deeper into the essential Reality, in which lies the Wisdom of God—looking into the measure, the number, and the inclinations of Creation, into the modes by which reality has constancy, the appearances by which it is discerned, and the order in which it is congruously arranged; for all of these are the *vestigia*, the foot-prints of the Divine Wisdom, which are not to be taken only metaphorically, as Plato thought of them, but as the existent essences or Divine Ideas in them which confer reality on them in a way that only the contemplative man who has entered into the Mind of God can apprehend. Thus, moreover, is surmounted the whole hierarchical dialectic of substance and accident, potentiality and actuality, and one comes directly to the 'representation' of the Trinity wherein the Father is the Origin, the Son is the Image, and the Holy Spirit is the binding of the Two together, that is, making the contemplative Return possible.

Bonaventure warns against "curiosity", that manner of dealing with things which would put God in a test tube and try by experimental method whether the contemplative method is the best or not. There is much work to be done in the right ordering of these respective methods, just as there is danger in confusing them. The wisdom of God, Bonaventure says, is to be considered according to number, weight, and measure, but even these words take on a whole symphony of overtones which are by no means mathematical only. The mode, species and order of God's operation are to be taken, like almost everything else under the influence of the illumination of the Holy Spirit, in analogical relation to the infinite 'joining' of the Blessed Trinity. Matter, form and adhesion are all subsumed under the divine operation in such a way that whatever the existent may be in its compositeness, it must be seen as containing not only in structure, but in relationality and in transcendence of relation, an inseparability from God. Substance, virtue and operation again only lead up to the effusion of the Wisdom of God. The Platonic *vestiguum* is topped by two other levels, the Image and the operation of Grace—and yet not levels only but interrelationalities which at once embody and bind and compel the Return into God. Memory, intelligence and will (the triad from Augustine) are seen not only as individual psychological functions but as divine principles, as universally operative in both microcosm and macrocosm.

These three again are harmonized with immortality, wisdom and joyfulness, leading to a permissible excess of zeal in which all things are seen within a Divine Light. The Love of God first sequesters the soul coming into this illumination, then induces a sort of soporific condition, at least as far as worldly matters are concerned, and then lifts it up to a new level of purely psycho-pneumatic activity. The word he uses here is *pertansit*. It is simply going across into a paranormal field of experience which most of modern 'scientific' psychology has not yet rediscovered. Every creature who has made the reduction of the conversion of the mind according to mystical discipline not only shares in the bliss of the Supreme but also comes to experience himself and all fellow-creatures as part and parcel of that open Unity, which, moreover, is open and fertile for the simple but profound reason that it is itself of the affective and not of the gnostic order. Hence also the impossibility of separating mysticism and logic, philosophy and religion, wisdom and theology. However, this cannot become completely clear until we have come all the way through to the final fruit of Perfection, of Beatitude. It is this that Bonaventure goes into under the nulliform, the *via negativa*, the *neti, neti*. Contrary to what might be expected, Bonaventure does not, as for example Eckhardt does, take this entrance into the Divine Obscurity, the Cloud of Unknowing, as an identity of being and knowing above or transcending love, but as the field of excess of the zeal of love.

Here Bonaventure is following Pseudo-Dionysius, but he seems to outstrip his *hegemōn* even as Dante goes on where Virgil must linger behind. This is, in short, a very high degree of contemplative prayer in which God is immediately seen as one, wise, and eternal. Now the meaning of the Word as the divine hypostasis of God's own giving of meaningfulness to creation is opened up. Now it is clearly and immediately known what is meant by God's understanding all things in understanding Himself. Now the realm of the Spirit is not understood remotely by faith, but in a 'second nature' the things of God are experienced as vividly as physical objects were handled before the transformation. This transmutation however, like the net in the *Laṅkāvatāra Sūtra*, leads not to any disturbance but to an understanding of the ultimate paradoxes of the relations of the metaphysical principles of stability and mutability, of the simple and the composite, and the most subtle and the most infinite. The formula *adequatio rei et intellectus* thus takes on an entirely different significance than in the other scholastics. It is not an adequation of formal logic but an immediate operation of the Eternal Word as the living truth, infusing both thing and intellect with significance which is not of themselves. Thus one speaks in metaphors, but the metaphors do not escape from material referents, are not mere embellishments but functional flying buttresses to lift the ceiling higher and higher until one is no longer aware that there is any ceiling at all, only an upsurge of spirit in response to a flood of light in which everything takes on a pictorial aspect.

In this light the old *ex nihilo* conundrum is resolved, for thus through the Word the 'hidden' things of the world—the reference is to Hebrews 11:3 but with full awareness that in this is included the entire corpus of Greek metaphysics—are understood so that from the One the Many, from the actual the composite, from the highest the lowest are made through the Word giving the principle "*de se, de nihilo, de aliquo.*" Elsewhere, however, he says *ex se, de nihilo, pro altero*. In this perspective the Word, in conjunction with the Holy Spirit, is understood to be the *purgator*, *illuminator*, and *consummator*.

According to Bonaventure, all the principles, otherwise thought of in the systems as outside the soul, are really only the structure and function and irradiation of what the soul of man must become. The hierarchized soul enjoys privileges which even the angels do not share, for they remain only like the pane of unstained glass through which the light shines without refraction, whereas the human soul is like the whole spectrum of prismatized light which shines through the stained glass of the world, giving it pattern and form and explicating the glory of God.

The traditional theories of causation are subjected by Bonaventure to some rather radical revisions. For causation is usually thought of only in terms of origin or as cause of motion. But Bonaventure sees this as only one-third of the picture at most. For origin, exemplar, and finish are again in perfect analogous functioning relation with the Blessed Trinity-in-Unity, so that notions or speculation about things, the causal capacity of things to be experienced, and the motives and affections of the soul toward doing things, are seen not as a static triangle that 'stays put' but as one which begins to spin on its centre so that the triangle is no longer seen but a circle appears! For Bonaventure, *māyā* is *līlā māyā* as much as for the Rāmānuja school. Substance, figure and nature are not merely appearances but are Being as infinitely self-caused in universal manifestation and as inexhaustible possibility of simplification. He does make a further division of Being according to substance and accident, universal and particular, potential and actual, one and many, simple and composite, cause and caused; but this traditional schematism comes to life in his hands, for herein the moral and aesthetic aspects of existence are in complete coincidence with the ontological.

In Bonaventure the Aristotelian virtues of truthfulness, nemesis, truth, wit, friendship, humility, chastity, fortitude, magnificence, liberality, magnanimity and others are subordinated to instruments of manifestations of God's own goodness, not merely the voluntary exercise of means of merit on the part of the aspiring or duty-bound individual. Art, prudence, wisdom, intellect and science are subjoined to the intertwining of necessity principle and divine cause of rectitude, in which "prudence ascends to wisdom through intelligence, descends into art through 'science'", in the same way that the speculative, practical and ecstatic virtues at once express the down-going of Word and the uplifting of Spirit. Aristotle would scarcely recognize himself in these garments, for all virtue in this perspective takes the aspect of sacrificial worship. The Church should not be merely a leaven within the state but an agent of the transformation of the whole of human existence into its rightful claim to God's own Providence, Prosperity and Plenitude. The animal, intellectual, and divine aspects of man's existence are thus taken up through exterior objects, interior virtues, and contemplative possibilities to the perfect union with God..

Following the Venerable Bede, Bonaventure does not see much in the world that is not subject to vanity, but we have come a long way from the pathological gloom of some of the earlier and more severe expostulators of the doctrine of original sin, which to Bonaventure has been *completely* overcome by the redemption of Christ. The way to the Fatherland is open. Mere human happiness as Aristotle sought to define it is not the end of man; rather we must pass on to salvation through sanctification to beatitude. These three stages are analogized to the three functions of the Holy Spirit in enabling us to follow the example of the Christ against infirmities: through the documents of truth against ignorance, through the incitements of enlivening love against malice, and through the remedies of the sacraments against concupiscence. Faith originates this ascent, hope uplifts us, and charity completes it. Charity enjoys the ascent even though it may appear that it has nothing to *do*. *Credens*, *fidens*, *fervens*: another of those little trilogisms which one can take along into one's solitude and into society also.

Faith for Bonaventure is not just another *prāmana* or means of knowing. It is an infusion of another dimension into human life affecting the whole being of man so that interior/exterior, even more than with some Vijñāna texts, is capped with the *superior* as the 'valid third' after the other two have failed in themselves. But these are also transformed into the superior once it is open. The illuminations are then inflamed with a seraphic fire of consummation in which there is, without disorder or confusion, one substance, one virtue, one operation, analogous to the role of the Holy Spirit in the Divine Economy.

Being entails participation, the full Platonic doctrine with the Simplicity of God at the apex and with the derived orders so related to it that even though they are involved in multiplicity there is never a departing from the possibility of their completion in that same Simplicity in which they had their origin. From this the Perfection of the Trinity is readily seen in the eternity, wisdom and beatitude of God Who is the Guarantor of the condition of perfection, of production, of diffusion, of the produced and of diffused delight.

Bonaventure's delineation in the *In Hexaemeron* of the varieties of unity is rivalled perhaps only by some pages from Rāmānuja's works. Here Bonaventure's panentheism is at its best. Essentially the same problem is encountered in the different schools of the Vedānta, as also of Islam and Neo-Confucianism vis-à-vis Māhāyāna Buddhism, where the condtion of perfection being linked with the ineffable (*anirvacanīyā*) is necessarily a descriptive limitation. In the Viśiṣṭādvaita, Bhedābheda and Dvaita schools, however, it is considered necessary to describe Being even if the description is nothing but that being is indescribable. But the further question is whether the description itself is only formal or whether it participates in the Being of That which it describes. Further, if we admit descriptibility, how far do we go, since somehow the perfection of Being in God entails an unlimited infinity of possible attributes and relations, but in a different mode from that which obtains in ordinary things. For in divine things this multiplexity does not compromise simplicity. This problem bothered most of the scholastics as much as it ought to bother us. Duns Scotus was considerably occupied with it, as were his Japanese Buddhist contemporaries. But whether Bonaventure completely resolves the paradoxes involved one must judge for oneself. At the minimum we are confronted with the proposition that "Being is full of being", without, nevertheless, falling into quantitative thinking, even though it cannot be denied that Being does contain the category of quantity along with all the other categories.

Bonaventure's treatment of the proper method of approaching the Scriptures will not be welcome to a great number of secularists, but those who have the patience will be rewarded by further enquiry. Essentially it is the same as that found in the

Vedāntic schools: *śravaṇa*, *manana*, *nididhyāsana*, *dhyāna*, i.e., reading or 'hearing', consideration, entrance, and passive contemplation with all hindrances removed. The analytical study must be followed by analogical enlargements and personal appropriation. One *enters*, becomes part of it, becomes *subject* to the truth involved and no longer the manager of the truth from the outside. Then one becomes the truth upon which one meditates. The anagogical must likewise follow the analogical. "It is necessary", he says, "to consider, to accept, to love the precepts of God." One thinks of St. Bonaventure somewhat as one does St. Francis himself, and the relation between them was a bit closer than that between St. Dominic and St. Thomas. His *ascesis* is not that of rigorous mortifications so much as that of adequate fruition. He speaks freely of various fruits of contemplation, but the highest remains, in all virginal simplicity, wisdom.

From contemplation of the Highest Good he proceeds to the consideration of the gifts of grace and supernatural charity. "Without charity there is neither grace nor justice nor wisdom", and "Without charity neither mysteries nor martyrdoms nor briefly anything else avails anything." Whereas other virtues may become exhausted, this same charity radiates in ever-increasing reciprocity between self, God and neighbor, between body, soul and spirit, between itself as charity and holy joy and in union with God in abundance of peace. For the fruits of the spirit are gifts, not possessions.

Bonaventure introduces the scheme of *scientia*, *sanctitas*, *sapientia*, which seems still rather universally applicable. This is followed with another subordinate scheme on the mode of study which should be according to order, assiduity, complacency and commensurability. Each of these is enlarged in turn although we may not follow in such detail. However, another little delicacy not to be passed by is the observation that the animals which chew the cud (of contemplation) are the most peaceful. Thus should the Scriptures be treated, not devoured voraciously nor violently cast aside.

The rest of the *In Hexaemeron* goes on into an esoteric field that will be very strange indeed to most of us, for it sounds like what Theosophy and the Rosicrucians propound or weakly echo today. It involves, as Bonaventure himself records, "things not allowed for man to utter." And yet he was only continuing a tradition long since firmly established even within the Christian fold by Dionysius and many others. This includes the range of astrology, expositions of the hierarchized Soul after it becomes fully microcosm, and a profound probing within the ranks of sound philosophical discipline of the depths and heights of the relation of God and the human soul as it approaches beatification. Those who are already familiar with Dante will not dismay overmuch.

Purity, 'actuality' and luminosity are grouped together to describe the Divine "Monarch" (there was not yet any democracy in the Kingdom of Heaven) Who is self-effulgent much in the same way as the Vedāntic schools describe. He takes Wisdom (Sepientia, the Hagia Sophia of Byzantine tradition whose role is like that of Sarasvatī, the *śakti* of Brahma, or Kuan Yin of Buddhist tradition in China and Japan) as the symbolic figure whose relation with God makes the ecclesiastical hierarchy possible, corresponding to the Celestial Hierarchy. Here we have an extreme instance of the heavenly *yang* and the earthly *yin* in harmony without the division-in-conflict which is so common in western tradition. The soul (*ātman*, not *jīva*) is made robust, jocund, adorned, corresponding to the *vīrya pāramitā* of the Mahāyāna.

The section on the militant Church, with its ranks hierarchized in accord with the total plan, may not interest many moderns except as a historical study. However, there is here an opening of a range of overtones of great significance for we have at base a definite sociology of religious types which affords a maximum of variations within a unified society, a society moreover with a purpose well defined, i.e., not the mere organization of the *zoōn politikon* of Aristotle but a body leading toward achieving a supra-mundane goal. This is parallel to the hymns of Shinran concerning the Amida Land, and is one of the best Christian counterparts of Ibn Khaldūn's efforts at a philosophy of civilization although it may not be quite so comprehensive.

The last section of the *In Hexaemeron* is likewise too floridly drawn for most modern streamlined souls, but the contents of the allegory are a gold mine of spiritual direction, of evidence that there was a new, creative, almost Promethian, fire in the world. Again there is a good typology of souls: the twelve sons of Jacob who become Israel, the twelve signs of the Zodiac, the precious stones in their astrological significance—all join in tracing the ascent to God, the trans-descent for the sake of the neighbor, and the *regressus in Deum* which he has traced in greater detail in the *Itinerarium Mentis in Deum.* Needless to say the angelic hierarchy is still there, and they now serve in the role of *nuntiatio*, *dictatio* and *ductio*. The ascent is through nature, industry and grace. The descent is more dangerous and the virtues must be treated *suseptivae*, *custodivae* and *distributavae* in order that they may be copiously borne, studiously guarded and liberally distributed. Here, needless to say, a great tranquillity in judging is counselled—*caveat* Nietzsche! Indeed here one seems to find the delicacies of the *Zarathustra* without the venom. But the Tantric systems of India and Tibet have the Divine Downwardness, the Śaktivāda, which, like the problem of re-entry in space travel, is the most dangerous part. Bonaventure counsels in effect that if the motive is humility then the re-entry will be safe and profitable to all. The *now no longer I* will be valid without any anxiety about it. The *regressus in Deum*, although it is only an enlargement on Gregory's commentary on Ezekiel, is very much like the distinction between *jīvan mukti* and *videha mukti* in Hindu tradition, or like the Bodhisattva stage and after in the Mahāyāna tradition.

This *regressus* completed, there follows a brief consideration of the things above itself on the part of the soul, to which it can scarcely attain without spiritual rapture. This must be sharply distinguished from secular ecstasy, such as Scriabin and Proust are concerned with, even though it is frankly erotic. One may observe the same motif in some of the Ṣūfīs, and it will be remembered that although those trained in the *Bhagavatam* tradition cultivated this to a very fine degree indeed, most of the Buddhists, except perhaps Honen and Shinran, distrusted it, putting the emphasis on the expansion of awareness rather than the heightening of the effections. Following on this the ranges of the operation of charity (*mahākaruṇā*) are enlarged by an indissoluable bond, an insuperable inflaming, an incomprehensible solace. It must not be thought that these things have no social extension.

as the Neo-Confucians accused the Buddhists of allowing. For the Holy Spirit will not be content with private affairs of the heart. The whole of Church and therefore the whole of humanity will still be benefited even after the *regressus.* For the beatified soul then belongs to the cult of the saints, and the Church is quite justified in sanctioning cults following in the wake of their charisma. In St. Bonaventure there is no simple good as such. All goodness *overflows*!

One of Bonaventre's favorite ways of distinguishing almost everything involved in the problem of perfection and imperfection, or of grace and glory, is the characteristic distinction of being in the way, *in via*, from being in the Fatherland, by which he means Heaven. In India generally the whole concept of *saṃsāra* is quite closely parallel to this, as is evidenced, for example, in the story in the fourth sūtra of the *Srī Bhāṣya* of the prodigal prince who does not know his true identity until he is recognized by others. The *valle lacrimarum* of European heritage carries the same semantic weight, not only in designating the nature of the world as such, but as indicating that the way out of it is a *way of return*. The attainment of Brahman, or the entrance into Vaikuṇṭha, is of the nature of a *rencontre*, a reunion, a regaining of what had been lost by the 'fall' into *avidyā* and *māyā*. *Karma* and *avidyā* are somehow beginningless, but they never completely mar the inherent nature of the soul, whose cyclic journey through the world(s) has no other purpose (at least for the Vaiṣṇava) than to quicken the eventual return and restoration of this inherent nature. The whole philosophy of Bonaventure will be misread if this doctrine of the return is not kept at the centre. This return moreover, is hierarchical; and although grace may speed the re-ascent from the Fall, still it can scarcely be done all at once.

The essential thing in the mediaeval systems is not "arguments for survival" but the inalienable and unavoidable consideration that man cannot but think of himself as capable of beatitude, and that this ideal is only partially realized in this present world, which must be only a *preparation* for the ultimate goal. The doctrine of the Fall, the obscuring of the Image, the involvement in the negative mystery of disobedience, ignorance, guilt, and delusion by the senses and appetites—the loss, in short, of the knowledge of divine origin—these remain indelibly in us, both individually and collectively. Somehow mankind has got into this condition, and we cannot know how until we get out of it. And yet the release, the salvation, the restoration, is not a somehow. The clarion call of the Buddha that *there is a way to end suffering* has its counterpart in every religion and is the taproot of every serious philosophy proposed by man. Even the dead-end frustration of a Kafka or a Sartre reaches some termination and still *seeks* for a solution: nihilism may not end in glory, but it cannot go on forever. The positivism of the Buddha ("Don't argue about the source and nature of the arrow that caused the wound, but take it out!"), the Biblical "Today is the day of salvation", the exigence of the Vaiṣṇava philosophy of grace whereby even the inevitability of karma's inexorable law can be superseded by divine intervention—these we must affirm, not so much by rational choice as by a deep movement of the soul, a primordial Need in the Unconscious.

At the end of much bulk of material patiently argued according to the tradition of his times (which is no more or less involved than that of Rāmānuja) at the end of Bonaventure seems to "throw up the book" and come out with his own personal convictions about proceeding towards perfection. The face and fervent spirit of St. Francis seem to break through the dogmatic formularies, in the same way that sometimes one senses Nammalwar's inspiration behind Rāmānuja's formal arguments. After all is said and done, and all theology with its involved technicalities is exhausted, the only thing that is of importance in the business of salvation, and all that follows after as well, is *bhakti*. *Mokṣa* can never be the end in itself, and certainly its attainment can never be automatic, much less reduced to a sure technique. Grace, dependence on God in ardent devotion—this is the whole story. *Bhakti* never comes to an end. And here the Vaiṣṇavas and the Franciscans alike have a lot to teach those of us who are too much tied up with a technological civilization which frustrates by exteriorization and alienation from our warmest and inmost movements of passion, reflection, and sincere enjoyment—too much technologizing of the psyche itself, too many "techniques" in all human relations, too much "psychology of adjustment", as though the all-too-immortal soul of man could also be put right by a simple twist of the screwdriver. The pilot of the jet plane may pass the sonic barrier, but he still has the same problems, he is still subject to the same spiritual urgencies, in his inmost heart, as the mediaeval pilgrim on the footpath.

23. Thomas Aquinas

Three keys for the understanding of Thomas Aquinas (1224-1275) can be presented in the phrase "Christian Aristotelian System". Thomas was an Aristotelian insofar as his fundamental metaphysical concepts and a large part of his philosophical vocabulary are taken from Aristotle, and the philosophical problems with which he deals are to a great extent those delineated by Aristotle. In Europe, Aristotle's *The Categories* and *On Interpretation*—translated into Latin by Boethius in the sixth century—were the only Aristotelian works known first hand before the twelfth century. Aristotle's metaphysics was known only second and third hand and in the paraphrases of commentators. In addition, what was known was a highly Neo-Platonized Aristotelianism. But in the twelfth century Aristotle's writings began arriving in Europe in the form of Arabic and Hebrew translations, and in the thirteenth century Greek texts began arriving from Constantinople. The "real" Aristotle was met with considerable hostility on the part of more conservative Christian theologians. However, efforts were quickly made to put Aristotelian metaphysics to use in the service of Christian theology. Thomas represents one of the first and greatest attempts to reconcile Aristotelian philosophy and Christian dogma and to explain the latter in terms of the former.

In speaking of Thomas as a Christian Aristotelian, the emphasis must always be placed upon "Christian". He was willing to reject Aristotle's teachings whenever they conflicted with the teachings of the Church. Finally, much more than with St. Augustine, it seems that one of the keys to understanding St. Thomas is the word "system". He did *construct* one on an

Aristotelian foundation. And like the architects of the great Gothic cathedrals of Europe, he leaves no detail of the plan unattended yet never gets lost in the execution.

One of Thomas' great skills is in presenting arguments according to the typical scholastic method. The question (always formulated so that it is answerable either with a yes or no) is first stated. Then come the most important arguments of his predecessors and contemporaries who have answered the question in the affirmative. Then comes the presentation of the arguments for a negative answer. Finally, the resolution of the question in which Thomas presents his own views, which more often than not are a synthesis of the opposing views rather than a simple acceptance of either position. This raises a basic question in interpreting St. Thomas, namely the relation of faith and reason. A parallel from the Advaitin tradition might be the relation between *jñāna* and *avidyā*, *māyā*, *adhyāsa* or whatever is postulated as covering Brahman with the double veil of *āvaraṇa* and *vikṣepa*, the ambivalence of being revealed while being concealed. Or in Rāmānuja's version there is the parallel relation between the *parajñāna* which follows *parabhakti*, that form of devotion which is all-consuming and leaves no room for any thought or deed whatsoever that does not redound to the praise of God.

With St. Thomas as with any Christian Scholastic, there is a certain inseparability of faith, hope and divine charity; but with him the theological pivot is faith. Natural reason can and must be trusted in all matters of experience, in the conduct of science, and in all ethical matters, and to a very great measure in the interpretation of faith itself; but it only leads to faith which *completes* it without being in conflict with it. The realm of faith does not coincide with the realm of metaphysics for that realm is completely conformable to the canons of reason. Metaphysics proceeds according to the method of demonstration, faith according to the method of revelation, which accepts Scripture as final authority. Faith takes over where opinion fails, being an opening of the strictly spiritual faculty, which to Thomas is still not necessarily mystical or intuitive but is of such an order of immediacy that there is no hiatus between being and knowledge. Faith in other words covers that realm where the adequation of intellect and being is complete and without any residue of probability. Hence faith gives more certainty than merely rational knowledge, yet without destroying natural knowledge which is only incomplete without faith.

Might reason even put to test what the Church was teaching? Surprisingly enough, most of the Scholastics replied yes! The Quodlibital Questions of Thomas are concerned with just this: the New Testament tested by Aristotelian logic! For Thomas, like the others, distinguishes faith from blind credulity even more vividly than the passages in the commentaries on the *Brahma Sūtras* distinguish between *śraddhā* and *tarka*. As Thomas puts it:

> Accordingly Christian theology may call on philosophy to perform three offices. First, to demonstrate the groundwork of faith, for the truths of natural religion—for instance that God exists, that there is one God, and so forth—can be proved by philosophy and are presupposed to religious belief and are necessary elements in the science of faith, or Christian theology. Secondly, to declare analogies common to nature and grace: thus Augustine draws illustrations of the Trinity for philosophical teachings. Thirdly to resist attacks on faith, by showing that they are either wrongly conceived or at least unsupported and cannot be pressed. Those who apply philosophy to the Christian Revelation should be on their guard against two faults. One is to invoke the tenets of unsound philosophy as Origen did. The other, which would confine the truths of faith within the bounds of philosophy, as though belief could not go beyond the reaches of reason, in effect turns things inside out, for philosophy should be kept within the bounds of faith: "bringing into captivity every thought to the obedience of Christ" (2 Cor. x 5).

This last point is Thomism's most vulnerable heel. Although Thomas himself is quite careful with this procedure, it has been made the basis of much intolerance, stupidity, and even fanatical persecution—Galileo, for example, and the inquisition at Goa, not to say the wrecking of the Jesuits' excellent work in India, Japan, China and Latin America by the Dominican and Franciscan friars only a few centuries after this great Dominican capitulated to this demand of orthodoxy. Surely he conceded this point unwillingly, for elsewhere he can be found to say explicitly that any truth that is irrefutably true must be in accord with the Truth of God, for truth can be only of God who alone knows no falsehood and who must necessarily therefore will that no single separate truth ever need to be subordinated to another insofar as it is true. Even if one grant that in the orders of truth there may be distinctions of value, just as there may be weights of semantical intention in different words used in the same manner or a single word used in many senses, nevertheless to insist that one must come under the subservience of another order is simply preposterous. Although the level of universality may make one truth more applicable, more invariably demonstrable, nevertheless, insofar as *any* proposition is true it must be equally true with all other truths. Revelation and reason may be concerned with different fields, different disciplines, different sciences, but there is no way of demonstrating that it is true unalterably that one should come under the censorship of the other. Let us therefore suggest that had Thomas been living in the twentieth century he might well have revised this to the effect that reason and revelation naturally and therefore according to Divine Providence are related as *yin* and *yang*—neither can assume the ascendency without eventually yielding to the other.

The reason why faith bears such a tremendous load in Thomism is because Thomas openly insists that all human knowing begins with sense perception. With Aristotle, he is an inveterate empiricist. It is because of this that he has to find the alternative to the Ideas of the Platonic tradition. Faith is just that. But just as faith must not overstep its bounds in asserting absolute certainty about details of divine truth, so faith is unnecessary in the procedures of natural science itself. Nevertheless, faith may spring from the conclusions of the natural sciences by the logic of proportion into well-established probabilities about the Unseen, just as science can confidently proceed with probabilities about the empirically determinable world. For the Thomist, faith may not, must not, contradict reason. Zen and Thomism are about as compatible as the square and the circle. They are perhaps irreducible types and there is no use in trying further to synthesize them.

As for the five proofs for the existence of God—from change ("motion"), efficient causality, contingency, degrees of perfection, and design—St. Thomas borrows heavily from Aristotle and Ibn Sīnā as well as from the traditional biblical and Augustinian sources. As demonstrations *quia* (moving from effect to cause) it is questionable whether they have the unconditional validity of a demonstration *propter quid* (which moves from essence to properties) and are thus only means to establish a high probability; or whether, more as one finds in the Vedāntic schools, they are only means for removing hindrances to the pure *darśan* or immediate 'seeing' of God in His Self-existence and Self-luminosity. It is interesting to note that the Indian tradition, with the exception of Sāṃkhya, rather consistently rejected the demonstrability of the existence of *Īśvara*. Rāmānuja's criticisms of such proofs are particularly insightrul and anticipate Hume in many respects. It is an especially serious question whether the being so "proved" as the Prime Mover and the *Actus Purus* is the same as the God of Abraham, Issạc and Jacob, not to mention the question whether it in turn is the same as Brahman or Tao.

Thomas rejects Anselm's ontological argument on the grounds that it is impossible to comprehend and thus define God. However, such a criticism seems little more than a quibble. Whether or not "that than which none greater can be conceived" properly defines God, as long as it is not self-contradictory and correctly characterizes Him, it can serve as the premise for a demonstration. For Thomas the difficulty lies in the appeal to self-evident truths, since one of the most obvious self-evident truths is that our minds are finite and can at best approximate absolute truth only by rational analogies and the operation of grace and faith. If the latter two were not necessary, then we might appeal to self-evident truth. But as long as we are dealing with rational proofs *as proofs*, we must adhere to the Aristotelian canons without exaggeration or alteration. Although he rejects Anselm, St. Thomas does not deny that the existence of God must be self-evident *in itself*, but this does not entail that it must be so *for us*. In other words, as creatures our existence involves a complexity which is inappropriate to the strictly theological realm. Only God's existence is truly simple, even though it is self-communicating. There are different orders of existence just as there are different modes. But the movement through them is really from the singular existence of God through them, giving them existence in a reduplicative manner which we can only dimly trace because (or as long as) we are involved in the complexity.

Each item in Thomas' system has its own contingent place, foundation, cause, and existence in an ordered if not particularly dynamic cosmos. There is no 'emptiness' or cult of chaotic creativity in Aquinas. Everything is *there*, precisely defined, and functioning in its own proper limited range of operation. Complexity for Aquinas is never a confused nexus of potentiality; there is no "night of Brahma", or even if there might be, the Cause of the darkness would be discovered if one proceeded rationally to investigate it. And if, at the other extreme, not everything irradiates in the self-effulgence of Divine Splendor, this does not mean that each individual is completely cut off from the potency of subserving the Cause of all Light according to its proper form and actuality—this quite literally, for St. Thomas does not like merely poetic metaphors. A further extension of this concept of causality is the teaching, again inherited from Aristotle, that everything in creation is a composite of potential and actual, and only God is completely Actual. At the other end of the spectrum is Prime Matter, which is (almost) pure potentiality. Although prime matter is almost devoid of qualities and remains wholly imperceptible, we must presuppose its existence if we are to explain the possibility of substantial change.

In addition to this traditional Aristotelian view of creatures as a composite of act (substantial form) and potency (prime matter), Thomas views creatures as a composite of act and potency in an even more fundamental way. They are all, he says with Ibn Sīnā, a composite of essence (potency) and existence (act). The two must be distinct, Thomas argues, for it is obvious that we can know *what* something is without knowing *whether* it is. In God alone is there no such distinction between essence and existence; the former essentially includes the latter. Thus God is pure act in a much more radical sense than simply being pure form. Even the angels are pure form. However they too are in poteney insofar as they are capable of accidental changes and insofar as their essence does not include their existence.

Thomas' four causes (material, efficient, formal, and final), which he inherited from Aristotle, can with some qualifications be compared to the four levels of *sat* in the Vedānta, viz., the *mithyā*, *pratibhāsika*, *vyāvahārika*, and *pāramārthika*. Rāmānuja's school sees the lower three as more or less intensive qualifications of the over-inclusive *pāramārthika*; but Madhva convincingly argues that if one does not rightly discern the difference between each of these he is violating every known law of logic and being known to man. Like Madhva, Thomas says that the fact that a possible object, a fact, a proposition, a theory, cannot be said to exist for the sake of another indicates a definite state of being different from the other although related to it, not by its own potency (*śakti*), but by virtue of origin, existence, position and operation. The world with all its differences is thus a "block" universe, a solid, four dimensional *reality*.

Aquinas holds no unusual views on predestination and contributes nothing new. Although he would have the reader believe that he is in essential agreement with Augustine, Thomas' view reflects the greatly modified doctrine of predestination of a Church which had remained willing to accept Augustine's language while becoming increasingly reluctant to accept its implications and increasingly willing to emphasize free will. The extreme form of the doctrine which later appears in Calvin can be viewed either as a return to a purer Augustinianism or else (for so Calvin was accused by Campanella) the result of Islamic influence (which was still quite strong at the University of Padua). Madhva also accepts predestination, but whether as a result of allowing greater scope for the Pūrva Mīmāṁsā in many points that do not override the strain of influence from the Vaiṣṇava *Purāṇas*, or simply as a logical consequence of his philosophy of difference, it is difficult to tell. At any rate, Bhagavan (God) has a will which cannot be opposed, and He wills that all who are not incorrigibly disposed by Him to try in vain to oppose Him shall be awakened to their true nature, which is to serve Him in this world and the next by performing their duties as realistically as they can. In spite of their belief in predestination, certainly neither Madhva nor Thomas wish to be fatalists.

Within the Christian tradition, the doctrine of predestination has tended to result from attempts to do justice to God's omniscience and omnipotence, as well as to some of Paul's ideas as expressed principally in Romans. However, having solved a problem at the level of deity, Christian theologians have been faced with the problem of finding a place for human effort in the attainment of salvation. In other words, they must also do justice to God's justice. Some traditions have avoided the problem of justice by rejecting an anthropomorphic highest reality. Thus, whether the universe is deterministic or not, there is no question of the fairness of a supreme being.

In the Advaita Vedānta, for example, there is a transcendence of this problem of choice, at least with respect to *nirguṇa* Brahman, although there remains a certain syncretistic vagueness (unless counter-balanced by the sharpness of dialectical skill) with respect to *saguṇa*-Brahman. Choice is still an activity within *māyā* which is to be transcended by a sort of "non-choosing" contemplation. Within the popular cults stemming out of this there tended to be too much apathy and acquiescence. This is exactly what the Neo-Confucianists, especially Chu Hsi and his disciples, were trying to counter with their critiques of Buddhism. Their greater emphasis on freedom of the individual and the inherent goodness of man left no room for the fatalism which has traditionally been attributed to the Chinese tradition. Although one does not always get what one deserves, whether fame or infamy, or a position within the imperial hierarchy, there is no question of the justice of a supreme being because of the Neo-Confucian rejection of anthropomorphism at the highest and most universal level. Within the Mahāyāna traditions most influenced by Nāgārjuna, such as Zen, the questions of human efforts to attain salvation do not arise because we are already "there", for *saṃsāra* is *nirvāṇa* and *nirvāṇa* is *saṃsāra* according to the traditional formulations.

For the most part the Thomistic theology depends more on faith while the Augustinian depends more on grace. This categorization applies to other religious traditions as well. Those who stress faith tend to stress effort to attain true beatitude, while those who stress grace tend to stress surrender and predestination. But seldom can a pure type be found. Though Aquinas stresses faith and effort, he certainly cannot neglect the doctrines of grace and predestination which had become Roman Catholic orthodoxy long before the thirteenth century.

For the realm of nature, Thomas' ethics follows Aristotle's philosophy of happiness, and the Aristotelian version of the doctrine of the Mean is applied even to interpreting some of the doctrines in the New Testament. As essentially rational, men have a natural tendency to act in accordance with reason. For Thomas as for Aristotle, an act is good insofar as it conforms to reason. Thus, in spite of the Christian doctrine of the Fall and its consequences, which was after all as much a part of Thomas' heritage as Aristotle, we find an insistence upon the natural goodness of man. The basic concern for Thomas as well as Aristotle is the formation of a permanent disposition to act in accordance with the practical reason. The tendency is there, but it must be strengthened lest it eventually become so weakened that it plays no part at all (much less the predominant one) in determining conduct. The primary concern of ethics then is not so much with the determining of the rightness or wrongness of individual acts, but with the formation and development of the moral personality.

At this level the comparison of Thomas' ethics with that of the Neo-Confucians is obvious. With them we have a return to a Mencian Coufucianism with its insistence upon the goodness of the nature coupled with the traditional Confucian emphasis upon character development. However, there is a contrast of major importance here as well. Although both traditions equate the good and the natural, within the Aristotelian tradition (of which Thomas is such a luminary) the natural is equated with the rational, at least for men, while within the Mencian tradition (of which Chu Hsi is such a luminary) the natural is equated with the altruistic. Thus there is here a possible criticism of Thomas by Chu Hsi. For all too often selfishness is rational, but it is always inimical to the harmony which is essential for the common good which is the common goal of both traditions. Perhaps Thomas would reply that upon careful examination the rational is always altruistic, or perhaps he would more likely reply that the subordination of the rational to the altruistic cannot be the result of rational considerations but must be the result of supernatural grace.

For Thomas the natural tendencies arise from the creature's essential nature, which is its participation in the eternal law, the divine reason which governs the universe. As a member of the hierarchy of being there is thus a place for everything and everything must properly fulfil the duties of that place. Insofar as one acts in accordance with reason or the other natural tendencies, one contributes to the maximization of harmony and thus happiness for all. For Chu Hsi the natural tendency to altruism arises from the *li* which far from being unique to human beings is shared by all things. But once again, insofar as one acts in accordance with the *li* one contributes to the maximization of harmony and happiness. Thus the emphasis upon hierarchy which we have noted in connection with Thomas is one of the most fundamental themes of the Confucian tradition as well.

During his earthly life natural man strives for happiness, and it is the job of ethics to tell him what this is and facilitate his access to it. However, the desire for happiness is only an expression of the natural desire for God, and nature alone cannot satisfy this desire. Truly supreme happiness, the Good, is attainable only after death and only with God's help; thus the necessity of revelation. It is in Thomas' more strictly theological treatises that the natural virtues are portrayed as only a foundation for the *edificio ecclesiastica* for the living of the supernatural life. The natural life appears to be sufficient and complete until the super-natural world is opened by the operation of grace. Then it is seen that although there is no conflict between them, the natural is only a preparation for, an adumbration of, what must be completed hereafter. The natural and the supernatural together contribute toward the perfection of man. Although pursuit of perfection cannot be binding on all, all must aspire *toward* perfection. This call for perfection finds its echo in the Mahāyāna Buddhist programme for the attainment of Bodhisattvahood with its systematic striving for the *pāramitās* (perfections) and the emphasis upon *mahākaruṇā* (great compassion). St. Thomas is not so great a contemplative as some on whom he relies for his discussions of contemplation, the Victorines for example, nor so much so as his Japanese Buddhist contemporaries, for example;

but he has no reservations about sanctioning that life for those who are called to it.

One of the most problematic points in Thomas' ethics is his delimitations of the conditions for a just war. According to most interpreters these conditions can no longer be fulfilled. Hopefully mankind has come into an era when the theological virtues as well as the cardinal virtues should be expected at the societal as well as the individual level. But Thomas for the most part seems to think that this cannot be demanded since the state is not a divine but a natural institution.

A crucial point is whether Thomas' virtual avoidance of the problem of the nature of the ego (*ahaṅkāra*) is deliberate or whether it is implicitly taken care of in his discourses on charity. For whatever elaborations may be made about the rest, charity remains the golden mean balanced by the entelechy of the whole of the ethical life, individual, in secular community, and in the *oikumenéke*, for it is the only virtue which is self-generating and not dependent on another virtue or tending toward another goal. Regardless of how elaborate the rest of the structure may be, the whole is comprised in the one virtue of charity, for God *is* charity. Even the angels know nothing higher.

A universal problem is that of the relation of the knowledge held by the human intellect and the knowledge which God has of things, souls and Himself. From outside the system the most crucial question or doubt that must be answered in order to satisfy the Vedāntin and the Vijñānavādin Buddhist is the extent to which, or the mode according to which, it may be said that God is knowledge itself, or at least consciousness-as-such; and further, the point at which these converge, if indeed they do; or whether the formula of the Aristotelian adequation of subject and predicate must still apply to God who is beyond the apex of the pyramid of universals which are operative in the unaided intellect. This latter becomes an especially knotty problem for Aquinas since he holds, as opposed to Bacon and the Averroists, that the Active Intellect is individuated. The Active Intellect is that part of the mind (or, as the mediaevals would say, soul) which forms universal concepts. If it is individuated, i.e., if each of us has one, then the question arises as to whether we can safely assume that different people will abstract the same universal concepts from experience. For example, can we assume that different men will have the same conception of humanity? If, however, all men in some sense share the same Active Intellect, then this problem does not arise, although a host of others do.

Thomas' doctrine of analogy is another of those topics which has been the focus of sharp controversy all through the centuries. For even if we can have knowledge of God only by analogy, the validity of analogy itself must rest in or be the operation of some Mind that makes the analogy available as a *pramāṇa* (source of knowledge). Suffice to risk the generalization that by contrast with Advaita but comparison with Navya Nyāya Thomas uses analogy as a means of enlarging the scope of affirmation rather than as a means of leading back through tautology to sheer identity. But even here one must be exceedingly cautious because of the differences between the strict Advaitins and the Navya Naiyāyikas whom the Madhva school followed on the question of the irreducibility of negation to analogy. Is there any analogy possible and inherently valid that is not, like every other form of predication, hemmed in by negations? St. Thomas and the Vedāntins seem to believe that there is, but the Navya Naiyāyikas and the predecessors of Ockham (Matthew of Aquasparta, for example) believed there is not.

Knowledge of God in the sense of "closing the gap" between knower and known is so completely foreign to Thomism that it is difficult for the Thomist to acknowledge the possibility of this manner of operation even in God's knowledge. Bonaventure is somewhat better. He simply says that in divine things we have to admit a different canon. The followers of al-Ghazālī likewise would insist that it is useless to go on further with this sort of procedure. Illumination is for them higher than ratiocination. Resorting to strictly mystical disciplines, it is better to seek for the Beatific Vision wherein God can *reveal* whether there is such a discrepancy of His manner of knowing and ours, or whether the veil might be lifted. And of course the Vijñānavādins claim to arrive at a perspective from which it is seen immediately in high yogic meditation that everything in its own nature *is* the transmergence of knower and known. Thus the discrepancy between changes in the things known and the knowledge about them is seen to be false by the side of the knowledge which they *are*. Everything, even this 'knowledge' itself, is in flux (although here is where the Advaitins sharply quit their company). Knowledge is the Ultimate Continuum, and to make propositions about it is as foolish as a bird's attempt to fly through a mirror.

Another serious objection to Thomism is the constant division—for it is that and not merely a distinction—between willing, being and knowing. If Thomas ever completely resolves this we have failed to find it. Whether even Madhva did better here is a matter of debate. He also admits the difference and asserts that God has so constituted the relation because He wills difference as the basic stuff of reality itself. There is no further reduction to be made. The Advaitin's claim to resolve the difficulty by asserting just the opposite thesis that reality cannot be other than absolutely non-dual and that therefore even the designation *sat-cit-ānanda* is still an *anirvacanīya* may be a little ambitious. The Viśiṣṭādvaitin simply admits that we cannot avoid relationality in God. However, it is not absolutely necessary to say that this entails either difference or identity as ultimate. Both are only harmonious qualifications of the supreme and overflowing Unity.

Is there not the possibility of an inseparable transmergence into pure identity of the Being, Knowing and Willing of God? The Being, as quiddity, is in danger of being left suspended as a non-functional, non-rational, and therefore absolutely unknowable or indescribable zero—the *Tathatā-Śūnya* of the Mādhyamika rather than the *sat-cit-ānanda* of the Vedānta—out of relation to anything else including itself. But Thomism doggedly refuses to admit any sort of transmergence like this. Here Aquinas might have found some resolution of some of his difficulties by conceding the identification of *sākṣi* with the Holy Spirit. St. Bonaventure comes much closer to this in his illuminationist passages, especially in the *In Hexameron*; and Duns Scotus tries to do the same sort of thing in his closer identification of a consciousness with the quiddity of existence.

Thomas does admit a certain identity of knowledge and will in God, but it is not clear to what extent this qualified identity is identical with the essence of God and/or to what extent it is merely attributive. Here the primary comparative references could be to Thomas' Islamic counterparts, although Madhva no less than Rāmānuja certainly is adamant in insisting on God's having the attribute of an unopposable Will. However, this seems for the most part to be only an attribute, distinguishable but not different from His nature according to Rāmānuja, different from but not opposed to His nature according to Madhva. The Advaita school for the most part takes the scriptures relating to this as metaphorical and for the sake of praise, for a sharp distinction between Will and any other quality compromises the Pure Identity which the indescribable *nirguṇa*-Brahman must necessarily be. In Chu Hsi and his followers we do not have the concept of the will of an anthropomorphically conceived God; but there is the Will of Heaven, which is not a 'personal' will but a supreme governing principle.

Thomas asks whether God will of necessity will whatever He wills. There are many serious systematic implications to this question since it involves the problem of whether and how necessity and freedom coincide in God. Such a question must be seen against the background of the Neo-Platonism from which Christian theology borrowed so much. The Neo-Platonic One transcends all anthropomorphisms, including personality and will, and the universe is not the result of a freely chosen creation *ex-nihilo* but an eternal and necessary emanation. For all the attributes they share, the God of Christianity is not such a One. Christian theologians like Thomas consistently opposed the complete rejection of anthropomorphism so characteristic of Neo-Platonism.

In denying that God is subject to necessity of willing what He wills, the question of God's unlimitedness has not been completely settled. If God's freedom and the resulting transcendence of all limitations are emphasized, then the question arises as to why He chose to command us to do certain things and refrain from others. If God's choices are absolutely without constraint, does the Mosaic law represent an arbitrary choice of rules for a game men cannot hope to understand? Could we have been commanded to commit adultery instead? Could the rules be changed? If one is uncomfortable with such possibilities, then one can insist that the laws men must live by are a reflection, as it were, of the divine nature, which while free to an extent men can hardly comprehend, is yet a *nature*, a limit of possibility. Although God has (rather, is) free will, there is that which He is not in fact free to choose, i.e., to do evil. However, if one continues to reason along these lines the possibility arises that in addition there are certain things God must do. If, for example, God is essentially loving and compassionate would He in some sense have been constrained by His own nature to incarnate Himself in light of the Fall? The basic problem here is the discomfort which *any* attempts to limit God (tame Him, as it were) tend to generate in the devout.

One's position with respect to this dilemma depends ultimately upon how one prefers to approach God conceptually: as a being unlimited in any way, or as a being of infinite perfection. Such problematic choices seem indemic to attempts to verbalize ultimate reality. Ordinary men seem more comfortable with a *saguṇa*-Brahman/Īśvara while theologians usually seem to be driven towards a *nirguṇa*-Brahman in spite of all attempts to preserve some meaning in theological language.

Analogous to the question of the freedom of God's will is that concerning the human will. Is free will even possible in light of God's foreknowledge and predestined grace? This is an ancient problem and a universal problem centering around such terms as *moira*, *karma*, and *ming*. Thomas insists that human freedom is in its sphere analogically quite as independent as God's Freedom, although in an infinitely more limited range. This is so for two reasons: in order that man may fulfil his moral nature it is necessary that God should will only that man *should* (not *must*) will what God wills; and secondly, since Thomas does not find any ontological relation between the unicity of God and the unicity of the human soul—except in the sense, loosely taken by comparison with Psellos and Erigena, that is strictly the analogy of *similarity* and not the analogy of *inseparability of essence*—it is necessary that there be an open possibility of freely entering into the relation of salvation and of blessedness as entelechy rather than as a realization of inherent permanent nature. Thus, for example, God wills that mankind should live in peace. But if man takes the initiative in making war, then for Thomas as much as for his Muslim predecessors, God must stand in judgment and man must bear the responsibility for his own acts before Him. He will assist man toward the virtuous life and pardon, but He does not compel obedience.

God's relationship to His own existence is the same as that to His other attributes. This results in a paradox that is difficult indeed to penetrate, although it is as unavoidable as it is illuminating. For it entails the answer to the possible objection that the God that is proved by Thomas' arguments is not the same as the God of all the attributes and Who is Trinity in Unity. At this point we are threatened by a controversy comparable to that between the Ash'arites and Mu'tazilites of the Islamic tradition or that between the upholders of a *saguṇa*-Brahman as opposed to a pure *nirguṇa*-Brahman within the Advaita tradition. It is a paradox which the structure of the Thomistic system, which is incompatible with paradox as such, does not easily allow. Thomas must insist that the attributes of God exist in precisely the same sense that God exists, for God can hold no duplicity or ambiguity. God *is* His own 'Act' (or actuality in the Aristotelian sense) of Existing as *Actus Purus* and His attributes are *inseparable* even though *distinguishable* from His essence: He *has* them, and He has them essentially. He would not be God without them.

The attributes of God are not merely constructions of the human mind for the sake of praise as the extreme Advaitins and Ash'arites argue, but necessary entailments from the fact that God is and therefore is all that pertains to the perfection, primacy omnipresence, and blessedness of Being, i.e., those qualities without which nothing could exist. Nevertheless, Thomas leaves a certain gap so that these attributes cannot be seen in transmergence. He chops off chunks of being, so to speak, and says to one attribute, "this is your share", and to another, "this is your portion". The method of ordered principation is never surrendered in the Thomistic system.

With respect to his views on the relation of God and His attributes, Thomas is definitely closer to his contemporary Madhva than to any of the Advaitins or Rāmānuja. God's unity is the unity of a being essentially One rather than the unity of a being simply *uniquely* One. Thus the emphasis is upon safeguarding transcendence more than emphasizing omnipervasiveness. The omnipervasiveness is that of the imparted act of being, not that of inseparable concomitance, much less that of denial of reality to that which is pervaded. For Thomas, in short, the world and God cannot be seen as parts of a continuum in any sense. Every possible and actual entity whether physical, chemical, psychological, logical, or theological, is just what it is, because God has constituted its *esse* in that degree which is fitting for its *existere*. There is no need to become involved in a formidable Indira's Net of infinitely complex interrelationalities. Thus the problem of the relatedness does not arise. Things exist and God supremely exists, but relatedness exists as only another existential characteristic of this whole of which God is not a part but the Creator of both whole and part in a mode that is proper and possible to Him alone.

As for the doctrine of the Trinity, it belongs primarily to the realm of faith and only secondarily to the realm of rational argument, whereas, God's existence belongs to the realm of rational proofs and only secondarily to the realm of faith. As Thomas puts it, a knowledge of God's existence is a preamble to faith. For Thomas, to speak of God as triune is not just an empty characterization. The usual superficial conundrums about the impossibility of being Three and One need not concern us for it is (as Rāmānuja long since had demonstrated) almost impossible to conceive of a completely unrelated self-identity which is not at least potentially distinguishable from some "other". Once this "otherness" is admitted, there must also be a "thirdness", a manner of referring this otherness back to its Source. The Advaitin attribution of *anirvacanīya* (indescribability) to Brahman is not an alternative to Trinity since even indescribability is subject to this same critique. In short, even if the primordial and final condition is the complete indistinguishability of the knower, the known, and their relation, as long as there are identities and distinctions to be made (or rather to be recognized), such negations and affirmations always demand at least a triadic scheme. St. Bonaventure takes his rhythm completely from the trinitarian dynamic and triadizes everything, for the interrelatedness of the Trinity is enough to generate any and all possible being and to bind all being inseparably to Itself and to bring all back to Itself.

Perhaps the quasi-mythological language of Father, Son, and

Holy Spirit is still too anthropomorphic for most of us. It is better to consider what these words signify even rather dwelling upon the symbols themselves. Is the Hindu Trinity of Brahma-Śiva-Viṣṇu, Creator-Destroyer-Preserver, a more balanced and more metaphysically systematic economy? Or is the Mahāyāna *Trikāya* preferable? If Thomas had known the terminology of the Vedānta, would he have had any disapproval of the *sat-cit-ānanda* trilogism which is the final characterization (*anirvacanīya* or no) of Brahman? Probably the only objection would have been that this should secondarily characterize equally each of the Divine Persons of the Christian Trinity, even though one might primarily assign *sat* to the Father, *cit* to the Word, and *ānanda* to the Holy Spirit. In fact this fits very exactly except for the hypostasizing as "persons" in the Christian formulation.

Something should be added about St. Thomas' doctrine of angels. It is as rationally posited as any scientific hypothesis today. As pure intelligences unencumbered by embodiment, they fit into the gap in the hierarchy of creation between man and God and are capable, under the authority of the Divine Will, of governing regions of nature. Although nature for the most part appears to behave according to determining 'laws', some element of freedom is still there. In other words, instead of the modern concept of natural law as something inherently operative in its own right, there is the at least suggestion that natural law is only the external manifestation of angelic intelligence or intelligences at work. Thus, as far as structure is concerned, they take the place in the scholastic systems of the *devatas* in the Hindu pantheon, although this does not mean that they are otherwise equatable with any pantheon. They are not mere symbolic functions, much less an abstract principle of pluralization within the range of the function of Spirit, but subordinate spirits who execute the Will of the One Deity.

It is difficult to criticize such a mountain as St. Thomas. The points or areas wherein he might be said to be vulnerable are in his theory of negation, his views of the relation between faith and reason, and in general on the right balance between dialectic, hierarchy and immediacy. He is not by any means a mystic but depends on the Victorines as authorities in this field. One does not find Thomas trilogizing so much as Bonaventure, but he is more a tetradizer, so to speak: the four causes and the four cardinal virtues of Aristotle explain almost more than the Scriptures reveal. Everything has its place in nature because God has appointed it that way. The mere relation of Creator and creature is enough. God's Omnipresence, omniscience, omnipotence, eternity and infinity do not force Him into a mystical heaven hidden from the view or understanding of the human mind.

Thomas never sees one idea, notion, definition, proof or counterproof as completely cancelling out another; rather, each has its place in the entire scheme of truth. He would meet no basic opposition from the Jainas in this regard. With their doctrine of *syādvāda* they too sought to reconcile rather than reject. One must only make the right distinction, find the proper interpretation, in order to "make it fit". The world to him is more like a jigsaw puzzle: he thinks in terms of entities, not processes; of combinations, not mixtures; *samyukta*, not *samavāya*.

Thomas' more solidly Aristotelian interpretation of the Final Cause and the entelechy of all things toward God may mark a turning point in the discernment of hierarchy within the Christian tradition. It is a theme which had its foundations as much in Aristotle as in Plato, but which had been beautifully and intricately developed and amplified by Aristotle's Neo-Platonic interpreters. Thomas' contemporary Bonaventure remained much more the Neo-Platonist and so tended to speak of the return to God in a more strongly mystical mode. In Thomas the structure of the hierarchy is such that one can no longer say that the *pravṛtti* and the *nivṛtti* are not in proper balance, as might be said of some Augustinians with their greater emphasis on the Creation and the Fall than on the inheritance of the Resurrection. Thomas is not an emanationist because as a structuralist he thinks of every individual as conforming to an upward looking and tending entelechy, and ultimately because it is irreconcilable with what had become the orthodox Christian view of a person-like God freely creating the universe *ex nihilo*. In this there is not so much a reflection of the Divine Glory as we find in Bonaventure and Suhrawardi but a proper fulfilling of function, all and each ordered in its own essence and existence by God as

Creator and Governor and Final Cause—cause in the sense of *ratio essendi* (imparting existence), not necessarily a *that into which* to enter and become re-absorbed, nor *pariṇamavāda* nor *kṣaṇa-vāda*, but, if we may coin a term, *bharavāda*. There is relatively little *sparśa-vimarśa*, nothing of the inter-enfolding complementariness of *yin* and *yang*, and nothing of the cyclic view of things. The world, the universe, is not eternal, contrary to what Aristotle, Ibn Sīnā and Ibn Rushd had taught. Here we are reminded that Thomas is a *Christian* Aristotelian, willing to reject the teaching of "The Philosopher" when he errs. Aristotle erred because reason fails us here. Neither the eternity nor the non-eternity of the world can be demonstrated. We can know that it is non-eternal only because this has been revealed to us, a revelation to which Aristotle unfortunately had no access.

Those who distinguish between an open system and a closed system—Bergson being one of the best examples of the open type in the modern West and al-Ghazālī an example in the mediaeval world—generally classify Thomas' as closed. However, it is a system that is extremely commendable because it is inherently expandable. No new scientific discovery is likely to require any radical revision of his metaphysical structure. Indeed, there is perhaps more justification (as there is also in Roger Bacon) for the scientific investigation of nature in Thomas than in Kant, and certainly more than in Śaṅkara, although not necessarily more than in Madhva. Since nature does not consist of essentially inaccessible essences, there is no danger of a Kantian transcendental illusion in the Thomistic realism. Of course, Thomas is not single-handedly responsible for such openness to empirical science; this is but one of the legacies of Aristotle. It is easy to overlook this because we still tend to view mediaeval philosophy from the perspective of the Renaissance, for whom the dominance of Aristotle was completely undesirable. For St. Thomas, at least a portion of the field of revelation must remain closed to scientific investigation. However, the transcendence is just that, a moving beyond rather than a rejection of, for there is ultimately no conflict between reason and revelation, science and religion. While nature remains totally accessible to reason, for knowledge of the supernatural, and in particular man's supernatural end, reason must bow to revelation.

24. Madhva

Madhva (1199-1278) belongs to our galaxy of writers of *Great Summas* or major works which set the pace as well as constituted the finished pattern for philosophizing for several centuries afterwards. It might be said of Madhva that, like Nichiren, he represents within Hinduism, which was until his time largely either mystical or ritualistic or scholastic in the dryer logical sense, the prophetic type of aggressive reformer rather than any of the other types. Tradition has it that Madhva was a champion heavyweight wrestler. Indeed, apocryphically, it is reported that sometimes he would offer his opponents the choice of a physical or an intellectual wrestling match, always confident that he could win in either case.

Madhva is another of those seminal thinkers who begin a tradition. His basic insight is universally but radically simple: *difference* is not only necessary but is unavoidable if one is going to think; and certainly if one does not admit difference there is the great danger of committing blasphemy against the Supreme Uniqueness of God. Even when Madhva was being schooled by the disciples of Śaṅkara at Śringeri he found their explanations of the *māyā*/Brahman ambivalence intolerable. Without at least admission of difference between *māyā* and Brahman monism falls apart. Mere qualification of the identity after the manner of Rāmānuja is, according to him, only a bad compromise. In order to preserve the true intention of the *mahāvākya ekam advaita Brahma* it is necessary to show that Brahman is absolutely different from any other possible (or impossible) reality, otherwise the *mahāvākya* would not have three words but only one. If strict monism were true there would be only one word, one language, and no grammar, at all, only OM ! Therefore difference is not only admissible but inherently the basic factor in all reality, even the reality of Unity. Once recognized, it follows that one should systematize the differences, showing how they differ from each other, for thereby one may come to a comprehensive grasp of the total pattern which is the marvellous work of God.

In many respects Madhva's system is more like Śaṅkara's than Rāmānuja's since essentially what Madhva does is to make the Śaṅkarites admit that their whole system is inextricable from the admission of the radical difference between *māyā* and *nirguṇa*-Brahman, both of which are claimed by them to be indefinable. Thus the basic formula is relatively similar: wherever Śaṅkara reads *māyā* Madhva reads *difference*—but difference which is real and not illusion or subservient to any other principle. Difference is the key to all reality, whereas Advaita tries to claim that difference, being unreal, is only the whirlpool of Unreality. The *pancabhedas*, the five differences, are the skeleton of Madhva's very living system—for skeleton it has, and as such it could almost accuse Advaita of being a sort of dangerous jelly-fish philosophy, beautiful but structureless except by virtue of the medium, the Oceans of Knowledge, in which it floats helplessly. These five differences are (1) God and soul, (2) soul and matter, (3) matter and matter, (4) matter and God, and (5) soul and soul. Madhva's difference is not a dynamic of polarization with a Tao as with the *yin/yang* principle but simply difference as such whether harmonious or conflicting or, as seems with him to be the case mostly, simply neutral.

Nagaraja Rao gives nine distinctions to be clarified in order to set forth the Madhva system as such:

> 1. Viṣṇu is the Supreme God mentioned in the scriptures. He is the prime import (*mahātātparya*) of them all. Madhva asserts that every word in the language primarily signifies Viṣṇu and refers only secondarily to other objects. This assumption greatly helps him in harmonizing the import of the scriptures. The Purāṇa-s which praise Śiva as the Supreme Deity are set at naught by him. Viṣṇu is the efficient cause (*nimitta-kāraṇa*) of the universe. He presides over creation, preservation and destruction. He is the liberator from, as well as the cause of, the bondage of *saṃsāra* (chain of existence). Nescience (*avidyā*), action (*karman*) and the subtle body (*liṅga-śarīra*) are the secondary causes of the chain of existence.
>
> 2. The external world is affirmed to be ultimately real (*satya*). It continues to exist at all times. The world process is beginningless and eternal (*anādi* and *nitya*).
>
> 3. The ultimate reality of the fivefold difference, namely, the difference between God and soul (*īśvara* and *jīva*), between

soul and soul (*jīva* and *jīva*), between God and matter, between soul and matter, and between matter and matter, is accepted.

4. All souls are dependent on God who alone is independent.

5. Among the souls there is gradation. There are three kinds of souls: those that are fit for liberation (*muktīyogya-s*), those that travel endlessly through the cycle of birth and rebirth (*nityasaṃsārīn-s*), and those that are fit to be eternally in hell (*tamoyogya-s*).

6. Liberation (*mokṣa*) is the realization of the soul's innate bliss.

7. Devotion is the means (*sādhana*) to it. Devotion is that kind of attachment to the Lord which is based on a complete understanding of His supremacy, transcending the love for one's own self and possessions and remaining unshaken under all circumstances. Besides devotion, the Lord's desire to protect the devotee is also necessary for liberation.

8. There are three means of valid knowledge: perception, inference and verbal testimony.

9. The existence of God is known only by correct methods of reasoning.[1]

The *Pramāṇa Lakṣaṇa* is Madhva's independent treatment of the *pramāṇas* so important for any and all Indian systems, and which to the best of our knowledge has not been excelled by any similar work in western Europe from the time of Aquinas to Merleau Ponty. This is probably the chief work stimulated by his controversy in his youth with his guru over the proper interpretation or correction of the distortions of Vimuktātman's *Iṣṭasiddhi*. Madhva rejects all but *pratyakṣa*, *anumāna* and *śabda*, and qualifies the dependent validity of *anumāna* since without being grounded in *pratyakṣa* and/or *śabda* it is on very shaky grounds. It is after all only a means of elaboration, not a function of some Platonic Ideas. In this he is remarkably close to the Muslim, Jewish and Christian Aristotelian scholastics as well as to those who followed Chang Tsai and those Byzantines who so intelligently opposed the extremes of the Hesychasts.

Madhva's pointed rejection of the Advaitin version of *māyā* comes primarily from his *Māyāvāda-Khaṇḍana*, which is short but incisively condensed. One is tempted to observe that it is only when philosophers are on the defensive that they become verbose, whereas, as with Madhva, if one is on solid ground a few words are really all that are needed. Such seems to be Madhva's way all the while, but especially in this exposure of the Advaita contradictions. The *Viṣṇu-tattva-nirṇaya* is perhaps Madhva's most brilliant and most impressive refutation or rather counterattack against Advaita while the *Tattvoddyota* is "one of the fighting works of Madhva" against the Advaitins. The latter covers basically the vindication of Difference as primordial and the misuse of syllogisms by the Advaitins. Madhva argues that Śaṅkara was after all a crypto-Buddhist, having failed to give adequate refutation of both Śūnyavāda and Vijñānavāda. He also defends theism, with the radical difference between man and God on the one hand and, on the other, the reality of the world of difference supported by the charismatic texts as well as by experience. Madhva explains the texts that use the term *nirguṇa* as simply meaning free from all taint and imperfection rather than as having no attributes at all (as Rāmānuja also had previously argued).

Both Madhva and Rāmānuja are very much devoted to the *Gītā*, so much so that wherever there is a possible discrepancy between the *Gītā* and the *Brahma Sūtras* the *Gītā* is likely to prevail with both of them. Madhva uses the *Gītā* as the basis of his devastating attack on Śaṅkara's indefinable arguments as well as on his insistence on the *nirviśeṣa* (unqualified denial of differences) characterization of Brahman. Correspondingly there is also an attack on Śaṅkara's notion of "self-luminosity" of knowledge, since even that must be knowable by the knower; and to try to assert that these three are identically one and the same is just to fall into the pit of complete incoherence.

Both Rāmānuja and Madhva put a primary emphasis on *bhakti* and are against Śaṅkara and his followers who are *jñānis*. All Vaiṣṇavas owe a debt to Rāmānuja for his opening the way of devotional theism with a very personal God, as well as his devastating critique of Śaṅkara's Advaita metaphysics. Of course the Madhvas think that Rāmānuja compromised too much in not going all out in affirming complete difference in the *bhakti* relationship and muddled it up, so to speak, with his qualifications which they consider as too much of a concession to Advaita. Madhva like Rāmānuja and most of the other Vaiṣṇava interpreters emphasizes that God is to be *worshipped*, "for He alone is free from sin". This worship certainly entails difference between the worshipped and the worshipper, so how can the Advaitins deny that; and where the texts obviously indicate emphasis on *bhakti* how can the Advaitins try to reduce it to *jñāna*.

Madhva was definitely and consciously committed to building his own system as such and not merely to making a refutation of the Advaita school. To the possible objection that one cannot build a system of *bhakti*, since that furnishes no more than devotional or even emotional relish to the knowledge and wisdom that one has acquired otherwise, the Madhva answer is very plain: *bhakti* presupposes, necessarily, the difference between the devotee and the object of his devotion; and this also entails the difference between the multitude of devotees and the Single Deity to whom they are devoted. The God thus worshipped must be independent and supreme, but not necessarily describable as an amorphous 'absolute'.

Of the most essential features of Madhva's system the first is the transcendence of the supreme Being as the personal God, free from all imperfections, who produced a real world as a supreme Act of Truth. The world is real because He made it so, and as such it manifests the greatness of the Lord, who therefore deserves our *bhakti* which is the unique way of salvation and which proceeds from knowledge of that grandeur. But this manifestation of the divine through the creation is not a theophany but rather the marvellous way that individual real things really fit together in all their remarkable diversity. The fact of the infinity of their interrelatedness should be enough to make us realize our finitude in the face of such marvellous power of the Lord to do such things.

Madhva's almost exaggeratedly radical difference between God and man is somewhat remarkable, so much so that some authorities have speculated as to whether it might be because of Christian influence. But this would not be the case since the Syrian Christians of Travancore not too far south of Udipi were basically Monophysites with strong monist trends in their metaphysics and by no means dualists. Islam is the much more likely candidate since Islam was making constant inroads in the North and already becoming Indianized.

Madhva emphasizes the transcendence of God more than Rāmānuja who tends more warm-heartedly to emphasize the compassion and availability of God's grace and his Presence everywhere as *antaryāmi,* which Madhva seems to substitute with his concept of the *sākṣi* consciousness. To Madhva an exaggerated sentimental pseudo-familiarity with God is just about as bad as assertion of atheism. Preserving the art of distinction, making and recognizing differences where they really exist, keeps the Madhvas from all extremes and therefore really makes life much more livable. Madhva realized the impossibility of doing full justice to the majesty of God, but Raghavachar gives four cardinal points: "(1) Viṣṇu abounds in all excellences. (2) He is free from all blemishes. (3) Everything depends upon Him, while He is absolutely self-dependent. (4) He is different from all else; otherwise, His freedom from blemishes cannot be true." Raghavachar adds: "With this Madhva would want us to conclude our synopsis of his philosophy of God."[2]

Madhva is almost fanatical in identifying God as Viṣṇu. This henotheism may be Madhva's weakest point, but even then his own logic can rationalize this quite well: there is a difference between the various sectarian cults, and it therefore behoves one to choose one and seek to improve it to the utmost rather than syncretize them. So Madhva does his best to vindicate the supremacy of Viṣṇu in what might be called a transition through henotheism to true monotheism, claiming that the other deities have defects which Viṣṇu does not have.

Another basic orientation-point for the whole system is the (necessary) affirmation of a very marked doctrine of grace, which is also absent in Advaita although it is fully present in Rāmānuja's philosophy and even very intensively present in the Tengalai school of Pillai Lokācarya and his followers. But this doctrine of grace leaves no room for dreamy idealism in metaphysics. The *pancabheda* skeleton is very real. Pluralist or not, realist Madhva certainly is; and his school never compromised on that point through the long history of their constant debates with the other schools, especially the Advaitins.

Madhva classifies human souls into a three-fold scheme of those who are predestined to salvation, those who are predestined to damnation, and those who will remain eternally in the endless cycle of rebirths. Some interpreters again have taken this as a possible tag of Christian influence, but again this is very unlikely since the Christians of Malabar were much further south and it is highly unlikely that they had any communication with the Udipi area. Moreover, the Syrian Christians were not dualists at all, but Monophysites, affirming an extreme form of Neo-Platonist metaphysics and indeed were often accused of Docetism, i.e., virtually *māyāvāda.* But on the other hand the hypothesis that this was due to Muslim influence is more tempting since there were occasional Muslim traders up and down the west coast of India enroute to what is now Malasia and Indonesia and even South China, and Madhva's meeting with Amir Khusrau could have had some unacknowledged influence. Nevertheless, this is not necessarily the only influence that could account for this theme of predestination since in Mīmāṁsā there is something very similar in the inexorability of karma doctrine.

Madhva insists that the individual soul is always dependent on God and on His grace. Indeed there is with Madhva a sort of doctrine of election such that God must choose the devotee before the latter can hope to attain Him. Some interpretations of Madhva put a lot of emphasis on this doctrine of election even to the extent of positing that in that respect at least Madhva is closer to Calvin than to Aquinas.

The 'gift' of bondage or imprisonment of the erring soul is not just to punish it but to evoke greater longing for the Lord so that the last Great Gift can crown the list namely *mokṣa,* which is defined not as *theosis* (as even some of his Byzantine contemporaries and many Ṣūfīs dared to assert along with the Advaitins and some Japanese Buddhists relying on the *Lotus Sūtra*) but as constant, abiding, uninterrupted consciousness of God's presence and marvellous qualities. The Madhva view of the *jīvātman* denies emphatically the Advaita notion of complete identity with Brahman, since although in both schools as in all varieties of the Vedānta the *jīva* shares certain attributes with Brahman, namely non-materiality, eternity, consciousness and bliss (at least in the ultimate state of *mokṣa*), nevertheless the *jīvātman* is clearly completely distinct from Brahman, and the Madhvas do not confuse similarity with identity.

The *jīva* is ignorant and the Brahman is omniscient; likewise, the *jīva* is incapable of fulfilling its own desires whereas the Brahman can create, sustain and/or destroy the whole world. Here the Madhvas would join forces with the most stalwart orthodox Sunni Muslims against any taint of Ṣūfī pantheism or even any Shi'ite Ishraqui like Suhrawardi. As Narain writes, though here we might hear Madhva himself thundering out with his stalwart voice, "In short, the very idea of the identity of the finite with the infinite is a negation of religion, ethics and all that is rational in the field of logic."[3]

Almost all systems of Indian philosophy can be classified as to their treatment of the relation between ontology and epistemology. The Madhvas separate them very distinctly, always objectively claiming that knowledge is always *about* something and that knowledge is merely an attribute of the *jīva*, and even of the *ātman*. At the other extreme Vijñānavāda, for example, claims that there is no *ātman*, and that reality itself is "knowledge", everything being merely an "appearance" of the *Ālaya vijñāna*. Advaita comes in for a very close second on that score, also claiming that once all the obstacles are removed there is the realization of the supreme non-dual Identity in which the gap between knowledge and knower and known is closed completely so that ultimately there can be no difference or distinction between ontology and epistemology. But in Madhva ontology and epistemology are not fused, or confused.

The categories according to Madhva are as follows: substance (*dravya*), quality (*guṇa*), action (*karma*), class-character (*sāmānya*) particularity (*viśeṣa*), qualified (*viśiṣṭa*), whole (*aṃśī*), power (*śakti*), similarity (*sādṛśya*) and negation (*abhāva*) Of. course Madhva must define *sādṛśya* very closely lest his emphasis on difference becomes clouded.

Śakti becomes increasingly important historically from this time on (or really a little earlier) in Indian tradition—especially in the Caitanya heritage among Vaiṣṇavas, who claim descent from (but not assent to) the Madhva heritage, but also heavily in the Tantric varieties of Śaivism—just as the theories of *potentia* and *actus* become increasingly important in western Europe and as the concept of Enabling is rather focal among the attributes of Allah, and of course *teh* remains important with Chou Tun-i. The word *śakti* is also used for the consorts of the deities, Śiva in particular, since these mythological figures symbolize the original tendency set up in the Sāṃkhya to identify *prakṛti* as the active female principle and *puruśa* as the non-active, contemplative male principle: they cannot easily get along without each other (whether this would still be true in a planet with no moon or more than one moon makes a fascinating speculation since this *śakti* principle is often identified with the astrological influence of the moon).

With *śakti*, *potentia* and *dynamis* we have a Sanskrit, Latin, and Greek semantic conjunction which is interesting indeed. Whether the Chinese were free of this ambiguity would constitute a very valuable study. For the word *śakti* like the word *potentia*—and probably even more closely *teh* in Chinese: *teh* is the *śakti* of Tao—carries the connotation both of power and of potentiality. In contrast to the controversies about the *potentia-actus* polarization among the Aristotelian scholastics, for Madhva the *śakti* concept has a causal connotation which makes unnecessary the division between actual and potential: the actual is brought forth by the potential, not vice versa. All *śakti* is God's. Without it His other qualities would lack existence. To the Aristotelians, however, to admit *potentia* in God would compromise His 'Actuality' even though this involves the almost insurmountable difficulty that *potentia* should be found anywhere aside from God's omnipotence. To say that possibility is not in God is to say that there must be some other source of the fact of possibility, which is absurd.

Another interesting study would be the extent to which Madhva's substances correspond with the concept of substance among the other scholastics, notably in regard to the problem of whether spiritual substance can be treated according to the same logic as material substance. They are: the highest self or/as God (*paramātman*), *Lakṣmī*, souls (*jīva*), unmanifested vacuity (*avyākṛtākāśa*), *prakṛti*, the three *guṇas*; *mahat*, *ahaṃkāra*, *buddhi*, *manas*, the senses (*indriya*), the elements (*bhūta*), the element-potentials (*mātra*), ignorance (*avidyā*), speech-sounds (*varṇa*), darkness (*andha-kāra*), root-impressions (or tendencies) (*vāsanā*), time (*kāla*), reflection (*pratibimba*). As for the qualities, Madhva accepts those of the Vaiśeṣika but also includes self-control (*śama*), mercy (*kṛpā*), endurance (*titikṣā*), strength (*bala*), fear (*bhaya*), shame (*lajjā*), sagacity (*gāmbhīrya*), beauty (*saundarya*), heroism (*śaurya*), liberality (*audārya*), and many more. As far as metaphysics is concerned it is difficult to say whether Bacon had a clear logical foundation for the scientific advances he made, whereas in Madhva we do clearly find sufficient ground in a philosophy of investigation according to difference which could have led to scientific inquiry and empirical studies but evidently for some reason or other did not.

Relatively Rāmānuja neglects the *sākṣi*, perhaps because of his preference for the *antaryāmi* which to him is not merely a concept but vividly the directing and even controlling *vyūha* of Viṣṇu in us and in the world, Immanence-alive, indeed, which Madhva minimizes and Rāmānuja maximizes. The typical Advaitin considers the *sākṣi* as a function or faculty of the *jīvātman-Brahman* equation such that it is anything else but individualized. It automatically guarantees the *svalakṣaṇa* of *jñāna* once *avidyā* is removed, and it can scarcely be said to be individuated at all. For ultimately in Advaita knowledge and Being are without division; and the *sākṣi* guarantees this, although only after the *via negativa*, the *neti neti*, is complete and all the veils are removed and the *koṣas* penetrated. But for Madhva, not so. Radically the *sākṣi* is definitely personal. It is the most subtle faculty, like a super-refined 6th sense, and therefore must have nothing to do with Brahman except to bear witness to its own dependence on Brahman/Viṣṇu.

Madhva puts more emphasis on the *sākṣi* consciousness than many other Indian philosophers, while Rāmānuja, because of his greater sense of the all-pervasiveness of God, takes the role of the *antaryāmi* as more important than the *sākṣi*. Madhva, also a devout Vaiṣṇava, adheres to the *panca-vyūha* doctrine and recognizes the importance of the *antaryāmi*, but he insists that one must recognize difference even in these hypostases of God. He does not subordinate *sākṣi* to *antaryāmi* for the reason that it is by virtue of the action of *sākṣi* that one perceives the differences that dialectically bind while they separate the different entities and spirits, including the different avatars. This is again a paradoxical difference from Śaṅkara who sees in *sākṣi* the final evidence for nondivision/nondifference everywhere and in everything and above everything. For according to the Advaitins, once the reduction to *sākṣi* is made everything else is seen to be *upādhi*, *adhyāsa*, *avidyā*. Indeed, there *is* nothing else, even this distinction being obliterated at the dawn of *Brahma-vidyā*, for this *sākṣi* as identical with the highest Brahman is of the essence of the Final or Total Cause of everything. But for Madhva this holds a hidden but fatal fallacy. The *difference* between this First and its antecedents, *māyā* though they may be in themselves, is irreducible. Śaṅkara is simply committing logical blunders and violating the evidence of the closest objective and introspective observation in trying to bridge that last identity. Observed and observer may be one in some fourth or fifth or *n*th dimension, but still we can certainly observe that even if that dimension were commonly available we would still distinguish between them even if the observed be the observer in self-observation, for the *sākṣi* is different from the *jīva*. At any rate, here we certainly have a remarkable analogue to the controversy over the Active Intellect among the Aristotelian scholastics.

As to the combination of *satkāryavāda* and *asatkāryavāda*, the Madhvas took a middle course such that, as Narain writes, "the cause and effect are therefore different aspects of the same principle. For example, when a necklace is made out of gold, it exists not as gold but as necklace, but prior to its manufacturing it was nothing else but gold. Thus according to the Madhva school the theory which can really claim to be logically valid is neither *satkāryavāda* nor *āsatkāryavāda* but both."[4] However, Narain adds that this applies only in the case of material causality and not instrumental causality. Narain claims that here there might be a partial compromise with the Madhva universal assertion of difference since between the material cause and its effect there is both identity and difference. Perhaps this is where the Aristotelian scheme might have come to the rescue since evidently the Madhva scheme does not include the formal cause, although rather obviously the material cause is essentially the same in both traditions as well as the instrumental or efficient cause. As to the final cause, that is always implicit although not always clearly stated except in terms of negation, as may be seen in the relation between Brahman and the world. At any rate, according to the Madhva point of view there is no excuse in attempting to reduce the material and the instrumental causes to one single transcendental ultra-final cause, denying any causal power except to the ultra-abstract, qualityless *nirguṇa*-Brahman as the Advaitins do.

As for the schemes of illusions, Madhva's argument is so simple that one marvels that the Advaitins try to ignore it or twist it completely out of proportion. In short, how can illusion be asserted without admitting the *difference* between illusion and reality? The Advaitin position is therefore self-defeating. Essentially the same line of argument is used in refuting the *ekajīvavāda* of some Advaitins since difference is already admitted with the assertion that all *jīvas* are one.

According to the Madhva theory the *svarūpabheda*, the autologous nature of difference, needs no extraneous validation because it is one of those basic presuppositions that any rationality has to presuppose as self-validating. The Advaitin argument is that if we have difference, then there must be a unity underlying the things that are different since it is *things* that are different and not difference-as-such which underlies unity-as-such. Hence difference-as-such can be corrected and thus shown to be invalid, since the things are within *māyā* and therefore the difference between them is also within *māyā* and therefore invalid, this invalidity being correctible by referring to the correcting counter-positive, since difference is rooted in negation, not in affirmation. The Madhvas simply counter that the Advaitins in making the distinction between identity and difference are already admitting the opposite of what they are trying to affirm. Indeed their very insistence on non-difference (*a-dvaita*) implies negation, and negation is always involved in difference. Therefore difference is prior to identity. And if one tries to assert what is based on negation of negation (the counter-example) that is still using negation, which is inseparable from difference.

According to some authorities the tension between Advaita and Dvaita Vedānta dominates the whole history of Vedāntic philosophy. Of course this is a slight exaggeration since there are also the *sampradayas* following after Rāmānuja, Śrīkaṇṭha,

Nimbârka, Vallabha and others. We do not yet have adequate information about refutations of the Madhva school by the Râmânujas or the Nimbârkas even though it is very difficult to believe that they did not exist. Our tentative speculation is that this has been due to the omission of such interests by Mādhava's *Sarvadarśanasaṃgraha*, which somehow seems to have dominated the scene among Euramerican Indologists out of proportion to its limited historical importance. At any rate, it is undeniably true that the specific controversy between the Madhvas and the Śaṅkarites did continue for many centuries, at least down to the time of Madhusūdana Sarasvatī and Jayatīrtha. Oddly enough the Hari Kṛṣṇa Caitanya-ites claim legitimacy from the Madhvas even though the difference between them is as much as the north polar ice cap is different from the mountains of Antarctica.

25. Nichiren

During the period when comparative philosophy was still in its first flush of enthusiasm, Nichiren (1222-1282) for the most part was neglected, partly because he had become even more unpopular with Japanese officialdom than in the previous centuries, but primarily because he just did not fit the stereotype of the "Wisdom of the Orient". He was entirely too aggressive. However, in recent years with the emergence of the Soka Gakkai, modernized and semi-westernized and definitely missionary (world-wide in ambition), interest in Nichiren himself has begun to be freshly aroused. Since we must establish a typology that applies fairly universally, we might well distinguish the prophetic and the priestly types just as we often distinguish the seminal or charismatic figure and the interpreters who come after whose job it is to present the contributions of a guru in systematized and rationalized form. Nichiren was not a systematizer but rather a powerful prophetic figure in constant opposition to virtually all of his contemporaries.

Most Japanese religious leaders were from aristocratic or

samurai families, but Nichiren was apparently the son of a provincial fisherman. Nevertheless he would come to see himself as the reincarnation of the Bodhisattva Jōgyō (Viśiṣṭacāritra), the protector of the *Lotus Sūtra*, and would make his famous vows: "I will be the pillar of Japan, I will be the eyes of Japan, I will be the ship of Japan." By the age of twelve Nichiren had encountered the two crucial questions that were to determine the course of his life. First, why had the Imperial family been allowed to suffer misfortunes, the child Emperor Antoku, for example, having been "allowed to drown and become food for fishes". Second, what is the one true version of Buddhism? As a nation cannot prosper under two rulers, neither can Buddhism prosper under a confusion of contending sects and sūtras. According to legend Nichiren studied Pure Land under Dai Amida, but when his master died in screaming agony Nichiren became convinced that all Pure Land followers were destined for hell and so he abandoned this way completely. On Mt. Hiei Nichiren narrowed his field of study to Tendai and Shingon and eventually to Tendai alone. He began to see himself as a restorer of Tendai to the ideals of its founder, Saichō. Once Nichiren saw the falsity of other faiths in comparison to the Tendai sect and the *Lotus Sūtra* he gained the answers to both his questions. The *Lotus Sūtra* alone could offer salvation. Neglect of it had caused the sufferings of the Imperial family. Furthermore, "although Śākyamuni was the leader of all sentient beings during his lifetime, now in the age of *mappo*, Nichiren alone was to be regarded as the rightful leader."[1]

The ambivalence and even hostility of some scholars toward Nichiren is perhaps best expressed by Renondeau who is more bluntly critical: "I have shown this monk to be intolerant and impetuous, fighting the existing sects, which he judged heretical, and exhorting the government, to the point of exasperation, to do its duty which according to him meant the radical suppression of the sects."[2] According to Renondeau, Nichiren considered the *nembutsu* recitation to be an act of hell; the Zen sect, the work of demons; and Shingon, a bad doctrine which makes the nation perish. He wrote to one official, "Ban the monks," yet elsewhere he argues for the universality of the Buddha, the presence of the

Buddha-nature in all beings and the certitude that we are all to become Buddhas one day.

Nichiren kept armed soldiers and weapons and stated publicly that heretical temples should be burned and the leading priests beheaded. Perhaps the government would not have moved against Nichiren for his intemperate religious statements alone, but when he surrounded himself with armed followers and seemed to threaten to burn down rival temples himself, the authorities moved against him and he was exiled to Sado Island. Nichiren's execution was secretly arranged but apparently something spectacular prevented the beheading from being consummated, one version saying that lightening struck the executioner's upraised sword. Perhaps because of his own experiences with persecution and suffering Nichiren gave particular value to affliction. In writing to a warrior he accommodates the word "affliction" in a way that all but removes it usual meaning. He says that when a man and woman chant adoration to the *Lotus Sūtra* while making love, "that is exactly in line with what we call affliction as nothing but enlightenment, mundane existence as nothing but Nirvāṇa."[3] Dear Socrates! What a merry time you must have been having in limbo all these centuries trying to get some coherance and unity and consistency out of these (nevertheless saintly and historically charismatic) sophists and sages which have followed you on this planet! As the *Lotus Sūtra* itself describes its message:

> Who hears and joyfully extols it
> Though but by a single word,
> Has thus paid homage to
> All Buddhas in the three realms. . . .
> Rejoice greatly in your hearts,
> Knowing that you will become Buddhas.[4]

That "single word" which can save all is, according to Nichiren, the title of the *Lotus Sūtra.* For Nichiren the title contained everything of importance in the *Lotus Sūtra* so that both study and chanting of the whole *Sūtra* could be replaced by chanting the *daimoku* (the sacred title) alone. Rodd writes:

> Nichiren countered the Amidist "sole practice" of the

> *nembutsu* with a sole practice of his own: he urged his followers to recite "Namu Myōhōrengekyō," "Homage to the Sutra of the Lotus of the Wonderful Law," instead of "Namu Amida Butsu," "Homage to the Buddha Amida." The practice was similar, but the theory behind the recitation was different. Whereas the *nembutsu* was an appeal to a humanized buddha, Nichiren's *daimoku* served as a mantra, or symbolic magical chant.
>
> Recitation of the *daimoku* was Nichiren's answer to the attraction of the *nembutsu*: it required no study or difficult religious training, and it was available to everyone. Nichiren advocated the *daimoku* as a combination of witness and meditation. Like the *nembutsu*, the *daimoku* was a simplified practice and a way to achieve enlightenment without long years of study of Buddhist philosophy.[5]

Nichiren's lifework can be seen as a project in religious simplification. He first simplified all of the religious complexities he knew down to one sect and one scripture. Next he simplified all of that scripture's meaning into its title. Finally, while exiled on Sado Island in 1273, he simplified everything into one visual symbol for his movement in the form of a *Daimandara* (Great Mandala).

According to the Tendai doctrine of Original Enlightenment, each human being is already intrinsically enlightened. What must be done is to manifest what is latent in each individual. The first part of the *Lotus Sūtra* concerns the need to begin the manifestation in spite of difficulties, while the second part deals with the "Origin" or "Absolute" itself. Nichiren emphasized the second section of the *Lotus*: "As a purist reformer . . . Nichiren sought to obliterate all forms of expediency and approach the 'Absolute' directly. . . . In both Shingon and Nichiren thought the impulse towards the 'Absolute' is so consuming that everything in its pathway is reduced in significance."[6] The "Absolute" is not something outside or above humanity but is identified clearly with the phenomenal world: "Nichiren's idealism was such that he believed perfect enlightenment possible for all beings and that as a result, the relative world could be transformed into a veritable Utopia."[7]

In one sense Nichiren's astounding conviction that his individual awareness contained the entire universe of the Eternal Buddha (Absolute Truth) was but a logical development of the Tendai concept of *ichinen sanzen* (one thought equals three thousand worlds). Nichiren believed "that his personal awareness that the *Lotus* was to be propagated at the present time was in fact the subjective awareness of the Eternal Śākyamuni of the Origin section of the sūtra."[8] This will seem even more logical if we realize that since *any* thought contains the three thousand worlds, Nichiren merely makes explicit concerning *his* thought what lay unemphasized in all the rest. We can find in Nichiren, even if it is not uppermost, some surprising sparks of insight into the most profound dialectics of Being and Becoming even though, as Nakamura points out, these are expressed almost entirely in concrete images and not in abstruse logical terms. As Satomi expresses Nichiren's sense of dialectic: "All beings on the one side are a mass of lust, but nevertheless they are, on the other side, Buddha in nature or Buddha in substance. Therefore if they should self-awaken to their true value and strain every nerve to get near their intrinsic Buddhahood, significant lives would be established."[9]

Nichiren's aspiration was to restore Buddhism to its original integrity and to establish once and for all its unity over against the sectarian fragmentation of the Buddhist Trinity. As a devout student of the *Lotus Sūtra* he regarded the three forms of the Buddha in the *Trikāya* as one and inseparable. However,

> What the prevailing schools of Buddhism had done was to emphasize one form at the expense of the others. Esoteric Buddhism stressed the Universal Buddha . . .; Amidism worshipped the Body of Bliss or Eternal Buddha, Amitabha. By thus dispensing with the historical Buddha, Shakyamuni (the Transformation Body), they committed the inexcusable crime of mutilating Buddha's perfect body. . . . The *Lotus Sutra* alone upholds the truth of the triune Buddha. And only in this trinity is the salvation of all assured.[10]

Of course Nichiren's opponents in turn saw their versions of Buddhism as being complete and his *Lotus* movement as merely a lopsided fragment.

No other person, Renondeau informs us, associated the destiny of his country so closely with the glory of his religion as did Nichiren. According to Nichiren, once the state is purged of its moral and religious pollution, something grand can stand forth in the union of the state and Buddhist Truth. In his powerful prophetic intensity Nichiren's goal was no less than to awaken a whole nation to its historic destiny:

> . . . Nichiren's vision of Japan (was) as the land in which the true teaching of the Buddha was to be revived and from which it was to spread throughout the world. The name Nichiren, which he adopted, symbolizes this exalted mission and his own key role in its fulfilment, for *nichi*, "the sun," represents both the Light of Truth and the Land of the Rising Sun, while *ren* stands for the Lotus.
>
> To accomplish this aim Nichiren urged all his followers to imitate the bodhisattva ideal of perseverance and self-sacrifice. In an age of utter decadence, everyone must be a man of Superb Action, ready to give his life if necessary for the cause.[11]

Nichiren was not interested in logic or in consolation, but in a prophetic action. The *Lotus Sūtra* was not merely for spiritual contemplation but should be "read by the body". Nichiren's famous shock-tactic for conversion is called *shakubuku* and means "break and subdue". It was revived in the twentieth century by Soka Gakkai which used the method to coerce and, in a surprising number of instances, to convert. Nichiren realized, as more moderate and detached philosophers may have failed to realize, that changes of the kind he envisaged can never come by means of mere sweet reasonableness.

Nichiren's intention is to demonstrate how the Eternal Infinite Buddha can and does come within the limited existence and experience of ordinary human beings. This is the only true, the only truly universal, Way, and thus all-embracing, and the way whereby any and all can be saved—democratically, as is taught in the *Lotus Sūtra* over and against the exclusiveness of the other ways, especially the Zen and Advaita trends which tend to be too esoteric for the general public. Nichiren was very much influenced by the Tendai, but emotionally and in many other ways he went far beyond their cultivated sense of decorum. Nichiren at times could be extremely compassionate as well as bombastically prophetic in his manner. His spirit of equality extends even to women in a way that reminds us somewhat of Rāmānuja's defying the exclusiveness of the Advaitins. But it was the spirit of the *Lotus Sūtra* that moved him rather than any merely rational principle of an abstract speculation.

26. Ippen

The ninth century monist trend was essentially aristocratic, but by the time of the Great Summas Era of the High Middle Ages to which Ippen belongs there was a spread of popular teaching of a high quality among the masses everywhere throughout Eurasia. The emergence of the Franciscans and Dominicans in Latin Europe and the increase in numbers and activities among the Sūfī orders in the Islamic world fit this description; and, in sharp contrast to Śaṅkara's exclusion of women and lower castes from the study of the Vedas, Rāmānuja's and Pillai Lokācārya's deliberate flouting of caste restrictions following the Ālvārs' example indicates that Ippen was certainly only an example of the general tenor of the time. Honen and Shinran also had effected popular movements among the common people, which others have called a "Protestant Reformation" but which we would rather liken to the contemporary rise of the Franciscans and Dominicans.

Ippen (1239-1289) belongs to the Amida cult. He was famous as an itinerant sage wandering around teaching and preaching, almost Franciscan style, which has always been what Buddhist monks are supposed to do. He advocated the *nembutsu* to Amida somewhat as Honen and Shinran. Ippen's following is known as the Jishū variety of Jōdoshū Buddhism because of its insistence on constant Recollection maintained by uninterrupted use of the *nembutsu* as well as specific prayers six times a day (instead of the five times for Muslims or seven times for orthodox

Christian monks). As with the Chaitanya cult and *many* others in world history of religion, dancing was common practice among them. Actually Ippen never intended to found another sect, although his following did constitute what is known as a *Ji* or Congregation. Like some sects that still thrive in India, they practised chanting of the Holy Name in shifts of six hours so that it would be uninterrupted throughout the twenty-four hours. Individually the ideal was that one should have it so harmonized or ingrained in one's subconscious mind that it would "do itself" without effort when one is sitting, standing, walking or even sleeping.

Ippen's family was of the aristocratic Samurai landowning class associated with a Shintō cult of the Kumano god. This partially explains his teaching that the omnipresent Buddha-nature is "even in Shintō shrines"; but it also is remarkable perhaps in demonstrating that Buddhism in Japan as in China, in contrast to Confucianism, had had a democratizing effect. Incidentally it is well known that Confucianism in Japan had essentially served as a strengthening of Shintō rather than as a leavening of Buddhism although both of them had been imported from China. Ippen's conversion had some radical socio-economic effects also since before him the local Shintō priests had kept the villages in fear that if they rebelled against their overlords the wrath of the local deities would be incurred. Ippen broke through this and his followers lost that fear in full faith that Amida regarded not only all human beings regardless of class or caste but even all living beings as equally meriting His plenary grace, so long as they simply used the *nembutsu.* Thus later on Rennyo (1415-1499) had quite a problem in handling this revolutionary liberation since increasingly the followers of Ippen had organized armed bands of rebellous peasants.

Having decided on renunciation of the world, Ippen lived for three years mostly in solitude on a mountainside practising the *nembutsu.* This again is a very common pattern among saints in all faiths especially in the High Middle Ages all across Eurasia. Very few people have ever found a sense of vocation or sense of mission without some such retreat, whether voluntary as in Ippen's case or involuntary as with Giordano Bruno in the Italian Renaissance and with Aurobindo more recently. Ippen's conversion was definitely of the traumatic type, liberating him from *ahaṅkāra* or ego—a sort of *fanā'* from the Ṣūfī point of view, or almost like St. Paul's, after which Ippen could also say, "now no longer I". It was a complete *śaraṇāgati*, to use the terminology common in Teṅgalai Śrī-Vaiṣṇavism in Rāmānuja's heritage. In fact one might find much in common between Ippen and Pillai Lokācārya (d. 1327) and others in the Viśiṣṭādvaita tradition. Just as Nammāḻvār before Rāmānuja sang, "Thou singest of Thyself through me", so Ippen says, "The *nembut*[illegible] itself chants the *nembutsu*".[1]

Ippen enforced rigorous discipline on all his intimate foll[illegible]ers, who were considered to be *sute hijiri*, sages who aband[illegible] all. Like many Indian yogis (a few even today), Ippen hoped [illegible] go to Heaven in his present body, transformed by the grace o[illegible] Amida. Since he had not intended to found a separate sect Ippen did not name any successor. At the time of his death there was such confusion that seven of his followers committed suicide by drowning. His most intimate disciple, Shinkyō, eventually became the leader, but only after a representative group of the faithful had gone to Mt. Tanjō where they intended to chant the *nembutsu* while fasting to death. Since Ippen's followers imitated his example of wandering around the countryside instead of settling in one place and composing high-level intellectual works, his influence was not very great among intellectuals. When the Tokugawa regime prohibited the practice of itinerant mendicancy, the number of the Ji sect dwindled considerably—another salient warning that censorship like lack of patronage can be more effective historically than intrinsic merit.

Just what was it that Ippen taught the masses? Did his teaching compromise sound Buddhist doctrine by allowing folksy superstition and magic; or was it more like the mission of Meister Eckhardt, who, in contrast to the scholarly and monumental work of Aquinas his fellow Dominican, wandered barefoot all over Germany teaching what was really heavy metaphysics but in a way that the common people could understand. Yanagi Sōetsu writes in his study of Ippen:

The scriptural basis for their doctrine was found mainly in

the eighteenth of the forty-eight vows set forth in the *Larger Sūtra of Eternal Life*:

Even if I were to attain Buddhahood, if the sentient beings of the ten quarters of this world who desire in true faith to be born in the Pure Land were to repeat the Nembutsu for even a few times, and yet not gain that rebirth, then would I not attain Supreme Enlightenment.

. . . The important point in the above passage is that which advocates the practice of the vocal recitation (*shōmyō*) or Namu-amida-butsu as the way of salvation for sentient beings—an "easy way" expressly provided for those of inferior endowment, who have only to pronounce the words. For them, there could be no more welcome teaching. . . .

Honen called himself "Honen of the ten evil deeds." Shinran spoke of himself as a "*gutoku*", or bald-headed ignoramus. "A man of humble capacity" was Ippen's term of self-reference. Without this realization of one's own ordinariness and lack of ability, there can be no refuge or genuine faith in the other power. Total, unreserved awareness that one is an ordinary, unenlightened man permits no traces of self-power. For the ordinary man, there is literally nothing else to do but to give himself up totally to the other-power. This "refuge" thus indicates a pure faith unadulterated by reasoning or traces of self-power.

What, then, was Ippen's teaching? In holding that man supplicates to the Buddha, or that the Buddha beckons to man, there remains a basic man-Buddha dualism. Even when salvation is defined as the mutual interpenetration of the two, the words "man" and "Buddha" are still separate. If we make out the Buddhist Dharma to be the nondualistic view, then it is desirable for us to seek a more profound standpoint. The Name (the pronouncing of the Nembutsu), which is able to eliminate this duality, contains within it man's actual rebirth in the Pure Land. So instead of man contemplating Buddha or Buddha contemplating man, one must attain the realm where Nembutsu is just Nembutsu, and nothing else. We may consider the following quotations from Ippen as the last word on Nembutsu teaching. A purer statement could not be made.

> At the instant of each calling of the Name, the Nembutsu recites the Nembutsu.

In the same way, the hearing of the Name is not man's hearing, neither is it the Buddha making man hear it.

> The Name hears the Name; there is nothing to be heard apart from the Name . . . You must know it as the Name that does not allow of other thoughts.[2]

It is perhaps surprising that we should find such an extreme 'advaitic' interpretation put on the *nembutsu* by Ippen. Although the basic trend was toward greater elaboration of what had preceded the period of the Great Summas in which Ippen did his work, nevertheless perhaps in his case greater elaboration after Genshin, Honen and Shinran was virtually impossible except by way of radical simplification. It would seem that the refinement on the meaning of the words in the *nembutsu* was carried by Ippen to an esoteric extreme that is a far cry from the historic Śākyamuni's original "middle way"; and indeed there may be a touch of *ex opere operato* magic attached to his Way. Ippen's radical intention is that through the *nembutsu* one makes the transition from instrumental or extrinsic to intrinsic transvaluation. In other words, he is dealing with *paramabhakti* and not with simple selfish devotion.

In contrast to Honen and Shinran, Ippen makes an appeal to *return* to what he believed to be the Buddha-nature in Man expressing itself without any human interference and without any regard to hierarchical differences in the world or in the realm of spirit. Sōetsu writes:

> One can also trace the transition from Honen to Shinran to Ippen in their respective interpretations of the word *Namu* (in Japanese, *ki-myō*). Honen took them as meaning that man entrusts (*ki*) his life (*myō*) to the Buddha. Shinran regarded "Namu" as the Buddha directing (*myō*) man to entrust (*ki*) himself to Buddha. For Ippen, it meant to entrust or return oneself (*ki*) to the nondualistic life-source (*myō*) that is prior to division into man and Buddha.
>
> A similar development appears in their concepts of merit-transference (*ekō*). The words *shishin ekō*, which appear in

the *Sūtra of Eternal Life*, were generally thought to refer to man transferring the merit he had accumulated in religious practice to the Buddha. . . .

But is this indeed the final, deepest significance in merit-transference? In the Buddha's act of merit-transference to man there still remains a distinction between man and Buddha. Both man and Buddha must be taken up within the dynamic working of merit-transference, which has been described as knowable "only between Buddha and Buddha," or as a "communication between one Buddha and another." The words of Ippen quoted previously about "Nembutsu doing Nembutsu" constitute perhaps the ultimate response. He says:

> "Though you put your mind into the Name, you must not put the Name into your mind."
>
> "Though you are ruled by the Name, you must not influence the Name . . . The Name does not depend upon meaning; it is a Dharma independent of man's mind."
>
> "There is no meaning in the Name of Amida. Namu-amida-butsu."

Therefore,

> "You may regard as gibberish all words other than Nembutsu."
>
> "Do not be preoccupied with knowledge about the Nembutsu."
>
> "Apart from this present Namu-amida-butsu do not cherish any distinction of before and after."

Here, thoughts about merit-transference versus no merit-transference vanish, leaving only the aspect of merit-transference transferring its merit and Buddha face to face with Buddha.[3]

If one gets the impression that here we are really only embroiled in petty theological disputes between the different branches of the Pure Land sect, then one might re-examine all the esoterics involved in the later Upaniṣads in interpretations of the mantra sound *ŌM*. Actually what emerges in Ippen is essentially the same radical paradox that one sign or sound includes *everything*, but in a transcendentally monistic way. One might also find here something closely resembling Dōgen's 'reductionist' efforts to get back behind all differentiation, even in grammar, which some have also compared to Husserl's attempt to get at pure consciousness-without-content, the difference being that Husserl and Dōgen were *jñānis* and not *bhaktas* as Ippen was. As may be seen in the Victorines, for example, such attempts were not at all uncommon in Latin Europe in the same century and are certainly in the Hesychast controversy in Byzantium.

Some members, especially in Shinran's Jōdō-Shinshū, taught that even if only once with complete sincerity one pronounces the *nembutsu*, one will attain the Western Paradise thus putting the emphasis entirely on faith rather than on works or practice. Such faith was likewise not uncommon among Muslims and Vaiṣṇava Hindus. Others put the stress on constancy of the recollection. Rāmānuja said recollection should be like a steady little stream of oil in a lamp that must keep steadily burning. Sōetsu writes of Ippen:

> Ippen is no different from Shinran in the belief that a single Nembutsu calling can assure Pure Land rebirth. But this "one calling" is not a numerical frequency. "One calling" is something that must come into play at each and every calling. Therefore, there is a continuity of such "one callings." And this is not a matter of many callings for their own sake, nor many callings intended as recompense or thanksgiving. It is a series of single callings that arise newly and freshly at every new moment. Hence, for Ippen there was numerically neither one calling nor many callings.[4]

The very strong 'advaitic' tendency in Ippen might be likened to the metaphysics even of, Citsukha his contemporary, except that again Citsukha is a *jñāni* and Ippen a *bhakta par excellence.*

If theology of grace is carried too far, neglect of the difference between good and evil might ensue. But if the emphasis goes too far in the opposite direction, then the Great Compassion of the Buddha or Deity is forgotten and we come into a sort of mechanical spiritual determinism like the rigorous versions of

Mīmāṁsā where the laws of karma are inexorable and operate on their own momentum. Sōetsu writes:

> . . . Is an other-power teaching unburdened by distinctions of men's good and evil, wisdom and lack of wisdom, justified in making the line between faith and lack of faith a matter of established doctrine? Are the doors of salvation closed to those suffering people who are unable to attain to faith? Is not faith too a power that is limited to a select group? Are the blessings of Pure Land rebirth not accorded to those without faith? This very question is the ultimate one that must confront anyone who would establish a Nembutsu teaching. It was Ippen who felt compelled to give it its most profound answer.
>
> Not only did he eliminate the distinction between good and evil, wise and dull-witted, in the face of Pure Land rebirth, he swept away differences of faith and lack of faith to boot.[6]

In Ippen's extreme doctrine of salvation by grace the historic Śākyamuni has evidently faded well out of the picture along with his own teaching "be a lamp unto yourself".

It is somewhat remarkable that neither Ippen nor any of his Japanese contemporaries show any evidence of influence from the Neo-Confucianism that had been prevailing in China really since the late ninth century and which had had its peak development in Chu Hsi who died in 1200, long before Ippen's birth. But all forms of Confucianism by this time had become quite elitist and for that reason, among others, may have failed to understand the real significance of Buddhism at its best. By the ascendency of the Tokugawa shogunate, after the purge of Christianity, when Buddhism was also suppressed, Chu Hsi's Neo-Confucianism became the official philosophy of the whole of Japan. But that comes later, long after the death of Ippen, Dōgen, Eisai and the others. Ippen as well as his contemporaries might not have understood the criticisms of Buddhism by the Neo-Confucians. Popularizers like Ippen just did not have time for such scholarly, gentlemanly pursuits. And yet the argument could still further be enlarged since Chu Hsi was also concerned with the welfare of the common people.

When Ippen realized his death was approaching, he took all the writings in his possession as well as works he himself had written in the course of his life and committed them to the fire. To his disciples in their profound sorrow he spoke the brief instruction, "The religious teaching of my entire lifetime has been reduced to Namu-amida-butsu."

> There the essence of the Pure Land teaching emerges in its entirety: to leave nothing at all behind and set the Name alone in bold relief. There can be nothing lacking if only we have the Name. The countless volumes spawned by the Pure Land tradition in China and Japan teach nothing beyond the pronouncing of the six syllables, Namu-amida-butsu. The Ji sect thus has no scripture for its followers to place their reliance on. For them it is the six syllables and the six syllables alone. No scripture could surpass that.[6]

Hence the simplicity of the teaching and practice, which is suited to one and all regardless of social status, occupation or level of education; and hence the lack of interest among metaphysical scholars. But sociologists might find here a very significant study of a democratic leaven in an otherwise rigid hierarchical feudal form of society. Ippen's egalitarianism gave the peasants social status and a sense of identity so that those who followed from his charisma did in some cases bring about some social revolution. Still one cannot but question whether his was not a sort of fanaticism as extreme in its way as Nichiren's was in his way. Fanaticisms, nevertheless, make history that humanists only study.

27. Roger Bacon

Roger Bacon (1212-1294) is a sort of transitional figure and for that reason a very controversial one. Yet as far as metaphysics is concerned he is not so different from the others of his century, in spite of his attempts at innovation and his creative restlessness. He had a very healthy curiosity—an inordinate one according to some of his superiors—about the rest of the world, with which Latin Europe was finally beginning again to have some contact and communication. We may remind ourselves that Western Europe was then still really only on the periphery of civilization. The conquest of Constantinople by the Franks in 1182, disgraceful though it was from the standpoint of fellow Christians looting and plundering a culture that was much more advanced than their own, did open to Western Europe much that had been lost through the puritanical funnel of Augustine and Pope Gregory and established a completely open road to China through the vast domain of Genghis Khan. Nestorian Christian pilgrims could travel all the way from Peking to France, gain audience and blessing from the Pope, and return. Evidently Bacon had little or no knowledge of China except what had come through the Nestorian pilgrims; but he specifically mentions India, Persia, the Tartars, the Babylonians, the Egyptians and almost everything else that had come into the possible range of learning in Western Europe at that time, and even argued in defense of those people whom some Christians would bring into subjugation for the sake of conversion. Throughout the Eurasiatic world in the thirteenth century there was trade and travel and exchange of ideas. Europe only later advanced to much that had originally come from other parts of the globe, as is evidenced by the travels of Ibn Baṭṭūṭah, and only later began to improve what it "discovered" in the rest of the oecumene.

At first it would appear that there is after all little that is strictly original in Roger Bacon. He depends on Boethius (surprisingly) and very largely on Avicenna, almost more than on Averröes. There is little of the mysticism of his contemporary and ecclesiastical superior, St. Bonaventure (who for some strange reason had to censure him somewhat), but there is not yet the positivism of William of Ockham, Buridan, or Nicholas of Autrecourt. What happens to Aristotle in his hands is certainly of a different genre than what happens in Aquinas. He is not in favour of the extremes of ecstatic contemplation of Richard of St. Victor, who even more than his predecessor Hugo rejoiced in those things which are above the mind; nevertheless, Bacon is by no means a materialist in the sense of the dogmatic insistence of the eighteenth century philosophers of science upon the primacy of observables. In short, as can be shown to be true of thirteenth century China, India, Persia, Samarkand, Baghdad and Damascus, Spain and Istanbul, in Western Europe also we still find the full spectrum of varieties and types of philosophizing.

According to Bréhier: "The most remarkable of the Oxonian scholars was Roger Bacon, the *doctor mirabilis,* whose impetuous, ardent, and indomitable spirit was reflected in his life as well as in his writings. No one was more critical than he of the ignorance and stupidity of the 'Parisian philosophers,' and particularly of their negligence in the matter of studying languages, mathematics, and the natural sciences."[1] Bacon is no doubt best known for his interest in scientific investigation, for which he has been called "the great prophet of modern science".

> His appeal to *experience* as the origin and justification of all philosophy and science, and as the final court before which their claims to validity must be tried, is novel. And his discovery that experience can be deliberately enlarged and deepened by *experiment* is original with him. He is the first thinker in recorded history to use the phrase "experimental science," and may be regarded as the father of the experimental method.
>
> In a sense, too, we may regard him as the father of European *invention.* To be sure, the discoveries attributed to him, as, for example, the telescope, the burning glass, spectacles, and gunpowder are doubtful, and in any case were not followed through. But the *spirit* of invention was there.[2]

Bacon himself writes:

> We have three methods of knowing, authority, experience, and reason; but authority does not contribute to our knowledge if it does not give us the reason for what is states. . . . Reason, in turn, cannot separate sophistry from demonstration unless its conclusions are verified by experience. The truth is, however, that no one today shows concern over this

> method . . . and that is why all or almost all of the secrets, and the greatest secrets, of science are ignored by most of those who devote themselves to learning.[3]

Bréhier adds that Bacon "also took up technical problems, ranging from the engineering techniques that caused him to imagine automotive machines and flying machines, and social techniques such as the problem of organizing work and providing for public welfare."[4] Of course we should not attempt to find in Bacon's efforts precisely the same elements as we now find in modern science after it has gone through its centuries of development. And while in Bacon "we find no precise method either for designing experiments or deducing laws from them," nevertheless we find an exploratory attitude which, with the help of others, could lead to those designs and laws.

The natural sciences had already made progress in both Islam and China, and the architecture of mosques, temples and churches, as well as fortresses and castles, had made remarkable advances. It should not be surprising therefore to find Albert the Great and Roger Bacon, following after Avicenna and Averroës and Chu Hsi's fellow-scientists, engaging in fresh investigations and making some original experiments. Far from Aristotle's being the chief hindrance to these, as it will later be charged in the case of Galileo, to a great extent it was Aristotle's philosophy which gave the metaphysical groundwork upon which the structure of these investigations could be built. In spite of some passages in Bonaventure in which there are references to the quieting influence or activity of the Holy Spirit, for the most part it may well be said that the period of quietism was over. Comprehensiveness was the rule, and the particular investigations and efforts at precision in everything from details of botanical classification to refinement of definition in the highest reaches of knowledge, essence, quiddity and existence, were only efforts at filling in the details of the total picture. The Gothic cathedral symbolizes much more, thus, than it reveals.

Bacon insists on the essentially composite nature of finite being; a simple finite being is a contradiction in terms. Only God is absolutely simple, and therefore any and all beings must be derived in their complexity from His Simplicity—quite the opposite of some more modern notions that would put the maximum of complexity and relatedness in God with the supposition that the atom is the simplest component (although increasingly the atom itself is beginning to appear as infinitely complex as a solar system). Matter to Bacon is not a stuff you can squeeze through your fingers. It is only a necessary, almost indemonstrable, supposition (*suppositum*) of all existent reality. As *suppositum* it can never be in manifestation except insofar as it is mixed with form. Although form also cannot be pointed to and handled as a thing, being immaterial and 'ideal', it is there and cannot become manifest except in mixture. In defending this structuring of all reality, even right up to the very essence of the Trinity which also must have 'matter' and form in order to become communicable, Bacon was more on the defensive than Madhva, who was on the offensive constantly in regard to his realism and logic of difference. They might have made hearty cohorts had they known each other, along with Ch'en Liang.

Bacon maps out the varieties of composition or compositeness quite clearly. They are (1) composition from form and being (*esse*), (2) composition of being and end (*ente*), (3) composition from genus and difference, (4) composition from what (*quod*) a thing is and how (*quo*) a thing is, and (5) composition from act and potency. These he has no doubt gathered from Avicenna. The first he rejects because form is cause, not the *actus essendi*, and form can enter into composition only with that which already has its *actus essendi*. That is, a thing must already have some existence in order to have composition at all. Its existence is not dependent on its nature, but the nature is commingled with its existence in the mixture *post rem*. The composition involved is only of a logical order. The second is also rejected for similar reasons. Being (*esse*) must be its own *actus essendi* beyond any dialectical involvement. Nothing can enter into composition with itself, therefore any ascription of being (*ens*) to Being is completely superfluous. No actual composition is really involved and the distinction remains only a logical one for there is no *otherness* involved, whereas all composition must involve otherness. The third is at best only instrumental. Definitions are not essential to the thing or intelligence defined. Especially is this true of the spiritual intelligences which make the definitions, which in themselves are incorporeal and are classified largely by negative delimitation, not by positive combination of descriptive characteristics. They are really forms, pure forms, involving no necessary conjunction, much less combination or mixture, with matter (as is the case especially with angels, for example). The fourth is also strictly logical. *Quo est* he equates with form and *quod est* to *ens*. The relation is merely that of the abstract and the particular instance of the abstraction involved rather than a composition of different distinct factors in the actual existence of the thing involved.

The fifth is demonstrated as hylomorphism, i.e., his viewing all logical operations as merely operative and not essential to the 'reason' of their existence. The combinations of actual and potential are all subordinate to the operation of the First Cause which is God, Who is purely spiritual and absolutely actual but commanding all potentiality. Nevertheless *act* in the second degree conforms to form while potency conforms to matter, so that there must be a distinction made between purely spiritual beings who need no matter or potentiality in order to exist and material things which are so mixed. But this does not explain how spiritual beings exist and become known without involvement in complexity. How he explains this is not absolutely clear and would require a detailed study. But one may surmise that he is almost anticipating Ockham in the distaste for multiplication of entities and would therefore rather reverse the question. The problem is not the non-involvement of spiritual beings in complexity, but the demonstration that the complexity ascribed to the *existence* of non-spiritual entities (as distinct from their nature) is also really essential to their being, even though the compositeness of their nature may be inseparable from that existence. Here he would probably concur with Chu Hsi and his followers.

This becomes somewhat clearer in his discussion of the unity of matter. This is a great puzzle to most beginners in scholastic philosophy—and admittedly to many experts also as perhaps to the scholastics themselves. The easier view inherited from Plotinus is that matter is of the essence of multiplicity, the last emanation from the One farther than which the evolutionary cycle cannot go, and must begin the return involutionary cycle towards

Spirit, Being and the One again. But the scholastic Aristotelians did not see it this way. Matter is the single principle, if not of reality as such, at least of Creation created by God *ex nihilo* (in sharp revision of Aristotle's teaching to the contrary that it is eternally coexistent with the First Form). Although nothing in itself, in combination with uncreated form, matter brings things into actuality out of the pure possibility that matter in itself is. The great body of problems growing out of the various possible combinations both as to degree and as to kind explains much of the bulk of the *summae* of the European scholastics, as, for that matter, is the case with Chu Hsi and the other interpreters of Chou Tun-i's *Diagram of the Supreme Ultimate*.

Can a principle which is nothing in itself still have unity? From our perspective Bacon is struggling with the old *māyāvāda* nut which is so hard to crack. Matter as such cannot be known except by abstracting away everything except what it must be in itself, and then you have 'nothing' left! Quite literally, matter is nothing (*māyā*) or at best the sheer undifferentiated impossibility of existing in separation from form. Thus to say that it has unity is really to say too much. Bacon, however, is not so naïve as to deny some sense of 'form' of unity to this sheer possibility in order to avoid the opposite trap of trimming down this possibility of existence to such an extent that it could not have the power of combining with form in order to bring existence into actuality. The question of whether this unity is essential to the matter itself or is of the essence of the form which combines with it forces him to admit a duplex nature to matter which evidently his contemporaries were not so willing to concede. Here perhaps he may be closer to Madhva than to some of his Christian contemporaries. Bacon's is a logic of difference, not of identity; a logic of matter, not of illusion.

The duplicity is that of matter as such and matter as existing in essential reality. This is his earlier distinction, and later he further distinguishes "material" matter from "spiritual" matter, as Madhva also does. The difference in the first case is that between the different *forms* of material things and the different *kinds* of material things. The chief emphasis is put, not on the division between potential and actual, but between form as such and the actuality which is produced by the combination of that form with matter. There is of course a sort of unity through these different species, these different varieties of matter, but the unity is only a logical unity, not necessarily an actual unity. Matter-as-such still is subject to the possibility of being or of not being. If matter is merely the quasi-unity of this possibility, we should run into the impossibility of matter being its own possibility, which is absurd. Even the possibility of the existence of matter, therefore, cannot be distinguished from the form of that possibility. However, this does not imply that the forms have any better condition than matter as far as composition is concerned. They are not self-existent, as some Platonists insist, any more than matter is self-existent. Both are created by the First Cause, and their combination produces the universe of spiritual and material existents, as Madhva also argued. Crowley summarizes Bacon's final position:

> There are thus three kinds of matter: prime matter, void of all form but capable of receiving all; natural matter (*materia naturalis*), which is prime matter plus the forms of substance and corporeity; and, finally, matter which is the substratum of substantial transformations (encountered only in the sublunary world) and which adds to *materia naturalis* the forms of the elements....It must be clearly understood that, for Bacon, the external agent contributes no more than this impulse or virtue which has for effect to arouse the active potency in matter. The incomplete form or active potency is not to be thought of as an accident of matter, nor is it identical with matter. It is a substantial form, essentially the same as the complete form. Between this incomplete form or active potency and the complete form there is only a difference of degree of actualization within the same essence.[5]

In Bacon's theory of privation, the absence of form is almost, if not entirely, synonymous with active potency, or with incomplete form. Unlike Navya Nyāya of India which insists on the possibility of an absence of an absence, Bacon evidently considers a pure absence sheer impossibility. God *is*, the angels *are*, creation *is*: there is 'nothing' anywhere.

Although one might expect a parallel of forms and matters, Bacon does not allow the same degree of plurality of forms as he does to matters. The actual modes of being in any given object, notably in plants and animals that grow, are already potentially in the form which it takes, even though that form be one of constant transformation. The unity of form is necessary in order to preserve the identity of the object, even though it takes on an increase or decrease of matter in its *actus existendi.* It is not quite clear to what extent this is analogously true of the whole of creation, not to say the whole of existence, including the existence of God (Bonaventure here differs from Aquinas and Bacon also). To be a *uni*verse the world must have a unity of form. Whether this unity of form is a *unity of unities* of forms of the individuals it contains, or whether this super-form makes the unity possible as a composite of the individuals of which it is composed; or whether the individuation is really an individuation that is 'not there' but is allowed only to our finite minds as a practical convenience; or whether this unity of form (or these unicities of forms) is superimposed on the matter by God in order to make existence out of non-being; or whether rather by a sort of non-mixing conjunctive touch of form and matter in their pure 'forms' the sparks that comprise creation are generated—these are possible questions common to Bacon and to Madhva and to the Islamic pluralists. Whether they exhausted all the possibilities is doubtful, however, for the possibilities themselves are infinite. One gets the impression that the Hindu and Buddhist scholastics were a little more aware of this infinity of possibilities than Bacon and certainly more so than Aquinas.

Whether or not Bacon realized this infinite possibility of an unlimited range of views—Leibniz' "possible worlds" is a weak echo of this *vidyā*—he did at least try to get some precision on what was within his grasp. As Crowley again summarizes:

> Bacon admits a progressive evolution of the substantial form, for generation embraces a multiplicity of partial generations. Between the incomplete form or the active potency and the ultimate specific determination, there are many intermediate stages. The whole essence of the substantial form is

> not realizéd all at once: hence Bacon's theory of the many grades in the *esse* of the substantial form. The Thomistic view that the intermediate forms are provisional and transitory is foreign to Bacon's system. For him they are not transitory but are constitutive grades of the substantial form.[6]

Bacon does not go quite so far into the translucency of all form as such, as the exemplarism of Suhrawardī or Bonaventure allows. Bacon, like the Madhvas and the Chu Hsi "realist" school, seems to hold a real "graspability" of form which rather holds things in their self-existence even though this may be only a logical holding, whereas Bonaventure treats form as only the instrumental means of infusing the divine essence into all matter insofar as it is capable of receiving it.

All this, however, is only a hurdle into the next field, that of the soul. Bacon follows Aristotle up to a certain point as almost everyone does. He not only allows that the soul is the form of the existence of the individual (body and all) but is a substance distinct in its own right. It seems that here he is following essentially the same structure, or attempt at a theory of possible structure, as in his treatment of matter-form connexity. The soul is composite: vegetable, animal and rational. These do not constitute separable entities within a whole that has been put together like a machine; rather they are formal distinctions within an organic whole integrally necessary to the existence not only of the organism as a whole but even to each of its thousands of individual cells and organs. The generic characteristic of this governing principle is not mere form, for in order to exist it must also be a composite of matter and form; but as a composite, it must constitute a single spiritual substance, otherwise its faculty of free will may be compromised. Whether Bacon distintinguishes the soul from the spirit as closely as Bonaventure does (and as St. Thomas does not) is another topic for intensive research.

Bacon runs into the difficulties of the problem of the origin of the different souls or levels of the soul, i.e., the vegetative, animal and rational. For it could be argued that the former two are simply part of created nature, i.e., that nature which tradition demanded to be created *ex nihilo*, and thus are not in themselves immortal. But the rational soul, which is the seat of the passive and active intellect, must be taken as immortal. Therefore what relation may it have with the other two in respect to origin? The Christian scriptures cannot allow pre-existent eternity to a merely human soul. If the rational soul is immortal, how then can it be created? Though it might be possible that God should create beings sharing His eternity, it does not seem appropriate that anything whatsoever should be eternal without being uncreated and co-eternal with Him.

This however would allow a greater measure of pluralism than anyone influenced by the Aristotelian or the Neo-Platonic tradition would be willing to admit. Spiritual substance? Perhaps, although this concept itself is somewhat ambiguous, and Bacon allows the further ambiguity of the relation of the soul as spiritual substance and as form of the organism to remain rather open. His only real recourse would be to allow a greater emphasis on the continuity of the active intellect between the Mind of God and the human individual. This necessitates designating the relations between this and the Holy Spirit, the former being an *a priori* given which is a part of the individual, and the latter being a gift that is greater than the individual to whom it is given. The former is created though inseparable; the latter is uncreated and separable. This of course is not altogether satisfactory, but it is about the best any scholastic can do. The net result is a compromise which neither Madhva nor Vimuktātman would like to make. Here Bacon may actually come close to Vallabha in 'pluralizing' the *antaryāmin*, the Holy Spirit. He cannot allow either a dualism or unqualified monism, but whether he really has a distinctive third view perhaps nearer to Nimbārka is not easy to judge. Because of his greater emphasis on the substantiality of the logical forms. and the self-identity of distinct substances, he is not so clearly the pantheist as Bonaventure, who resolves the difficulty with an illuminationism which Bacon evidently is not willing to allow or simply cannot follow.

Bacon, Bonaventure and Thomas were not alone, for there were many others who took all the possible positions from the view wherein the soul is a composite and the form of unity which holds it together is not a substantial form but only a 'logical' one, to the extreme Augustinian doctrine that the soul is the *imago Dei* without any possible qualifications. Bacon appears to be trying to find a middle way between these extremes. But he is evidently more aware than most of the others that the real crux of the problem is not so much in the structure of the various faculties and 'departments' of the soul, with the concomitant difficulty of the nature of the form that unifies them, but rather the *fact of change* within that unity, whether the change be habitual or accidental, caused from relation to outside influences, or internally generated. And since this factor cannot be denied, Bacon leaves a large measure of pluralism in his middle position. Some interpreters might take this point to emphasize Bacon as an innovator and a beginning of a new spirit, if not a harbinger of a new age, in which change will gradually gain precedence over structure and permanency.

But to other more traditional interpreters this is not so important as the observation that the shift in turn is from that on the unity of the soul to the perfectibility of the soul in its attainment of immortality. Bacon follows Aristotle here, but probably more nearly Avicenna than Aristotle himself, in putting the vegetative and animal souls in a completely subordinate position as concerns immortality. At best they only participate in the immortality which is inherent in the intellective soul, which is immortal because its nature is pure act unmixed with any potentiality. We are reminded afresh of the similar controversy in the *Brahma Sūtras* over the question whether the departing soul takes the *prāṇas* with it when it leaves the body. There again there was not complete accord. It seems that one is always compelled either to some deliberate extreme or to some compromise.

Is the intellective soul intrinsically immortal, substantially and formally, while the other two are potentially immortal according to moral merit, i.e., according to their proper subordination or hierarchical progressive elevations and assimilation into the active intellect? Is the active intellect separable from the rest of the soul or completely one with it? Crowley writes:

> The intellect is not the act of any part of the body but of the whole body. It is difficult to define exactly its relations to the vegetative and sensitive souls. Bacon speaks of all three faculties of the soul but it is clear that in his conception they

> are in the nature of essential parts. The word 'soul' is . . . merely a name, and even those who admitted that the nutritive, sensitive and rational principles were three distinct substances still spoke of the soul as one. Bacon, though he holds for the substantial unity of the soul, cannot speak of the nutritive, sensitive and rational powers as accidents or properties: he can speak of them only as essential parts.[7]

According to Crowley, Bacon joined the forces that condemned the monopsychism of Averroës, although there were many Christians who followed Averroës in his virtual denial of individuation to the intellectual soul.

Bacon goes on to teach that the possible intellect does not share in the immortality of the active intellect. How then are the possible intellect and the active intellect related? In what manner does the active intellect work on the possible intellect when the latter is the seat of the senses and imagination, which are the only means whereby man may conceive of the nature of the active intellect? The species imprinted on the possible intellect evidently become confused and blurred when they come into operation in the actual world of name-and-form. Are they acquired, infused or intuitively perceived? Bacon says that the possible intellect is a *tabula rasa* and the active intellect "imprints"—patterns of knowledge on it. But it is not clear, in spite of the duplicity which he assigns to it, to what extent the capacity of the active intellect to do this is innate in the human individual. It is further still not completely clear what the relation of the active intellect is to the Mind of God.

Regarding the question as to the manner whereby man may have knowledge of God, it must not be supposed that Bacon is necessarily representative of his time. The answers ranged from the strict Aristotelian method of abstraction of universals out of particulars to the most universal possible, which must be God, to the extreme Augustinians who considered man's nature so corrupted by the Fall that only Divine Illumination could possibly give any knowledge of God: man could not acquire it; it must be given directly, immediately and intuitively apart from reason, by God, from God alone, and for the sake of God alone, *in spite* of man's ingratitude and as the crown of the *via negativa*. Again

Bacon takes a relatively moderate position: the knowledge of God may be mediated or immediate, but this does not exclude the possibility, whether as a third factor independently or in a mediating role, of an imprinted knowledge which is objective but imparted by God through the agency of the active intellect in a structured 'scientific' mode without any necessary mystical overtones, nor yet unconditionally determined by rules of logic but conforming to them for the sake of appropriateness.

This may put Bacon in a more pluralist light than we have thus far allowed, although it still might be argued that he was trying for a middle ground. The fact is that the whole trend of the era historically was an enlargement of the pluralistic ground, and the great problem was that of keeping some overall comprehensiveness in spite of this tendency. This is patently true not only of Europe but of India, China, Japan and the Islamic world as well. This trend is very obvious in art and architecture; but it is strange that so few have thus far seen it also happening in philosophy and the "liberal" arts. The usual thesis was that this did not happen until the Renaissance, but that is completely mistaken. As the pluralizing continues to increase, the asceticism attempts to preserve or recreate art as *re*-creation in the sense that painting and architecture are "re-creating" the unity which is no longer there.

For Bacon all human ratiocination is quite objective; man must proceed according to scientific method, for there is no other course. What, then, is left for the active intellect to do? Bacon denies that it is the giver of forms in the sense that Avicenna had allowed. Bacon taught that it still illuminates the phantasm, although its operation of the possible intellect is more limited than some others would allow for otherwise there would be too much limitation of the independence of the investigating, rational faculties of man. Bacon guards even more closely than Avicenna, but not more closely than Madhva, the distinction between this sort of illumination and revelation. Evidently in all cases Bacon's theory was that the active intellect renders the forms of things and their position in the order of the universe capable of being perceived and theorized about in the human intellect and sense faculties, making the *adequatio intellectus et rei* possible. But how he can posit this without some inherent connection between

God and the human soul in operation within and upon the world of things is still not too clear.

In the following passage the basic factor is in congruence with most of the Hindu tradition, namely, that truth needs only that the hindrances be removed rather than that truth must be asserted. His list of hindrances is about as good as any in his century:

> There are, indeed, four chief hindrances to the understanding of truth, which stand in the way of every man, however wise, and permit hardly any to arrive at the true title of wisdom; to wit, (1) the example of frail and unsuited authority, (2) the long duration of custom, (3) the opinion of the unlearned crowd, and (4) the concealment of one's own ignorance in the display of apparent wisdom. Every man is involved in these difficulties, every condition of man is held by them. For every one in all the acts of life and study and every occupation uses three of the worst arguments to the same conclusion; namely, (1) this has been exemplified by our ancestors, (2) this is the custom, (3) this is the common belief: therefore, it must be held. But the opposite to the conclusion follows far better from the premises, as I shall prove in many instances by authority and experience and reason.[8]

Philosophy then to Bacon as to many of his contemporaries in India is the removal of these difficulties. Science takes over towards new investigations once these obstacles have been removed. May theology not also be considered a science? The answer is an almost unqualified yes. Far anticipating Hume, his argument about the existence of God start with what we now call "natural" religion; but he finds nothing of the reasons for scepticism which Hume did.

Bacon's tendency to divide the natural and divine and thereby make room for further and more free scientific investigation of nature was rather strong, and in this he parallels the transition in India from Rāmānuja to Madhva and the further development of rationalism in China in the triumph of the Neo-Confucians over the Buddhists as well as the ascendency of the

Chu Hsi tradition over that of Lu Hsiang-shan. Bacon's achievements in philosophical psychology and metaphysics were really not so original, but his unusually wide erudition has put him in a place of brilliance considerably greater than most of his contemporaries. His scientific achievements were scarcely more than a continuation of what Avicenna had done, although for the most part those were new to the Latin mind. His interest in astronomy and other sciences was corrupted, from our point of view today, by a detailed exaggeration of the importance of astrology, but this was very common universally not only in his own time but well after Galileo and Copernicus. Although in more than one place he states explicitly that metaphysical speculation is only a preface to the establishment of good ethical systems, his moral philosophy is largely if not almost entirely a reiteration of what he finds in Seneca and Boethius. In political philosophy he again follows Avicenna and Averroës for the most part, not quite advocating universal democracy, but expecting that legislation should keep business ends and all other human affairs subordinated to justice, reason, and concern for the common good. He does not expect the social order to lag behind the religious standard of perfection of charity. His affirmation of the Christian Faith—here he might be considered not only far ahead of his time but really breaking new ground—was based not so much on the traditional statements of the mystery of the Trinity, the Fall, and the Redemption in the Atonement of Christ as on the beginning of *critical* study of the Bible and a schematic study (primarily from Avicenna and Averroës) of comparative religion, the first reappearance of this field of study since the days of Clement of Alexander (except for a few abortive gestures in Byzantium, Psellos, like Pletho after him, only reiterating what could be found in the Greek classics and in John of Damascus rather than making any new investigations). Bacon also made some contribution to the study of comparative philology, and his mathematical treatises are such that they might well be re-examined.

Roger Bacon has been too much neglected, even by his fellow Franciscans, and perhaps at the other extreme too nearly made into a martyr on the part of some like Bertrand Russell. Prudently seeing that his work was new, he wrote largely in cipher in order to survive in obscurity; this has only recently been deciphered. His concern remained primarily with the further advancement of scientific investigation, although in this he remained terribly impatient and dissatisfied, if not often downright disgruntled, because he could not get enough freedom, much less equipment and moral and financial support, to carry out his experiments as he would like to have done. As De Wulf says, he was a brilliant meteor all too inadequately observed. He remained in relative obscurity until 1733 when Jebb brought his *Opus Majus* into light, and ever since then he has been and still remains perhaps the most controversial figure in the whole history of Western European philosophy.

28. Duns Scotus

The Franciscan metaphysician John Duns Scotus (1265/66-1308) may well be the most difficult of European scholastic thinkers, as is suggested by his titular epithet, *Doctor Subtilis*. Scotus wrote voluminously but did not produce a finished *Summa* like that of Thomas, and so his views which together make a cogent and systematic position are scattered here and there within his arguments and criticisms. The mere bulk of his labours is formidable, but his style is even more so, having been variously described as obscure, verbose, and redundant, so that Duns is, according to Harris, "if not the most difficult, yet without doubt the most irritating of mediaeval schoolmen."[1] But the greatest difficulty in reading Scotus is that he becomes so involved with complicated dialectics using such subtle distinctions and delicately balanced argumentation that one may well lose patience even before losing one's way. According to Taylor, "No man ever drove either constructive logic or the subtilties of critical distinctions closer to the limits of human comprehension or human patience than Duns Scotus."[2] McKeon writes that "no modern language is constructed to carry the force of his distinctions, and in restatement therefore either distinctions must be blunted by approximate translation, or new expressions must be invented as strange and as difficult as the Latin terms of Duns."[3] Although his style of scholastic discourse was less clear and simple than Thomas', and less beautiful and luminous than Bonaventure's nevertheless Scotus had a greater following than they into the seventeenth century. Unfortunately his students were too often attracted only to the subtle ways of the Doctor, and instead of trying to elaborate and clarify his insights merely tried to outdo him in subtlety. For the most part they only became more obscure and inane with their circus of syllogisms, earning for themselves the name "dunce" (a Duns-man).

Duns Scotus was born in Scotland, studied at Paris and Oxford, and died at Cologne. Few details about his life are certain and until recently there was a great deal of uncertainty about which of the works attributed to him, and how much of those, were actually his. Scotus seems to have been more familiar with both scholastic and pre-scholastic thinkers than any other mediaeval philosopher. He had all that was available from Aristotle and knew the Arabic and Jewish commentators as well as the Byzantines. He knew Bacon, Bonaventure, Aquinas, the Victorines, Anselm and virtually all of the scholastics from the eleventh through the thirteenth centuries. He cites Cicero, Augustine, John Damascene, Porphyry, Democritus, Epicurus, Empedocles, and others. Scotus is not strictly confined to a tradition but seems to take positions as his analyses require. While he is true to the Augustinian tradition on some points, he rejects illumination, seminal reasons, and innate knowledge. On the other hand he departs from the Thomistic/Aristotelian positions with his doctrines of matter, individuation, and will. Scotus was imbued with all the currents of scholastic thought but was not writing an apologetic for any set of doctrines either traditionally propagated or eclectically bunched together. He seems genuinely motivated to discern the positions required by critical and dialectical inquiry into philosophical and theological problems. Even with his vast erudition his solutions to some very old and well-worn problems are often original with him.

Scotus is a Christian scholastic *par excellence*. He takes up all the major scholastic themes and treats them against the background of the scholastic traditions. He differs from his predecessors like Thomas Aquinas virtually not at all in spirit, and he must be listed along with such other great scholastics as Anselm, Abelard, and Bonaventure. These men are all of a kindred spirit even though they differ on particular themes. But it must also be emphasized how Scotus differs, namely, in his super-refinement of the scholastic positions, and in his up-setting of the balance between philosophy and theology. Because of these two characteristics Scotus is seen both as the apex of European scholasticism and also as the beginning of the end of mediaeval scholasticism and the transition into the fourteenth century *via moderna*.

After the work of Thomas Aquinas there were limitations as to just how much more scholasticism could do. Scotus reached these limitations and, so to speak, pushed them a bit. After Thomas there was room for Scotus to offer corrections and refinements, but after Scotus there was not much more an orthodox Christian scholastic philosopher could do. Taylor writes that the works of Scotus were "impressed with qualities of finality, signifying that in the forms of reasoning represented by him as well as Thomas, thought should advance no further." Taylor continues:

> Throughout the academic world, thought still was set to chords of metaphysics; and although men had never listened to quite such dialectic orchestration as Duns provided, they liked it, perceived its motives, and comprehended the meaning of its themes. So his generation understood and appreciated him. That he was the beginning of the end of the scholastic system could not be known until the manner of that ending had disclosed itself more fully. We, however, discern the symptoms of scholastic dissolution in his work. His criticism of his predecessors was disintegrating, even when not destructive. His own dialectic was so surpassingly intricate and dizzy that, like the choir of Beauvais, it might some day collapse. With Duns Scotus, scholasticism reasoned itself out of human reach.[4]

The subtle Doctor had raised the entire scholastic enterprise into a realm of such subtlety that only "dunces" would continue that course.

Duns Scotus separates theology and philosophy into different realms. They do not deal with the same things and they are not the same kind of sciences. Theology is for Duns a "practical" science concerned with the will and not the intellect. That is, theology is concerned with how men should *act* in order to attain the goals of the Christian teaching. The truths of theology stand on revelation, and philosophy cannot demonstrate these theological truths. According to Scotus philosophic speculation cannot prove conclusively the existence of God, the immortality of the human soul, or the truth of the Trinity. Nor can unaided natural human season prove certain of the divine attributes, such as that God is omnipotent. These truths are known by something *stronger* than natural reason, namely, revelation. Knowles writes that with Scotus "the realms of philosophy and theology are beginning to fall apart each into its own focus, in a way unfamiliar to the traditions of both Bonaventure and of Aquinas.... Though himself a metaphysician, he narrowed the scope of metaphysical attainment; it was left to his successors to begin the flight from metapysics as such".[5] Jones writes.

> ...Duns upset the delicate balance Thomas had established between reason and revelation and so prepared the way for the thesis that reason is strictly a secular instrument. The final result of trying to save theology by excluding it from the field of rational inquiry was, ironically enough, its relegation to an increasingly inconsequential role in the coming "Age of Reason." By initiating this policy, by upsetting the Thomistic balance, by emphasizing the role of revelation, Duns helped to produce precisely the state of affairs that he would have most deplored—the isolation of religion.[6]

In his breaking up the union of metaphysics and theology and in other ways, Scotus is a precursor of William of Ockham and his much more radical positions.

Scotus is well known for his doctrine of *haecceity* ("thisness"), which is his view of the knowability of the individual, the particular, the singular. For Aquinas and the Aristotelians matter is the principle of individuation. But matter is potential and unknowable, and so by this view individuals cannot be known since all we can know is the form, the universal. This view also presents Aquinas with a difficulty concering personal immortality since without the individuation of the material body there would seem to be no individual, i.e., with the loss of the individuating matter (the body at death) there is the loss of the individual too. Scotus takes the position that it is not matter but form which individuates, and since we can know form we can know individuality. Form gives both the *quidditas* ("whatness") and the *haecceitas* ("thisness"). For example, form gives us not only Man but *men* through what Scotus calls "contraction" of form. It is of the nature of form to be particularized as well as universalized, and so particulars are as real and as knowable as species, genera, and universals. Jones writes:

> Every form is *this* form, is (to use Dun's technical term) "contracted" into this, that, or the other singular. There is not merely a form "man," which is individualized as Plato, Socrates, and Aristotle by being embedded in different bits of matter. There is a form "Platoneity" (which is the form of Plato and the knowable aspect of Plato); there is a form "Socrateity" (which is the knowable aspect of Socrates); there is a form "Aristotleity" (which is the knowable aspect of Aristotle)....
>
> Duns's name for this individual contraction, the terminus of the process of logical division, was *haeceitas*, or, as we would say, "thisness" as opposed to "whatness" (*quidditas*). The *haecceitas* of any singular is not mere potentiality, not mere matter. It is a positive element, formally distinct from the other positive elements (such as species and genus) and precisely as real—no more, no less—as they are.[7]

The *haeceitas* is not the particular form but the "thisness" of *this* form. As Copleston writes: "A human being, for instance, is *this* composite being, composed of *this* matter and *this* form. This *haecceitas* does not confer any further qualitative determination; but it seals the being as *this* being."[8]

One of Scotus' primary philosophical concerns was to safeguard the objectivity of human knowledge, that is, to show that the human intellect is capable of claiming real and valid knowledge. In Scotus' view it is therefore necessary that particulars be knowable since it is from particulars that we abstract universals. As Scotus writes: "It is impossible to abstract universals from the singular without previous knowledge of the singular; for in this case the intellect would abstract without knowing from what it was abstracting."[9] The human intellect in its present state, according to Scotus, does not have a perfect intuition of the singular essence as such, but it does have an intuition of the singular *as existing*. The main point of Scotus' analysis of singulars seems to be his argument that, since form individuates (not matter) and since form is intelligible, it follows that singulars are also intelligibles, even if the human intellect in its present state does not have a complete and clear knowledge of singulars. Scotus also argues that God and the angels certainly know singulars and therefore singulars are intelligible, whether clearly so to the human intellect or not. Copleston writes:

> If two material things were deprived of all difference of accidents (of place, colour, shape, etc.), neither sense nor intellect could distinguish them from one another, even though their "singularities" (Scotus's *haecceitas* remained and this shows that we have, in our present state, no clear and complete knowledge of the singularity of a thing.... Scotus did not mean to reject (he makes this quite clear) the Aristotelian doctrine that human science is of the universal; but he considered it essential to supplement that doctrine by accepting our intellectual intuition of the singular thing as existent, and he considered that this supplementation was necessitated by the facts.[10]

In other words as Copleston again writes, "The intellect can have an intuitive knowledge of the singular as existent, even if its knowledge of the essence is knowledge of the universal."[11]

Although it is not original with him Scotus makes great use of the "formal" distinction, which is a distinction which fits between a real or objective distinction and a virtual or rational distinction. A *real* distinction obtains between two things which are separable, while a *rational* distinction is in the mind only and does not indicate any real distinction in the thing itself, as in the case of a thing and its definition. The *formal* distinction obtains between two things which are both real but which are inseparable. For example, there is a formal distinction between the soul and its faculties. Again, there is a formal distinction between the divine attributes. Mercy and justice in God, for example, are inseparable and yet are formally, logically, distinct. Scotus applied this doctrine of the formal distinction to the question of universals. According to Scotus, the distinction between the universal and the particular is not a real distinction as the realists maintain, nor a rational distinction as the nominalists claim, but a formal distinction. Jones writes of Scotus: "We do not, he held, have to choose between asserting that genus is wholly objective (that there is a 'real' distinction between particular and genus) and admitting that it is only subjective (that there is merely a 'rational' distinction between particular and genus). There is a third possibility, namely, that the distinction between particular and genus is 'formal', that there is a real difference between them but that they are not separate entities."[12] The formal distinction also applies to the *haecceitas*, as Fuller and McMurrin explain:

> But it is the nature of "this" to be "not that". Logically and formally, then, "this" is "not-that." Tom by virtue of being Tom is logically not Dick. In short, the difference between Tom and Dick is a difference not of *matter* (as with Aristotle and Aquinas) or of *essence* and nature (as in the case of Aquinas' angels) or of *individual forms* (Plotinus) or of mixture of *substantial forms* (Alexander of Hales and Bonaventure). It is of a new sort original with Scotus—the formal and logically necessary difference of any "this" from all "thats" or, in other words, of any one *individual* "contraction" of a given Form from all other contractions.[13]

Although the distinction among particulars of a genus is a formal distinction, that distinction is really *there.* Thus Scotus has been favorably viewed by those with a concern for the reality of the individual, for each individual is *this* individual, has *haecceitas*, and is real and knowable. Scotus also says that the fact that we love individuals argues for the knowability of the individual, for love presupposes knowledge.

Another major theme in Duns Scotus is the doctrine of the univocity of being. Though he differs from Aquinas in other ways, Scotus remains an empirical Aristotelian. Man does not have innate ideas and does not rely on illumination; rather, human knowledge is derived through reflection on experiences of the senses. Thus man has no present intuitive knowledge of God in his essence for God is not an object of sense. Scotus did think that man had a natural knowledge of God but that this natural ability was frustrated in our present condition in the world, perhaps because of sin. Thus man in his present condition can have only an *a posteriori* knowledge of God. Furthermore, a present intuition of God in his essence would be "precisely that form of knowledge which places a man *extra statum viae*."[14] In this life man must be able to move from a knowledge of creatures to a knowledge of God, or else no knowledge of God would be possible at all. But the obvious difficulty is how one can move from the finite, material and imperfect creatures to a knowledge of the infinite, immaterial and perfect God. Against Henry of Ghent who held that the being of God and the being of creatures is equivocal, that is, different and without a true meeting place, Scotus argues that being is univocal, that is, that the being of God and the being of creatures is, in an important metaphysical sense, the same. Copleston explains:

> ... Scotus is maintaining the existence of a univocal concept of being which is applicable to God and creatures, so that one can say that God is and the creature is, using the word "is" in the same sense. He is perfectly well aware, of course, that God and the creature are actually opposed to nothingness in different ways, and he does not mean to deny this; but his point is that if you mean by "is" simply the opposite of nothingness or not-being, then you can use the word "being" of God and creatures in the same sense.... Though they are opposed to nothingness in different ways, they are nonetheless both opposed to nothingness.[15]

Having established a univocal concepts of being Scotus goes on to say that we can also form univocal concepts of attributes applicable to both God and creatures. In other words, because of Scotus' metaphysical position regarding the univocity of being, he is now able to make the epistemological assertion that we can gain knowledge of God by an examination of the creatures. Copleston writes:

> Scotus affirms that "creatures which impress their own ideas (*species*) on the intellect, can also impress the ideas of transcendent (attributes) which belong common to them and to God"; but it would not be possible to proceed from a knowledge of creatures to the knowledge of God, were we not able to form from creatures univocal concepts. When the intellect has formed these concepts, it can combine them to form a composite quidditative idea of God. Just as the imagination can combine the images of mountain and gold to form the image of a golden mountain, so can the intellect combine the ideas of goodness, supreme and actuality to form the concept of a supremely good and actual being.[16]

Scotus argues that Aquinas' doctrine of analogy really presupposes univocity, for even analogy requires a commonality between the creatures and God. With his views of univocity as with his views on the knowability of individuals and his use of the formal distinction, Scotus' concern is primarily epistemological. We must be able to know particulars if our abstraction of universals from particulars is to be validated; we must have the formal distinction in order to claim knowledge of things which are distinct but inseparable, such as the divine attributes; and we must have a univocal concept of being in order to justify metaphysical knowledge derived from sense knowledge.

Scotus follows the Augustinian-Franciscan tradition in placing emphasis on the will rather than the intellect in both man and God. This reflects his emphasis on freedom in God since freedom resides in the will, as well as his emphasis on "practical" theology in that the will is primarily responsible for the attainment of beatitude. The will is a free power and can direct the intellect. For the Aristotelian, man is by definition the rational animal, and the intellect is the supreme faculty; but for Scotus, love is higher than knowledge and love resides in the will, thus the will has primacy over the intellect. The will, is also more important for man in that to hate God, which would come from will, is worse than not to know God, a defect of intellect. Since divine volition has precedence over divide intellect, it follows that God does not will the good because it is good, but what God wills is good because He wills it. Copleston writes:

> The free choice of God is the ultimate reason of contingent things, and we cannot legitimately go behind God's free choice and seek a necessary reason determining that choice. God's intellect does not determine His creative work by necessary reasons, since creation is free, nor is He determined by the goodness of objects, since the objects do not yet exist: rather they are good because He wills them to be. That God can create only what is an imitation of His essence and that He cannot, therefore, create anything evil is understood.[17]

The divine will is subject to the law of contradiction; God cannot for example, will a square circle. Scotus sees the distinction between the divine intellect and divine will as a *formal* distinction and not as a real distinction. While Sctous does not mean to deny the place of intellect in God or man, will must be seen as "free" from the intellect since will is a more essential expression of God as Free, and for man will (howbeit with intellect) is the primary factor in attainment of his highest destiny.

Although Duns Scotus is a continuator of the scholastic attempt to establish a more nearly perfect metaphysical and theological basis for an orthodox Christianity, he is often seen as primarily a critic of Aquinas. Scotus differs from Aquinas only on those points where he truly thought he found weakness or error in the Thomistic positions. In his presen tation of the Christian teaching along the lines of the Peripatetic structures Aquinas naturally had some difficulty finding perfect reconciliation between the two. Indeed, according to Harris, "the Thomist philosophy with its orthodox Aristotelian cosmology and its peripatetic intellectualism was ill fitted to serve as a philosophical basis for the dogmas of the Christian Church."[18] Scotus' 'corrections', therefore, should have qualified him to become the official doctor of the Church in place of Thomas —or so it might be argued, according to Harris, who says that "it is manifest that Scotus' teaching is more in harmony with the Christian faith."[19] Harris writes:

> Had he ever completed the superstructure in all the minute detail of the *Summa Theologica* of Thomas, he might have eventually become the official doctor of the Catholic Church. But by an irony of fate his work has lain neglected since the beginning of the eighteenth century, and the current of modern thought has passed it by, while the Roman Church in more recent times has devoted herself almost exclusively to the study of the Thomistic philosophy and disregarded a system which in many ways is more suited to serve as the speculative basis for the Catholic faith.[20]

Harris concludes: "It is in Scotus rather than in Thomas that scholasticism reaches its maturest development."[21]

John Duns Scotus ranks among the greatest metaphysicians in the world history of philosophy. His influence was not so very great though he did have a following for quite some time, and of course Thomas Aquinas now has the position in Latin Scholasticism to which Duns could also make a claim. Knowles writes:

> ...Though Scotism claimed more followers in the schools than Thomism from 1350-1650, with the consequence that Duns men (or 'dunces') were the prime objects of obloquy to Erasmus and the Reformers, Scotus fell into an eclipse even more complete then that which overtook Aquinas in the age of enlightenment, and when scholasticism again became the mode eighty years ago Thomism took pride of place. John Duns, though in fact Aquinas was only one among the many predecessors and contemporaries whom he criticized, had always been the adversary *par excellence* for the Thomists, the *fons et origo mali*, the first exhibit in the chamber of horrors, and it was some time before he was presented anew to the modern world.[22]

One might say, not so much speculatively but to make a point about Duns, that had there been no Thomas Aquinas there still would have been in Duns Scotus a consummate metaphysician who would have and perhaps would have presented a Christian system comparable in depth, breadth and value to that which Aquinas did produce. But the lack of a finished system in Scotus, and his position historically as a critic and corrector of Thomas, not to mention his "bad image" due to the "dunces" who followed him, do not diminish his standing as a truly remarkable metaphysician. One would never expect Scotus to be in any sense popular, for he is more the metaphysician's metaphysician, and he is a *scholastic* metaphysician *par excellence* who encompasses more than any other Christian scholastic the entire of scholastic philosophy. McKeon argues that Duns is relevant to contemporary philosophizing and should not be seen as an historical figure only: "Contemporary logical and phenomenological inquiries are returning to a formulation of these problems in many ways similar to the statement of them made by Duns Scotus. It is unfortunate that the remarkable subtlety of his analysis of formally certifiable truths has been forgotten in large part. . . ."[23] Wolter points out that many modern existentialists "find his views on intuition, contingency, and freedom refreshing. Soctus' doctrine of haecceity, applied to the human person, invests each individual with a unique value as one wanted and loved by God, quite apart from any trait he shares with others or any contribution he might make to society."[24]

No doubt Duns Scotus will continue to be known for the intricacy, subtlety, and formidability of his metaphysics—"Yet there have always been a hardy few who find the effort of exploring his mind rewarding. Even a poet like Gerald Manley Hopkins regarded his insights as unrivalled 'be rival Italy or Greece,' and the philosopher C.S. Peirce considered Scotus the greatest speculative mind of the Middle Ages as well as one of the 'profoundest metaphysicians that ever lived.' "[25] But though a profound metaphysician, Scotus was also a *theistic* metaphysician, and for him the final end of metaphysics is the love of God. As Scotus writes, "Thinking of God matters little, if he be not loved in contemplation."

29. Raymond Lull

The Spanish mystic Raymond Lull (1232-1316) is revered by Franciscans as *Doctor Illuminatus.* Lull's writings in the field of what may now be recognized as Neo-Platonic mysticism in Christian guise have remarkable similarities to some Ṣūfī literature. That, we gather, was the chief reason for his being accused as a heretic: his apologetics to the Muslims sounded too much like their own. A major feature of Lull's character and career was his ardent disapproval of the use of violence to force conversion. He very much wanted conversion of the Muslims, but by dialogue and persuasion and not by coercion. In that he furnishes a noteworthy model for our own time and may well be ranked, for example, with Vidyāraṇya who had essentially the same attitude toward Islam from the Hindu perspective. Lull was born in Mallorca three years before it was recaptured from Muslims by Christians. He wrote most of his works in Catalan rather than Latin and thus was the first mediaeval Christian writer to use the vernacular for his major writings. Lull's style has been called "instinct with life", and in his style and his relative independence of scholastic authorities he seems to have presaged the Renaissance, the famous *Ars Lulliana*, for example, adumbrating much that later bursts forth in Giordano Bruno's perspective of the orders of Infinity.

Lull received the education of a knight of thirteenth-century Spain, married. wrote a manual of chivalry, and apparently was something of a troubador. In an illuminative experience he beheld Christ five times, and came to believe that God had appointed him to convert the Muslims to Christianity. Lull's passionate commitments caused him to withdraw from wife, family, and worldly affairs and devote nine years to the study of philosophy and Arabic and ultimately to produce about three hundred works (some in Arabic). In 1287 Lull began travelling to the courts of kings and popes trying to convince them to support his vast missionary plan. The Council of Vienne (1314-1315) did accede to his importunate arguments to the extent of creating chairs for Hebrew and Arabic in five different centres. Lull not only tried to persuade others to support missions to Jews and Muslims but personally undertook missions to Tunis and

Algeria. Although his actual martyrdom at the hands of Muslims is disputed, his willingness to die for his faith is not. Lull wanted to revive the formal dialogues among Christians, Muslims and Jews, both because of his desire to convert and because of his respect and appreciation for his intellectual adversaries. Heer writes: "Lull thought it an advantage for the children of Christian Europe.to gain some insight into the Jewish and Islamic worlds. He was convinced that European Christendom needed to be educated afresh so that people's eyes might be opened to the beauty of alien worlds."[1]

One reason why Lull's visionary ambition to convert Islam was not entirely unrealistic was that Neo-Platonism, the philosophical basis from which he was working, was shared by Latin, Greek, and Islamic cultures. The principal elements of Neo-Platonism shared by these cultures were a ladder or hierarchy of creation, theories of the four elements and the spheres, a view of reality organized according to a numerical-geometrical symbolism, and the idea of man as a microcosm.[2] All of these elements are found in Lull in his continuance of the Augustinian Neo-Platonic tradition.

History has not been kind to Lull. Although he is remembered by some as a great alchemist, he was not an alchemist at all but rather an opponent of alchemy. Contrary to some exaggerated claims, he did not invent the field of artificial intelligence, though one of his ideas may have prefigured the computer. According to James Michener[3] he did the intellectual groundwork for the increased eminence of Mary in Catholic devotion, but most histories seem to ignore this aspect of his work. According to one incomplete list of Lull's accomplishments outside of philosophy and theology, he dealt with geometry, astronomy, physics, chemistry, anthropology, as well as law and statecraft, navigation, warfare, and horsemanship; he foresaw a major problem of thermodynamics, invented the astrolabe, predicted a Tartar invasion, and believed in the existence of a great continent where Columbus eventually discovered one. While he did not have the scientific temperament of Roger Bacon, his fellow Franciscan and contemporary, he certainly encompassed and increased the available knowledge of his day.

Leibniz envisaged a combinatory machine or art which would

enable disputants to say, "Let us compute", and so in a more or less mechanical way resolve disputes. Similarly, Lull believed in a combinatory art based on the self-evident categories common to all sciences without which no science could exist. He developed a symbolism in which he assigned letters to concepts and invented a mechanical means for grouping and cataloguing these symbols. On seven discs he placed his main concepts and questions in such a way that by manipulating them he could produce answers. In *Ars generalis* Lull, enumerated nine absolute predicates: goodness, greatness, eternity, power, wisdom, will, virtue, truth, glory. These express the attributes of God called "Dignities". Nine other concepts express relations: difference, agreement, contrariety, beginning, middle, end, majority, equality, minority. In addition, Lull described three fundamental questions which are related primarily to virtues and vices: how, when, and where. Through combination, he believed, we can discover the principles of the particular sciences (philosophy is the general science) and even discover new truths. This combinatory mechanism won a large and enthusiastic following for the "great art" down to the seventeenth century, but neither the device nor the philosophy supporting it succeeded in converting the Muslims or stopping the further drifting apart of philosophy and theology. Lull's "logical algebra" was deficient, but his thought that the sciences are combinations of general principles is Leibnizian, and Leibniz himself acknowledged Lull's influence on his work. Also like Leibniz, Lull believed that God is most perfect and that there is the greatest harmony between God and what He has created. Lull was concerned with moral and metaphysical concepts instead of what modern logicians call truth-functionality of complex sentences. Apparently "on-off" can generate more logical power than "goodness", "wisdom", or "glory".

In any comparison of faith and reason, Lull gave the higher priority to faith. Against the Averroists he argued that philosophy is the servant of theology. Faith he compared to oil which continues to rest unmixed on water even if the water is increased. Although philosophy is subordinate to theology, reason can make articles of faith acceptable by "necessary reasons". Faith has to deal with objects which human reason cannot understand. Nevertheless, Lull wanted to show Muslims that Christian beliefs are not contrary to reason and that reason can meet objections to faith. No "double truth" theory such as the Averroists held, one for philosophy and another for theology, is necessary. In fact, such a theory contravenes the meaning of truth and hence is absurd. Furthermore, some of the Averroists following Aristotle believed that reason denied any ultimate or immortal status to the individual human consciousness though faith asserted such a status. They argued for a unitary consciousness or active intellect which explains, activates, or maybe even explains away the individually separate consciousness. Against this Lull argues from experience, faith and reason that our consciousnesses, acts, and wills are our own.

In *Blanquerna*, which is one of the first philosophical-social novels of Europe, Lull sketched both the contemplative life and his plan for a *Pax Christiana* headed by the pope. His sketch is a fusion of clear reasoning illuminated by flashes of religious ecstasy. In *The Art of Contemplation*, one part of *Blanquerna*, the hero Blanquerna is a larger-than-life Lull and, more significantly, a promise of what every spiritually disciplined and graced person may become. By means of an odyssey which is geographical, intellectual and spiritual, Blanquerna faces the main doubts and obstacles in his spiritual path and eventually achieves his destination. Lull the mystic never seemed to doubt the efficacy of the monastic, ascetic and solitary way for the attainment of ultimate truth, but he did let his spiritual hero Blanquerna doubt some theological beliefs such as how God should have justice, liberality, etc., before the world was. Blanquerna eventually reasoned that God could have these virtues before there was any other person in order to *enjoy* them.

The spiritually awakened Lull vowed to live from that time forward by only one rule: "He who loves not, lives not." The Catalan verb for will (a central reality in Lull's thinking) and love is the same. In his well-known *The Book of the Lover and the Beloved*, which is the other part of *Blanquerna*, love and service to God constitute the core of man's life: "The Lover cried aloud to all men, and said: 'Love bids you ever love: in walking and sitting, in sleeping and waking, in buying and selling, in weeping and laughing, in speech and in silence, in gain and in loss, in short, in whatsoever you do, for this is Love's commandment."'[4] For love in Lull we may understand *bhakti* following the pattern we know he was familiar with, namely that of al-Ghazālī (whose *Logic* he translated) in refutation of Avicenna.

Raymond Lull was a truly intercultural figure who put great emphasis on the importance of action. He was perhaps really more of a prophet than a philosopher in the usual sense. There is the story of a devoted one who approached heaven and asked to be admitted because of his complete enfatuation. Reply: Well, if you do really love Me that much then go back down there and *Get To Work*!—i.e., sooner or later the Bodhisattva vow becomes necessary and the mystic becomes a prophet, at least, ideally.

30. Nicephorus Chumnos

Nicephorus Chumnos (c. 1250/1255-1327) and Theodore Metochites (1270-1332) are only representative of a very rich and deep tradition of Byzantine thought which unfortunately has yet to be explored and given its proper place among the other great philosophical traditions in the world history of philosophy. Before giving a brief discussion of Chumnos we should mention other Byzantine thinkers who are really of equal merit. *Nicephorus Blemmides* (1197-1272), whom Basile Tatakis regards as the most eminent example of thirteenth century Byzantine scientific and philosophical thought, was born in Constantinople, completed his studies in Nicea, and embraced the monastic life quite irreversibly in 1235. Blemmides twice refused ecclesiastical promotion, once to the bishopric of Ephesus and once to the patriarchal throne. His brilliant studies quickly made him a great savant well-versed in both science and philosophy. His compendium of Aristotelian logic became a basic educational text in the Latin Occident as well as in the Greek Orient. Blemmides used logic and tradition to create a hierarchy of abstractions ascending always toward more permanent patterns, in a way that sought to reconcile virtue and asceticism, Hellenism and Christianity, realism and nominalism, Plato and Aristotle, and, in sum, to educate the higher tendencies of humanity while disciplining the lower. Orthodoxy ("right opinion") he regarded as the synthesizing mean between extremes. Blemmides had the Emperor Theodore II Lascaris as a student. He advises the ruler to look after the common good since all the people form a single body. Royalty and philosophy are very much the parents of the people, the one at the summit of rank and the other at the summit of the arts and sciences. Like Plato and the Neo-Confucians, Blemmides thought that, ideally, wisdom and political power should be fused in one individual. After summarizing Blemmides' contributions, especially in logic and physics, Tatakis writes, "However, the work to which Blemmides seems to have consecrated his life is not science or philosophy but education and teaching."[1]

Theodore II Lascaris, Emperor of Nicea (1254-58), tried to be a philosopher-king in accordance with Blemmides' model. He believed that it is good for everyone to commune with philosophy since it can most perfectly reveal both the knowledge of nature and the noble virtues which accord with nature. For Theodore the communication of wisdom is fully as important as wisdom itself. In his six discourses on natural communion Lascaris anticipated Spinoza's geometric demonstrations, his emphasis on the moral and the scientific, and his use of the old distinction between a dynamic nature and the individual beings it spawns—or, in Latin, *natura naturans* ("nature naturing") and *natura naturata* ("nature natured"). Tatakis characterizes these discourses as "bold, profound and obscure". A kind of *yin-yang* polarization seems to permeate Lascaris' thought. This philosopher-king tells us that "the universe owes its unity to nature, the common ground of all beings. All is one, and it is this one (nature) that particular beings divide, distinguishing themselves and distributing themselves."[2] One becoming many seems to be Theodore's formula here. At any rate, he sees two basic orders of communion: *kata physin* (according to nature) and *kata krasin* (according to combination). The first mode designates what is common to all, whereas the second mode differentiates animate or inanimate beings and confers on them their proper individuality. It is interesting to note that this second mode is aided by the category of nonbeing. Nature for Lascaris occupies a position comparable to the One in Neo-Platonism; individual beings are nature's emanations. Nature contains quality (a capacity for intensity and relaxation) and quantity (a lack of capacity for intensifying or relaxing). Since nature is always good and has never produced evil, it provides a model for moral and spiritual nobility. The idea that while human laws must designate certain things as evil nature itself contains no evil, is considerably different from most of Latin Christianity and most of Islam, coming closer to some varieties of Hindu and Chinese ways of looking at the world. Nobility, according to Lascaris, means an emulation of nature rather than of conventional goodness. The wise ruler knows how to utilize a communion with science and nature in order to bless his people. The specific form of this communion is a triad of disciplines most necessary for the people's welfare: philosophy, strategy, and medicine. Only a very good nature (in this case, the character of the monarch) can acquire the true nobility of nature. This is done by acquiring science well, for the more humanity is informed by education, the more it achieves perfection.

Nature develops in time, is evolutionary. Nature for Lascaris seems to be primarily viewed as a web of what we would call "natural processes". However, there is this difference from some of the more mechanistic interpretations of nature then or now: Lascaris evidently had full confidence that the natural order both in its own right and in its manner of relating genera (or generalities) to individualized species in the evolutionary scale still left the way open for the mind to trace back that total process to its divine origin. Yet Lascaris does not see this openness to the general, the purposive, the integrative, and even the divine, as any kind of excuse for neglect of the intricacies involved in the study of either nature in general or human nature in particular. In respect to the latter, for example, Lascaris finds ninety-two *syzygies* (capacities and actualities) in the psychological make-up of human beings.

The great humanists *George Pachymere* (1242-1310) and *Maximus Planudes* (1260-1310) make the reader believe he or she is living in classical times. They both did work in history and literature as well as in philosophy. Pachymere sets an exacting standard for history. "The soul of history, to express myself thus, is truth. Whatever substitutes the false for the true is a consummate sacrilege. It would be better to remain silent than to speak the facts in any way other than that in which they have come to pass."[3] When giving exposition to the history of thought Pachymere shows the power, as it were, to take up Aristotle's pen so as to express or extend the thinking of the great Stagirite himself. What is even more surprising considering the restrictions of Byzantine culture is that Pachymere, working as he must within his role as commentator, retains a totally personal character in what he writes. The devotional (*bhakti*) element was stronger in Pachymere than in Aristotle or most of the Greeks he commented on. As for Maximus Planudes, he was the first Byzantine to be rather thoroughly familiar with Latin classical and Christian writings. For example, he translated some of the works of Cicero, Augustine, Boethius and perhaps also Aquinas. This work of translation began a trend toward better intercommunication between Greek and Latin Christianity. But Planudes was quite important in his own right. He used some methods developed by Hindu mathematicians, incorporating the figure zero from them, and he also presented his own method for extracting square roots, a method which yielded a better approximation.

Joseph the Philosopher (d.c. 1330) was a monk who carried forward the program of Michael Psellos (eleventh century) to bring together into one encyclopedic work all human and divine branches of learning: ethics, the sciences, metaphysics and of course theology. Evidently some of the savants of Constantinople were experts in their specialties but had lost all sense of the ties existing among the branches of learning. Joseph not only made an effort to synthesize Plato and Aristotle but gave a synoptic exposition of all branches of knowledge. The whole of his work was infused by what Tatakis calls the merit of wishing to show the interior unity of all ways of knowing. Joseph attempted to order them in such a manner that each would contribute the better to their common task, the elevation of the soul to God. Contemplation linked with the study of the various sciences assures such elevation of the soul. Joseph had little of his own to submit, whether due to a sense of selflessness or a sense of inadequacy, following as he did in the shadow of Psellos and other great minds. His merit lies in his faculty of integrating comprehensively a vast literature preceding him and bringing it into a unified focus.

Nicephorus Chumnos (c. 1250/1255-1327) was one of the leading Byzantine humanists of the fourteenth century. His tendency to criticize Hellenistic sources (especially Plotinus) and to revert to Hellenic sources (especially Plato and Aristotle) characterized the Byzantine Renaissance of which he was an outstanding example. George of Cyprus, the teacher of Chumnos and whom Chumnos regarded as worthy of the ancients, instructed him in syllogistics, analytics, rhetoric, and physics, as well as in the quadrivium of mathematical science: arithmetic, geometry, music and astronomy. A man of good fortune who inherited a fortune, Nicephorus Chumnos was largely independent of patronage save that of the patriarch and emperor; yet he showed a strong desire, one might almost say compulsion, to be orthodox in the eyes of the True Faith. Chumnos' work contains no system, only a discussion of the questions and problems debated at his time. His importance lies less in the ideas he expressed than in the spirit he conveyed as he drew eclectically from the different philosophical systems of antiquity in order to reconcile their teachings with Christian doctrine. Besides his philosophical works he also addressed such issues of physics and cosmology as the quality of the air, the existence of superior waters, the problem of vision, and the nature of the celestial bodies. In oratory Chumnos, honored a tradition going all the way back to Demosthenes. As a matter of fact, his entire life was in a sense devoted to this art while only a relatively few years were spent in the composition of scientific, philosophical or religious works.

In his philosophical essays Chumnos criticises Plato's ideas about "ideas" as well as about matter, and his "On the Soul" is a telling criticism of Plotinus. Unfortunately Chumnos' critical writings have still not been edited for modern use though they were influential in his own era. Aristotle was definitely his chief philosophical model. Chumnos was a realist in the modern, not the Latin scholastic sense. His realism extended to a denial of the pre-existence of ideas before individual things come into actuality. Matter, he taught, is never without form or without beauty. Its beauty either can be seen already or will be seen when its potential is realized. However, Chumnos could be critical of Aristotle too. He rejects the Aristotelian idea of the eternity of the heavens, implying as it does the eternity of time and thus relativizing the Christian doctrine of an absolute beginning not only *in* time but *of* time as well. While Chumnos accepts Aristotle's ideas on celestial movement and the immobility of the earth, he condemns the Aristotelian conception of celestial bodies as infinite, unengendered, incorruptible and, therefore, not at all capable of any augmentation or alteration. In his realistic tendencies Chumnos would find himself in sympathy more with Gaṅgeśa than with Śrīharṣa, and with Chu Hsi rather than with Lu Hsiang-shan.

While Chumnos draws upon many notions and themes common to the Byzantine spirituality of his time, he scarcely refers to mysticism at all. The spiritual currents swirling around Mt. Athos seem to leave him untouched. We do not find references to "divine energies" or light from Tabor in his *On the Holy Transfiguration of Christ.* On the other hand, his writings reveal a familiar and profound knowledge of the holy scriptures and an unwillingness on his part to separate philosophy from scripture. Chumnos was not a theologian, and so no controversial theological problem was touched on even in his work on the transfiguration. He held himself largely aloof from all mystical intensities such as erupted twenty-five years later in connection with Hesychasm, but he did nevertheless place mystical contemplation at the highest level in the hierarchy of the modes of knowledge.

Chumnos abandoned many Platonic and Neo-Platonic ideas on the soul and immortality, for example, that knowledge is a kind of Platonic recollection from a previous existence. Like Aristotle, Chumnos believes that knowledge of first principles is neither completely acquired nor completely latent. It starts from sensation (*aisthesis*) and rises, by our effort, from relative confusion and uncertainty to the knowledge of intelligibles (forms or universals). Body and soul combine in producing scientific knowledge by means of sensation, imagination (*phantasia*), discursive explication (*dianoia*), and belief or opinion (*doxa*). These are the four instruments (*organa*) of knowledge, and they (especially the first two) cannot be separated from the body, which serves *nous*. Agreeing with Plotinus that the *nous* (mind, thought or intelligence) is a simple, non-composite thing which possesses life independently and in itself and so is stronger than all corruption and death, Chumnos nevertheless refuses to follow Plotinus when the latter goes on to assert that souls exist before bodies, coming into them from the height of heaven. If the soul pre-exists the body, Chumnos argues, then either it communicates life itself to the body or else it communicates another kind of life than its own. In the second case, since the soul is incorruptible, from where does bodily corruptibility come? Chumnos seems to imply an argument to the effect that even if the life of the body is another kind of life from that of the soul, if it is in the slightest degree derived from the soul, it should not be so far removed from the soul's excellence as to be corruptible, mortal.

Following Aristotle, Chumnos accepts the thinking, sensitive, and vegetative aspects of the soul. These aspects are not divisions and so do not interfere with the simplicity or indivisibility of the soul. The soul does not pre-exist the body nor the body the soul, but both exist together, as the metaphor of the plant, the chaff, and the grain suggests. Does the grain exist before the chaff, and the chaff after the plant, or all together? If the grain existed before the rest, from what did it originate? And so on and so forth. While this metaphor sometimes limps, what is clear is that Chumnos thought it illustrated how a body and soul form a unity in human life.

Chumnos is Aristotelian more than Platonic in insisting on the linkage of the soul and body in the knowing process, even after death. The soul, by means of the resurrection, revives with the body. In the judgment both body and soul are punished; in life each awakening of the ensouled body from sleep is a prefiguring of the "waking up" from the great sleep of death. "In effect," explains Verpeaux, "waking is born from sleep and sleep gives birth to waking, life engenders death and from the latter life is engendered."[4] There is an almost Taoist balancing here, a recognition of the fluctuations of life in death and of death in life. Yet the thread of continuity is neither lost nor denied as it seems to be in some Buddhist schools, for "The sleeper who awakes is not different from the one who went to sleep."[5] However, above the normally body-dependent awareness, awakeness, or knowledge, there is, Chumnos avers, a certain *intuitive* consciousness which accounts for the insight and outlook of the great mystics. But, as we have said, Chumnos knows little of that, except that it is a function of *nous* in the universal sense of mind as described by Aristotle and the Neo-Platonists. The function of *nous* is contemplation, an even higher function than action; yet Chumnos does not support the extreme mystic tendencies associated with Hesychasm.

For Chumnos time is very real in life, death, and resurrection, and it presents two aspects—or perhaps two kinds which are in some tension and are simply among the binary opposites: time and eternity, space and void, matter and spirit, earth and heaven. The flux and transformations of the world lie at the base of time. The periodic cycling of such things as the moon and stars allows the introduction by humanity of boundaries such as days and years into an otherwise unmarked flow of things. This first type of time is tied to movements of physical objects and hence to sensation, whereas the other Time is the unmoving principle of time and is itself immobile, unchangeable and perpetual. Chumnos seems close to Plato and Plotinus here in that the Platonic and Neo-Platonic traditions taught that time is the moving image of eternity.

In Chumnos' cosmology each of Aristotle's four causes interacts with the other three in pairs and in the flow of time to form the natural phenomena of the world. Creation and revelation represent the descending order of reality, just as the purification or rarefaction of gross objects into the ultra-fine constitutes the ascending order of reality. The key to every particular phenomenon is the *predominance* of something—the Chinese might say, some *yin* or some *yang*—in the specific mixture which is evolving, revolving or devolving through time and space. The see-saw of life is seldom balanced but always tilting to one side or the other, with the various effects depending on the length of the 'lever' on each side and the weight and activity of the partners in the swaying dance of the metaphysical teeter-totter.

With the revival of Greek thought it was inevitable that heroic self-assertion would again swell its chest, but Chumnos resisted this secular, overreaching aspect of the Renaissance.

Chumnos also stood squarely against those monks who bragged that "the monastic life has received the name of the science of sciences and the art of arts" and who clearly felt that no other "art" or "science" was either necessary or permitted to the godly. Such monks, as even the great Palamas later, opposed the currents which flowed into the Italian Renaissance.[6] Still, Nicephorus Chumnos had more affinity with the classics-reviving work of the Renaissance than with the other more creative vibrations of that era.

31. Eckhart

When God looks at the soul he laughs. When the soul looks at God the soul laughs back at God. In this way the Trinity is begotten. Or . . . when the Father and Son look at each other they laugh. Their laughter gives rise to pleasure and their pleasure, to joy, and their joy, to love, and love gives the Trinity of which the Holy Spirit is one.[1] In words such as these Meister Eckhart (c. 1260-1327/1328) establishes himself as the first and greatest speculative mystic of Germany and one of the few philosophical theologians in world history who places love and laughter at the heart of the universe. Eckhart's words and what we know of his life bespeak the joy and freedom of a smiling Buddha or a laughing Trinity.

The visionary scope of Meister Eckhart makes his thought difficult to categorize. His flight of the alone (the soul) to the Alone (the Godhead) is distinctively Neo-Platonic in its quest for the One and in the emotional detachment and intellectual abstraction required to enter into the One. But while Plato had thought of God as the supreme mathematician and the Neo-Platonic tradition generally mediated a love of mathematical forms to Kepler and Galileo, Eckhart's interest in mathematics was limited to a kind of shared unity. Also Neo-Platonism is not incarnational but emanational; God or the Godhead overflows in the various emanations. But Eckhart saw God's "becoming flesh and dwelling among us" to be the elevation of man and matter, or even the realization of the divine spark of being which is already immanent within the created world. Neo-Platonic detachment pulled Eckhart one way and a worldly spirituality named compassion another.[2]

One of the most interesting influences on Eckhart was the movement of lay women known as Beguines among whom he worked and preached along the Rhine. Fox writes:

> He reached his maturity not in academia but in his activity along the Rhine preaching in convents and churches and counseling and listening to lay women who were known as Beguines. If much of Eckhart's spiritual vision is profoundly feminist—and it is—that is because he listened and read what women had to say about the spiritual journey. And they listened to him as well, for it was from women—both Beguines and nuns—who took down his sermons that we have the German texts of his preaching.[3]

Those influenced by Eckhart include Martin Luther, Ignatius Loyola, George Fox, Hegel, Marx, Josiah Royce, Erich Fromm, Carl Jung, Martin Heidegger, and D.T. Suzuki. From Luther and the Quaker movement through Marxism and idealism to existentialism and modern Zen—quite a range in time, space, and viewpoint!

In 1302 Eckhart assumed the same chair of theology (reserved for non-Frenchmen) occupied earlier by his fellow-Dominican Thomas Aquinas. Both men helped develop the new Christian Aristotelian philosophy of being which was slowly winning its way as the official Roman Catholic teaching after many hard battles under dark suspicions of heresy. If Thomas was the analytical systematizer of mediaeval Christian philosophy, Eckhart was its poetical teacher. As Fox writes: "Eckhart was first and foremost a preacher—that is, an artist. Here lies the key to his language, his ambiguity, and his genius."[4] For Thomas words were the oxen to pull forward the heavy carts of knowledge, faith, and institutional stability. For Eckhart words were the wings of meaning, the lilt of God's creation, the joy of his laughter, the ova in souls he created for the birthing of high vision and warm compassion—but Eckhart expunged all suggestions of the erotic from the mystical language he inherited.

A complete philosophy of art can be found in Eckhart, along with a youthfulness and spiritual overflow that supports the exuberance of true artistry: "being and being young are one," and, "My soul is as young as it was when it was created. Yes, and much younger! I tell you it would not surprise me if it were younger tomorrow than it is today!"[5] The following seems to characterize Eckhart himself rather well: "Human beings should turn their will to God in all their activities and keep their eyes on God alone, marching along without fear and without hesitancy about being right or not doing anything wrong. For if a painter wanted to consider every stroke of the brush when he made his first stroke, no picture would ever result."[6]

As artist-preacher, Eckhart searched ceaselessly for new, more effective images and even for ways of moving beyond images to the eternity in the soul. The tension in Eckhart the artist produced what surely sounds like a Ṣūfī prayer: "I pray God to rid me of God." In such dramatic paradoxes as this Eckhart seems to warn his listeners that the Godhead must never be fenced in by "God", or eternity by time, or the soul by the self. It is little wonder that such a vivid and surprising speaker was both a threat to institutional stability and a shaper of the German language. The flavor of Eckhart's teachings is caught in his frequently repeated, "Now pay attention! I am now going to say something I never said before." Then he would say something like, "God enjoys himself."

Eckhart distinguished error from heresy: "I may err but I am not a heretic, for the first has to do with the mind and the second with the will." It was perhaps inevitable that Eckhart be condemned, but like other inevitabilities the condemnation was, according to Fox, tragic nonetheless:

> Something ceased. . . . It was prophecy *with* mysticism, that is, a compassionately oriented spirituality that included social justice along with deep growth in consciousness; it was deep reverence for the artist in us and among us in our midst; it was laughter and joy as core elements of spirituality; it was simplicity instead of fanciful spiritual methods; it was the

> conviction that lay persons can be mystics and not just professional religious. In short, what had been lost was creation-centered spirituality. Eckhart invites us back to this rich and wholesome, indeed holistic, tradition.[7]

But Eckhart himself never simply calls us back to a worthy tradition but forward to unheard of possibilities. Since no one knows which possibilities will be actualized or in what combinations, Eckhart speculates without benefit of consistency, complete coherence, or sober realism. He is in this respect the great possibilist. One way in which the theologically orthodox have been able to reclaim Eckhart for themselves is to emphasize the importance of his more sober and precise works in Latin

Eckhart clearly recommends detachment yet admonishes us to be 'attached' in love, passion and compassion, not only to God and other creatures but even to ourselves. Eckhart said, "All deeds are accomplished in passion. If the fiery love of God grows cold in the soul, it dies." Yet in the same sermon he insists, "If the soul is to be united or become one with God, it must be removed from all things and must be alone just as God is alone." The paradoxical image emerges of the fruitful virgin as Eckhart writes, "The word 'virgin' means a person who is free of all false images, and who is as detached as if he or she did not yet exist."[8] We are reminded of the famous words of Nishida, "The bottom of my soul has such depth; neither joy nor the waves of sorrow can reach it." Not passivity but activity, not withdrawal but robust involvement, are the ways to show God's passion in the soul, "for God has sheer delight and laughter over a good deed." But we must leave the *results* of our actions to God. While Schürmann[9] has Eckhart cap, his spiritual stages with abandonment and breakthrough, Fox finds love and justice at the peak. However Eckhart plainly says, "But I praise detachment more than all love. First, because the best thing about love is that it forces me to love God. On the other hand, detachment forces God to love me."[10] The inner man, Eckhart explains, dwells in immovable detachment. A door opens and shuts on a hinge. The hinge is the immovable detachment; the door is sorrow and death. God suffers with us, yet is above suffering. A man suffers, yet detaches himself from suffering.

When God made all the creatures they were so narrow that he could not live or work in any of them. So he made the soul in such a way that he could give himself to the soul. Eckhart says, "The blessedness he (Christ) brought us was our own." Furthermore Eckhart tells us that when people asks him to pray for them, he says, "Why don't you stay within yourselves and grasp your own blessings? After all, you bear essentially all truth within yourselves." Eckhart emphasizes the inness or immanence and availability of God at all times and all in places. When people through lack of spiritual maturity insist that God needs churches, it is as though "they wrapped a coat around God's head and shoved him under a bench."[11]

The theme of God-createdness is sounded so loudly and clearly for Eckhart that no discordant notes struck by sin or the fall can drown it out. Despite the considerable number of times he quotes Augustine, that God created the soul is communicated by Eckhart more often and more energetically than that the soul has turned away from God. God has made us for himself and therefore has planted us all deep within his own being, consciousness and compassion. Eckhart's most striking way of saying this is, "Judas does not want to be someone else, whether in heaven or in hell. Why? Because if he had to become another, he would have to abandon his existence, he would become nothing." The Judas remark is somewhat parallel to the comment, "My mouth expresses and reveals God but the existence of a stone does the same." While Thomas Aquinas taught that God is being, Eckhart went further: being is God. Echoing and deepening the thought about Judas, Eckhart explains that a person suffering the torments of hell would still love being, for being is God.

Ninian Smart, following Rudolf Otto, sees a strong similarity between Eckhart and Śaṅkara.[12] Eckhart stresses eternity as real and time as illusory, and says of the eternal nameless aspect of the soul, "It is and has no existence of its own, since it is neither this nor that, neither here nor there,"[13] and Eckhart also places man in God and God in man without minimizing the reality of either. Eckhart says:

God becomes God when all creatures express God: There

> he becomes "God." When I was still in the core, the soil, the stream, and the source of the Godhead, no one asked me where I wanted to go or what I was doing. There was no one there who might have put such a question to me. But when I flowed out from there, all creatures called out: "God!" I was asked, "Brother Eckhart, when did you go out of the house?" For I had been inside. In this way all creatures speak about "God." And why don't they speak about the Godhead? Everything within the Godhead is unity, and we cannot speak about it. God accomplishes, but the Godhead does not do so and there is no deed within the Godhead. The Godhead never goes searching for a deed. God and the Godhead are distinguished through deeds and a lack of deeds. When I return to "God" and then do not remain there, my breakthrough is more noble than my flowing out. I alone bring all creatures out of their spiritual being into my understanding so that they are one within myself. When I come into the core, the soil, the stream, the source of the Godhead, no one asks me where I'm coming from or where I've been. No one has missed me in the place where "God" ceases to become.
>
> If anyone has understood this sermon, I wish him well....[14]

Certainly it is difficult to hold Eckhart's expressions in a systematic framework, but here we see a distinction between God and Godhead very suggestive of the distinction between *saguṇa* and *nirguṇa* Brahman. In reference to the tradition of Plotinus and Erigena, Pringle-Pattison writes:

> In Meister Eckhart, the devout mystic, there is a similar distinction between 'God', the knowable Creator, and the original ground, beyond Being and Knowledge, which he calls 'the Godhead' and which he also characterizes by predilection as the Nothing, or 'unnatured nature', not only unknown and unknowable to man, but unknown also to itself. The Godhead, as he says in the extremity of his paradox, dwells in the nothing of nothing which was before nothing, and it is apprehended only in the knowledge that is a not-knowing.[15]

As Eckhart himself states this *via negativa*: "You should seek him in such a way that you never find him. For it is when you do not seek him that you find him." "For God is nothing. . . . Therefore the way in which we must love him has to be *without a way*." "This is why I pray God to rid me of God; for my essential being is above God insofar as we consider God as the origin of creatures."[16]

Orthodox Catholic interpreters of Eckhart tend now to doubt that he was ever really a pantheist, though some of his language was certainly pantheistic. Pantheism generally means that God is all and all is God. Nothing "hangs out" or laps over from either sphere; they are congruent. Eckhart's position seems to be more precisely a form of panentheism. The world is in God but some important "deeps" and heights of God's transcendence extend beyond the world as "superabundant riches" and as such are scrupulously protected by Eckhart from any reductionism. For example, God's potential for creativity always exceeds what he has actually created till this moment. God is not identical with the world because he contains it and always goes beyond it. In a paradox Eckhart intertwines the immanence and transcendence of God: "The more God is in things, the more he is outside of things."[17] For God to be both in and out is no more difficult than for the sea which passes through the gills of a fish. In a short statement which suggests panentheism he says that God "is a being that has in itself all being." And Eckhart also says that "to be in God is to be God." Always Eckhart brings to such themes, even when their orthodoxy can be clearly documented, a freshness and vitality that quickly overflows boundaries and categories. Eckhart says, "God enjoys himself. In the same enjoyment with which God enjoys himself, he enjoys all creatures, not as creatures, but he enjoys the creatures as God."[18] Whatever else interpreters do for or to Eckhart, they must not try to excise completely his radical non-dualism and thorough-going immanentism. "What is truly mine I have received from no one."[19] God in making man remade himself as the Trinity, but in the eternal, timeless perspective, nothing was accomplished.[20]

Are mystics only refugees from objectivity? Is there an inner life that is closer to God than that of the scientist who is using objective instruments and making objective measurements of things which he is sure are 'there', distrusting introspection altogether? The answer may be, if answer there can be, made in terms of metaphors: The whirlpool in the water sucks one down to destruction; the cyclonic funnel in the whirlwind lifts everything en masse. The mystic defies any scientist to continue his 'objective' observations when caught in either! The mystics will say that the Love of God is like such disturbances: one is loosed from one's normal moorings and things begin to happen which are not in the course of everyday natural phenomena. Perhaps another metaphor—for in this field metaphors seem to be the normal language; therefore let us not discard them but try to find some method of getting better ones—is that of the problem of re-entry in space flight: after one is "in orbit" everything is fine. Perhaps the mystics are already there in the Region of No Return. But do not ask them to come back for they will burn, they will burn ! The real challenge still remains: Further out! Further out!

Probably the best criteria of validity in choosing a mystic for a guide are (1) the extent to which he focuses his devotion on that God rather than still being wrapped up in the warm blankets of his own ego; (2) the extent to which his supreme personalism is really that, with systematic considerations either consciously by-passed or tried and found wanting, and not merely the retreat to childish piety; (3) the beauty of his poetical expressions; (4) the impact the individual makes on history; and (5) the generosity of his compassion toward humanity as an out-pouring of his knowledge and love of God.

32. Metochites

It has been the fate of Theodore Metochites (1270-1332) along with many fellow-Byzantines to remain largely unedited and untranslated even though some of his works were translated into Latin. Metochites wrote *commentaries* on Aristotle, over one hundred *Miscellaneous Essays*, an introduction to astronomy, some speeches, and some poems which are often more of the character of self-reflective epistles. The best known of Theodore's works is *Commentaries and Moral Judgments,* commonly referred to as *Miscellanies.* It is a kind of encyclopedia in which philosophy occupies the largest place. In his preface Metochites acknowledges that his studies led him to see that the great men of the past have all spoken with such perfection that "they have left nothing for us to do." We hear in these words the voice less of Metochites than of Byzantine traditionalism, for he proceeds to say, "Are we then condemned to remain mute? I will write some commentaries, some thoughts that I have had for myself, as they have come in the course of my life." Commenting on this, Tatakis explains, "Now one finds that these thoughts lack nothing in originality; it is therefore in an effort to deliver himself from this tradition which he admires that Metochites hides under this presentation of his work."[1]

Metochites considered his main scientific feat to be the renewal of astronomy, and as a part of this project he meticulously restated Ptolemy's *Almagest.* Astronomy for Metochites was a way to purify the mind, detaching it from the sad spectacle of vain human agitation and preparing it for music, the way of harmony which ultimately leads to God. According to Tatakis, Metochites purified astronomy of its "oriental monstrosities" as he grasped its mathematical purity. Certainly he saw no conflict, as others did, between astronomy and faith.[2]

To understand Metochites properly, it is necessary to remember that he was not a monk or friar philosopher but an all-around scholar, scientist, literateur, and public servant. In Sanskrit he would have been termed a "pundit". Such, for example, were the advisors of rulers in South India, and no doubt Hemachandra followed that pattern as well as Gaṅgeśa. We find this same role and distinction in Islam but especially with the Neo-Confucians of China. Indeed, Metochites is closely parallel to the Confucians and Neo-Confucians in their mutual abhorrence of monasticism. "Metochites dares condemn the contemplative life as a lie and as a deceit. If it were not possible for men to be Christian while living in the ordinary social way, then Christian life would lead to the destruction of humanity."[3] A strong sense of Greek identity had been evoked by the threat of Muslim, not to mention Bulgarian or Slavonic, conquest. Thus Metochites records, "When the fatherland is in danger, it is only the indifferent who dare to remain aloof from political life." This sentiment has often impelled philosophers to come out of their meditative towers and assume some responsibility in public affairs. We might remind ourselves that once even Dōgen felt this responsibility, although not for long.

After bitter quarrels and personal rivalry Metochites wholly displaced Chumnos at court and at the same time reduced the political influence and scholarly respect accorded Chumnos—or so, at any rate, Chumnos perceived matters. Metochites' political career began in 1305 when he became prime minister or, more exactly, chief intermediary for the emperor. That career interrupted the contemplative life (in the scholarly, not the monkish sense) which he tells us he had to abandon. Nevertheless one contemporary wrote of Metochites: "From morning till night, he applies himself completely and very carefully to the affairs of state, as if science did not count for him; but late at night, after leaving the palace, he plunges himself into science like a learned man who is absolutely a stranger to any preoccupation."[4] There is no doubt that there existed in Metochites a tension between the contemplative life of the scholar (or really even the monk) and the active life of the noble pursuer of wealth and power. In one of his poem-letters he confesses that he is admiring and even jealous of an archbishop retired to a monastery. At any rate, he never solved the dichotomy between political involvement and intellectual or spiritual detachment. The catastrophe of 1328 solved it for him, however, in that his patron, the emperor, fell, leaving him politically exposed. Metochites was banished for two years, then settled in his monastery of Chora in Constantinople. There he reread his works, wrote some more, contemplated the transiency of fame and glory, and died in 1332.

Metochites vacillates on the relative excellence of Plato or Aristotle as philosophers, now preferring "clear Plato" to "obscure Aristotle" and then, again, preferring Aristotle as "better than all those born before or after him."[5] As a basis for commentary Metochites clearly preferred Aristotle; but as an anticipator of things to come he seems to have preferred Plato. What attracted him most was Plato's philosophy of mathematics.

Metochites placed mathematics above physics in the hierarchy of sciences because its objects are precise, unlimited in number, unchanging, and unambiguous. The practical utility of mathematics is that it forms the base of mechanics, but astronomy especially attracted Metochites as the most important sphere of mathematics. He was also fascinated by numerology, believing with Pythagoras that number is the primordial nature of each and every entity.

Metochites regarded philosophy as "the supreme part of culture" because it consists of thinking God's thoughts after him. Things are reasonable by divine design; nothing is by accident. While some people utilize mere perception as do the lower animals, philosophers and those inspired by them engage in "assiduous reflection on the character of things." They realize that things are orderly and in a permanent manner. Metochites writes in Poem 4 that "man had this great thing whereof to boast; that whatever God has devised, he has inquired after and found out; he has come to understand every creation, and has construed God's well-contrived plans. Also, he has thought out coherent pronouncements concerning the sciences of the Nature of Reality and essences."[6]

Metochites' affirmation of history is a value much needed in our own time. History, he insists, enlarges our perspectives on present crises and problems, if not our intelligence as such, including our perception or insight into being and becoming. "It is impossible says Metochites, to do something great in the doma in of wisdom, without the close study of the experience acquired from history. For anyone who aspires to wisdom, time is a great pedagogue. History enlarges the mind greatly and elevates the eyes of reason to the comprehension and perception of beings, to the knowledge of events."[7]

In his philosophy of government, Metochites shows his indebtedness to both Plato and Aristotle. Monarchy, by which he evidently means what we would call a constitutional monarchy, is the best form of government because it is capable of preserving a balance between general regulations and more personalized applications. "Although it seems that democracy is the regime appropriate to free men, the egalitarianism which is inherent in democracy does not permit people to be led or governed by those among them who are superior."[8] Perhaps Metochites would agree with Thomé Fang that there must be a democracy of "levelling up" and not a democracy only of reducing all to the lowest common denominator.

What Theodore Metochites did and said reveals to us a great egotist who in his quest for cultural immortality chose to try to preserve for posterity not only his own writings but the writings he most treasured from others. Sevcenko and Featherstone write:

> He tried to realize this ambition for himself both by writing and by restoring and lavishly decorating the monastery of Christ Savior of Chora—*chora* means keep or treasury—his own residence toward the end of his life and, as Poem 4 informs us, the dwelling place of his protégé Nikephoros Gregoras. Metochites succeeded. . . .His works are still studied and his Chora, now a museum, is among the Byzantine treasures of modern Istanbul . . .
>
> We listen to a self-centered man, to be sure, presenting his egocentricity as a universal trait of human nature, but also to a man able to rise above self-pity and concern for himself and to deplore the plight of "our nation," to foresee—somewhat prematurely—the imminent collapse of the remnants of the Byzantine Empire, and to be deeply distressed by that prospect.[9]

Again, we must remind ourselves that twentieth-century popularity of historical figures is a poor measure of their real importance. Metochites summarizes his bequest to posterity in the conclusion to Poem 4:

> Therefore receive you these products of my wisdom, even as a keep (*chora*) endowed with a safe harbor, sheltering them for countless ages to come from foul and envious ruin that may threaten them, as well as all the many other books that I have collected in this place, of both sacred and profane wisdom. Here are contests of Oratory; here sacred visions of Philosophy; here exceedingly lovely works of Poetry, bound in each and every metre. With a willing mind, keep you all

these, too, safe in the monastery, both for my sake and for that of all lovers of wisdom—that trusty companion—who shall be born hereafter.[10]

33. Ockham

The Franciscan longician William of Ockham (c. 1285-1349) separates the realms of reason and revelation completely, so that if reason contradicts the revelational dogmas of faith, which it sometimes may, we must still go with faith. Ockham's central position is the omnipotence of God, according to which God is *truly* omnipotent and human reason cannot hope to encompass this omnipotence; however, reason can function in its own finite realm, and without any special illumination or transcendental aid. By separating theology from 'science', Ockham began the examination of reason strictly on its own terms and its natural ability to know the natural world. Ockham is still primarily a logician, and his science is primarily deductive; however, with Ockham science has also become completely secularized. Popularly Ockham is best known for what has come to be called "Ockham's razor": "What can be explained on fewer principles is explained needlessly by more"—which principle of simplicity is still operative in modern science.

Ockham and Gaṅgeśa, the founder of the Navya-Nyāya, should be extensively compared for they represent contemporaneous developments along the same line, that is, the triumph of a certain logical positivism over the older metaphysical vertigo and reversion to purely intuitive mysticism. The intuitive foundations of all intellection, nevertheless, remain, just as that has been already modulated in Duns Scotus and Nimbārka. With Ockham and Gaṅgeśa, faith, which is not considered as intuitive so much as simply the necessary admission of what tradition has taught, is considered quite independently from logic; and logic threatens to overstap its boundaries, at least as limited by the older notion that the best it can do is *tarka*, sophistical refutation of refutations. For Ockham and Gaṅgeśa discover with had been *almost* obvious in their predecessors, namely that *formal* distinctions in the management of syllogisms do not necessarily concur with actual distinctions as they appear in nature. The falsehood of sophistical syllogistic reason comes to the surface and threatens to block all other approaches to the truth. Truth then becomes, in a definite sense, a *function* while that which the truth is about remains beyond a dubious bridge, which later dialecticians will be called upon again to cross. However, a more moderate interpretation is that in these developments we have only a continuation of the older trends wherein logic simply eliminates itself in order to make room for the necessity of voluntarism and the prayerful awaiting of the Beatific Vision, *only* after which it may be hoped that all epistemological as well as other types of problems may be solved.

In Ockham we find a definite three-valued logic: true and false must admit a fellow along with them, the *neutral*. This is essentially new in the history of European tradition, although we have seen something like it in the Buddhist schools which insist on getting beyond good-and-evil, true-and-false, positive-and-negative subjective-and-objective, etc. True enough in some remote corners of Plato's mind there is something like it; but since Aristotle had discarded this it lost much chance for further exploration, in spite of Plotinus' attempt at designating the One as beyond these antinomies. However, here the *neutral* is not necessarily the Ultimate as in the other systems but is universally operative merely as a logical function.

A necessary presupposition follows, stubbornly irreducible, that everything is true contingently—contingent on God, of course. But in what manner? And by what is the universal contingency known? Is this also known only as a contingent truth? If so, do we have any access to any certainty, any *a priori*? Ockham seems almost afraid to answer yes or no lest he be tossed out on his ear as a heretic; but he does not really find any other answer within the realm of logic as such. Thus faith is brought in, not as the completion of what is validly operative within nature and reason, but as the *sine qua non* of all cognitive efforts as well as all other human enterprises. But faith as the inevitably necessary relation provided by God whereby we are enabled to operate, howsoever uncertainly, in a positive manner in the world is itself only a sort of Big Contingency after all.

Ockham arrives at a logic of *demonstration* rather than a logic of 'proof'. The distinction here is very revolutionary indeed. Although there had been many others ever since Abelard's *Sic et Non* who had seen that proofs can be constructed for almost anything you want to prove or disprove, not many had clearly seen that they were not *proving* anything but only *constructing demonstrations* of relativistically connected integers in a vast set of individuations. As contingent, proofs are *not* guarantees of existence, and this applies to all existents except—and here comes the somersault which Kant was later unwilling to make—God, since unlike all other existents, which are existential 'demonstrations' of His existence, His existence is not limited to any net of connexity or demonstrability.

Ockham warns against the delusion that in making logical operations we are making truth also, as it were—an attitude which has plagued too much of modern European tradition in spite of Ockham's razor. All we can do is show with some very minute degree of approximation the proper divisions of the fundamental Unity which must be presupposed. Inferences supposedly guiding outside this or jutting beyond it or leading to supposed speculations about that One are *adhyāsa*, delusory and unnecessary superimposition. Why do you want to give more unity to what is already unified?, the Zen Master might ask. Actually this movement toward simplicity is what is behind much of Ockham, although he makes the move rather impetuously, even recklessly at times, and still insists that it can be done *as logic*, for he is still in a very large measure Aristotelian in spite of some deference to Boethius and St. Augustine. The idea that only by better logic can logic be rectified is, as it were, the other edge of his famous razor that the multiplication of entities beyond necessity is a great source of error. Nevertheless he is not by any means unaware of the absurdities into which merely formal logic can lead one; he is always impiously popping them in when one expects some great insight into somethiag truly profound.

For the specialist Ockham offers as many challenging developments as any philosopher between Aristotle and Leibniz. The crux of his logic is planted in his theory of the *suppositio* by which he seeks to bridge the gap between existential entailment and formal operations. This is another of those matters which could constitute a large specialized study in itself both in reference to his contemporaries and to the present day recurrence of the same problem in only slightly different dress. Signification is the other side of the coin of the *suppositio*, the relation of the two being the real problem, as in any system. Of course the signification also must have a *suppositio*, and the *suppositio* must have a signification, if it is to be known. How much of the Ultimate *Suppositio* can be signified is no simple problem either, just as there is always the danger of an infinite regress of significations which only play around that *suppositio* like the electrons around the nucleus of an atom.

On the old scholastic question of the univocity of being Ockham disagrees sharply with the Thomists, to whom essence and existence are not the same except in a very closely qualified sense in God. But for Ockham at each node of individuation there is some mode of conjunction of essence and existence or a *thing* could never *be*. Only being is common to all things, although it is supremely applicable to God since all other things are only participants in God's Being. Pure perfections are those whose formal aspect does not include any imperfection, even though the empirical exemplification of them may be imperfect: the attributes of God, goodness, wisdom, justice, love, etc., have no imperfection in themselves but participate in the perfect Existence of God. Even though insofar as we experience them we do so imperfectly, we can still characterize them formally (even if not actually) in a perfect way. Here again Ockham's positivism (too often lightly referred to as 'nominalism') comes out: we can give signification to any logically deducible *suppositio* even though we may not be able to give its existential referent. But whether Ockham can adequately further renduce or bridge this paradox remains problematical. He is not willing to give up the subject-predicate manner of thinking, at least as long as he remains a *viator*, even though by the same logic he is able to insist that in the perfection of the Beatific Vision there will be a form of intuition which will bridge this gap. I may be that the univocity of being, which makes all these speculations about perfections beyond our inclusive comprehension, is only formal, but it nevertheless is valid, since without it there would be no way of knowing any form of unity.

When one turns to Ockham's tract *On Predestination* one does not find a pious work intended to arouse the fear of God and penitence before the Day of Judgment strikes, but instead one finds an exercise in three-valued logic! Necessity is neither true nor false, but neutral. God cannot contravene this sort of necessity since it would not be to His interest nor the interest of anyone else to do so even if He could. Moreover there is no use arguing about the truth or falsity of propositions like God and only God knows a round square, God could make three days into one, God could make everything that necessarily exists to not exist, since they involve statements of necessity and *a priori* impossibility which have nothing to do with truth and falsehood. They simply are or are not; like the *abhāva* and *abhāvapratiyaga* of the Navya-Nyâya, there is simply an absence of a counter-positive. There is no question of futurity and contingency until that future becomes present. And the same thing happens in terms of his distinction between metaphysics and (natural) theology. Here perhaps he is closer to Avicenna who also does the same sort of thing but with even less emphasis on the purely (positivistic) logical manner of proceeding.

The positivistic logical formulations can never give us the immediate certainty which the mystics claim to have achieved by other means, but at least they can give us a sufficient reduplication of what they are trying to express in their metaphors and analogies. The *anirvacanīyā*/indescribable characteristic of God's nature—does not entail therefore a silence which may be confused with that which remains simply unknown because undiscovered or unexplicated. We may and must try to designate what is meant about the Inexplicable, even though by *a priori* definition we cannot expect to exhaust the infinite regressus which it seems to hold, but which is really only the middle ground between our finite ways of postulating and the Absolute that is beyond the Infinite, so to speak. This paradox is irreducible, but we must not therefore abandon it. Rather, we must be constantly aware that whatever we postulate is not a *proof* in the sense of *our* dealing with that which is far more perfect than ourselves, but an effort to *demonstrate* that That, which is God as the identity of Truth, as Being, is, howsoever indirectly, the Supreme *Subject* for every possible predicate, whether or not He be an object to be 'proved' or 'disproved'. As subject, as the existence of everything that is, including logical operations, He must be involved in these proofs and disproofs in a way that cannot be completely controlled by finite minds.

Ockham never 'came to rest' in his ontology because he could not get into a pure ontology; he was too much tied up in logical apron strings. Through this failure at finding peace in metaphysical speculation and logical manipulation and his refusal to resort to contemplation, one might very well argue that his logic and ontology are only propaedeutic to what turns out to be a typical Franciscan Voluntarism after all, but with sufficient pressure built up behind it to anticipate much that will appear in full blossom in Hume concerning the possibility of a purely *natural* theology, and with a vehement zeal for moral reform which anticipates Hus and Wyclif in their pre-Reformation efforts at collapsing the social and ecclesiological hierarchy in the same way that Ockham cuts away much pseudo-metaphysics with his logical razor. In Ockham there is the constanty threatening inference that since simple intuitive knowledge is available to us only after death, in this life we must not expect to build theology on supernatural concepts; rather, we must keep our speculations well within the confines of good logical operations wherever those may lead us. The metaphysical vertigo of twelfth and thirteenth centuries is gone, and the flowering of the *Great Summas* is ripenning in the form of a *scientific* spirit which will soon turn the world upside down.

From such a mind we should not be surprised to find some advances in the physical sciences. Certainly Ockham dealt with the classical problems of space, time and motion. Even if he did not make any radically new discoveries, Ockham did begin to pave the way for the ideological bases of the scientific revolution which was soon to flourish in the Renaissance; for his position in regard to the problems of ultimate certainty and the subsequent freeing of the realm of Nature from unnecessary involvements in theological speculation left him completely unhindered in considering these problems on their own grounds. Even though God, of course, is the "prime mover", nevertheless we need not consider this at every turn when we are investigating motion as such. However, it appears that in spite of this, Ockham is still most interested in the purely logical aspects of the subjects he is dealing with more than the empirical investigations which will later follow. For Ockham, precise knowledge of terms and proper definitions of terms is essential to beginning a problem correctly and to finding its final solution. Thus his physics is closely linked with his theory of demonstration. Again, we are not concerned to 'prove' anything; we are only concerned, for the most part, at arriving at proper and well-defined concepts which are logically consistent. For example, motion and mutation must not be confused. Neither may be hyposticized; they are not things, but what happens to things. The outcome remains that Ockham is after all more interested in the *formal* problems than the empirical ones; the categories by which motion may be considered are really more important to him than motion itself!

It is the will that is the link between intellect and motion. The Prime Mover is not so much *Intellectus Purus* to Ockham as it is to Aquinas since it is the Will of God that is the cause of all motion, not the Mind of God. The voluntarism here is, of course, Franciscan, but it also has the advantage of joining directly his physics and his ethics. Even more than with Kant and most of the Vaiṣṇavas and some of the Buddhists, where the intellect fails to arrive at ultimates, the will must take over in the here-and-now, directing to or driving towards the best possible end under present circumstances. If dissatisfied with its failure to attain the Beatific Vision, the soul must nevertheless accept as the second-best the proper manner of dealing with matter, nature, and law. But with Ockham more than with the others, it is more the *manner* of dealing that is important, the setting up of an adequate canon of logical consistency, howsoever formal, than the material dealt with. The will is more concerned with means than with ends, which is the realm of the intellect. Ockham is at least not inconsistent!

Virtually the same structure belongs to time. Time and motion are limited to the realm of phenomena, even though this be unlimited in extent. Time-as-a-whole is not simultaneous, since then it would not be a measure for phenomena. It is not different in its parts from its nature as a whole. It is not a thing, for it is infinitely divisible and infinitely extended. Like motion in almost every particular—for time also *moves* in addition to being the measure of motion—it is basically quantitative. According to some interpretations Ockham offers a declaration of independence of science from unnecessary theological implications and metaphysical presuppositions. Even if we cannot answer Aristotle's demand for First Principles, we can and must proceed 'positivistically' with what we do have at hand. Time is within *this* range; it is nothing metaphysically strange. Ockham demonstrates that time and phenomena are inseparable, whether or not there is really anything that constitutes a *prius* to them. The quidditizing of Duns Scotus must be shaved off; it is only epiphenomenon. For time itself, to a great measure is that by which all phenomena are known.

Ockham does not go so far as John of Jardun and some of his co-scholastic fellow-travellers who were still further stretching the "double truth" manner of adjusting to the demands of the Church, building on the foundation left by Averroës; nevertheless, Ockham does not hope to escape from this relativity. We simply must go on as best we can, as positively possible, even though we do not yet and may never find that Ultimate point of reference beyond the relative. Man is in a ridiculous condition here—Ockham laughs his way out of the end of the Mediaeval cycle in almost the same way Aristophanes and Diogenes had laughed at the failure of the Greeks to reach the sun directly. The forms remain, and we can and must deal with them as forms. We simply do not ask the ultimate questions. Probably Ockham will be found to be closer to his Theravāda contemporaries in Thailand, Ceylon and Burma than to the Thomists who are bold enough to say that we not only may and must ask the ultimate questions but that faith does give the definitive answer. The Ockhamist simply replies that this is crucifying faith, which is, and remains, and cannot be expected to be otherwise than, "the substance of things hoped for, the promise of things unseen." The matter rests, again, primarily in the will, in effort, not in the mystical operation of grace. The instant, the moment, is that within which we must work, even though we are also in that; or rather, simply because we cannot expect to get outside of the instant, the 'part' of time which is our lot in this *valle lacramarum*, we must deal even with the *primum mobile* as also only a temporal moment, but as conformable to a logical mode of predication.

Ockham's treatment of *place* becomes involved in an implicitly tangled dialectic which Ockham himself does not allow to become dialectical, or tries not to allow it to become so by virtue of his positivistic dodging the question of ultimates and absolutes. We are immediately confronted with the paradox, which he does not like to allow to be recognized as such, that although place "takes place" in space, nevertheless space cannot be designated as such except as what is derived from, is an extension of, place. What Ockham is doing, perhaps too much without realizing it, is playing with definitions; or at least he might be accused of such a thing, because what he makes again is a formal, not an existential, distinction. We are dealing with nominal definitions only. Is there some realm of Spirit in which we are liberated from these formalities and the freedom to re-question them? Of course the Zen answer is, No realm; but you are already there. Ockham's answer is, in effect, We are not angels and it is better not to try to be what we are not. Maybe we are limited by our formal way of proceeding, but it is better not to get lost in the Void! And here Ockham is much closer to Navya-Nyāya than to Zen.

In short, for Ockham as for Bruno later on the universe is a system of systems. But no matter how many worlds or systems one is dealing with, and no matter with what methods, one is or increasingly becomes still the observer of one's own dealings with them. If Ockham met this problem of the self, the observer, the evidence for such a conclusion is slender. He rather seems to stay quite clear of it and keeps his intensive focus on the formation of an adequate canon of consistency of possible statements about nature rather than the investigation into the things behind the veil which nature may or may no be, which is after all a matter of faith. The elimination of abstract ideas (universals) entails not an *as if* but a system of deliberate construction of conceptual schema, arguments, and other linguistic instruments for the statement of general truths about the things of our experience, which must be brought to the bar of logical consistency. The judge is not the intellect but the will, which then turns with fervent zeal to *moral* problems (the reform of the Papacy, for example) as the focus of empirical endeavor. The judge, so to speak, need not leave the courtroom and go out and harangue the mob, trying to convert them to the new gospel of science; but at least the same consistency must be maintained in the body politic as in the laboratory. Truth in either case is not necessarily revealed, although there are the traditional dogmas to which, or rather against which, one should not dare to make assertions. In short, truth, as system, must not commit the only unpardonable sin of inconsistency, whether in morals, physics, or theology.

Ockham came very close indeed to anticipating the reforms instituted by Wycliffe and John Hus. He was not quite as vehement as Marsilius of Padua in his denunciations of the abuses into which the Papacy had fallen, nor was he quite so extreme his secularizing tendencies; but he was by no means a 'university recluse' completely engaged in juggling logical propositions. He travelled considerably and was in the midst of many politico-ecclesiastical entanglements, and even took part in contesting the election of Charles IV when he declared his independence of the Papacy. Like Kant, but much more so, Ockham failed to find the answer to his enquiry in the purely intellectual field and turned to the ethical; but unlike Kant, who, in spite of his enthusiasm when he read Rousseau, only gave moral support to his sovereign's reforms leading toward 'Enlightenment', Ockham entered the fray actively and won the day. He reprimands the Pope no less than Marsilius, saying in the words of scripture, "Pasture thy flock"—don't try to *rule* them like a secular potentate. This seems to be the central burden, although with typical logical consistency he derives many correlates therefrom. It does not necessarily entail the separation of Church and State but only the right distribution of responsibility between them. The Pope has no business in trying to meddle with the matters dealing with the body politic; his function is that of the leadership of the soul, not the body. His charisma should be of such an order that he can lead the members of the Corpus Christianum, in its role of the Body of Christ, out of the Old Law into the "Perfect Liberty of the Sons of God" as taught in the New Testament, Quite against the rising tide of schizm and splintering of the ecumenical universalism that typified the Mediaeval state, howsoever feudalistic, there follows the challenge to establish a *single standard* of charity for all, rather than the exercise of the cardinal virtues at the secular level with the theological virtues being left over for those with a special vocation for a 'holy' life. Ockham is not quite a Luther, not emotional; he only expects consistency in both standards and practice. Revolution should not be necessary, but repentence and reformation are always binding on any Christian soul.

It is perhaps too much to claim that Ockham instituted the beginnings of the Reformation for the transition to this was very gradual; but the biginnings of the transition are certainly there. The Mediaeval universalism was breaking up, just as the proto-organism subdivides itself in order to propagate itself. Internally, renovation; externally, multiplication—such is the formula for civilizations as well as for biology! Whether the cyberneticists will work out these 'single principles' and be able to reduce them comprehensively again to One', we yet have to see. But it does appear that the outward-spiralling, the splintering of the Mediaeval Synthesis that leads through the Renaissance right on down to the Atom Bomb, had its beginnings in the fourteenth century.

NOTES

Śrikantha

1. Surendranath Dasgupta, *A History of Indian Philosophy,* vol. IV (Cambridge: Cambridge Univ. Press, 1949), p. 67.
2. Ibid., pp. 78-9.
3. Ibid., pp. 84-5.
4. Ibid., pp. 85-6.

Bernard of Clairvaux

1. Jean Leclercq, *Bernard of Clairvaux and the Cistercian Spirit,* trans. Claire Lavoie (Kalamazoo, Michigan: Cistercian Publications, 1976), p. 11.
2. Etienne Gilson, *The Mystical Theology of Saint Bernard* (London and New York: Sheed and Ward, 1940), p. 7.
3. Thomas Merton's Foreword to *St. Bernard of Clairvaux Seen Through his Selected Letters,* trans. and ed. Rev. Bruno Scott James (Chicago: Henry Regnery Co., 1953), p. vi.
4. Leclercq, *Cistercian Spirit,* p. 56.
5. Ibid., pp. 20-21.
6. Jean Leclercq, *The Love of Learning and the Desire for God: a Study of Monastic Culture* (New York: Fordham Univ. Press, 1961), p. 67.
7. Ibid., pp. 128-29.
8. Gilson, *Mystical Theology,* p. viii.
9. Richard S. Storrs, *Bernard of Clairvaux: the Times the Man and His Work* (New York: Charles Scribner's Sons, 1912), p. 302.
10. Cited from A.C. McGiffert, *A History of Christian Thought,* vol. II, *The West: From Tertullian to Erasmus* (New York: Charles Scribner's Sons, 1950), p. 231.
11. W.T. Jones, *A History of Western Philosophy,* 2nd ed., *The Medieval Mind* (New York: Hercourt and World, 1968), p. 200, citing *de diligende Deo,* 28.
12. *de diligende Deo,* 28, cited in Dom Cuthbert Butler, *Western Mysticism,* 3rd ed. (New York: Barnes & Noble, 1967), p. 109.
13. Ibid., p. 107.
14. Etienne Gilson, *The Spirit of Medieval Philosophy,* trans. by A.H. Downes (New York: Scribner, 1940), pp. 299-300.
15. Butler, p. 114.
16. Watkin W. Williams, *The Treatise of St. Bernard Concerning Grace and Free Will* (London: SPCK; New York: Macmillan, 1920), pp. 82-83.
17. Anne Freemantle, *The Age of Belief: The Medieval Philosophies* (New York: Mentor, New American Library, 1954), p 101.
18. Storrs, p. 465.

19. Ibid p. 473.
20. Ibid., p. 475.
21. Ibid., p. 477.
22. Ibid.
23. McGiffert, p. 228.
24. Merton, p. viii.

Hemacandra

1. William Theodore de Bary, *et al*, *Sources of Indian Tradition* (New York: Columbia Univ. Press, 1958), p. 86.
2. Jagdish Sharma, "Hemacandra: The Life and Scholarship of a Jaina Monk", *Asian Profile*, vol. 3, no. 2, 1975, p. 211.
3. Ibid., p. 209.
4. Satkari Mookerjee, *Hemacandra's Pramāṇa-Mīmāṃsā* (Varanasi: Tara Publications, 1970), pp. ix, xii.
5. Ibid., pp. ix-x.
6. Hari Satya Bhattacharya, *Pramāṇa-naya-tattvālokalaṃkara of Vādi Devasūri* (Bombay: Jain Sahitya Vikas Mandal, 1967), p. vi.
7. Sarvepalli Radhakrishnan and Charles A. Moore, *A Source Book in Indian Philosophy* (Princeton: Princeton Univ. Press, 1957), pp. 260-61.
8. Mookerjee, pp. x-xi.

Nimbārka

1. Surendranath Dasgupta, *A History of Indian Philosophy*, vol. III (Cambridge, 1940), p. 440.
2. Ibid., pp. 413-14.
3. Ibid., p. 428.

Ibn Ṭufayl

1. Lenn Evan Goodman, trans., *Hayy Ibn Yaqzan* (New York: Twayne) p. 3.
2. Bakhtyar Husain Siddiqi, "Ibn Ṭufail", in *A History of Muslim Philosophy*, M.M. Sharif, ed. (Wiesbaden, 1963), pp. 528-29.
3. Ibid., p. 534.
4. Ibid., pp. 533-34.
5. Sami S. Hawi, "Ibn Ṭufayl's Appraisal of His Predecessors and the Influence of These on His Thought", Islamic Studies, no. 13, 1974, p. 143.
6. Ibid., p. 166.
7. Siddiqi, p. 530.

Suhrawardī

1. Seyyed Hossein Nasr, "Shihāb al-Dīn Suhrawardī Maqtūl", in *A History of Muslim Philosophy*, M.M. Sharif, ed. (Wiesbaden, 1963), p. 396.

2. Henry Corbin, in *The Encyclopedia of Philosophy*, vol. 7 (New York: Macmillan, 1967), p. 486.

3. Seyyed Hossein Nasr, *Three Muslim Sages* (Cambridge: Harvard Univ. Press, 1964), p. 68.

4. Corbin, p. 486.

5. Ibid.

6. Nasr, *Three Sages*, pp. 61-2.

7. Nasr, *History of Muslim Philosophy*, p. 376.

8. Nasr, *Three Sages*, p. 66.

9. Majid Fakhry, *A History of Islamic Philosophy* (New York: Columbia Univ. Press, 1970), p. 327.

10. Ibid., pp. 337-38.

11. Nasr, *Three Sages*, p. 69.

12. Ibid., pp. 70-71.

13. Ibid., pp. 73-74.

Lu Hsiang-shan

1. Lyman W. Cady, *The Philosophy of Lu Hsiang-shan* (Pacific Cultural Foundation, Academy Books, 1977).

2. Ibid.

3. Siu-chi Huang, *Lu Hsiang-shan* (New Haven: American Oriental Society, 1944), p. 39.

4. Ibid., pp. 33-36 passim.

5. Ibid., pp. 30-31.

6. Ibid., p. 55.

7. Ibid., p. 43.

8. Ibid., p. 44.

9. Cady, p. 74.

10. Huang, p. 48.

11. Ibid., p. 50.

12. Ibid., p. 51.

13. Cady, p. 116.

14. Ibid.

15. Ibid., p. 335f.

16. Huang, p. 69.

Ch'en Liang

1. Hellmut Wilhelm, "The Heresies of Ch'en Liang", Asiatische Studien, vol. xi, 1958, p. 102.

2. Hou Wai-lu *et al*, *A Short History of Chinese Philosophy*, trans. by Wang Cheng-chung (Peking: Foreign Language Press, 1959).

Ibn Rushd

1. Majid Fakhry, *A History of Islamic Philosophy* (New York: Columbia Univ. Press, 1970), pp. 304, 307.

2. Ibid., p. 311.

3. Mohammad Jamilur-Behman, trans., *Faṣl al-Maqāl fi ma bain al-Ḥikmah w-al-Sharī'ah min al-Ittiṣāl* (Baroda: Gaekwad series XI, 1921).

4. Ibid., p. 66.

5. Ibid., p. 188.

6. Ibid., p. 202.

7. Ibid., p. 205.

8. Ibid., p. 257.

9. Ibid., p. 266.

10. Ibid., p. 287.

11. Simon van den Bergh, trans., *Tahāfut al-Tahāfut* (London, 1954), p. 269.

Chu Hsi

1. Wing-tsit Chan, "Chu Hsi's Completion of Neo-Confucianism", Études Song-Sung Studies, Ser. II, no. 1, 1973, p. 63.

2. Ibid., p. 64.

3. Ibid., p. 75.

4. Ibid., p. 81.

5. Joseph Needham, *Science and Civilisation In China*, Vol. II (Cambridge: Cambridge Univ. Press, 1956), p. 480n.

6. Ibid., p. 558.

7. Chan, p. 67.

8. Ibid., p. 68.

9. Ibid., p. 69.

10. Ibid., pp. 71-2.

11. Toshimidzu Goto, "The Ontology of the 'Li' Philosophy of the Sung Dynasty of China", Philosophical Studies of Japan, no. 2, 1960, p. 121.

12. Ibid., p. 125.

13. Ibid., pp. 128-29.

14. Ibid., pp 132-33.

15. Ibid., p. 133.

16. Ibid., pp. 133-34.

17. Ibid., p. 142.

18. Ibid., pp. 142-43.

19. Wing-tsit Chan, trans, *Reflections on Things at Hand* (New York: Columbia Univ. Press, 1967).

20. Ibid.

21. Ibid.

22. Chan, "Completion", p. 73.

23. Wing-tsit Chan, *A Source Book In Chinese Philosophy* (Princeton: Princeton Univ. Press, 1963), p. 653.

24. Kenneth Ch'en, *Buddhism in China* (Princeton: Princeton Univ. Press, 1964), p. 399.

25. Chan, *Reflections*, p. 282.

26. Li Chi, "Chu Hsi The Poet", p. 100.
27. Ibid., p. 60ff.
28. Ibid., p. 103.

Maimonides

1. John F. Wipple and Allan B. Wolter, eds., *Medieval Philosophy* (New York: Free Press, 1969), pp. 244-45.
2. Isaac Husik, *A History of Mediaeval Jewish Philosophy* (New York: Atheneum, 1969), pp. 240-41.
3. Ibid., p. 300
4. Guttman and Rabin, eds., *Guide of the Perplexed* (London: East-West Library, 1952), p. 63.
5. Ibid., p 65ff.
6. Ibid., pp. 86-7.
7. Ibid., p. 88.
8. Ibid., p. 111.
9. Ibid., p. 127.
10. Ibid., p. 130.
11. Ibid., p. 160.
12. Ibid., p. 163.
13. Ibid., p. 165.
14. Ibid., p. 169.
15. Ibid., p. 172.
16. Ibid., p. 188.
17. Husik, pp. 306-7.

Honen

1. Masaharu Anesake, *History of Japanese Religion* (Rutland, Vermont: Charles E. Tuttle, 1963), pp. 171-73.
2. Junjiro Takakusu, *The Essentials of Buddhist Philosophy* (Hawaii, 1956), p. 171.
3. Daigan & Alicia Matsunaga, *Foundation of Japanese Buddhism*, vol. II (Los Angeles: Buddhist Books International, 1976), pp. 71-2.
4. Anesake, p. 178.
5. Ibid., p. 178n.
6. Ryugaku Ishizuka, *Honen the Buddhist Saint* (Kyoto, 1949), p. 340.
7. Ibid., p. 343.
8. Ibid., p. 349.

Eisai

1. Daigan & Alicia Matsunaga, *Foundation of Japanese Buddhism*, vol. II (Los Angeles: Buddhist Books International, 1976), pp. 214-16.
2. Dale Saunders, *Buddhism in Japan* (Philadelphia: Univ. of Pennsylvania Press, 1964), p. 221.

3. Daisetz T. Suzuki, *Zen and Japanese Culture* (Pantheon Books: Bollingen Series LXIV, 1959), pp. 94-111ff.

4. Robert Aitken, in private correspondence.

5. *Sources of Japanese Tradition*, vol. I, compiled by Ryusaku Tsunoda, Wm. Theodore de Bary and Donald Keene (New York: Columbia Univ. Press, 1958), p. 242.

Śrīharṣa

1. Surendranath Dasgupta, *A History of Indian Philosophy*, vol. II (Cambridge: Cambridge Univ. Press, 1961), pp. 127-28.

2. Ibid., pp. 142-43.

3. Ibid., p. 147.

4. Ibid., p. 146.

Ibn 'Arabī

1. S.A.Q. Husaini, *The Pantheistic Monism of Ibn al-'Arabi* (Lahore: Ashraf, 1970), p. 37.

2. Ibid., p. 26.

3. Ibid., p. 28.

4. Ibid., p. viii.

5. Ibid., p. 1.

6. Ibid., p. 46.

7. Ibid., pp. 55-6.

8. Abul Affifi, *The Mystical Philosophy of Muhyid Din-Ibnul Arab* (Lahore: Ashraf, 1964), p. 10.

9. Ibid., p. 11.

10. Ibid., p. 24.

11. Husaini, p. 146.

12. Ibid., p. 149.

13. Ibid., p. 151.

14. Affifi, p. 25.

15. Ibid., p. 26.

16. Ibid., p. 29.

17. Ibid., pp. 34-5.

18. Ibid., p. 40.

19. Ibid., p. 46.

20. Ibid., p. 163.

21. Husaini, pp. 104-5.

22. Affifi, p. 171.

23. Ibid., p. 173.

24. Ibid., p. 173.

25. Ibid., p. 13.

26. Mehmed Ali Aynī, *La Quintessence de la Philosophie de Ibn-i-Arabī*, trans. by Ahmed Rechid (Paris, 1926).

Citsukha

1. V.A. Sarma, *Citsukha's Contribution to Advaita* (Mysore: 1974) p. 30.
2. Ibid., p. 221.
3. Ibid., pp. 8-9.
4. Ibid., p. 193.
5. Ibid., p. 194.
6. Ibid., pp. 195-6.
7. Ibid., p. 196.
8. Ibid., p. 112.
9. Ibid.

Dōgen

1. Daigan and Alicia Matsunaga, *Foundation of Japanese Buddhism*, vol. II (Los Angeles-Tokyo: Buddhist Books International, 1976), p. 242.
2. Ibid., pp. 241-42.
3. Kōsen Nishiyama and John Stevens' Introduction to Dōgen's *Shōbōgenzō* (*The Eye and Treasury of the True Law*). I, xii, (Sendai, Japan: The Daihokkaikaku Pub. Co., 1975). Hereafter cited as N & S.
4. Dōgen, *Shōbōgenzō Zuimonki* (not to be confused with the more famous *Shōbōgenzō*), trans. by Reihō Masunaga as *A Primer of Sōtō Zen* (Honolulu: Univ. of Hawaii Press, 1975), p. 66.
5. Hee-Jin Kim, *Dōgen Kigen Mystical Realist* (Tucson: University of Asian Studies, 1975), pp. 2 and 8.
6. N and S, p. xix.
7. Matsunaga, II, p. 256.
8. Ibid., p. 257.
9. *Shōbōgenzō* (hereafter SBGZ), Bodaisatta-Shishōbō, as cited and translated by Kim, p. 270.
10. Matsunaga, II, p. 258.
11. Ibid., p. 241.
12. Ibid.
13. Ibid., p. 246.
14. Ibid., p. 240.
15. Ibid., p. 305.
16. Kim, p. 55, citing SBGZ. "Raihai-tokuzui".
17. N & S, II, p. 162.
18. Kim, p. 52.
19. SBGZ, N & S, II, p. 83.
20. Ibid., p. 162.
21. Ibid., p. 83.
22. Hajime Nakamura, *Ways of Thinking of Eastern Peoples*, revised (Honolulu: East-West Center Press, 1964), p. 540.
23. Ibid., p. 554.
24. Kim, p. 229.

25. Matsunaga, II, 237-38.
26. N & S, II, pp. 185-86.
27. SBGZ, N & S, II, p. 178.
28. Ibid.
29. Ibid., pp. 107-110.
30. Ibid., p. 178.
31. Ibid., p. 161
32. Matṣunagas, II, p. 240.
33. T.P. Kasulis, "The Zen philosopher: A review article on Dōgen scholarship in English," Philosophy East & West, 28, no. 3 (July 1978), pp. 358-59.
34. Matsunaga, II, p. 244.
35. Kim, p. 111.
36. Bardwell L. Smith, ed., *Unsui: A Diary of Zen Monastic Life* (Honolulu: The University Press of Hawaii, 1973), p. xxvi.
37. Ibid.
38. Ibid., p. xxv.
39. N & S, p. 42.
40. Ibid.
41. Ibid., p. 41, n. 1.
42. Ibid., p. 46.
43. Ibid., p. 40.
44. Nakamura, p. 370.
45. Kim, p. 201.
46. Ibid., p. 82.
47. N & S, pp. 98-99.
48. Kim, p. 80.
49. Matsunaga, II, p. 325, n 47.
50. Ibid., p. 248.
51. *A Primer of Sōtō Zen*, p. 25.
52. Matsunaga, I, p. 100.
53. Ibid.
54. Ibid., p. 101.
55. Ibid., p. 103.
56. Ibid., p. 105
57. "One Bright Pearl," trans. by Normon Waddell and Masao Abe, *The Eastern Buddhist* (New Series), 4, no. 2 (Oct., 1971), pp. 113, 117.
58. Ibid., p. 117.
59. N & S, p. 81.
60. Matsunaga, II, 249.
61. Ibid., p. 251.
62. Ibid.
63. Kasulis, p. 360.
64. Matsunaga, II, p. 252.
65. Ibid., pp. 253-54.
66. Ibid., p. 255.

67. Ibid.
68. Kasulis, p. 368.
69. Ibid., pp. 94-95.
70. Ibid.. p. 98.
71. Ibid., p. 91.
72. Kim, p. 8.
73. Ibid., p. 235.
74. Ibid., p. 236.
75. Ibid.

Shinran

1. Hajime Nakamura, *Parallel Developments: A Comparative History of Ideas* (Tokyo and New York: Kodansha Lts., 1975), p. 395.
2. Nishi Utsuki, *The Shin Sect: A School of Mahāyāna Buddhism* (Kyoto: Bureau of Buddhist Books, 1938).
3. Alicia & Daigan Matsunaga, *Foundation of Japanese Buddhism*, vol. II (Los Angeles and Tokyo: Buddhist Books International, 1976), pp. 33-34, summarizing *The Meditation Sūtra*.
4. Ibid., p. 57.
5. *Sources of Japanese Tradition*, vol. I, compiled by Ryusaku Tsunoda, William deBary and Donald Keene (New York: Columbia Univ. Press, 1964), p. 209.
6. Hee-Jin Kim, *Dōgen Kigen—Mystical Realist* (Tucson: Univ. of Arizona Press. 1975), p. 197.
7. Nakamura, p. 391.
8. Hajime Nakamura, *Ways of Thinking of Eastern Peoples: India-China-Tibet-Japan* (Honolulu: East-West Center Press, 1964), p. 515.
9. Nakamura, *Parallel Developments*, p. 393.
10. Ibid., p. 397, citing Bertrand Russell's *History of Western Philosophy*, p. 405.
11. Nakamura, *Parallel Developments*, pp. 387, 396.
12. Nakamura, *Ways of Thinking*, p. 499.
13. Matsunaga, p. 501.
14. Ibid., p. 87.
15. Hyakuso Kurata, *Shinran*, trans. by Umeyo Hiramo (Tokyo, 1964), p. 63.
16. Ibid., p. 54.
17. Ibid.
18. Alfred Bloom, *Shinran's Gospel of Pure Grace* (Tucson: Univ. of Arizona Press, 1965), p. 84.

Rūmī

1. Reynold Nicholson, *Rūmī: Poet and Mystic* (London: Allen & Unwin, 1950), p. 26.

2. Khalifa Hakim, *The Metaphysics of Rūmī* (Lahore: Institute of Islamic Culture, 1965), pp. 3-4.

3. Ibid., p. 9.

4. Nicholson, pp. 18-21 passim.

5. Khalifah Hakim, "Jalāl al-Dīn Rūmī", in *A History of Muslim Philosophy*, ed. by M.M. Sharif (Wiesbaden: Harrassowitz, 1966), p. 827.

6. Hakim, *Metaphysics*, pp. 38-41 passim.

7. Ibid., p. 122.

8. Ibid., pp. 109-12.

9. Ibid., p. 114.

10. Afzal Iqbal, The Life and Works of Muhammad Jalal-ud-Din Rumi (Lahore: Institute of Islamic Culture, 1974), pp. 100-101.

Naṣīr al-Dīn Ṭūsī

1. G.M. Wickens, trans., *The Nasirean Ethics* (London: George Allen & Unwin Ltd., 1964), p. 12.

2. B.H. Siddiqi, "Naṣir al-Dīn Ṭūsi", in *A History of Muslim Philosophy*, vol. I, ed. by M. M. Sharif (Wiesbaden: Harrassowitz, 1963) pp. 565-66.

3. Wickens, p. 74.

4. Ibid., p. 81.

5. Ibid., p. 144.

6. Siddiqi, p. 569.

7. Ibid., p. 569.

8. Wickens, p. 126.

9. Siddiqi, p. 569.

10. Wickens, p. 129.

11. Ibid., p. 141.

12. Ibid., p. 142.

13. Ibid., p. 145.

14. Siddiqi, p. 566.

15. Ibid., p. 580.

16. Ibid., p. 570.

Madhva

1. Nagaraja Rao, *The Epistemology of Dvaita Vedānta* (Adyar, 1976), pp. 2-3.

2. S.S. Raghavachar, *Dvaita Vedānta* (Madras, 1977), p. 57.

3. K. Narain, *A Critique of Madhva Refutation of the Samkara School of Vedanta* (Allahabad: Udayana Publications, 1964), p. 150.

4. Ibid., p. 72.

Nichiren

1. Daigan & Alicia Matsunaga, *Foundation of Japanese Buddhism*, vol. II (Los Angeles and Tokyo: Buddhist Books International, 1976), p. 150.

2. G. Renondeau, *La Doctrine de Nichiren* (Paris: Presses Universitaires de France, 1953), pp. 3, 7, 6 and pp. 266-67.

3. Hajime Nakamura, *Ways of Thinking of Eastern Peoples* (Honolulu: East-West Center Press, 1964), p. 379.

4. Ryusaku Tsunoda, *et al*, eds., *Sources of Japanese Tradition* (New York and London: Columbia University Press, 1958), II, 224.

5. Laurel R. Rodd, *Nichiren: Selected Writings* (University Press of Hawaii, 1980), pp. 41-2.

6. Matsunaga, p. 157.

7. Ibid.

8. Ibid., p. 161.

9. Kishio Satomi, *Japanese Civilization* (London: Kegan Paul, Trench, Trubner and Co., 1923), p. 82.

10. Tsunoda, pp. 213-14.

11. Ibid., p. 221.

Ippen

1. Daigan & Alicia Matsunaga, *Foundation of Japanese Buddhism*, vol. II (Los Angeles and Tokyo: Buddhist Books International, 1976), p. 120ff.

2. Yanagi Sōetsu, "Ippen Shōnin", The Eastern Buddhist, pp. 43-4.

3. Ibid., pp. 44-6.

4. Ibid., p. 48.

5. Ibid., p. 53.

6. Ibid., p. 56.

Roger Bacon

1. Émile Bréhier, *The History of Philosophy: The Middle Ages and the Renaissance*, Wade Baskin, trans. (Chicago: Univ. of Chicago Press, 1967), p. 167.

2. B.A.G. Fuller and Sterling M. McMurrin, *A History of Philosophy* (New York: Holt, Rinehart and Winston, 1955), p. 428.

3. Bréhier, p. 170.

4. Ibid.

5. Theodore Crowley, *Roger Bacon: The Problem of the Soul in his Philosophical Commentaries* (Dublin, 1950), p. 104.

6. Ibid., p. 110.

7. Ibid., p. 164.

8. Richard McKeon, ed., *Selecions From Medieval Philosophers* vol. II (New York: Charles Scribner's Sons, 1930), pp. 8-9.

Duns Scotus

1. C.R.S. Harris, *Duns Scotus*, vol. I (New York: The Humanities Press, 1959), p. 267.
2. H.O. Taylor, *The Mediaeval Mind*, vol II (Cambridge: Harvard Univ. Press, 1966), p. 544.
3. Richard McKeon, ed., *Selections From Medieval Philosophers*, vol. II (New York: Charles Scribner's Sons, 1930), p. 304.
4. Taylor, pp. 539-40.
5. David Knowles, *The Evolution of Medieval Thought* (New York: Vintage Books, 1962), pp. 308-9.
6. W.T. Jones, *The Medieval Mind* (New York: Harcourt, Brace and World, 1969), p. 316.
7. Ibid., pp. 310-11.
8. Frederick Copleston, *A History of Philosophy*, vol. 2, pt. II (New York: Doubleday, 1962), p. 240.
9. Ibid.
10. Ibid., pp. 216-17.
11. Ibid., p. 216.
12. Jones, pp. 303-4.
13. B.A.G. Fuller and Sterling M. McMurrin, *A History of Philosophy* (New York: Holt, Rinehart and Winston, 1955), pp. 411-12.
14. Copleston, p. 242.
15. Ibid., p. 226.
16. Ibid., pp. 242-43.
17. Ibid., p. 255.
18. Harris, p. 111.
19. Ibid., p. 306.
20. Ibid., p. 303.
21. Ibid., p. 112.
22. Knowles, p. 309.
23. McKeon, p. 311.
24. Allan B. Wolter, in *The Encyclopedia of Philosophy*, vol. II (New York: Macmillan, 1967), p. 436.
25. Ibid.

Raymond Lull

1. Friedrich Heer, *The Medieval World* (Mentor, 1961), pp. 306-8.
2. Jocelyn Hillgarth, in *The Encyclopedia of Philosophy*, vol. V (New York: Macmillan, 1967), pp. 107-8.
3. James Michener, *Iberia* (Connecticut: Fawcett, 1968), pp. 725-35.
4. E. Allison Peers, trans., *Blanquerna* (London, 1926).

Nicephorus Chumnos

1. Basile Tatakis, *La Philosophie Byzantine*, ed. Émile Brehier (Paris: Presses Univ. De France, 1949) pp. 232-35.
2. Ibid., p. 236, citing *Patrologia Graeca*, 1270 A.B.

3. Ibid., citing *Patrologia Graeca*, 143, 444 A:445A.

4. J. Verpeaux, *Nicéphore Choumnos*: *Homme d'État et Humaniste Byzantin* (Paris: Editions A. et J. Picard & Cie, 1959), p. 143.

5. Ibid.

6. Ibid., pp. 169, 192, 200.

Eckhart

1. Paraphrased from *Breakthrough*: *Meister Eckhart's Creation Spirituality in New Translation*, Intro. and Com. by Matthew Fox (New York: Image Books, 1980), p. 155, citing Raymond Bernard Blakney, Meister Eckhart: A Modern Translation (New York: Harper Torchbooks, 1941), p. 245.

2. Matthew Fox, *A Spirituality Named Compassion and the Healing of the Global Village, Humpty Dumpty and Us* (Minneapolis: Winston Press, 1979).

3. *Breakthrough*, p. 35.

4. Ibid., p. 15.

5. Ibid., pp. 111, 113.

6. Ibid., p. 409.

7. Ibid., p. 49.

8. Ibid., p. 284.

9. Reiner Schürmann, "Eckehart", *Macropaedia*, VI, 187-88, *Encyclopaedia Britannica*.

10. James M. Clark and John V. Skinner, *Meister Eckhart*: *Selected Treatises and Sermons translated from Latin and German* (London: Faber and Faber, 1958), p. 160.

11. *Breakthrough*, pp. 144, 201.

12. Ninian Smart, on Eckhart in *The Encyclopedia of Philosophy*, vol. II, p. 450.

13. *Breakthrough*, p. 103.

14. Ibid., pp. 109-10.

15. A. Seth Pringle-Paattison, *The Idea of God in the Light of Present Philosophy* (New York: Oxford Univ. Press, 1917), Lecture XVI, p. 314, n. 1.

16. *Breakthrough*, pp. 169, 203, 217.

17. Ibid., p. 65.

18. Ibid., p. 76.

19. Ibid., p. 68.

20. Ibid., p. 75.

Metochites

1. Basile Tatakis, *La Philosophie Byzantine*, ed. by Émile Brehier (Paris: Presses Univ. de France, 1949), p. 250.

2. Ibid., pp. 252-53.

3. Ibid., p. 255.

4. Ibid., p. 249.

5. Ihor Sevcenko and Jeffrey Featherstone, *Two Poems By Theodore Metochites* (Brookline, Mass.: Hellenic College Press, 1981), p. 2.

6. Ibid., p. 33.

7. Tatakis, p. 254.

8. Ibid., p. 255.

9. *Two Poems*, pp. 3-6 passim

10. Ibid., p. 45.

GLOSSARY

abhāva: (Sanskrit) non-existence, negation, absence.

ācārya: (Sanskrit) one who knows and teaches.

Actus Purus: (Latin) 'pure act'; pure actuality as opposed to potentiality; a Thomist doctrine traceable to Aristotle's conception of divinity as 'pure act'; absolute reality.

adhyāsa: (Sanskrit) superimposition.

adṛṣṭa: (Sanskrit) unseen force or power, potential form: destiny. Advaita Vedānta Hinduism: Upaniṣadic-based school developed by Gauḍapāda (fl. 530) and flowering in the ninth century philosopher Śaṅkara.

Āgamas: (Sanskrit) non-Vedic Indian treatises, dated first century A.D. and following, considered authoritative by Vaiṣṇava and Śaiva Hinduism.

agapé: (Greek) spiritual altruistic love; charity.

ahaṅkāra: (Sanskrit) ego; asserting self (distinct from *ātman*, which may be termed 'selfless self').

ahiṃsā: (Sanskrit) non-injury, non-violence; reverence for life.

ajñāna: (Sanskrit) negation or absence of knowledge (*jñāna*); ignorance.

ākāśa: (Sanskrit) space, ether; most rarefied or 'etherial' element in nature.

Ālaya or *Ālayavijñāna*: (Sanskrit) cosmic mind, great storehouse of consciousness, self-evolving Thought.

Allah: in Islam, the One God.

Ana'l-'abd: (Arabic) I am the servant of God.

Ana'l-Haqq: (Arabic) I am God.

ānanda: (Sanskrit) supreme joy, bliss, serenity.

anātman: 'no soul' or 'no self' (a Buddhist concept).

anirvacanīya: (Sanskrit) indefinability.

antarātman: (Sanskrit) inner Self; *antaryāmin*.

antaryāmin: (Sanskrit) the internal controller: *antarātman*.

anupalabdhi: (Sanskrit) perception of absence, one of the traditional *pramāṇas* (means of cognition) of Hindu thought.

'aql: (Arabic) systematic reasoning.
Arhat: (Sanskrit) the ideal saint of Theravāda Buddhism.
asatkāryavāda: (Sanskrit) theory of causation which holds that the effect does not pre-exist in the cause.
ascesis: (Greek) pattern of discipline for achievement of mystical or spiritual transcendence of bodily limitations.
ātman: (Sanskrit) soul, spirit, Self; 'selfless self'.
āvaraṇa: (Sanskrit) veiling, concealment.
avidyā: (Sanskrit) ignorance, not-seeing.

bala: (Sanskrit) strength.
baqā: (Arabic) abiding (in God).
bhakta: (Sanskrit) devotee.
bhakti: (Sanskrit) affective devotion to the divine being or another object of contemplation.
Bhedābhedavāda: (Sanskrit) referring to the philosophy of Nimbārka, the theory of Brahman as unity-in-difference.
Bodhisattva: (Sanskrit) the ideal saint of Mahāyāna Buddhism; one who renounces final *nirvāṇa* and returns to the world to exercise compassion (*mahākaruṇā*) and thus deliver other suffering beings from *saṃsāra*.
Brahman: (Sanskrit) Ultimate Reality; God.
buddhi (Sanskrit) intellect, intelligence.

Cārvāka Hinduism: early materialist, atheistic Hindu school; Lokāyata.
Ch'an (*Zen*) *Buddhism*: school which seeks oneness with the Buddha Mind (enlightenment, *satori*) through meditation (*zazen*, 'silent sitting') and paradoxical sayings (*koans*).
ch'ang: (Chinese) invariables; universal and eternal laws or principles running through the phenomenal changes of the universe.
ch'i: (Chinese) vital force, breath, air, ether; 'materializing tendency'.
cidākāśa: (Sanskrit) intelligence or higher mind as faculty of *ātman* (*citta*) with *ākāśa*: hence, identity (especially in Advaita) of the rarest material element with ideation or intelligence, transitional to complete transcendence.
citta: (Sanskrit) mind, consciousness, intelligence.

contuition: in contrast to 'exterior' intuition of the divine, an 'interior' participation and abiding in.

diamoku: (Japanese) a mantra or symbolic chant.

darśana: (Sanskrit) literally, 'perception'; intuitive vision.

dharma: (Sanskrit) law, duty, virtue, merit, order; body of teachings; element; motion.

Dharmakāya: (Sanskrit) the third or Unmanifest Body of the Buddha; see *Trikāya*.

dhimmī: (Arabic) protected subject, follower of a religion tolerated by Islam.

dhirk: (Arabic) recollection of God's presence.

dhyāna: (Sanskrit) intensive meditation.

dianoia: (Greek) discursive explication.

dik: (Sanskrit) space.

doxa: (Greek) belief or opinion.

dravya: (Sanskrit) substance, as a substratum of qualities (*guṇas*), accidents or modes.

ecstasis: (Greek) enlightenment and/or the enraptured state sought by mystics; ecstasy.

ekajīvavāda: (Sanskrit) theory that there is really only a single Individual, a single Self.

epoché: (Greek and Latin): suspension of judgment.

ex nihilo controversy: question of the origin of the world; controversy between the Greek view of the eternity of the world and the view of the world as created by God in time.

Falsafah; (Arabic) Islamic philosophy based on Greek tradition.

fanā: (Arabic) 'passing away', dying to self by transmutation, union with God.

fiqh: (Arabic) jurisprudence; the discipline of elucidating the *Sharī'ah*.

geist: (German) spirit, mind.

gnosis; (Greek) knowledge, often with the implication of esoteric knowledge, as in Gnosticism.

guṇa: (Sanskrit) quality, attribute.

ḥadīth: (Arabic) tradition going back to the Prophet Muhammad based on a chain of transmitters of reported sayings or actions of the Prophet.

ḥajj: (Arabic) ritual pilgrimage to Mecca.

ḥāl: (Arabic) rapture.

Ḥaqq: (Arabic) Ṣūfī term for God, The Real.

Hesychast controversy: Eastern Orthodox quietist mysticism originating with the monks of Mt. Athos.

ḥikma: (Arabic) wisdom.

Hīnayāna Buddhism: see Theravāda Buddhism.

hsing: (Chinese) human nature; form.

'ilm: (Arabic) knowledge, science, of divine things.

imām: (Arabic) leader in public worsnip in Islam.

ishrāq: (Arabic) illumination.

Īśvara: (Sanskrit) Lord, personal God as determinate, *saguṇa* Brahman; most often associated with Śiva.

jāti: (Sanskrit) logical class, universal as distinct from particular (*viśeṣa*); hereditary caste.

jen: (Chinese) humanity, humanness, benevolence, human-heartedness; virtue.

jihād; (Arabic) literally, 'contest' or 'war'; a Muslim holy war against unbelievers or enemies of Islam; 'mystical striving'.

jīva: (Sanskrit) soul, in the sense of vital principle; distinct from Self (*ātman*).

jīvanmukta: (Sanskrit) one who attains spiritual emancipation while still living; one who attains embodied liberation.

jñāna: (Sanskrit) knowledge, wisdom.

kojogo: (Japanese) everyday language is the whole universe.

kāla: (Sanskrit) time.

kalām: (Arabic) scholastic theology, in Islam.

kalpa: (Sanskrit) cosmic cycle.

karma: (Sanskrit) action deeds; the results of good or bad deeds; with *bhakti* and *jñāna*, one of the three *yogas* (as in the *Gītā*).

kasb: (Arabic) acquisition, personal initiative.

koān: (Japanese) in some forms of Zen, a puzzle or exercise used to release one from that which prevents *satori*, as, for example, dualistic thinking.

kokoro: (Japanese) mind and heart seen as a unitary whole; egoless consciousness achieved by arduous discipline.

koṣas: (Sanskrit) sheaths: bodily, vital, mental, intellectual, and the sheath of bliss.

ko wu: (Chinese) investigation of things.

kṣaṇa: (Sanskrit) moment, instant.

kṣaṇavāda: (Sanskrit) Buddhist doctrine of momentariness.

kufū: (Japanese) a mere means to enlightenment; in some forms of Zen, also the end of meditation.

li: (Chinese) principle, metaphysical principle, rational principle, law, pattern, order; propriety, decorum, ritual ceremony, good form, courtesy.

logos: (Greek) reason, word, principle; as used by the Stoics, the rational principle of the universe; as used in the Gospel of John, the eternal Word, the Son of God, the pre-existent Christ.

Mādhyamika Buddhism: see Śūnyavāda Buddhism.

maḥabba: (Arabic) reciprocal love between God and His creations.

mahākaruṇā: (Sanskrit) the great compassion of the Buddha and the Bodhisattvas.

mahāparinirvāṇa: (Sanskrit) the final, ultimate *nirvāṇa*, entered only after death.

manas: (Sanskrit) mind, understanding; the unifying principle which analyzes and synthesizes sensation.

mantra: (Sanskrit) a prayerful utterance repeated often, for meditative purposes.

marga: (Sanskrit) way, path, road.

ma'rifah: (Arabic) mystical intuitive knowledge.

māyā; (Sanskrit) ultimately unreal; illusion.

meden agan: (Greek) middle way, the 'golden mean' of Aristotle.

Mīmāṁsā Hinduism: a school founded c. 400 B.C. and concerned with the fulfilment of the ritual prescriptions of the *Brāhmaṇas*, the first of the *Vedas* (Vedānta being concerned with the more metaphysical *Upaniṣads* which form the last part of the *Vedas*).

ming: (Chinese) destiny, fate; the decree of Heaven; often associated with *hsing*, human nature.

mithyā: (Sanskrit) falsehood; varying degrees of falsehood.

mokṣa: (Sanskrit) emancipation, liberation, salvation, release.

murīd: (Arabic) aspirant.

mushin: (Japanese) no-mind.

Mu'tazilite Muslims: 'seceders'; philosophical trend, school or tradition in early Islam, dating from the eighth century, with emphasis on rationalism towards interpretation of the Qur'ān, nature, and the problem of free will; opposed by followers of al-Ash'arī, the ultra-orthodox and literalists.

nafs; (Arabic) lower self, the animal-spirit soul.

nāmarūpa: (Sanskrit) name and form; mind-body complex; appearances.

nembutsu: (Japanese) *Namu Amida Butsu* (I take refuge in the Buddha); calling the 'Name' in adoration; a chant (appeal) to Buddha.

neti neti: (Sanskrit) 'not this, not that'; a Upaniṣadic passage on the nature of Brahman.

nirguṇa: (Sanskrit) without attributes, qualities of qualifications; indescribable.

Nirmāṇakāya: (Sanskrit) Earthly or Incarnation Body of the Buddha; manifestation, transformation or mind-made body of the cosmic Buddha.

nirvāṇa: (Sanskrit) literally, 'blowing out' as of a candle flame; extinction of desire-and-ego; emancipated state, salvation (heaven); non-finite existence; opposite of *saṃsāra*.

nirvikalpa pratyakṣa: (Sanskrit) indeterminate perception.

niṣkāma: (Sanskrit) desireless; as in the *Gītā*, *niṣkāma karma*, selfless action.

noesis: (Greek) the exercise of *nous* or reason; the activity of intellectual apprehension and intuitive thought.

nous: (Greek) mind; reason, intellect.

Nyāya; literally, (right) argumentation; Hindu school of logic, founded by one Gautama (c. 400 B.C., not the Buddha

Gautama); closely associated with the Vaiśeṣika school of metaphysics.

oikumenéke: (Greek) community as a whole, usually refers to the Christian community.

Parama-Puruṣa: (Sanskrit) the Supreme Person, usually associated with Viṣṇu or Śiva as a personal Deity.

pāramārthika: (Sanskrit) relating to ultimate reality, opposite of *vyāvahārtika*.

Paramātman: (Sanskrit) Supreme Self, as associated with the doctrine of the unity of *ātman* and Brahman.

pāramitās: (Sanskrit) the six virtues of perfection in Mahāyāna Buddhism: *dāna* (giving), *śīla* (moral precept), *kṣānti* (forgiving nature), *vīrya* (energy), *dhyāna* (meditation) *prajñā* (knowledge or wisdom).

parousia: (Greek) presence, in the sense of the essence; appearance in reality, 'arrival'.

pīr: (Persian) elder, master.

pneuma: (Greek) vital breath; associated with spirit, as in *Hagion Pneuma*, Holy Spirit.

prajñā: (Sanskrit) wisdom, knowledge, insight, intuition.

Prajñāpāramitā: (Sanskrit) in Buddhism, the perfection of knowledge or intuition; the name given to seminal *sūtras* of Mahāyāna Buddhism dating from c. 100 A.D.

prakṛti: (Sanskrit) original, uncreated matter or substance consisting of the three *guṇas*.

pralaya: (Sanskrit) periodic dissolution of the world; cosmic involution.

pramāṇas: (Sanskrit) means of acquiring valid knowledge; means of cognition; measure.

prāṇas: (Sanskrit) vital breath; energy.

pratibhāsika: (Sanskrit) illusory, imaginary.

pratibimba: (Sanskrit) reflection.

pratītyasamutpāda: (Sanskrit) the chain of endless causation; dependent origination.

pravṛtti: (Sanskrit) activity, effort; volitional resolution; energy; *via positiva* as opposed to *via negativa*; opposite of *nirvṛtti*.

psyché: (Greek) soul; World Soul; spirit.

puruṣa: (Sanskrit) the 'person' in the sense of observer-consciousness; observer-enjoyer consciousness.

pūrvapakṣa: (Sanskrit) literally, 'prior view'; the first step in a logical argument, stating the view which is to be refuted.

rasa: (Sanskrit) literally, sap, juice, nectar; in Indian aesthetics, pleasure, enjoyment charm, sentiment, beauty.

ra'y: (Arabic) personal judgment in working out jurisprudence rules.

riḍā': (Arabic) pleasure, satisfaction with the state in which God keep the Ṣūfī.

rūḥ: (Arabic) spirit.

rūpa: (Sanskrit) form.

śabda: (Sanskrit) sound as a metaphysical concept; word, especially the divine or cosmic word; testimony as a source of valid knowledge.

sādhaka: (Sanskrit) practitioner of *sādhanā*.

sādhanā: (Sanskrit) spiritual discipline or exercise.

saguṇa: (Sanskrit) qualified, determinate; opposite of *nirguṇa*.

Śaivism: post-Buddhist form of theistic Hinduism devoted to Śiva.

sākṣi: (Sanskrit) the subject, perceiving consciousness, the witness, spectator.

śakti: (Sanskrit) strength, might, of feminine gender; capacities of the human soul or mind, or that which brings potentialities into actualities; female generative power worshipped as the wife of a male deity, e.g., Durgā and Pārvati.

samādhi: (Sanskrit) concentration, trance; highest stage in yogic meditation.

samavāya: (Sanskrit) inherence.

Sambhogakāya; (Sanskrit) Subtle or Enjoyment Body of the Buddha.

Sāṃkhya Hinduism: a school of 'right knowledge' founded, according to tradition, by Kapila and forming the theoretical background of Yoga.

saṃsāra: (Sanskrit) cycle of death and rebirth; the continuing transmigratory rounds through mundane existences and opposite of *nirvāṇa*.

samvṛtti: (Sanskrit) relative, empirical truth.
saṃyoga: (Sanskrit) conjunction.
saṅgha: (Sanskrit) Buddhist (and sometimes Jaina) monastic community; brotherhood.
sannyāsa: (Sanskrit) one of the four Hindu *āśramas* or stages of life; the stage of renunciation, mendicancy; ***sannyāsin***, a mendicant.
sat or *sattā*: (Sanskrit) Being, existence.
sat-cit-ānanda: (Sanskrit) being-consciousness-bliss; a Vedāntic definition of the highest, all-inclusive reality (Brahman) but also of the Self (*ātman*) once it has attained full realization.
satkāryavāda: (Sanskrit) theory of causation holding that the cause is inherent in the effect.
satori: (Japanese) Zen enlightenment.
satya: (Sanskrit) actual, real, true, valid; the real.
savikalpa pratyakṣa: (Sanskrit) determinate perception.
Sharī'ah: (Arabic) the path of exoteric revelation; jurisprudence; rules guiding the life of a Muslim.
siddhānta: (Sanskrit) demonstrated conclusion to an argument/refutation.
siddhis: (Sanskrit) 'supernatural' powers, auxiliary to the attainment of the highest stages of yogic practice.
skandhas: (Sanskrit) aggregate of elements.
smṛti: (Sanskrit) scriptures, sacred writings.
śraddhā: (Sanskrit) faith, confidence.
Sūfī: a Muslim mystic.
sukr: (Arabic) spiritual intoxication.
Sung Dynasty: Chinese dynasty (960-1279) famous for artistic and literary achievement; encompassed the high tide of Neo-Confucianism.
śūnya: (Sanskrit) empty, void; zero.
śūnyatā: (Sanskrit) 'emptiness', conceived or presented as a principle.
Śūnyavāda Buddhism or Mādhyamika: a branch of Mahāyāna first systematically expounded by Nāgārjuna in the second century A.D.; emphasizes the Buddha's teachings on the inability of intellect to comprehend Reality and the inability of language to express Reality.

sūtra: (Sanskrit) literally, 'thread'; aphorisms expressing the essence of a teaching.

sva-dhatma: (Sanskrit) one's own individual duty.

svayaṃ-prakāśa: (Sanskrit) self-illuminating.

syādvāda: (Sanskrit) literally, 'perhaps-way'; the Jaina seven-fold logic or multi-valued logic.

T'ang Dynasty: Chinase dynasty (618-907): the various schools of Chinese Buddhism had their best development and flowering during this dynastic period; printing proliferated, art and literature flourished.

Tantra: exoteric and meditative practices, wedded to the use of sexual and other polarized energy.

Tao: (Chinese) Way; cosmic order; Nature; the moral order; ineffable Reality.

ṭarīqa: (Arabic) the Ṣūfī path; a mystical path or school.

tarka: (Sanskrit) reasoning, logic; associated with the Nyāya.

Tathatā: (Sanskrit) 'thatness', 'suchness', ultimate reality.

tattva: (Sanskrit) 'true principle', as opposed to metaphysical vision (*darśana*); 'thatness', 'whatness'.

tawakkul: (Arabic) trust, mystic abandonment into God's hands.

tawḥīd: (Arabic) the unity and unicity of God.

teh: (Chinese) power, virtue; Tao as manifested; Tao particularized; character.

theosis: (Greek) identification with or absorption into transcendent reality or deity.

Theravāda Buddhism: Hīnayāna; a post-Mahāyāna Reform "going back to the Fathers".

Three-Treatise school: Chinese Buddhist version of Mādhyamika or Śūnyavāda in India.

T'ien-t'ai Buddhism: highly popular Chinese Buddhist school from the eighth to the fifteenth centuries, based on meditation, intellectual comprehension, and ritual observances.

Trikāya Doctrine: the threefold doctrine of Buddhahood whereby the Buddha was considered to have had three levels of embodiment: the Earthly Body (*Nirmāṇakāya*), the Subtle Body (*Sambhogakāya*), and the Unmanifest Body (*Dharmakāya*).

'ulamā: (Arabic) body of orthodox or ultra-orthodox scholar-theologians in Islam who rule on questions of heresy and rightness of governmental procedures.

upamāna: (Sanskrit) analogy.

Upaniṣads: the last part of the *Vedas*, containing monistic speculations and providing the basis for the Vedāntic philosopies.

vairāgya: (Sanskrit) disgust, aversion, repulsion; renunciation of worldly things.

Vaiśeṣika Hinduism: a realist but not materialist school of metaphysics, founded by Kaṇāda (dates uncertain); associated with the Nyāya school of logic.

Vaiṣṇava Hinduism: sect treating Viṣṇu as the personal deity.

Vedānta Hinduism: literally, 'the end of the Veda' (i.e., the *Upaniṣads*); philosophies based on the *Upaniṣads* or on the *Brahma Sūtras*: of Bādarāyaṇa; sometimes wrongly equated only with Advaita Vedānta.

via media: (Latin) with respect to the nature of Christ, the view that Christ was both human and divine, and in both respects perfect.

via negativa: (Latin) method of philosophical and theological argumentation based on first determining what is not the case.

viator; (Latin) traveller, wayfarer.

vidyā: (Sanskrit) knowledge, seeing.

vikṣepa: (Sanskrit) the creative, revealing factor of *māyā*.

Viśiṣṭādvaita: school of qualified monism (Rāmānuja).

Vijñānavāda or Yogacāra Buddhism: Mahāyāna school of idealism.

Viṣṇu: the Preserver God.

vyāvahārika: (Sanskrit) relating to practical or empirical matters; opposite of *pāramārthika*.

wu: (Chinese) eternal non-being, non-manifestation; the first principle of Tao; matter, things, creatures; opposite of *yu*.

wu ch'i: (Chinese) Extreme Nothing.

wu wei: (Chinese) non-assertion, spontaneity, naturalness; accomplishment without effort.

yin-yang: (Chinese) passive (*yin*) and active (*yang*) cosmic principles, contrasting yet complementary.

yu: (Chinese) being; the 'mother of all things'; space; desire; opposite of *wu*.

zazen: (Japanese) seated meditation.

Zen Buddhism: See Ch'an Buddhism.

zuhd: (Arabic) devotion, renunciation.

INDEX